AF519379

Svayambodha
and
Shatrubodha

Advance Praise

'I have known Shri Pankaj Saxena for over seven years now. Having closely followed his work and views on Bharat, its past, present and future, apart from his encyclopaedic knowledge of world history, I believe his work needs to be consumed by a global audience of Hindus and others. In particular, his exposition of Svayambodha (understanding of the self) and Shatrubodha (understanding of the adversary) has been deeply educative for me personally, and from which I have drawn in the course of my own work. That he has finally captured his thoughts on the subject in writing for wider consumption is a matter of both pride and joy for people like me because of its civilizational relevance and candour alike. In the interest of their own survival, I urge every Sanatani to read, internalise, and disseminate the message Pankaj ji has been articulating with scintillating clarity for a while now. I wish Pankaj ji all success in this auspicious and audacious dharmic endeavour and pray that the devatas bless his mind, pen, and tongue with more power to do Their Work.'

J. Sai Deepak, senior lawyer and author

'Pankaj's *Svayambodha* and *Shatrubodha* explores the intricate relationship between social ethics, culture, and ideologies. It emphasizes on understanding the essence of being Hindu (Svayambodha) as well as on understanding others (Shatrubodha) to navigate today's conflict-ridden world and reflect on the society we wish to leave for future generations. It is a must-read!'

Ami Ganatra, author

'Pankaj's book talks about the major problems that plague Hindu society today and gives us intellectual solutions to fight the threats that Sanatana Dharma and Hindu society face. Without mincing words or ideas, he gets to the point very clearly and tells us what it means to be a Hindu and who are the enemies of Hindu society and Sanatana Dharma.'

Anand Ranganathan, author and scientist

'No proper cure without accurate diagnosis. In this book, Pankaj Saxena analyses the besieged Hindu society's twin failures regarding self-knowledge and knowledge of the battlefield, including its various unsolicited adversaries. In case any Hindu is interested in winning the struggle for survival, this book offers him an indispensable roadmap.'

Koenraad Elst, author and Indologist

Svayambodha and Shatrubodha

Hindu View of Self and the World

PANKAJ SAXENA

ink | OCCAM

Cover art by Niharika Singhal
Cover pic by Ramakrishna Kongalla
Figures in pp. 110, 446, and 479 by Srushti Joshi

ISBN: 978-93-6547-379-7

First published in India 2025
This edition published 2025

BluOne Ink Pvt. Ltd
A-76, 2nd Floor, Sector 136, Noida
Uttar Pradesh 201301
www.bluone.ink
publisher@bluone.ink

Printed and bound in India by Thomson Press India Ltd.

Kali and Occam are imprints of BluOne Ink

To my guru, Shri Shashimohan Ganjoo, the fountainhead of everything good in me. He is that quintessential banyan tree the shade of which is the extent of my knowledge. Just as the roots of a banyan tree descend from above and become independent trees on their own, his thoughts descend from above in my mind and become theories and pathways of action in my life. All the good that I have, comes from him.

Contents

Introduction ix

SECTION A: SVAYAMBODHA

Chapter 1: Fundamental Axioms of Sanatana Dharma 5

Chapter 2: The Ascent and Descent of Consciousness 27

Chapter 3: Diversity in Unity 49

Chapter 4: A Dynamic Balance of Opposites 69

Chapter 5: We, the Hindus 111

SECTION B: SHATRUBODHA

Chapter 6: Enemies of Sanatana Dharma 133

Chapter 7: Fundamentals of Prophetic Monotheism 167

Chapter 8: Hindu View of Prophetic Monotheism 249

Chapter 9: The Long Arc of Christianity 295

Chapter 10: The Long Arc of Islam 343

Chapter 11: Weaponization of Life 385

Chapter 12: Hindu View of Secular Modernity 409

Chapter 13: The Svayambodha–Shatrubodha Scale 447

Prologue to the Hindu Renaissance 481
Acknowledgements 491
Notes 499
Bibliography 529
About the Author 539

Introduction

'There are many Hindus who are legitimately proud of Hindu art, architecture, sculpture, music, painting, dance, drama, literature, linguistics, lexicography, and so on. But they seldom take into account the fact that this great wealth of artistic, literary and scientific heritage, will die if Hindu society which created it is no more there to preserve, protect and perpetuate it.'

—Sita Ram Goel

Kalicharan's Question

On that extremely hot day of June 2014, while I was on my way to an ancient temple site, I saw an ocean of Muslims in skullcaps, protesting in a huge march. One slogan, tearing through all the noise, reached me very clearly: '*Israel murdabad*!' The Muslims of Vidisha, Madhya Pradesh, were protesting in thousands against Israel's attacks on Gaza in response to Hamas's (Harakat al-Muqawama al-Islamiyya [Islamic Resistance Movement]) abduction and massacre of three Israeli teenagers. The sides were clear. Muslims versus the rest. Not one placard sympathized with the three innocent Jewish teenagers who were murdered brutally by Palestinian Islamists. The Muslims of Vidisha were supporting the Muslims of Palestine with no ethical or moral judgement involved. Very few of them would even know exactly where Palestine was. The criterion to choose sides was clear—Islam, the necessary and sufficient condition. Hamas was a Muslim organization. Palestine was a Muslim state. And the protestors in Vidisha were Muslims. Muslims of India were taking out a massive rally in a state with a heavy Hindu majority to support their 'Muslim brothers' in Palestine. Along with Israel, they were also protesting against the Indian state for not supporting Palestine enough.

Kalicharan, the 23-year-old driver who was taking me to the site, was also silently observing. He was a proud Hindu, and the spectacle of the Muslim strength for a transnational Islamic cause held his attention deeply. Breaking long silence, he asked a deep question, the essence of which was: 'Why is it so that Muslims unite across national and geographical boundaries but fail to unite with the land they live in? And why are Hindus not like that?'

To answer Kalicharan's question simply: Muslims unite worldwide with their co-religionists, because for them, religion is more important than country, geography, civilization, or even ethics and morality. But this answer is not fundamental, for it asks other more fundamental questions like: Why do Muslims consider religion (Islam) as their primary and overarching identity, subsuming all other identities like State, race, ethnicity, language, humanity, etc.? And why do Hindus and other pagan, polytheistic, and native religionists all over the world identify more with land and other concrete markers, like language, race, ethnicity, food, etc., unlike Muslims?

Before we attempt to answer these questions, it would be pertinent to ask whether Muslims are alone in this or if there are other communities that unite over an abstract idea. The answer is yes. In another event, almost a decade later, rivalling the one quoted above, the Chhattisgarh Christians (minuscule in number) called for and achieved a state-wide *bandh* protesting the 'killing of their brothers and sisters in Manipur' during the Meitei–Kuki riots in Manipur in late 2023.

They were supporting the Kuki-Chin-Mizo tribes of Manipur, which are Christian in religion. The question is: How are the Christian Kuki tribes of Manipur and Mizoram 'brothers and sisters' of the Chhattisgarh tribes? There is nothing common in them, including race, ethnicity, language, food, culture, etc. The only common thing between them is their religion, Christianity.

Another case is that of Jews and Judaism, who upon the creation of Israel gathered from more than sixty countries with wildly different languages, food, and cultures to unite with people with whom the only common thing they had was religion. A common thread runs through these three cases. The religions under question here are Islam, Christianity, and Judaism. They are collectively known as prophetic monotheistic religions. Their followers—Muslims, Christians, and Jews—are called 'People of the Book' since they derive their supreme, overarching identity from their religious books—the Bible for Jews and Christians and the Quran for Muslims.[1]

To come back to Kalicharan's question, what differentiates the behaviours of Muslims and other prophetic monotheists from other followers of natural religions like Hindu dharma is their ability to gather together under an abstract idea like a belief or a dogma, anchored in a Book. Hindus, on the other hand, identify more with concrete identities rooted in land, language, food, and culture. Thus, what differentiates the two sets of people is the monotheist habit of considering religious dogma or belief as their overarching identity and the ability to band together under it. They have monolithic, homogenized, and universal views about religion, society, and the world. Hence, it is easy for them to unite across all real geographical boundaries. But the question remains: why and how are they able to do so?

Kalicharan's question made me go beyond secondary answers. My earlier studies in comparative religion had taught me 'how' the Hindus were different from the followers of Islam and

Christianity. But they hadn't given me any satisfactory answer as to 'why' that was so. This book, in a way, is an attempt to answer Kalicharan's question in all its 'whats', 'hows', and 'whys'. To expand his question to include other variants as well as other aspects of differentiation, these would be the most fundamental questions that I will try to answer in this book:

1. Why are Muslims (and Christians) able to unite globally over an abstract idea (religion), but Hindus cannot?
2. Why are Muslims (and Christians) not able to unite with the land they live in and rather have extra-territorial loyalties?
3. Why have Christianity and Islam spread all over the world, becoming global religions, while pagan religions remained local?
4. Why do they (Muslims and Christians) convert and make us a part of them, while we cannot?
5. Why is it that Hindu disunity harms Hindu causes and Hindu society but the internal discord of Islamic and Christian societies does not affect their overall progress as religions all over the world?

What Is the Primary Problem of Hindu Society?

Kalicharan identified the source of Muslim power in their great unity. In comparison, he saw Hindu society as deeply disunited. And he was right, at least as far as India was concerned, where Muslims are far more united than Hindus. However, this opinion does not hold if we look at Islamic countries. There are more than fifty Islamic countries all over the world. Many of them are completely Islamic in their demography, and yet they cannot unite under one command. The divisions are far from just political.

The Muslim world is divided into many religious factions, the most common being Shia and Sunni, but there are other sects like Ibadi and Ahmadiyya. Between 85 and 90 per cent of

Muslims the world over are Sunni. Some of the most important Islamic countries, like Saudi Arabia, Turkey, and Indonesia, are all Sunni. Iran, Iraq, and Azerbaijan have a Shia majority, and there are Shia minorities in many other countries of Western Asia. Oman calls itself an Ibadi country, which is a Kharijite sect, closer to Sunnis than Shias but not quite Sunni and thus classified as separate. Ahmadiyyas and Bahais do not have any separate countries but are minorities in a few countries.

Even within the Shia and Sunni worlds, there is no absolute unity. Saudi Arabia and Turkey are both overwhelmingly Sunni, and yet they are bitterly divided over ethnicity. The Turk vs Arab conflict is millennia old. While Turkey and Azerbaijan are both Turkish in ethnicity, they are divided over religion, as Turkey is Sunni and Azerbaijan is Shia. While Iran and Azerbaijan are united in religion, as both are Shia-majority, they are divided over ethnicity. In Iraq, a Shia-majority country, Shias are divided between Arab Shias and Iranian Shias. Sunnis of Saudi Arabia look down upon Pakistani Sunnis for being of 'inferior stock'. The Pathans of Afghanistan too look down upon the Pakistanis, and vice versa. The Pakistanis are also divided over the Shia–Sunni conflict, but there are many other divisions over ethnicity, like Punjabi vs Sindhi, and divisions based on recent history in which the immigrants from India during the Partition, like the Muhajirs, are hated for not being 'original Pakistanis'. Indonesia is the largest Muslim and Sunni country in the world, and yet they are racially discriminated against by West Asian and Arab Muslims as '*chinkis*'. The African Muslims from West Africa, like Nigerians, are of course looked down upon as the racially inferior '*habshi*', but even within Africa, the 'Black Africans' south of Sahara are considered inferior to the 'superior and fair Arab stock' of countries like Egypt, Algeria, Tunisia, and Morocco. Even within Algeria, the Arab Muslims hate Berber Muslims and call them nomadic barbarians of the desert. The Berber Muslims call the Arabs the invaders who never left.

In short, the Islamic world is as divided as any other group on earth. There are religious, racial, ethnic, political, and other divisions in all Islamic countries. The Christian world is as or even more divided. Apart from the three major divisions of Catholicism, Protestantism, and Orthodoxy, there are many other smaller sects. According to some estimates, there are 24,000 Christian sects all over the world. So, the Christian world too is deeply divided.

Yet, their internal divisions do not result in a total loss to their respective religions. Both Islam and Christianity keep growing all over the world in leaps and bounds, mostly through conversions and a better birth rate. Islam is the fastest-growing religion in the world. Muslims are more than two billion in numbers now, forming around one-fourth of the world population. Christians, the largest group in the world, hover at around 32 per cent, or one-third of the world population.

While Islam is gaining numbers in almost every part of the world, Christianity is losing to Islam in the West and in some African countries due to the better birth rate of Islam and due to immigration from Muslim countries. If we ignore cases where Islam and Christianity are locked in a combat head-to-head, Christianity too is perpetually growing, especially in non-Muslim and non-Christian countries like India, China, and Southeast Asian countries. While East Timor and the Philippines were converted during the colonial era to Christianity, South Korea now has Christians as the largest religious group, and the change happened in the last seven decades only.

Somehow the internal conflicts of Christian and Muslim societies are not detrimental to the overall growth of Christianity and Islam, while divisions of Hindu society result in the loss of Hindu dharma. It is easy to conclude that unity cannot be the primary cause of the victory of Islam and Christianity because their societies are also deeply disunited. So, what is that which gives a prophetic monotheistic religion like Islam and Christianity an edge?

It is their deep sense of the enemy—their *Shatrubodha*.

Yes, what makes Islam or Christianity win is their Shatrubodha. For both Shias and Sunnis, Hindus are a greater enemy than any Muslim sect or individual. This acute sense of the enemy and his inferiority is deeply embedded in the Muslim and Christian psyche. It is epitomized by the Ali brothers and their opinion about Gandhi. When asked about the respect that he had for Gandhi compared to his Muslim brothers, he said:

> However pure Gandhiji's character may be, he must appear to me from the point of view of religion inferior to any Mussalman, even though he be without character. Yes, according to my religion and creed, I do hold an adulterous and a fallen Mussalman to be better than Mahatma Gandhi.[2]

This explains the acute Shatrubodha in Islamic society. For them, the religious outsider can never be good, even if he does all the good deeds in the world. For Muslims and Christians, belief is everything; action is nothing. Even when there is infighting in two Islamic groups, it is always clear that the non-Muslims are always the enemy for all Islamic sects, and when it comes to supporting a Muslim faction on the one hand and a non-Muslim faction on the other hand, the choice is always clear. A Muslim is always to be favoured over a non-Muslim. In case of any inner conflict, the pyramid of priorities is always clear for a Muslim or any other monotheistic believer. The non-believer is always of lower priority than the worst kind of believer.

Shatrubodha, coupled with the pyramid of priorities guaranteeing the favour of insiders over outsiders, solves the problem of inner divisions or lack of unity. But there is another critical element that makes Islam and Christianity perpetually victorious. What guarantees their perpetual growth is their conversion agenda. They do not just think that others, like Hindus, live in sin. They also believe that it is the sacred duty of a Muslim or a Christian to convert a pagan Hindu to their religion.

What makes the prophetic monotheistic religions of Islam and Christianity dangerous for dharmic communities like Hindu society is this deep Shatrubodha, coupled with a pyramid of priorities and a conversion agenda.

Shatrubodha makes sure that the other is always identified as the enemy, and every insider knows that the outsiders are enemies. The pyramid of priorities makes sure that any internal conflict is not detrimental to the global agenda and overall growth of the religion. And the conversion agenda makes sure that the prophetic monotheistic religion does not remain stagnant but keeps growing. This is why Christianity has converted and won over continent after continent since its inception. This is why Islam has converted and increased in population ever since its advent, and this is what Hindu society lacks.

The primary problem of Hindu society, and of any other pagan polytheistic society, is its lack of Shatrubodha. This does not mean that Hindus do not need to unite. We do need to unite, of course. Hindu unity is a necessary goal. But it is not sufficient. What makes it sufficient is Shatrubodha. We need to know who the ideological enemy is and what it thinks—a clear idea of 'us' and 'them' and their modus operandi. Sita Ram Goel, the great Hindu thinker and historian, said that if we refuse to fight ideological enemies, then we have to fight physical enemies on the streets. So, we need to know our ideological enemies, and we need a plan to settle our internal differences so that they do not damage our dharma and society. We also need to come up with a plan to convert 'them' into 'us', so that the slow bleeding of our side is stopped, and a balance is created.

Shatrubodha is to know the other, to know where the boundaries lie, where the limits of our culture and civilization end, and where the outsider, the other, begins. We often gather an idea of who we are from knowing who we are not. Shatrubodha is thus not just a tool to fight the enemy. It is also a means of knowing our boundaries, and thus, by this indirect method, to know who we are. But to know the other is not enough. To know the boundaries is not enough. It is equally important to know who we are and where our centre lies.

Svayambodha, the knowledge of our own dharma, culture, and civilization is also important. Shatrubodha is to know the peripheries and what lies beyond the peripheries of our civilization. Svayambodha is to know our centre, our roots, our fundamentals, from which the sense of 'us'—our own sense of identity—emerges. Without knowing who we are, we lose our anchor and risk becoming the other.[3] Some Hindus today, impressed with Islamic success, recommend becoming like them in 'strictly following dogma'—to be anti-science and anti-technology and to treat women like they do. This is a sure way to doom. Svayambodha is necessary so that we do not turn into the 'other'. This does not mean that we do not learn anything from our ideological enemy, but only that part should be learnt which does not fundamentally change our own identity.

Only a good balance of Svayambodha and Shatrubodha will create a healthy society. Lacking any one of the either will result in severe disability. At many points in our history, it is the critical lack of Shatrubodha that has defeated us. The misplaced magnanimity and chivalry of our Kshatriyas, who would let the Islamic invaders go free after defeating them on the battlefield, proved fatal for them and everything they held dear. They could not see that the ethics they were extending to the enemy were not the same as those practiced by the enemy. Even after showing mercy and chivalry to an invader many times and letting him go after defeating him on the battlefield, when the same invader defeated them once, he would behead him, molest and enslave women and children in his civilization, and destroy all that the Hindu king loved.

This happened because of the loss of Shatrubodha at a critical juncture. Here, Svayambodha would not help, for no amount of Svayambodha for a Hindu would prepare him for the inhuman barbarity that was practiced by the invaders. The ethical system that the Islamic invaders brought into Bharatavarsha was something we Hindus were totally unfamiliar with.

A Hindu believes that respecting women, children, elders, saints, temples, and ecology are fundamental benchmarks to be followed. But the new enemy followed none of these practices. They targeted women and children, fought during the night, killed innocents and unarmed, desecrated and destroyed temples, and massacred cows and Brahmins. Everything that the Hindus did, they did the exact opposite. Islamic ethics and modus operandi had no precedence in Bharatavarsha. No amount of learning more Svayambodha from his co-Hindus would ever prepare them for the barbarity that was beset upon them during the Islamic invasions of India. One cannot prepare for every single emergency like this *a priori*. One can prepare for it only after exposure.

The only possibility for a culture facing an existential threat from a barbarian enemy with a completely different ethical standard is to study the new enemy upon first exposure and prepare a response that is emergent at first and then institutionalized later. For sheer survival, the defending culture and society should be able to absorb the first impact of such an enemy and prepare its society with behaviour, institutions, and mechanisms to fight for survival. The *purva paksha* of such an enemy should be thorough and should be defined in clear and simple terms that are capable of seeping down to every last person of the 'in' group.

To be able to formulate a response, create institutions and even scriptures instructing for the emergent situation, and spread it to every individual of the native society is called Shatrubodha. And there is no substitute for it.

To investigate the other possibility: What happens when Svayambodha is missing in a society? Many Hindus with highly developed Shatrubodha in the past few decades have correctly identified that they are culturally and civilizationally 'different' from Islamic and Christian civilizations. They have condemned the barbarism and arbitrariness of Shariat-like legal systems and rightly so. But this has led them to believe that just because they are different from monotheists, Hindu society has no customs, rituals, or traditions at all, and that it is a free-for-all system with no identity of its own. On the other hand, some Hindus, impressed by the power that Islamic and Christian societies hold, start recommending that Hindus should be like them in being dogmatic. This is also a way to destruction. That is why Svayambodha is also important, along with Shatrubodha. It is equally critical to know 'who we are' and not just 'who we are not'.

In 2024, the Hindu resurgence is evident in India. The grand Ram Mandir has been rebuilt, and the quest for regaining the lost temples of Hindu dharma is on its way. The Indian State has acknowledged its Hindu civilizational character for the first time since Independence by bringing in the provision for CAA (Citizenship Amendment Act). The Indian media scene is waking up to the atrocities heaped on Hindu society, and gradually, issues like Love Jihad and Christian conversions are coming to light. Impartial historians of India like Sita Ram Goel, who wrote the correct, unbiased history of India, are being acknowledged in mainstream media. Movies are no longer unequivocally anti-Hindu, and movies like *The Kashmir Files*, *The Kerala Story*, and *Kantara* are seeing the light of the day. Stand-up comedy is also witnessing the rise of proud Hindus who are no longer interested in Hindu bashing. The ad industry and OTT platforms are becoming more sensitive to Hindu issues. In foreign policy, India is emerging as a confident nation with vision and nuance. Hindu meditational practices are no longer exoticized and have become part of mainstream discussions.

In short, the Hindu renaissance has again picked up speed, and fundamental changes are happening to the Hindu psyche and society, sufficient enough to reclaim the lost glory of Bharatavarsha.

And yet, one cannot help but remember the first line of Dickens' *A Tale of Two Cities*: 'It was the best of times, it was the worst of times.' If we look at the other side of things, the 'woke' virus has plagued our society, and our youth is being enamoured by a self-destructive ideology. Hindu populations are declining everywhere, and in states like Kerala, West Bengal, Assam, and even Andhra Pradesh, Tamil Nadu, and Punjab, they are facing an existential threat. There is no end to Bangladeshi Muslim infiltration in India, and the CAA without NRC (National Register of Citizens) remains a paper tiger. Christianity is having unprecedented success in India like it never had in its history, and its rate of growth in Andhra Pradesh, Tamil Nadu, and Punjab is frightening. Every major institution of India, including the judiciary, is still anti-Hindu, and the best intentions of Hindu politicians are struck down by the Supreme Court or any other such institution. Our country is on the verge of caste riots instigated by all major political parties of India except one, and the churches and the corporates of the world are stoking these internal fault lines in India so that they can divide Hindus into a million pieces and consume us into Christianity or Islam piecemeal. China, the only other major country with a dharmic population, is ruled by an adharmic communist government and is blocking India's and Hindus' advance on world stages. The ecological crisis has hit the ceiling, and the disaster unfolds as we speak. The Vatican and the Waqf Board continue unbridled, and their hold on India's real estate increases frighteningly. The left-liberal deep state remains strong, and one political defeat of the Bharatiya Janata Party (BJP) might unleash a communist–missionary–mullah terror on Hindu activists and thinkers. The list is endless.

To ensure that the Hindu renaissance started by Swami Vivekananda and continued by the likes of Shri Aurobindo, Veer

Savarkar, Shri Ram Swarup, and Shri Sita Ram Goel continues, and that Hindus and Sanatana Dharma gain their rightful place in the world, we need a clear intellectual framework of Svayambodha and Shatrubodha.

To be clear, Shatrubodha is not about individuals; it is only about ideas and ideologies. *Shatru* is far from an individual. Shatru is the ideology that inspires individuals of a particular group to perpetually fight with other groups. While reading this book, this critical fact must be kept in mind.

This framework becomes critical for a crucial reason: any society experiences internal clashes. If there are one billion people, like the Hindus, internal clashes are inevitable. But when external enemies are bent upon the destruction of Hindu society and civilization, we also need a united front against the enemy forces. So Hindus need a framework by which they can sort out their internal differences and unite against the external threat. For this, they need to understand the pyramid of priorities, which makes sure that in no case an enemy ideology is favoured over an 'in' group. This book is an attempt in that direction. Svayambodha and Shatrubodha framework makes sure that the pyramid of priorities is clear for the Hindus whenever they face an external threat.

So let us embark on the journey of defining ourselves, our friends, and our enemies; let us learn what is Svayambodha and Shatrubodha for Hindus. From here, we proceed.

SECTION A

SVAYAMBODHA

In an incident that is etched deeply in my memory, just months after having met my guru in 2003, I was looking in his library while he was not home. I pulled out a volume, which he kept talking about and which piqued my curiosity. It was *Tripura Rahasya*, the great Tamil spiritual classic, which was the favourite of Shri Ramana Maharishi. I started reading it. In a few minutes, he came and took it from me, saying I would not understand it. Feeling slightly offended, I asked why I would not understand it, to which he said that it is not a subject of thought but of action. The contents of a classical Hindu text like that will open up to me only if I have the requisite meditational practice and have been practicing it for a while. It would not make much sense to someone who has no experience or accompanying meditational practice. In short, he told me that it was not a matter of mind but of experience, practice, and meditation.

Over the next two decades, during my study of prophetic monotheism on the one hand and my experience of Sanatana Dharma through the *anugraha* of my guru on the other, I realized that on that day he had told me about a fundamental binary that divides the two worldviews represented by Sanatana Dharma on the one hand and prophetic monotheism on the other. While Sanatana Dharma is all about experiences and practices, prophetic monotheism is all about dogma and belief. This deep binary has caused all the differences between the two systems.

So let us begin by investigating Sanatana Dharma with this understanding that it is primarily experiential in nature. The texts support the experience and are not independent of it. Even the axiomatic truths that this chapter is going to talk about serve as props to help the seeker's experience. As far as my own grasp of Sanatana Dharma is concerned, whatever I understand about it is through the anugraha of my guru. I claim no expert knowledge of dharma. I base my understanding upon the experiences of other great experts of Sanatana Dharma, of *jnanis* and *jivanmuktas*, as well as the experiences of my guru. It is with this understanding that we delve into some fundamental axioms and practices in Hindu dharma.

This section is on Svayambodha—what it means to be a Hindu. It is not an attempt to decide who is a Hindu and who is not; far from it. Instead, it is about what it means to be a Hindu in practice. It will discuss some of the most fundamental axioms and practices of Sanatana Dharma.

Chapter 1

Fundamental Axioms of Sanatana Dharma

'Be as you are.'
—Shri Ramana Maharishi

Shiva Dakshinamurthy, *Kailasanathar Temple*, Madhu Jagdhish, 27 Oct. 2018. In this form, Shiva is seen as the greatest of teachers, and thus an apt metaphor for Sanatana Dharma[1]

Rta, Satya, Rna, Dharma

There is a natural order in the universe: a certain way matter and energy interact, stars form and die, planets orbit stars, and satellites orbit planets; life is born and evolves on a planet. This order works in cycles that are so large they are not immediately perceptible to a human observer. But they are universal and all-pervading. Life perpetuates in many of these cycles: species rise and fall; day turns into night, night into day; summers give way to rains, rains to winters, and so on. There are many of these cycles that govern our lives, even though we are not always conscious of them. These natural cycles can be called the cosmic rhythms of the universe. These cyclical patterns are to be seen in every aspect of nature and culture:

> Looking at nature, the most striking thing we notice is how the same pattern repeats over and over again in a seemingly infinite cycle; much like a well-oiled machine. Sun rises in the east and sets in the west as night follows day and day follows night, the waxing and waning of the moon, the high and low tides at sea, the progress of the seasons from the bountiful spring to the barren winters and back again, the northerly and southerly movements of the sun, the periodical movement of stars and constellations; all of these seem like against cosmic orchestra repeating itself over and over again. In fact, there are several nested cycles within one another like the cycle of a day within a fortnight, which is nested within a month and seasons. There is a full cycle of seasons within a year and cosmic cycles spanning over several years.[2]

We witness these patterns in every aspect of our lives. Life itself is such a cycle at many levels. We are born, are taken care of by our parents, then grow up, marry and produce children whom we take care of, and then when we get old, our children take care of us. The legacy continues with our children, who have already spawned off another cycle before we die. Although we disappear as individuals, the cycles that gave us birth and the cycles that we helped perpetuate continue. In nature, one creature feeds off another, and the cycle of the circulation of energy continues. Not just living beings, but these cycles can be seen in inanimate objects on Earth too. Colliding oceanic tectonic plates create mountains; mountains are worn off by weathering by wind and water and disintegrate into rocks; rocks weather down into sand and then mud, which is carried back to the ocean once again, and the cycle continues.

These cycles are eternal. They have always been. No one governs or administrates them. They are perpetual hidden potentialities of the universe that are always there and manifest whenever they find fertile ground to do so. These cycles are called '*rta*' in Sanatana Dharma. Rta is a term 'denoting the order underlying and controlling the harmony of the cosmos'[3]. It is the 'natural order inherent in nature that sustains and keeps it running'[4].

Rta is one of the most primordial concepts of Hindu dharma, finding mention in the *Rig Veda*, which expands upon rta in various verses, showing its all-pervading influence. Rta becomes clearer when we discuss a related concept, *satya*. The *Rig Veda* makes clear that 'creation is nothing but the emergence of a beautiful set of interrelated cycles, in time and space and what lies at its root is rtam-satyam'[5]. When rta manifests, it becomes satya. To take the analogy of seed and tree: a seed with the potentiality of a tree is rta, while the very act of sprouting that seed into a sapling and then a tree is the manifestation of satya. If rta is the latent reality, then satya is the manifest reality. In other words, rta is the potentiality of satya.

Rta also signifies dynamism in Sanatana Dharma. Our culture and dharma have been described by many great scholars as '*Sanatana Ganga Pravaha*', the 'eternal flow of the river Ganga'. This comparison is very apt and particularly meaningful for describing Sanatana Dharma. A river is forever changing and yet always the same. It is never the same again, for every instant the molecules of water in it are changing, yet the channel and the pattern remain the same. Similarly, Sanatana Dharma or the Eternal Tradition is forever changing and yet always the same. While keeping the universal patterns alive, it keeps adapting to the exigencies of time, place, and context. Like a river, it is unceasing and eternal. Rta symbolizes this dynamism.

Sanatana Dharma is to be found more in the processes rather than specific institutions or concepts. The concept of rta is thus very helpful in realizing the core of Sanatana Dharma in practice. It is not in ideas or concepts. It is not in institutions. It is in the preservation of eternal cosmic cycles. Shatavdhani Dr R. Ganesh and Hari Ravikumar indicate towards the dynamic aspect of rta:

> It (*rta*) refers to the dynamism inherent in the universe. Even in nature, dynamism means life and stasis means death—a man is deemed to be alive only if he is breathing, his heart is beating, and blood is flowing through his veins. *Rta* is the order behind the whole of creation. It symbolizes universal vibrancy and a sense of belongingness to something bigger than oneself.[6]

Rta-Satya is thus the natural order of the universe. But this order is very delicate, and any potential disturbance to it might lead to its breakdown and great disturbances down the cycles. And man, as a species, is entirely capable of disturbing these natural cycles, or rta, due to his greed, desire, and unbridled use of technology. So there is a need to protect the order of rta-satya, which brings us to dharma. To protect the order of rta-satya is dharma:

> *Rta* comes into contact with the world to become *satya*. When *satya* is practiced, it becomes dharma.... The wise understand *rta* as a system inherent in the universe, *satya* as a manifest reality of that system, and dharma as the work that is done with

> a firm understanding of the system and its manifestations. So, *rta* corresponds to an inner realization, *satya* corresponds to an external manifestation, and dharma corresponds to an action leading to a result.[7]

When we strive to uphold the natural order with understanding and the intent to do so, it is called dharma. Hindus considered it their sacred duty to protect the order of nature or what we called the order of rta-satya. As beneficiaries of the order of nature, our ancient *rishis* felt indebted to it and thought it only natural that it was their duty to protect nature from the rapacious side of human beings. Dharma, very simply, was anything that restored natural balance. Adharma, as a corollary, was anything that disturbed the natural balance. Dharma is thus, eternal balance. 'Dharma is that which sustains or preserves the order of rtam-satyam.'[8]

Dharma maintains the cosmic order or the order of rta-satya. One way to do this is to reinforce the natural order by aligning our lives to the natural cycles. For example, there is the natural cycle of day and night, and so we should align our cycles of sleep and waking to the natural cycle of day and night. To do so is dharma. Conversely, to not do so is adharma. Contemporary science is reinforcing this ancient dharmic way of living. Electricity and modern ways of living have made us defy the natural sleep and waking cycles, resulting in many chronic diseases among us. Now science confirms that human beings will be at their healthiest if they follow their 'inner circadian rhythm', which is defined as 'the physical, mental, and behavioral changes an organism experiences over a 24-hour cycle.'[9] Dr Ganesh sums up this aspect of dharma very clearly:

> In a nutshell, we can say that dharma is the principle of sustenance. If we are forced to provide a single-word equivalent in English, we may use the word 'sustainability'. The literal

> meaning of Sanatana dharma is 'eternal sustainability' and a reasonable approximation of the implied meaning is 'ancient Indian way of life'—or even 'Indian Culture', roughly speaking.[10]

Restoring a disturbed cycle to its natural order is another way to do dharma. For example, the Hindu science of architecture, *vastu*, ordains that when a site is chosen and levelled by felling of trees for the building of a temple, then ten times the number of trees should be planted as were cut down while levelling the *bhumi*, or the land for the temple. Thus, we see dharma here as the principle that restores the disturbed cycle of nature. Any act like reforestation that reinstates the natural cycle and heals the disturbed or damaged ecosystems is also dharma. Thus, dharma is to maintain the natural order and to restore it if it is disturbed.[11]

Sanatana Dharma considers it the duty of human society to restore the balance of nature, as it is human activity that has disturbed it. Any such restoration is considered a great act of dharma. Sanatana Dharma has oriented all individual and social activity of human society towards this goal. Through various customs, practices, and cosmological stories, it is ensured that social and individual activity is oriented towards creating balance in nature and life.

The *Rig Veda* makes this aspect very clear while elucidating the concept of 'rta'. While on one hand, rta is the 'general order of the cosmos', it is also called in the texts the 'correct way of the gods' and also the 'moral conduct of man'. The *Rig Veda* mentions that the gods exist as the guardians or protectors of rta. Mitra, Agni, and Varuna are the charioteers of rta. It suggests that all human activity in service of divinity is an attempt to flow in line with the rhythm of the cosmos, to align the world of culture with the world of nature. This becomes clearer when we see how rta in the *Rig Veda* is also associated with the idea of *paapa* or sin. P.V. Kane mentions that rta is mentioned in the earliest of texts, such as the *Rig Veda*, as having threefold aspects: '*Rta* had a threefold aspect. It means "the course of nature" or "the regular and general order in the cosmos"; with reference to sacrifice it means "the correct and ordered way of the cult of the Gods"; thirdly, it also means the "moral conduct of man".'[12]

To not follow rta, or to not flow in line with the natural order of rta, is considered a sin. This makes it clear that the greatest quest of human society, according to a dharmic culture like Hindu dharma, is to create and manage a society that flows with the natural order of the universe, not against it. By linking adharma with the violation of rta, the ancient sages made sure that following dharma would mean the upholding of rta, or the natural order of the universe. The *Rig Veda* also mentions a phrase '*rtena rtam*' where 'rtena' means the correct course of sacrificial rites and 'rtam' the settled order in the universe. It shows how dharmic activity makes human activity flow in tune with the cosmic rhythm.

The Mahabharata defines dharma similarly. 'Dharma supports everything, it bears everything, and it is the foundation for everything.'[13] It is not unlike the thermostat, which maintains the temperature in the room at a certain level. If the temperature goes above that level, then it is brought down. If it goes below, then it is brought up. Increasing or decreasing the temperature in itself is neither good nor bad. What makes it good or bad is whether it is moving towards balance or away from it. Dharma thus is not what sounds good to the ears or what looks good in the short run. Dharma is that which sustains in the long run, even though it might feel harsh or unpleasant in the short run.

The civilization of Bharatavarsha operating under the principles of Sanatana Dharma has been a civilization that always keeps trying to achieve balance or sustainability. When society becomes too orthodox, dharmic forces move liberally towards the mean. When it becomes too open to protect any dharmic systems or laws, dharmic forces move conservatively towards the mean once again. In both cases, it is neither of the extremes, but balance that is sought. Similarly, dharma balances social security and individual freedom, progress and conservation, hierarchy and equality, technology and culture, *samsara* and *vairagya*, and many other such opposites. To say it in another way, dharma is the dynamic balance of opposites. It is the principle of harmony.

Another way to understand the idea of dharma is by understanding the idea of '*rna*'. Rta is omnipresent, but it is easier to understand it when we see it closer to our lives. Take the example of the birth of an individual. When we are born, we cannot take care of ourselves. Neither can we feed ourselves nor relieve. Someone else—our mother, father, and other members of the family—has to take care of us. When we grow up, we need the order of the society, including a safe neighbourhood, educational institutions, hospitals, and public institutions that maintain law and order. We stand on the shoulders of the sages and scholars who created the knowledge base for us. We are indebted to them. We build on the work of our ancestors, who created, fought, and defended a society and a land that is capable of sustaining a knowledge society like ours.

All of this creates a debt on us; the rta of the universe creates a rna on us. And to repay that debt is dharma. Dharma is simply the force that gives back to the universe what we have taken from it while growing up. In other words, it is the force that maintains balance. What is very perceptive is that in Krita Yuga, there was no need of dharma, as rta and its workings were perceivable to everyone. Rta was not in imbalance, thus there was no need to restore it. Everyone naturally followed rta and flew in its rhythm, thus removing the necessity of a force like dharma, which makes rta felt and which makes us flow in rhythm with it. Rta, undisturbed, is dharma. When disturbed, it is the force that restores it, which we call dharma.

Pancha Rnas

The Vedic tradition defines five kinds of rnas: *deva rna*, *rishi rna*, *pitra rna*, *nru rna*, *bhuta rna*—the debt paid to deities, sages/scholars, ancestors, fellow human beings, and nature. These debts are redefined as duties for individuals and groups. To fulfill these responsibilities is to repay those debts to nature and culture. The Hindu cosmos functions on the basis of duties and responsibilities that individuals and groups have to fulfill. It is through the fulfillment of these *kartavyas* (responsibilities) that Hindus do dharma. Rituals are one of the ways in which dharma makes itself tangible to us.

It is this *kartavyabodha*, the sense of duty towards nature and culture, that is the driving force behind Hindu society. We need a sense of kartavyabodha in human society, for the natural laws no longer hold on their own, and we need a divine–human order that protects rta. It is impossible for everyone to perceive where and how the rta is disturbed and how to correct it. But if their dharmic duties tell them to behave in a way that restores the balance of rta, then its restoration and natural order are automatically taken care of. Dharma achieves this restoration through kartavyabodha.

The Hindu worldview, in this way, governed by the laws of rta, rna, and dharma, works on kartavyabodha and *pancha rnas*. A Hindu lives a life that preserves nature and, at the same time, transcends its limitations spiritually by understanding rta and eventually overcoming it by attaining *moksha*, or release from the cycle of birth and death. Let us now delve a little deeper into each of the pancha rnas.

The first rna (debt) is the deva rna. This rna means that our world is what it is because the higher beings, the deities, have bestowed their grace on it, and thus we exist and find sustenance due to *deva kripa* (the grace of the deities), which creates a deva rna on us. It is a sacred contract between the deities and the devotees. Hindus repay deva rna by worshipping and meditating upon these *devatas*. They worship the deities by incorporating them in daily rituals with prayer and meditation, celebrating particular festivals dedicated to them, and maintaining the temples or shrines that are devoted to them. By paying the deva rna, it is ensured that the continuity of the indigenous tradition is maintained and the dharmic character of the land is upheld.

Deities are important to Hindus for various reasons. When an individual takes *deeksha* (initiation in meditation) from a guru, he meditates upon a deity, which helps him concentrate his mind, remove the layers of ignorance, and attain a higher state of consciousness, which opens the path towards moksha a little more. Without a form to meditate upon, it is almost impossible for a majority of individuals to withdraw their tendencies inwards. Thus, deities are central to *dhyana* or meditation.

They are also the visible and tangible form of many cosmic rhythms that exist but are not easily visible to us. They represent many aspects of nature. Hindus worship all aspects of nature, like mountains, rivers, and oceans, but in the form of a deity, so that without having to understand the complexities of how ecosystems work, they treat nature with respect. By respecting and worshipping them, Hindus accede and submit to the larger laws of nature and life. To worship a deity is a humbling activity that accepts that man is not the centre of all creation but one species among many. The deities also reflect many inner realities on higher planes of consciousness, where they represent many functions that are critical in meditation. By repaying deva rna, we also open ourselves up to the possibility of attaining knowledge about higher realities.

The second great rna in the Hindu worldview is the rishi rna. Humans function upon the knowledge base created by their ancestors. Hindu society is even more indebted to its saints and scholars because India was fundamentally a knowledge society. The most sacred scriptures of Hindus are called the Vedas—the texts of knowledge. Thus, the debt of the great saints and scholars who created the great tradition of the Indian Knowledge System through generations of hard work is heavy upon the shoulders of Hindus. That is why repaying rishi rna—the debt to the saints and scholars of the past—is the second greatest kartavya, the second great contract, or rna, that Hindus hold sacred. It is considered their sacred duty to support the community and saints and scholars who have devoted their entire lives to the pursuit of knowledge, so that this pursuit can be preserved as an exclusive and specialized endeavour.

The third rna, pitra rna, says that Hindus must be grateful to their ancestors for enabling our existence in this time and space, for preserving dharma and civilization through the ages, and for handing them over to the current generation. Tradition is that which continues. Without respecting one's ancestors, no culture can expect to continue the good in their civilization; and without continuing anything from the past, one cannot hope to call oneself tradition. That is why worshipping ancestors is the third great rna, or sacred debt, that Hindus must repay.

Worshipping our ancestors also keeps us connected to the land. And a deep connection with the land and the space makes us respect it, love it, care for it, and preserve it. Wendell Berry, one of the foremost natural thinkers to come out of the contemporary West, says that a major reason for the degradation of ecosystems the world over today is that so many people are now uprooted, constantly shifting between cities and towns, and feel no connection with either their place of birth or their place of adoption. The lack of ownership incubates a careless attitude towards the place they are living in, leading to the degradation of the cultural and natural ecosystem around them. In Bharatavarsha, the pitra rna ensured that nobody felt disconnected from their native place, nobody felt uprooted, and everyone had a sense of involvement, inclusion, and ownership in the place of their birth and the place where they lived, making them care for it more. Pitra rna creates a sense of belonging, and that is why it is so central to being Hindu.

Nru rna or *manushya* rna is the fourth great rna in the Hindu worldview. We have already discussed how we are indebted to our parents and family for taking care of us and helping us grow into self-dependent individuals. However, this debt does not stop at the immediate family. As a famous saying goes, 'It takes a village to bring up a child.' It hides in itself great truths, and more so about the Hindu society. It shows us how interdependent we are and how it is the wisdom, support, and vigilance of the entire society that helps us lead safe and fulfilling lives.

Even though we know this rationally, it can be hard sometimes to keep the human bonds alive apart from our immediate family due to many reasons. But Sanatana Dharma made sure that we would remember to keep these human connections in the form of a kartavya. We may not feel individually obliged to keep our connections alive with the wider *kutumba* or society, but if we are reminded of doing that as our sacred kartavya, as one of the pancha rnas, then we make sure that we do it as our dharmic duty.

The fifth rna, bhuta rna, is the most critical rna from the point of ecology and sustainability. Bhuta rna is the debt of nature on human beings. We are indebted to the flora, fauna, and the larger ecosystem that sustains us through our lives. In an all-encompassing view, Sanatana Dharma does not neglect nature and its role in sustaining life. We are encouraged to take care not just of our fellow human beings in society, but also of animals and plants in nature. Kindness is taught towards all animals, and even plants are said to have '*jiva*', so care is taken that they are not unduly harmed or 'disturbed at night'. Many Hindus have heard the 'myth' in their childhood that plants should not be disturbed at night, as it is considered a sin against the deities that reside in them. These 'rights' of jivas, other than human beings, stem from the belief that man is not the ultimate focus of all creation, as he is in monotheistic religions. Sita Ram Goel says:

> The view that is fostered in a devotee of Advaita, is that all that is there in the universe, animate or inanimate, manifests different limbs of the One Vast Being and, while using those limbs for sustenance and right livelihood, a feeling of friendship should be cultivated towards all of them. Human superiority lies only in this much that birth as a human being facilitates the attainment of supreme truth. Man in his ordinary state is not the master of the universe. Man should consider himself indebted for all the help and cooperation he gets from various components of the universe for his subsistence and his physical, intellectual and spiritual development. And man should repay these debts according to his opportunity and capacity. The Hindu doctrine of repaying the five debts—to *rishis*, ancestors, gods, humans, all other animate and inanimate creatures—is expressive of the same principle.[14]

To take care of ecology, if it is presented to us as a dharmic and divine duty, is easier than understanding the complex scientific phenomena behind it. An easy example presents itself to us. Today, we are more conscious of how ecosystems work and how ecological damage is caused by human activity. The current generation knows more about ecology than any previous generation, and yet it is the present generation that causes more ecological damage than any other generation before it. Clearly, simple rational knowledge of a subject does not necessarily translate into changed behaviour.

There is a very simple way of translating knowledge into behaviour: ritual and meditation, which convert knowledge into action and behaviour. Our ancestors had figured this out and converted the actions incumbent upon us as human beings into sacred duties, kartavyabodha. This is how they ensured that an overall balance was achieved in life, both between humans and nature, and among human societies. It is easy to put dynamite in a mountain and blow it up if it is considered just a mountain, but it is much harder to do so if it is considered a god. As long as this sense of the sacred remains in human life, ecology is also preserved. Wade Davis, an ethnobotanist, expresses a universal truth when he comments on the eco-sensitive nature of Native American tribes:

> A child raised to believe that a mountain is the abode of a protective spirit will be a profoundly different human being from a youth brought up to believe that a mountain is an inert mass of rock ready to be mined. A Kwakwaka'wakw boy raised to revere the coastal forests as the realm of the divine will be a different person from a Canadian child taught to believe that such forests are destined to be logged.... Herein, perhaps, lies the essence of the relationship between many indigenous peoples and the natural world.... What these cultures have done, however, is to forge through time and ritual a relationship to the earth that is based not only on deep attachment to the land also on far more subtle intuition—the idea that the land itself is breathed into being by human consciousness. Mountains, rivers, and forests are not perceived as being inanimate, as mere props on a stage upon which the human drama unfolds. For these societies, the land is alive, a dynamic force to be embraced and transformed by the human imagination.[15]

To a Hindu, this makes intuitive sense. It is no revelation to him that a mountain is the abode of the gods, or even the god himself. Himavana is the father of Parvati, the wife of Shiva. The Shivalik mountain range is thought of as the locks of Shiva himself. Ganga is not simply a river, but a great goddess. The ocean is not just the greatest body of water; it is a deity whose permission must even be sought by Lord Rama, a Vishnu avatar. The wind is not just air; it is Lord Pavana. The breath that flows in our lungs is Hanuman. The sacred hill in Tirumala is Vishnu himself, just as the sacred hill of Arunachala in Tiruvannamalai is Lord Shiva. The Dandakaranya forest is where Lord Rama spent much time and planned to defeat the *rakshasas*. The forest of Dangs in Gujarat is where Shabari received Shri Rama. The hills of easternmost Arunachal Pradesh are the native place of Rukmini, the wife of Shri Krishna. Wind, air, and water are all sacred elements. Every pond and lake have deities and divine beings dwelling in them. Every tree hosts countless deities. The world is so thick with the divine that one can never truly find oneself alone. And this wonderful sacralization of geography is the conscience keeper of traditional folks like Hindus. Even the uneducated behave in an eco-sensitive way without even knowing about it, because it is their divine duty. We need to understand how deeply ecological the Hindu point of view was—that this sense was embedded as one of the core duties of Hindus—through the concept of bhuta rna. It made us aware of the deep but hidden truths of life. Shri Ram Swarup speaks of the deep sacralization of every aspect of life:

> Sanatana dharma teaches that there is an interchange going on between Gods and men, between heaven and earth, between men and men, between the past, the present, the future, and they each owe one to the other. It thinks of life as a *yajna*, an interchange, between different forms and modes, and transformation.[16]

This was the worldview of pancha rnas that is central to Hindus. Apart from making them responsible towards the divine, the knowledgeable saints, the ancestors, fellow human beings, and nature, it also gave them multiple levels of identities. Identity crisis is largely a phenomenon of the modern world. A traditional Hindu society did not have much space for it. Every Hindu was secure in his personal deity. He knew the tradition and land he belonged to. It gave him a rootedness in the space and culture in which he lived, making him more responsible towards nature and culture.

In classical Hindu society, there was another great psychological dimension to the worldview of kartavyabodha. In a Hindu universe, happiness was a function of one's duties and responsibilities and did not depend merely on material possessions. One derived happiness from the fact that he had fulfilled his responsibilities. It mattered little what the responsibility was. In this way, everyone was a hero. The sense of having done one's part for society and nature was everyone's right and not the privilege of a rare hero. A king, after having saved his kingdom, and a poor man, having fed his family, would sleep with an equal sense of satisfaction at night. It was a democracy of happiness.

In the Shatrubodha section, we will explore what happens to those cultures that do not have the concepts of pancha rnas and kartavyabodha.

Karma and Punarjanma

One might argue, however, what if one does not want to follow through with any of these responsibilities? One might call such a person unethical, but what if the questioner replies that he has no problem with being unethical and has no desire to repay the debts? How will the rnas or the debts be enforced then? Will there be an external agency like the State to punish such a behaviour and attitude in Sanatana Dharma? Or are there internal mechanisms to correct this behaviour and make it more responsible and ethical?

Sanatana Dharma responds to most fundamental behavioural problems by instituting mechanisms that change the individual from within. That is how it changes the world. In Hindu dharma, the problem of behavioural irresponsibility was solved by the recognition, codification, and celebration of a most fundamental and axiomatic truth—the phenomenon of *karma* and *punarjanma* (reincarnation).

The *karma-phala siddhanta* is at the centre of Hindu *darshana* and Hindu cosmology. It is impossible to understand the Hindu point of view if we do not understand the idea of karma. This principle of karma says that our actions set in forces subtle motions that propel us towards our future course. Every action begets karma. Good action (karma) accrues good karma-phala, and bad action accrues bad karma-phala. Our actions create a chain of cause and effect that does not stop at the death of the body but continues beyond it, as we are reborn as someone else, and the cycle continues. In the Mahabharata, when Arjuna becomes heavy with sorrow at the prospect of killing his own kin and gurus and refuses to fight, Shri Krishna reveals to him the secret of life and death:

> वासांसि जीर्णानि यथा विहाय नवानि गृह्णाति नरोऽपराणि।
> तथा शरीराणि विहाय जीर्णा न्यन्यानि संयाति नवानि देही।।

> Like a person discards worn-out clothes and accepts others that are new, like that, the soul discards worn-out bodies and attains others that are new.[17]

This tale of birth, death, and rebirth continues over aeons, until one does *sadhana* and contemplates the nature of reality under the guidance of the guru. Then the cycle breaks. In thought, this cycle can be stopped by not identifying with the actions done. The *Isha Upanishad* says, '*Na karma lipyate mare*',[18] which means that action (done with the consciousness that everything in the universe is Brahman or the 'god') does not lead to the causal chain. If karma is done with *drashta bhava* (mere witnessing the act and not identifying with it), then the effect of the results of our karma does not reflect back upon us, and the causal chain is broken; the cycle of life and death is broken, and liberation from this samsara is achieved.

The ultimate goal of Hindu life is to break the cycle of life and death, to come out of the play that causes people to be born again and again. This liberation from the cycle of life and death is called moksha or self-realization. Moksha is one of the four *purusharthas* and the ultimate goal of human life.[19]

The idea of karma and punarjanma makes an individual realize that he is indebted to the deities, wise men, ancestors, fellow men, and nature in not just this life but in many lives. This realization makes him follow his duties and fulfill his responsibilities more deeply and diligently, as individual accountability is not confined to just one life but follows through many lives. No one can escape one's destiny, and thus fewer individuals attempt to have a free lunch in life and digress from the pancha rna worldview. Very few try to avoid fulfilling their duties because they realize it is impossible to shirk your responsibility once you see life through many perspectives. The many lives perspective thus makes one more responsible towards nature and society.

Karma and punarjanma are thus the axiomatic foundation of all Hindu thought. It is on these fundamental truths that all Hindu cosmology, darshana, and rituals stand. Punarjanma means repetition of the cycle of birth and death and continuation of suffering. Moksha means a release from this cycle. But who exactly gets this moksha? And what is the nature or feeling of moksha? That brings us to the next important set of axioms in Hindu dharma.

Atman and Brahman

The quest for moksha is the search for that element that never dies, that which always is, and that which is beyond death. We all realize the impermanence of the world and yearn for that which is permanent, that which always was, is, and will be. For finding this element, we need not take a spaceship and go where nobody has gone before; rather, we have to turn inwards and take an inner journey so that we go beyond the lower reality that we perceive through our senses and the mind. Shri Ram Swarup, in his work *On Hinduism*, talks about the greater truths that the ancient Hindu sages found when they took upon this inner journey:

> The ancient sages studied man and for that they started with themselves; they turned their gaze inward and found there a vast internal life. Going still deeper, they discovered, beyond their more external being, another life or principle which takes another language to describe it; they found it self-existent, bodiless, pure, luminous and conscious; they found that it is in some way unborn and undying; that it does not come along with the body nor does it die with it; that it is beyond sorrow and decay; that it shines from within and it knows itself as self-evident. They found that it is their very essence, their true Self; they called it atman, which is pure, immortal, and untouched by evil. They found that this innermost truth of their being is also the truth of all beings that it is inside as well as outside, that it pervades all; that the atman is also Brahman, that the immanent divine principle is also the transcendental principle and divine ground of all.'[20]

Shri Ram Swarup is not speaking metaphorically. The 'inward turning of the gaze' is not a philosophical take but an actual journey that any *yogi*, or seeker, takes when he sits for meditation or yoga. This method of involution, of withdrawing our senses and turning them inwards, was perfected in ancient Bharatavarsha, and this is what we know as yoga or meditation. Meditation is the method by which we find our true selves—*atman*. Shri Krishna tells Arjuna that it is the atman that is imperishable in everyone's body.

> न जायते म्रियते वा कदाचिनायं भूत्वा भविता वा न भूय:।
> अजो नित्य: शाश्वतोऽयं पुराणोन हन्यते हन्यमाने शरीरे।।

> The soul is neither born nor does it ever die; nor, having once existed, does it ever cease to be. The soul is without birth, eternal, immortal, and ageless. It is not destroyed when the body is destroyed.[21]

And it is our duty to realize that we are not the body or the mind. We are the atman, and the true nature of atman is 'Brahman'. The *mahavakya* of the *Mandukya Upanishad* says:

> अयम् आत्मा ब्रह्म।
>
> This Self (Atman) is Brahman.[22]

Brahman is the Supreme Consciousness from which all universes and all beings emerge. We are all Brahman. The *Brihadaranyaka Upanishad* declares in another Upanishadic mahavakya:

> अहं ब्रह्मास्मि।
>
> I am Brahman.[23]

The *Shiva Sutras* declare:

> चैतन्यमात्मा।
>
> Awareness, which has absolute freedom of all knowledge and activity, is the Self or nature of Reality.[24]

This realization: that we are atman, that atman is Brahman, and Brahman is everything, is moksha. The *Avadhuta Gita* says:

> न जातो न मृतोऽसि त्वं न ते देहः कदाचन।
> सर्वं ब्रह्मेति विख्यातं ब्रवीति बहुधा श्रुतिः।।
>
> You are not born, nor do you die. At no time do you have a body. The scripture declares in many different ways the well-known dictum 'All is Brahman'.[25]

Brahman is the Hindu idea of 'god'. It is important to make clear that the very concept of the supreme godhead in Hindu dharma is not that of an extraterrestrial male god. For us, the purest form of 'god' is not an individual or a specific entity. For us, 'god' is pure consciousness, which can take any form. This pure consciousness is known as Brahman, which we also know as ultimate knowledge or wisdom. One of the four great mahavakyas of Upanishads, from the *Aitareya Upanishad* says:

> प्रज्ञानं ब्रह्म।
>
> Ultimate Wisdom/Knowledge is Brahman.[26]

All sects centred on a deity worship him or her in the form of supreme consciousness. In Vaishnava sects, Vishnu is the form of supreme consciousness; in Shaiva sects, it is Shiva; in Shakta sects, it is the Goddess; and so on. In each of these sects, the supreme deity is imagined as Brahman (supreme consciousness), and human beings and all other beings are seen as jiva having an atman. The Hindu idea of Brahman, as discussed, is very different from the monotheistic idea of 'god'. Shri Chandrasekharendra Saraswati Swami says:

> The Reality (*Sadvastu*) is one. That it manifests itself as countless beings is one of our cardinal tenets. It follows that it is this one and only Reality that transforms itself again and again into all those beings that are subject to birth and death. Also it is the same Reality that is manifested as Isvara to protect this world of sentient beings and insentient objects.[27]

Moksha is therefore another name of the process of realizing that atman is Brahman; that Many are One; that all we see in this universe, all living beings and inanimate objects, have come from Supreme Consciousness, Brahman.

Atman and Brahman are thus two of the most important axioms on which Hindu darshana and worldview stand.

It is the relation between atman and Brahman that is the foundation of Hindu darshana and, as we will know later, even the social order. Brahman 'forgets' its true non-dual nature, and thus, in this forgetfulness, the dual world is created. One becomes two and then many, and ultimately all the universe and creation descend from this one true reality, the supreme consciousness. To reverse this process, to 'remember' one's true nature is moksha.

The impact of this basic darshana about life and reality on the Hindu worldview is profound. The Hindu sees a fundamental unity of being. This unity is not something stitched together artificially. This unity is not something that is attempted by human beings. This unity is more fundamental than anything else. It is at the very level of being. We are not one because we are favoured by a god. We are not one because the sociopolitical realities need us to be. We are one because there is nothing else in the universe except what is our true nature—Brahman or the Supreme Consciousness. Shri Ram Swarup says that Hindus have no concept of one true God. For us, God only exists. It means that only the Supreme Consciousness is the absolute and ultimate reality, and everything else is the veil of *maya*—'*brahma sat jagat mithya*'.[28]

This seems to be a very philosophical view of life. How can something as concrete as Hindu social order emerge from this? But Sanatana Dharma incorporates the most impossible set of binaries within. From the formless emerge all forms. From the attributeless emerge all attributes. From the nameless emerge all names. From nothingness emerges everything. From a very transcendental point of view emerges the immanent view of life. From a philosophy of 'god' and divine emerges a worldview of society, polity, and everything else in life. But how is this transition achieved seamlessly? For that, we need to understand something called the 'Ascent and Descent of Consciousness'.

Chapter 2

The Ascent and Descent of Consciousness

'On uniting the energy in the chakras,
the universe ceases to exist.'

—*Shiva Sutras*

Siete [Seven] *Chakras*, Pieter Weltevrede, 01 Feb. 2007[1]

The ultimate goal of life in Sanatana Dharma is happiness. But this happiness is not to be found solely in material objects and sensory pleasures. While they provide some delight, it is neither ultimate nor lasting. Sanatana Dharma says that it is possible to find everlasting and unending bliss and stay in it forever. Finding that everlasting bliss is the ultimate goal for a Hindu. This does not mean that everyone must abandon all other worldly pursuits. In the Hindu universe, all worldly pursuits are organized in such a way that they eventually lead towards the path of finding ultimate, never-ending happiness.

But didn't we discuss in chapter 1 that the ultimate goal for a Hindu is to attain moksha? Yes, that is true. But moksha is nothing but attaining ultimate knowledge, and attaining ultimate knowledge is what gives one ultimate happiness. Thus, in Hindu dharma, knowledge and happiness are one and the same. The quest for one necessarily leads to the other, ultimately making the seeker realize that they are one.

Not just in individual life, but all of Hindu society in the Hindu cosmos is also arranged in a way that maximizes happiness. This does not mean that there is a bacchanalia of all material pleasures. Higher pleasures are always sought by limiting lower pleasures. In the process, happiness is maximized and optimized at all levels. This is how Hindu society and Bharatavarsha were organized.[2] This way of living, practised and passed down through generations by *guru-shishya parampara* is Sanatana Dharma.

So, what is the source of this happiness? It is clear that happiness is not external, as the memory of a pleasure also triggers happiness within us. Thus, happiness is not located in the five senses. It is not even located inside the mind or the brain. Our senses trigger happiness, which is already within us. Ancient Hindu sages had gone to this inner source of happiness and codified many ways in which to reach it. Like all Hindu quests, this one too starts with the body and leads towards the atman and Brahman.

The Four States of Consciousness

First, let us restate the problem. The ultimate goal of human life is unending happiness, which is also ultimate knowledge. The source of this knowledge and happiness is nowhere else but within us. It is our truest nature, which is Brahman or the Supreme Consciousness. This true nature of ours is occluded from us due to the layers of ignorance or impurity that have accrued over multiple lives due to our deep identification with our own actions and falling into the twin traps of *raga* (attachment) and *dvesha* (grudge). These layers of ignorance occlude the ultimate reality, which is within us. This state of impurity in knowledge can be seen in many ways, including as darkness and ignorance. Thus, the journey towards knowledge, happiness, and moksha is the journey from darkness to light, from ignorance to knowledge, from suffering to bliss, from the lower states of consciousness to the highest state of consciousness, and from the individual self to Brahman. So, there is a journey to be made. The path of this journey is portrayed in many ways in our texts and by our sages. One way is to portray it through the states of consciousness.

But before we delve into the states of consciousness, it is important to note that reality has always been perceived in Bharatavarsha at three levels: *adhibhautika*, *adhidaivika*, and *adhyatmika*.[3] The first level refers to the reality of the material world. The second level refers to the higher realms of existence, which are subtle and not given to the five senses. The third level of adhyatmika is the highest level of reality, where truth, knowledge, and beauty exist in their purest form. The reader should keep in mind the three levels while reading this section.

The *Mandukya Upanishad* states that atman has 'four quarters' or four states of consciousness. Three of these are common experiences for everyone: *jagruta*, *swapna*, and *sushupti* (waking, sleep, and deep sleep). Waking and sleep are self-explanatory. In waking state, our mind and body are both active. In sleep, our body comes to rest, but the mind keeps working, resulting in dreams. In deep sleep, both the body and the mind come to rest, halting even the dreams. All our pleasures, sorrows, and identities, including all our raga and dvesha, disappear during deep sleep. Deep sleep, sushupti, is thus the dreamless state. Shri Anirvan, in his great commentary on the *Mandukya Upanishad*, says that the mind stops functioning in the deep state: '[W]e are conscious of deep sleep only when we come out of it.'[4]

Our sages, seeking ultimate truth, asked a most potent question keeping sushupti at the centre: that if both the body and the mind (ego) disappear during sushupti, then what remains? This sense of existence, which never disappears, is the real self. The problem is that the cycle of waking, sleep, and deep sleep is beyond our control. Just as waking leads to sleep and sleep leads to deep sleep, deep sleep eventually ends, and we find ourselves once again back in the waking state, with all its limitations.

The great sages of ancient Bharatavarsha, however, found a way to break this cycle and stay in a fourth state of consciousness where we realize the true nature of our self, where atman becomes Brahman. This fourth state of consciousness is called *turiya*, where all three earlier stages of consciousness are transcended and one stays in eternal bliss, which is our true nature. This state is the most permanent, and all other states of consciousness emerge and merge into it. Shri Anirvan says that 'to attain the fourth (*turiya*) or transcendent consciousness is the highest and final goal of human life'[5].

The goal of all meditation or sadhana is to raise our state of consciousness to a higher level until we are permanently situated in the highest state of consciousness—turiya. Just like sadhana, under the guidance of the guru, breaks the cycle of life, death, and rebirth and situates one in one's true nature, which is Brahman, it also breaks the cycle of three states of consciousness where jagruta, swapna, and sushupti go on in endless cycles and places the individual permanently in the fourth state of consciousness—turiya. In this state, one realizes one's true nature, that all that is, is Brahman, and that 'I am Brahman'.

Hindu cosmology, art, and iconography are replete with stories and depictions portraying this eternal truth and the journey from lower states of consciousness to the highest state. The *Padma Purana* mentions the story of three sons of Tarakasura: Tarakaksha, Kamalaksha, and Vidyunmali. They appeased Lord Brahma and received in boon three floating cities for each of them, one of gold, one of silver, and one of iron. The boon said that they would become undefeatable until someone shoots an arrow through all three of these floating cities at the same time. Only Shiva is capable of doing that, and by shooting an arrow through all three of them simultaneously, he destroys the three cities and the power of the three *asuras*, relieving the world of their terror. This form of Shiva, who destroys the cities of the three demons, is called Tripurantaka Shiva. The story is also mentioned in the *Tattiriya Samhita* of the *Yajurveda*. And Tripurantaka Shiva has been a favourite theme of Hindu sculptors over the ages, and one can find profuse depictions of this form of Shiva in Hindu temples all over Bharatavarsha.

The story is highly symbolic, where the three floating cities are the three states of consciousness that have to be transcended to reach the state of turiya. Shiva's arrow is the grace of the deity and the guru through which one engages in sadhana or meditation and breaks the cycle of alternating states of consciousness and gets permanently situated in the fourth state called turiya.

Hindu temples feature thousands of sculptures depicting Shiva shooting the arrow that destroys the three cities of the three demons. Shiva is thus the great lord whose anugraha (grace) results in the stoppage of the cycle of jagruta, swapna, and sushupti and makes one get situated in the fourth state of consciousness-turiya.[6]

The process of the merging of the three states in turiya, where a seeker does sadhana, increases his state of consciousness, and situates himself permanently in turiya, is called the ascent of consciousness. We can also call this process involution or the method by which we turn our senses and the mind inwards to the point of dissolution of our differentiated identity and where we realize that our true nature is Brahman.

There is a complimentary process to this. Just like the three states merge into turiya by ascent, they also emerge or descend from it in a process called the descent of consciousness. In this process of evolution, the supreme, undifferentiated consciousness, or Brahman, forgets its true nature and, becoming differentiated or many, becomes many individuals and creatures. In this process, One becomes Many, and undifferentiated reality becomes differentiated beings. Together, these two processes are called ascent and descent of consciousness.

The Seven Chakras

The Hindu tradition considers the body as the vessel that can be used to attain knowledge and happiness. This is why much attention is given to the body processes, which are vital to the ascent and descent of consciousness. Great attention is given to the care of the body, but in a way in which that attention is gradually diverted towards the atman, or the real self.

Prana is the vital breath, or the life force that flows through the body. The channels through which it flows are *nadis*. They are elaborated upon in *samkhya*, *tantra*, and yoga. Ayurveda also builds upon pranas and nadis. It is by paying attention to the flow of prana and controlling its flow that one progresses in meditation. The three important nadis that flow through the spine are called *ida*, *pingala*, and *sushumna*. Sushumna is in the centre, while ida is towards the left, and pingala is to the right.[7]

It is said that while prana flows through ida during the day and pingala during the night, at dawn and dusk it flows through sushumna. As sushumna is the main highway of prana, which reaches up to the highest seat of consciousness in the human body, it is highly advised to meditate at dawn and dusk, as it is easier to reach higher states during these times. As one meditates, his consciousness level reaches higher states. In the body, it is represented by the upward ascent of prana through sushumna nadi. If one meditates constantly for a long period of time, one is permanently situated in the highest state. This is *jnana*, or the state of *turiya*. The *Shiva Sutras*, one of the most fundamental texts of Kashmir Shaiva darshana, says:

शक्तिचक्रसन्धाने विश्वसंहारः।

On Uniting the Energy in the *Chakras* the Universe Ceases to Exist.[8]

This *shakti*, or the power that is within us, with the potentiality to reach higher states of consciousness, is denoted as *kundalinishakti*. It is depicted as lying dormant, coiled at the bottom of the sushumna nadi, near the lowest *muladhara chakra*. When it is awakened, it starts its ascent, passing various chakras on its way until it reaches the highest, *sahasrara*. While the nadis are located in the *sukshma sharira* (subtle body), their physical or gross representation is the spine. That is why it is important to keep the spine erect while meditating. If the spine is erect, the flow of prana in nadis becomes easier.

This journey of ascent between the lowest and the highest state (turiya) is broken down into many parts with intermediate seats of consciousness in the spine or the sushumna nadi. These seats are called chakras and are elaborated upon vividly in Hindu texts. They are named, and their position in the spine or the sushumna nadi is specifically mentioned.

> There are seven important *chakras*. *Muladhara chakra* is the lowest *chakra*, located near the base of the spine. For men, it is located between the genial organs and the back passage. In women, it is situated at the beginning of the cervix. The next *chakra* is *Svadhishthana chakra* located above the *Muladhara chakra* at the base of the spine, in the region we call the tailbone. After *Svadhishthana* comes the *Manipura chakra*, which is situated in the spine, directly behind the navel. Higher up in the spine, directly behind the sternum, is the *Anahata chakra*. Further up in the spine, behind the throat pit, is the *Vishuddha chakra*. Next is the *Ajnachakra*, located behind the eyebrow center. Finally, there is *Sahasrara chakra*, situated at the crown of the head.[8]

The chakras can be imagined as pit stops of consciousness in the spine during its ascent to the highest state of turiya, which is the state described as jnana or moksha. The lower the location of consciousness in the chakras, the more occluded reality is. The higher the location is, reality gets more and more illumined, and the permanent location of consciousness in the highest chakra of sahasrara results in the disappearance of all layers of ignorance and the self-illumination of ultimate knowledge or happiness, which is always within.

Yoga or meditation is the process by which one achieves this. An object of concentration, like the name or image of a deity or a *mantra*, is used to still the ever-distracted mind. While we learn the yogic method somewhere from the outside, the potential to raise our consciousness lies within us. It is this inherent power to realize our true self within us, which the texts have spoken about as the kundalini shakti lying at the bottom of the spine in the muladhara chakra. Dr Raghavan explains what happens when consciousness in the form of the kundalini starts its ascent:

> [B]y first pulling the focus of the mind and senses back from the external objects; by progressively cutting off the mind

> from the body and focusing the mental faculties on a carefully chosen object immersing oneself into the state called variously as *samadhi*, yoga or *jnana*. The tantras and yoga describe this as a journey from the *muladhara*—base of the spine—towards the *sahasrara*—the crest (within the brain). The ultimate state itself consists of the experience of effulgent light and immense joy.[9]

As the mind turns inwards and becomes *ekagra* (focused on one object), the layers of ignorance that occlude reality start disappearing one by one. The yogi or the seeker becomes increasingly oblivious to the samsara with all its sights, sounds, and experiences. As this *prakriti* recedes from experience, the yogi becomes less and less aware of the gross bodies and more aware of the subtle body, or the atman. This process of involution, of consciousness turning inward, is also the process of the ascent of consciousness through the seven chakras.

While Yoga darshana (in *Yoga Sutras*) mentions this process of involution or the ascent of consciousness through meditation, Samkhya darshana (in *Samkhya karakas*) and Kashmir Shaiva darshana (in *Shiva Sutras*) also describe the process of descent of consciousness. In other words, while yoga describes the process of involution, where samsara disappears and many become one, Samkhya and Kashmir Shaiva darshanas also describe the process of evolution, where the one undifferentiated reality—the *purusha*, the Brahman, or the *Parashiva*—becomes many and creates samsara (different jivas and inanimate matter) through the process of evolution.[10]

And the most beautiful and compassionate thing about Sanatana Dharma is that while it tells us that everyone must find the ultimate truth for oneself, it also assures us that in this process of self-discovery, we are not completely alone. While the guru shows the path and showers his anugraha, the deity (in mantra or image form) helps by aiding the *chitta* become ekagra, the Shakti (consciousness) itself intervenes and descends through the chakras to pull the consciousness of the individual from lower states to higher states. Thus, the individual does not have to walk the entire path alone without any help. Shakti, by descending herself, shows the seeker that the pathway that she used to descend can be used by him to ascend. If he takes deeksha from a great guru of a great tradition of meditation, then his path is made easier by constant guidance by Shakti herself. This process of ascent and descent of consciousness is portrayed in various ways in our tradition. We briefly talked above about gross body and subtle body. It is another way of describing the process of involution and evolution.

The Five Koshas (Sheaths)

In Christianity, the body is detested as the source of sin. In Hindu dharma, it is taken as the means by which one realizes the ultimate truth. Instead of just denying that body is not real, Sanatana Dharma tells us that the flesh and bone body that we see is only one body, which is at the gross material level. But there are other bodies that are subtler and are the source of this body, and if we trace the source of these subtle bodies, we will reach the source of our origin, which is far from material or physical. This is the theory of *koshas*, or sheaths.

The *Taittiriya Upanishad* explains that the atman, which resides in our body, is enveloped or covered by five koshas (sheaths). These sheaths envelope the atman in concentric layers, like the layers of an onion. The body of flesh and blood that we are all aware of is not the only body that exists. It is only the gross body, which is perceptible through the five senses. It is called *annamaya kosha*. It is gross because it is nourished by food, and that is why it makes us identify with flesh, blood, and bones. The annamaya kosha is subject to death and decay. Therefore, it is called the *sthula sharira* (made up of physical matter). That is why it is not our true self. In the language of the Upanishads, it is *anatma*, or non-atman.

The second kosha is the *pranamaya kosha*. It is composed of *prana*, the life breath or vital force that flows through our body and keeps it alive. It pervades the whole body of the individual. This kosha is subtler than the annamayakosha and wears it as a body. The third kosha is the *manomayakosha*. It consists of the mind and five sense organs. It is the mind that creates the sense of 'I' and makes us identify with the body. This kosha is subtler than the annamaya and pranamaya but is still not the true self. The fourth kosha is the *vijnanamayakosha*. It consists of the intellect and the sense organs. It is subtly different from the manomayakosha and is associated more with the organs of perception. All these three koshas are the 'sukshma sharira' or the subtle body of the self.

The fifth and innermost kosha is the *anandamaya kosha*, and it consists of nothing but unending, unlimited bliss, or *ananda*. It is the *karana sharira*, (causal body) of the self and gives birth to all the other four koshas. In other words, all four koshas descend or evolve from the anandamaya kosha. It is closest to our truest self, or the truest nature of the atman.

In the case of the chakras, the ascent of consciousness or the process of involution comprises the rising of the kundalini shakti from muladhara to sahasrara. In koshas, the equivalent process would mean a successive identification with the higher koshas, starting from annamaya and ending in anandamaya. This process would be involution. The evolutionary process of the descent in the case of koshas would mean the creation of all other *koshas* from the causal body, or the karana sharira of the anandamaya kosha, which is the substratum on which all other koshas exist. The *Tattiriya Upanishad* says that a person on the path of meditation realizes that he is the atman at every kosha successively until he realizes that he is the anandamayakosha:

> The Reality in the core of man and the Reality which is in the sun are one. He who knows this, on leaving from this world, first attains the Atman made of food, next the Atman made of *prana*, next attains the Atman made of mind, next attains Atman made of *buddhi* and lastly attains the Atman made of Bliss.[12]

There are many other ways in which the process of involution and evolution is explained. *Shrimad Bhagavada Purana* explains the principles of *srishti*, *sthiti*, and *laya*, or evolution, sustenance, and involution. The trinity of Brahma, Vishnu, and Mahesh also signify the same process where Brahma creates, Vishnu sustains, and Shiva dissolves the world of maya. This is another way of depicting the cycle of involution and evolution, like many discussed above. Dr Raghavan sums up many other ways in which this process is described in our texts:

> These processes of involution and evolution are associated with the principles of *Purusha* (or male or *shiva*) and *prakriti* (or female or *parvati*). These terms are used as a pair of principles most famously in the *sankhya* system where *prakriti* refers to the evolved state or one where all the senses have emerged and are active. *Purusha* is outside the scope of *prakriti* and watches silently. Thus in our scheme, *Purusha* is best approximated by the antipole of a fully evolved state, i.e., the fully involved state of *samadhi*. This schema is attested even in the Vedas, but as the pair Mother-Father, where Mother is *bhuh* or *prthvi*, Father, the *dyaus*. In the cycle of seed to tree to seed in the external world, the seed is the Male or *Purusha*, while the full grown tree is the female or *prakriti*. This terminology is also extended to call the process of *vistara* or expansion of seed to tree as a feminine process and the involution process of tree to seed as a masculine process.[13]

Wherever one looks in Sanatana tradition, one finds the discussion of the states of consciousness and how to attain the highest state of jnana. The goal is to explain how samsara comes into being and how we realize the ultimate reality through meditation. The *Mundaka Upanishad* commands to 'seek the indivisible through meditation'. Yoga and tantra have evolved various techniques for meditation. All of them focus upon the stilling of the activity of the mind, as this is what creates ignorance and hides reality, which is always within. Thus, all yoga, meditation, and even rituals are still the activities of the mind. The *Yoga Sutras* start by declaring this to be the goal of yoga:

> योगश्चित्तवृत्तिनिरोधः॥
>
> Yoga is the stilling of the changing states of the mind.[14]

This is the goal of all meditational practices. The activities of the mind occlude reality. Yoga stills the activities of the mind, and as a result, the reality, which always is within, appears. Different traditions of meditation use various methods of stilling the mind. Chanting a specific mantra in a particular intonation provides a particular stimulus to the mind, gradually quietening its tendency to stillness. Paying attention to the activity of prana of the life breath does the same to the activities of the mind, as do various other methods that were developed by different sects to offer the widest variety of options to the individuals suiting their own *svabhava* (nature). This is why yoga is a process of involution, or the means by which the senses are withdrawn, and the tendencies of the mind are stilled.

Samkhya, one of the six darshanas in Sanatana Dharma, on the other hand, explains the process of evolution of the world in different creatures and elements through twenty-four elements. Trilochan Sastry says:

> Samkhya describes twenty-four tattvas or principles. *Purusha* is pure Consciousness and causeless and is not counted as a principle or tattva. The first tattva is *Prakriti*, which is also

> causeless and goes on to describe how evolution takes place. The juxtaposition of *Purusha* and *Prakriti* gives rise to *mahat* or the entire universe in its potential form. This forms the basis from which everything evolves.[15]

Samkhya explains the descent of consciousness by talking about how the juxtaposition of the two primary elements of purusha and prakriti results in the creation or evolution of the world into myriad creatures and different elements. It has four sets of five: five *jnanedriyas* (instruments of knowledge), five *karmendriyas* (instruments of action), five *tanmatras* (mechanisms of storing impressions on the mind), and five *panchabhutas* (five elements). Even though Samkhya mostly talks about descent or evolution, it also says that the goal of the individual is to realize its true nature through meditation. Sastry expands:

> Samkhya says explicitly that *Prakriti* exists for the individual *Purusha* to gain experience and has no other purpose. *Purusha* in a way forgets its true nature when united with *Prakriti* and identifies with the *Ahamkara* and *Buddhi*. Liberation is achieved when the *Purusha* realizes its own true nature.[16]

Kashmir Shaiva darshana expands on Samkhya and increases the number of elements to thirty-six. A non-dualistic darshana, it is very similar to *Advaita Vedanta*. The most primary and causal element of all existence is Parashiva. Parashiva is in Kashmir Shaiva darshana, what Brahman is in the Vedanta. With the first disturbance in it, Parashiva divides into two elements: Shiva and Shakti. Shakti, it is said, is bored with herself and wants to play. It is the play of Shiva and Shakti that then creates the universe, down to the animate and inanimate objects. Just like Shakti limits herself and creates the differentiated universe in descent or evolution, an individual can also ascend the ladder of consciousness and realize that he is nothing but Parashiva himself. As it descends, so we can ascend.

Ascent and Descent of Consciousness in the Hindu Temple

This process of ascent and descent of consciousness is the centrepiece of Hindu temple architecture. This is not surprising since every Hindu discipline reflects the greatest of darshanas. The Hindu temple is built and perceived in the image of Mount Meru, which represents ultimate knowledge, and climbing it symbolizes attaining moksha. The temple, as Mount Meru, facilitates the spiritual journey of man, from being an individual to realizing his oneness with the Supreme Consciousness.

The vertical dimension that is seen in the chakra imagery in the human spine is replicated in the Hindu temple. The most important part of the temple is the *garbha-griha*, where the *vigraha* (icon) of the deity resides. Exactly on top of the vigraha is the *shikhara*, which is topped by a *kalasha*, which contains *navagraha* symbolizing the seed of the universal or Supreme Consciousness or Brahman. Similarly, exactly beneath the vigraha, underground, is buried another kalasha, which again has navagraha, symbolizing the seed of the individual consciousness or the atman. When an *archaka* invokes the deity through rituals, he is virtually initiating the process of the descent of consciousness from above and the ascent or germination of consciousness from below, which meet in the vigraha of the deity. Just like the human body is a vessel of the ascent and descent of consciousness, so the Hindu temple and the vigraha of the deity in the garbha-griha of the temple are the vessels of the ascent and descent of consciousness.

There is another symbolism connected to the architecture of the Hindu temple that shows the same process. The Hindu temple is imagined as a union of two trees. One growing upright from the seed that is underground, and the other inverted tree that descends from the seed above in the kalasha at the top. In this imagery too, the ascent and descent of consciousness is represented.

This process of involution and evolution is reflected in the horizontal profile of the temple too. While the outermost parts are full of sculpture depicting all activities that take place in samsara, as one goes deeper into the temple, the number of sculptures decrease, and finally, in the garbha-griha, only the vigraha of the presiding deity remains. Similarly, the outermost parts of the temple have ample light, but it keeps decreasing as one proceeds inside, and in the garbha-griha, it is almost completely dark. The passage of the devotee from the entrance of the temple to the place in front of the garbha-griha is a process of involution, where senses are withdrawn, and samsara disappears successively until it all dissolves in the oneness of Brahman in the garbha-griha.

The symbolism of descent of consciousness is replicated not just in architecture or sculpture but also in the rituals that are practiced. *Abhisheka* is one of the most important rituals in any temple where the vigraha of the deity is bathed in various liquids and scented essences. In the ritual, the liquid is poured at the top of the vigraha of the deity, right where the sahasrara chakra is supposed to be. The liquid then runs down the entire body of the deity until it comes down at the bottom. This process is exactly how descent of consciousness has been described, in which once the kundalini has ascended to the top, meeting sahasrara, the nectar at the top is released, and then the entire creation (body of the deity) is bathed in the same nectar. This ritual is visualized and enacted in the process of abhisheka.

It is the greatness of Sanatana Dharma that it has transformed some of the most concrete of mediums—stone—into a vehicle of transmitting some of the most abstract of darshana or philosophy. Every day as millions of Hindus throng millions of the temples all over Bharatavarsha and even abroad, they look at the architecture and sculpture and have the opportunity to be transported to the realms of the greatest of philosophies ever created on earth.

A Civilization in Pursuit of Knowledge

Jivanmukta is a highly significant word. It means an individual who has realized moksha, or the highest state of turiya in this life, and has become stable in the Upanishadic sense of 'I am Brahman'. Such a person has risen above all duality and has become one with all creation and existence. So, he is situated in the knowingness of undifferentiated reality. But to others he is a living Brahman and therefore an icon of knowledge and wisdom and someone from whom one can seek guidance in every walk of life.

Shri Ramana Maharishi was such a jivanmukta who had realized the 'Shiva-state' or moksha in his lifetime. He had become a guiding light to many who sought moksha, and he is still guiding many through his words that were recorded by his disciples. But since this book is about Svayambodha and Shatrubodha, one might ask how a jivanmukta, a jnani like Shri Rama, is useful in solving sociopolitical problems like we face today: Islamic terrorism, Christian conversions, etc. In short, the question is: How is a jnani, whose quest is internal, useful to the outer and wider world?

Shri Ramana was asked this very question once by one of the visitors in his *ashrama*. Someone asked how a jnani or a *mumukshu* (one desiring and on the path of moksha) helps the wider world. To which Shri Ramana replied that a jnani or jivanmukta helps the world immensely and fundamentally just by meditating. While one might believe that spreading knowledge and wisdom in society is a good cause overall, at the same time one might also doubt that there is a direct correlation between a *sadhaka* meditating and the solution to the problems of the world.

But Shri Ramana is absolutely correct when he said the above statement, and it is not very difficult to understand it once we understand the process of involution and evolution a little more deeply.

A jivanmukta, or *brahmajnani* (knower of Brahman), sees the world in a different way. Having climbed to the highest chakra of sahasrara and attained the state of turiya, he sees the entire creation in a new effulgent light. The effect of the turiya state persists even in the waking. Thus, everything in samsara is suddenly illumined by the light of the Brahman or the highest state of consciousness. It is like climbing the highest vantage point in a particular geography and looking at all that exists from the highest point of view. One has a commanding, holistic, and long-term view of everything. Solutions that are impossible to see from a lower ground are suddenly obvious from a higher ground, just like a trek in a rainforest, which is very difficult to follow on ground, is immediately visible if one sees the view from above. A jnani, like Shri Ramana, who overlooks the process of evolution or descent of consciousness from above has this vantage point of view.

The process of involution or ascent of consciousness gives a seeker access to the ultimate reality and knowledge, and with this vantage point, he once again overlooks the process of evolution or creation of social customs, practices, institutions, and principles. 'In the process of evolution, the faculties of action (which also include speech) bring forth into the external world, the experience that was within.'[16]

Buddhism has a similar concept in bodhisattva. A bodhisattva is an individual who has delayed his enlightenment and stopped just before *nirvana* or the highest state of consciousness, in order to help those who are not yet enlightened and help them climb the ladder of consciousness. It is described as a great act of compassion and empathy for the world where a mumukshu, or someone desiring nirvana delays the highest goal of life so that others can be helped. And indeed, it is an act of compassion.

But Sanatana Dharma goes one step forward. Here, we have the concept of jivanmuktas, who have reached the highest state of enlightenment, who have achieved moksha while still alive, and thus, with the perspective of the greatest wisdom that ever can be, they guide others who ask them about cosmos, life, and the paths to achieve jnana or moksha. While in Buddhism, the goal of enlightenment is temporarily compromised for empathy, in Sanatana Dharma, neither is compromised, and other individuals are helped in their quest, but with the greatest vantage point of wisdom that ever can be.

Sanatana Dharma, its practices, and its texts are generated, nourished, and guided by none other than its jivanmuktas, these jnanis and rishis who went through the entire process of involution, having ascended to the highest state of consciousness. When these jivanmuktas, who are nothing but Brahman in the human body, look upon the world, they see through all darkness and ignorance and see what exactly is right for any given situation at any given time. Hindu disciplines, practices, and texts are created and nurtured by these jnanis. This is why we did not create a civilization based on dogmas. Dr Ganesh says:

> The idea of *jivanmukta* presupposes the futility of holy book, prophet, heaven, hell, last judgement, apocalypse, etc. *Moksha*—the highest ideal—can be potentially attained by anyone, anywhere, anytime. It is within our reach without a mandatory middleman nor divine intervention. This is a lofty lesson.[18]

Even if all the 'books' of Sanatana Dharma are burnt, even if all the temples are destroyed, even if all the universities are decimated, even if all its institutions become degenerate, Sanatana Dharma will not disappear until there are jivanmuktas and jnanis who continue the Eternal Tradition by transferring the secret of the Vedas, the secret about the ultimate reality, from one generation to another. Jnana, or knowledge, that is supreme, is not located in one or the other 'book'. Sita Ram Goel writes with his usual eloquence:

> What for do we need a book? The whole spiritual truth, every *shastra*, is secret in the human heart. Anyone, anywhere, at any time can have access to the spiritual realm provided one seeks for it sincerely, and prepares oneself for entering it. Many seers and saints have seen it in as many ways, spoken of it and in as many languages and by means of as many metaphors. The Vedas provide one version of it, the *Jainagama* another, the *Tripitaka* yet another, and so on down to the latest Hindu saint such as Sri Ramakrishna, or the latest Hindu sage such as Raman Maharshi.[19]

This is why Swami Vivekananda also said, 'Of all the scriptures of the world, it is the Vedas alone which declare that the study of the Vedas is secondary.'[20] Swami Vivekananda is far from trying to dismiss the importance of the Vedas. The Vedas are of central importance to Hindu civilization, as we will see in chapter 3. He is simply stressing the point that our dharma, Sanatana Dharma, being eternal, does not depend on any text for its survival. The Vedas, existing as they always were, were seen by the jivanmuktas in their flights of meditation. What is most central to Sanatana Dharma is the guru-shishya parampara, where jivanmuktas guide others in the process of achieving jnana or moksha. Until this remains, Sanatana Dharma will remain.

The *Rig Veda* talks about the experience of jnana or moksha, which is confirmed by countless jivanmuktas in one of its most famous legends, the legend of Indra slaying the demon Vrtra. The legend says that Vrtra was holding the life-giving waters. Indra slew him and released the waters, restoring the life cycle on earth. Like always, this Hindu legend too has a deeper meaning hidden underneath. It is depicting what happens when kundalini reaches sahasrara and unites with Brahman. It is depicting what the jivanmuktas feel upon moksha. Dr Raghavan explains:

> When the *prana* reaches *brahmarandhra*, the subject experiences the highest state of nectarine bliss and effulgence, which combine the characteristics of the sun and moon. This ascent of the spinal cord is a half cycle of involution. From here starts the counter-half cycle of evolution. The moonlike sensation described above also has a nectarine quality that oozes and then turns into a steady flow of nectar, downwards into the lower spheres. This downpour is quite naturally described as rain, as the release of waters that were held up; its experience resembles the sweetness of nectar, the nourishing effect of milk, and ghee.[21]

This nectar of ultimate knowledge continuously flows in the mind of a jivanmukta or a jnani, and whatever he speaks, writes, or creates has a direct imprint of the Brahman. Everything that Sanatana Dharma and Hindu culture are known for—Hindu deities, Hindu knowledge systems, Hindu arts and aesthetics, Hindu science, and Hindu social order—are all creations of that supreme reality. Hindu deva, *vidya*, *kala*, *vijnana*, and yajna are all creations of Brahman in the form of jivanmuktas, known as rishis in Bharatavarsha.

Sanatana Dharma not only took care to lead individuals to jnana; it also made sure that samsara would be led by these jnanis so that a society wedded to the pursuit of knowledge and happiness is created. We, the Hindus, saw the world from the point of view of non-duality or *advaita* and then proceeded to create a *dvaita jagata*, a dualistic world that was conducive to individuals who wanted to search for advaita or non-duality. This is the Hindu way of life.

In this way, we created a civilization that balanced the pursuit of sensory pleasures with higher spiritual pleasures; we created a society that neglected neither the material nor the spiritual aspects of individuals and groups; we created social systems based on such deep principles of harmony that binaries, which are conflicting in all other cultures, became deeply complementary in Bharatavarsha.

This resulted in the greatest civilizational harmony the world had ever seen, which managed complementary binaries, which in most other cultures were conflicting, leading most outsiders to believe that India is a civilization of contradictions. Bharatavarsha is, however, not a bundle of contradictions but a dynamic balance of opposites, which is dharma.

By following *artha* and *kama*, we would turn towards moksha. We would engage in karma in a way that would make us free of all karmic debt. By taking utmost care to create human units like *kula* and *kutumba*, we would proceed towards a stage in life where we could transcend even our own individuality. By giving our individuals multiple identities, we made sure they would transcend all of them. By creating dharmic diversity, we made sure it would all come back to the unity from which it arose. By engaging in the world, we would transcend it. By creating the greatest diversity of languages, texts, communities, customs, practices, rituals, food, and culture, we never lost sight of the vision of the greater unity that our sages had envisioned.

Our sages had realized the unity of thought, knowledge, and being. We had realized that not only were we all one in our true identity as the greatest self or Brahman, but all the diversity we see also descends from this unity. This is how, despite understanding and experiencing the greatest unity, we did not go for uniformity of expression since we knew that all the forms come from formless, all the names come from nameless, and all the attributes come from attributeless. This is the vision of the Vedas and their unity of deities. We realized how all deities expressed the same Brahman, but we also focused on presenting as many deities as possible to man so that the one appropriate for one's own svabhava is able to guide him in his quest for knowledge. This was the vision of Diversity in Unity of the great civilization of Sanatana Dharma, which we are going to explore in chapter 3.

Chapter 3

Diversity in Unity

'The Hindus do not call their Gods either One or Many. According to them, what they worship is One Reality, *ekam sat*, which is differently named. This Reality is everywhere, in everything, in every being. It is One and Many at the same time and it also transcends them both.'

—Shri Ram Swarup

Vishnu Vishvarupa, Victoria and Albert Museum, London, approx. 1800–1820. This form of Vishnu contains all the universe within him symbolizing diversity in unity[1]

The Fundamental Unity of Knowledge

Our sages realized some deep, seemingly contradictory, but complementary truths. They realized that the nature of ultimate truth is impossible to convey in any human language. It can only be experienced. Yet, in the greatest act of compassion in the history of humankind, they created mechanisms that would help the individual in realizing that ultimate truth. Our sages, once having realized the supreme, stayed in the world for some time to create a vast body of literature as well as institutions, resulting in the greatest knowledge civilization the world has ever seen. The most wonderful aspect about Hindu disciplines and institutions was that they all reflected the greatest truth of the Upanishads. Like Dr Rajnish Mishra says, 'All Hindu disciplines, take one from *bheda* (dualism) to *abheda* (non-dualism).' These disciplines were nothing but vehicles of realization of the Supreme Consciousness or the ultimate truth.

Our sages realized how the world descends from Brahman. This process of evolution was expanded upon by various darshanas like Samkhya or Kashmir Shaiva darshanas. Therefore, some of the most important concepts of these darshanas are reflected through all Hindu texts, disciplines, and even institutions. First is the idea of purusha. While Brahman, as the transcendental reality, has no attributes, it is known as purusha upon manifestation. The *Rig Veda* itself has *Purusha Sukta*, which invokes purusha, the cosmic being. He is described as omnipresent and enveloping the world from all sides. He pervades all living and non-living beings. All the devas, rishis, and the Vedas come from him. After describing how the entire world came out of purusha, the *Sukta* ends by explaining that the outer reality of samsara is just a reflection of the inner ultimate reality:

यज्ञेन यज्ञमयजन्त देवास्तानि धर्माणि प्रथमान्यासन्।
ते ह नाकं महिमानः सचन्त यत्र पूर्वे साध्याः सन्ति देवाः।।

> The *Devas* performed the external *Yagna* by meditating on the real *Yagna* (i.e., contemplating on the *Purusha* Who is Shining behind everything); And thus they first obtained the Dharma (based on the Oneness of the *Purusha*), by Meditating on the Greatness of the *Chidakasha* (Blissful Spiritual Sky behind everyone, which is the essence of the *Purusha*), during those earlier times, the Spiritual Aspirants became the Shining One themselves.[2]

It says how dharma is that principle by which the realized sages reflect upon the world through the nectar of wisdom that they received while meditating on the inner ultimate truth. The Vedas are 'the spontaneous flow of words from such (realized) state of experience'.[3]

Purusha in this way is a central concept in dharma. It has nothing to do with gender. It can be understood as the *siddhanta*, or the supreme principle, by which everything is governed on its own. The concept of purusha is reflected in all Hindu disciplines. Samkhya builds upon the concepts of purusha and prakriti. While purusha is the siddhanta, or the principle, prakriti is the *abhivyakti*, or manifestation. In a way, purusha signifies the principle of involution, and prakriti signifies the principle of evolution. Together they make any idea or discipline complete. The concept of purusha is repeated in many Hindu disciplines, and thus we find *vastu purusha*, *shilpa purusha*, *sangeeta purusha*, *natya purusha*, and so on, making sure that these disciplines never lose sight of the ultimate truth. The concept of purusha thus works as the pole star of dharma, making sure that even worldly subjects such as *natya* or *nritya* never become completely free of their spiritual moorings.

There is a deep organic unity in Hindu disciplines. They are not isolated disciplines. They are connected to each other with a shared vocabulary and universal metaphors that pervade all the disciplines of art, philosophy, and science. It is impossible to study Hindu temple architecture without studying Hindu sculpture, which necessitates the study of Hindu iconography. And one of the primary texts that discusses iconography is the *Natyashastra*, a text that is primarily devoted to theatre and drama. It is an example of the inner connectedness of Hindu disciplines. Any deep study into one will lead one to another, making the seeker realize the deeper unity.

Let us take the case of Hindu arts. The same metaphors that are common in Hindu darshana carry over seamlessly into Hindu iconography. The stories that the devotees listen to and narrate in their daily lives are the ones represented on the temple walls. The mantras that the devotees daily recite are the ones that invoke the exact same attributes of the gods depicted on the temple walls and in the garbha-griha.

The darshana with which a Hindu was familiar through the various epics, stories, *kathas*, mantras, daily worship, and the general art of storytelling was the darshana that dictated the hand of the sculptor too. And while Hindu philosophy was called darshana, the act of temple going was also called darshana, as both involved not the activity of the mind but to see the divine and to fall silent with the activity of the mind subsiding into stillness, which illumines the inner knowledge.

This shared vocabulary arises from the *yogic chitta bhumis* of jivanmuktas or jnanis who had experienced the ultimate truth and were looking back on samsara through this knowledge. As we discussed above, Hindu *shastras* and disciplines were guided by the insights of these jivanmuktas. But how did they make sure that they would be understood by others? Sanatana Dharma made sure of that by instituting meditation as a great practice widely spread in society. Those who were not privy directly to deep meditational techniques did *japa* and other daily rituals, which also worked towards stilling the activity of their mind, letting the inner knowledge illumine, even if partially.

Meditation and ritual focused on stilling the activity of the mind was the common point where the creators of the great sculpture and the onlookers met. The experience by which the sculptor peeked into higher reality was also democratically available to anyone else who wished to explore the path of knowledge, and many did. The thread of consciousness running through Hindu darshana enlivened every one of these disciplines, institutions, and individuals. So, there was a horizontal unity between different Hindu disciplines and a vertical unity with Hindu darshana. Sanatana Dharma in this way had made access to knowledge democratic and commonplace, leading to an entire civilization devoted to the pursuit of knowledge.

The Centrality of the Vedas

The Vedas have always held central importance to Sanatana Dharma. The word *Veda* comes from the Sanskrit root *-vid*, which means to know. Thus, the most important texts of Hindu dharma are purely knowledge texts. They are *apaurusheya*, which means that they are not human creation. They were 'seen' or 'witnessed' by great rishis during meditation.

One is prompted here to compare them with the 'revealed texts' of some prophetic monotheistic religions like the Bible and the Quran. And many Hindus do compare them. But that would be utterly wrong. We will discuss the nature of the Bible and the Quran in the Shatrubodha section, but in short, they are revealed by an extraterrestrial god to his prophet, who gives them to his 'chosen people'. Neither the prophet nor the people have done anything specific to be 'chosen'. Their candidacy is entirely the whim of God.

The Vedas are far from this kind of 'revelation'. They are self-revealed since the knowledge that is 'revealed' always resides within the heart of the yogi. Upon the clearing of the layers of ignorance through meditation, this knowledge starts shining. This is the 'revelation of the Vedas'. There is no revealer here, just the revelation. There is no external agent, like the Biblical God, revealing it. No chosen or last prophet. No chosen people. Any rishi to whom the Vedas have been 'revealed' has undergone long and hard meditation. There is no randomness involved in the revelation.

Another fallacy arises when it is mentioned that the Vedas are *shabda pramana*, which is then compared to the 'revealed' nature of the Bible and the Quran once again. The Vedas are indeed shabda pramana, meaning that they are taken as literally true, but in a very different way from the Bible and the Quran. The Vedas are shabda pramana in a similar way to scientific texts. Scientific truths are based on experiences that can be replicated by anyone. Upon replication, anyone, anywhere, and at anytime will find the same results. However, not all of us test all scientific theories for ourselves; we trust the text of the scientists who have experienced the reality firsthand. But if we were to gain those skills, learn those disciplines, and conduct those tests, we would find the same results as the scientist has explained in his text.

In a very similar way, the reason the Vedas are called shabda pramana is because they are the spontaneous outpourings of rishis and *atmajnanis* who have experienced the ultimate reality themselves and have recorded their experience. These experiences are open to anyone who chooses the path of involution through meditation and lends himself to the process of the ascent of consciousness. Upon reaching the greatest state of consciousness—turiya—he will find that what is written in the Vedas is indeed true. Countless jnanis and jivanmuktas have done so over thousands of years, ever since the Vedas were first codified in human language, and every single one of them has confirmed the depiction of the ultimate truth mentioned in the Vedas. Thus, the Vedas are shabda pramana, or to be believed as they are, because they are the collection of *apta vakyas*, the truth speech of the jnanis or jivanmuktas. Apta vakya is the greatest *pratyaksha pramana*, as it is the direct experience of the jnani and does not need any external prop.

To compare the Vedas to the Bible and the Quran is utterly wrong, because not only is there no value placed on individual experience in the monotheistic traditions but no investigation is allowed at all. Experience is not a valid proof or pramana. Dogma is necessary and sufficient. To question the 'word of god' or the 'revelation of god' is considered a great sin and has been severely punished in the prophetic monotheistic traditions. The Vedas, on the other hand, are based on the spontaneous outpourings of jivanmuktas who see reality as it is. As Dr Raghavan says:

> In the process of involution, the faculties of speech (and action) and other mental processes are progressively suspended. In the process of evolution, this same faculty of speech—*vak*—faithfully brings forth into the external world the experience that was within. It is thus the words that flow during the phase of evolution from the inner states of realization hold a special place in Indic Knowledge Systems and has resulted in the body of knowledge called Vedas and its auxiliary sciences—collectively termed *vidya*. The Vedas are held in great esteem and accorded the highest status within Indic Knowledge Systems.[4]

It is because of the acceptance of the wisdom of jivanmuktas, or jnanis as apta vakyas, that Sanatana Dharma never descended into blind dogma or belief. Whenever such tendencies arose in Bharatavarsha, these living and walking Brahman, like Shri Ramana Maharishi, Shri Ramakrishna Paramhamsa, and Shri Nisargadatta Maharaja, weeded those tendencies out by telling the folks, through their direction experience, what the truth was and what was not. This feature is deeply embedded in the very design of Sanatana Dharma, the agency by which we never became dogmatic, blind believers who could not look beyond the 'Book'. In fact, our Vedas themselves declare that when in doubt, we should listen to the 'men of wisdom' or 'jivanmuktas'. The *Taittiriya Upanishad* declares:

> In situations of confusion, consult people who have imbibed wisdom and are capable of thinking with clarity. They should not have views on dharma that are extreme and dogmatic, but should have the power of discerning right from wrong. When in doubt, one must follow their advice and their actions.[5,6]

The influence of turiya, or the highest state of consciousness, on *vak*, or speech, results in vidya, or knowledge systems, while its influence on non-speech modalities results in kala or art. This is how deeply the *atmavidya* (science of the self) in Hindu dharma influences other vidyas (sciences of other disciplines). This is the reason there is a greater unity in Hindu disciplines. For this unity is forged in the turiya state.

There is one more way to understand why the Vedas are shabda pramana and how they can illumine the highest reality to anyone who seeks earnestly. For that, we first need to understand the levels of vak. Just like there are four states of consciousness, seven chakras, and five koshas, there are four levels of vak (speech or language): *para*, *pashyanti*, *madhyama*, and *vaikhari*. The highest level is para, where there are no words, and the lowest level of vak is vaikhari. Human speech, even Sanskrit, is in vaikhari.

Shri Ram Swarup writes in *The Word as Revelation* that the names of things are not arbitrary. There is a greater and deeper connection between words and their meanings. He says that words are not inert and lifeless. They have an inner life and a personality of their own. They have 'movement, warmth, vibration, aura—even temper, personality and character'. Names and forms, or *nama* and *rupa*, have a greater connection between them, and nama is even more important than rupa from a Hindu point of view. 'An object is merely an outer expression, a material representation of the more internal and essential nāma.'[7]

Vaikhari is human speech, but the words and the ideas behind them—the names that are—are long in the making. Even before they are uttered and take form in our body through our vocal cords, they have an existence in our thought, and before they take form in our thought, they are in our consciousness. Shri Ram Swarup traces their origin back from vaikhari to para:

> The *vaikhari* level is the level that we ordinarily know, where the sound is formed, *sabda nispatti* happens. Its seat is the throat. Behind it, and supporting it, is the *madhyamavaka* with its seat in the heart region. It cannot be heard by all but the more attentive can hear it by closing their ears. It can always be heard by the inner ear, *srutigocara*. Here the sequence and form, *krma-rupa*, are not the same as we see them in ordinary speech. Beyond this lie two other levels, *pasyanti* and *para*, with their seats at the navel, *nabhi*, and the solar plexus, respectively. They are beyond the ken of the ordinary mind and they can be seen only by Yogis in states of deep trance. In *pasyanti*, there is no sound but only meaning, *dyotitartha*. In this state, the speech is indivisible, *avibhaga*, and the forms and sequence are fused or concentrated, *sarvatah samhrta-krama*, as in a seed. In para the speech is established in its own luminous form, *svarupajyotiha*, and in its original, primal form before any modifications start. Here sound becomes silence, *asabda*, and only a potentiality, *avyakta*.[7]

Para is the highest state of vak where no words remain, yet it holds the potentiality of all words. It is wordless and yet is the source of all words. Para is the vak equivalent of Brahman. It is the origin and destination of all speech. Just as there is an ascent from jagruta to turiya, from muladhara to sahasrara, from annamaya to anandamaya, so is there an ascent of consciousness from vaikhari to para. The ancient Hindu sages realized this truth that words can be traced back, in meditation, to their origin in the wordless sphere of para. But like every involution has a complementary evolution process, so these same sages, having experienced the thoughtless and wordless state in para, came down to other states of vak with the wisdom of para and created Sanskrit and the Vedas for us.

This is why the language that they chose as their vehicle—Sanskrit—is considered a *devabhasha*. It is not said to be the creation of human intellect, but just like the Vedic mantras, it is supposed to be 'revealed' to the sages in higher-state consciousness. That is why, even though the expression is still in vaikhari, Sanskrit retains the memory of the earlier and higher stages of vak, and even of para in some sense, making it the perfect vehicle for talking about any spiritual process.

Shri Ram Swarup asserts that this 'memory' of the absolute truth that co-exists with the para state of vak is preserved in the roots of the words, even at the stage of vaikhari. While words keep changing according to times and needs, the roots remain almost unchanged and continue the same darshana or same parampara (tradition) through ages. Old roots converse with new ideas and change old words slightly to adapt to the new need and new meaning. Thus, the link continues unbroken. The soul of language, carrying the memory of ultimate truth, travels through the roots of the words, through the ages, to us. In this way, Sanskrit, just like Sanatana, is eternal.

A language that retains its memory of para state of vak more clearly, like Sanskrit, illumines everything that it speaks upon with the light of the supreme consciousness and the fundamental unity that comes from the realization that all is Brahman. There is a greater unity of vak, exhibited at the level of the unity of sounds, unity of roots, unity of synonyms, and unity of meaning. Sanskrit throbs with this deep and fundamental unity of words, roots, sounds, and meaning. Language itself becomes a vehicle of jnana or the ascent of consciousness. There is a reason why, out of six *Vedangas*, four are directly related to language. Language is considered a valid vehicle of jnana or knowledge. The *Mundaka Upanishad* and various other texts, including the *Yoga Sutras*, speak on how 'Om', the primordial sound of creation and dissolution is shabda Brahman. Hindu dharma does not restrict the idea of Brahman to darshana but converts every discipline into a vehicle of conveying the greatest knowledge, which is none other than Brahman. And just like almost all disciplines have the idea of a purusha, so do many disciplines have the idea of Brahman. So, there is a shabda Brahman and an *akshara* Brahman.

Mantras have power because they have the capacity to activate pathways towards knowledge or ascent. Words have sounds; sounds have vibrations; and these vibrations are not arbitrary. They reflect reality at a higher plane of consciousness. By chanting these mantras in the way they are meant to be, the kundalini begins to awaken, consciousness starts its ascent, and the practitioner begins to gain sight of reality at a higher state. As the yogi ascends and his chitta reaches ekagra bhumi, the words also drop their lower meanings and acquire meanings luminous with greater truth. In the words of Shri Ram Swarup:

> *The Rgveda* speaks of secret words, and secret Names. It says that the Speech, surrounded by a thousand syllables, sahasraksara, resides in the highest region of heaven. According to this tradition, a word has deep roots in our being and its greater life is hidden there. Like an iceberg, it shows only a part of itself. The *Rgveda* says that a word exists at four levels and three of them are hidden in the cave of the heart.[9]

Sadhana or meditation unlocks the real power of words. They are vehicles of consciousness, but this is hidden as a secret in them. When a yogi gets initiated in meditation by a guru, chants and meditates on the mantra, and goes through the eight stages of meditation[10], the secret meanings of these names of deities open up to him.

The names of the gods in the Vedas are the greatest vehicle of the ascent of consciousness and thus indispensible to a yogi seeking truth. These names help the yogi in making his mind become focused, and once it is situated in the ekagra chitta bhumi, they open their greater meaning. This is how mantra japa works. A mantra descends from Brahman and is a capsule that aids the ascent of the yogi.

The names of the gods are imbued with all aspects of reality. This is the reason that there are many gods, and each god has many names. It is a tradition in Sanatana Dharma to chant the *Sahasranamas* (thousand names of the gods) of many deities like Shri Vishnu, goddess Lalita, etc. The names are multiples to denote that absolute reality is one. While every name dwells on a certain aspect of the deity, it also pushes the seeker to realize that the names, forms, and beings originate from one source. The Brahman descends and creates all the forms, names, and beings in his image, and all of these names and forms of gods are capable of leading their disciples in their ascent towards the realization that they are Brahman; all are Brahman. As Shri Ram Swarup Ji beautifully explains:

> If we look at the Names of the deities, we are struck by certain features:
> Each God is also the other.
> Each has the attributes of the supreme Godhead.
> Each combines all the opposites.
> Each is also the source, the embodiment and the secret Self or truth of everything.
> Each is also the Gods and the elements of Nature.
> Each is beyond time, yet it gives names to all the planets and all the measures of time.
> Each one is full of valor, vigour and beauty.

> Each is everywhere.
> Each is also the great goal, the wide gate, the way and the knowledge that leads to the destination.
> Each is a great teacher, protector and saviour.
> All are equally worshipful.
> They are healers and bearers of all gifts to their worshippers.
> All have their seats in the secret cave of the heart and are difficult to realize.
> On the other hand all of them are said to be easily attainable.
> They are also the Great Questions, the Key to all the answers, the Great Exposition of Everything.[11]

The names of the gods are the vision of Advaita, the realization that Brahman only is. This is the secret of the Vedas. That is why the Vedas have a central importance of Sanatana Dharma, Bharatavarsha, and the Hindu civilization.

Hindu Unity: The Source of All Diversity

Hindu sages, very early in the history of humankind, had realized that all the diversity that they see in nature is deceptive. They saw in flights of meditation that all that diversity originates from one source—that many are one and one is many. This led them to create a society that was most tolerant and protective of diversity of nature and culture because they understood that their real nature was one. Realizing the inner unity of being, there were very few attempts at a political unity that is forced from above. Whenever social unity was sought, it was sought in the names of the gods. India's diversity, in this way, was anchored in the greatest unity that is. With the inner unity of being always present in our subconscious, the Hindus set about creating a civilization of complementary binaries, which were usually conflicting in other cultures and civilizations.

A cursory glance at the history of civilizations will reveal a fundamental fault line around which some of the most important conflicts have revolved. On one hand are the centralizing or centripetal forces that keep trying to centralize and unify the people of a certain country or nation into a sociopolitical identity centred in a national consciousness. They attempt to impose upon their subjects a homogenous and one-stop identity, making it easier to keep them united and easier to control. The fundamental appeal of these forces is centred on the concept of a state-administered unity of the various peoples ruled by the civilization, resulting in a 'peace' that facilitates trade and prosperity.

On the other hand, there are the regional or centrifugal forces, which keep trying to stress upon the diversity of every small region controlled by the centralizing forces and advocate the independence and independent expression of all these regional forces even if it results in disunity, infighting, and even secessionism of the various regions from the state. Independence, freedom, and diversity are the fundamental appeals of these forces, centred in the regional, local, and indigenous micro-identities.

Historically, these two forces—centripetal and centrifugal—have always been in constant struggle with each other, resulting in great strife, violent clashes, and immense human suffering. Great empires like Rome have crushed various nations and regions under the unifying power of the Roman Empire and offered prosperity, peace, and trade in return.

The history of the world can also be seen as a clash of these two forces. Sometimes, the centralizing forces get the better of the game, resulting in the rise of great empires like that of the Mongols; at other times, regional and secessionist forces get the upper hand, resulting in the slave revolts in Rome, the period of warring states in China, and modern Europe, where weak but independent regional identities reign supreme.

Whether it is the pharaohs of Egypt, the Khans of Mongolia, the emperors of the Incas, the great colonial powers of late mediaeval and early modern Europe, or the First Emperor of China, they have all steamrolled their subjects into state-enforced unity. And when these empires have grown weak, it has resulted in myriad warring states with independent identities.

The bottomline is a constant struggle between the two opposing forces, resulting in great violence and strife. This violence can be seen at many levels, not just at the sociopolitical level. In language, Europe has seen a great clash between the classical language of Latin and the vernaculars like Spanish, French, and English. One has always tried to suppress the other. If we talk about culture, the classical culture in any country has always seen the folk culture as unrefined, unorganized, and underdeveloped, while the folk culture has seen the classical as artificial, forced, and rigid.

The most significant and perhaps the bloodiest manifestation of this faultline has religion at its centre. No other clash has resulted in more violence and bloodshed in the world than the clash between Christianity and the pagan, polytheistic, indigenous religions of Europe, the Americas, Africa, Australasia, and now Asia. While ancient, mediaeval, and early modern history of this clash involved great physical violence, modern times have seen this violence take the place of ethnocide, where Christianity converts the followers of pagan religions all over the world and results in their absolute destruction and disappearance of their religions. The same is true of Islam and its clash with native religions wherever it went.

An important point to remember is that it is the centralizing force of the state religion of Christianity that has brutally and most violently suppressed the vernacular, folk, and indigenous faith systems and belief systems of its subject peoples.

The same clash can be seen between nature and culture in history, as most of the cultures defined by either Judeo-Christianity or Islam have seen nature as a cruel force working against the interests of man, and hence culture is seen as a force by which man uses technology and social institutions to control the forces of nature for man's use. Once again, the paradigm has been one of conflict.

This fault line cannot at all be seen in Bharatavarsha and Sanatana Dharma. In this sacred land, these two forces exist, of course, for they are universal and fundamental forces, but here they exist in fundamental balance with each other. In *Bharatiya* culture, these two cosmic forces are called *Margiya* and *Desiya*, symbolizing the highway and the country. Margiya represents the siddhanta, while desiya represents the abhivyakti. However, they are not seen as separate from each other with separate origins. Far from being opposite forces, they have always been complementary to each other, with one nourishing and enriching the other.

The complementary nature of this binary is seen even in language. The binary of margiya and desiya unfolds as the binary of Sanskrit and *Prakrita* in the arena of language. Prakrita, as the name explains, is the language of any region that naturally evolves on its own. Sanskrit was 'seen' by the sages in meditation and presented to others as the vehicle of jnana and moksha. Sanskrit is the principle that descends from above, while Prakrita is the manifestation that rises from below. And as they are one and the same in their most fundamental nature, there is an inherent unity between them. Here we would do well to remember the binary of atman and Brahman and how they are one and the same; similarly, the same principle, the same siddhanta works at the level of language in Prakrita and Sanskrit.

Another such binary is prakriti (nature) and *sanskriti* (culture). Sanskriti, or culture, is the *sanskarana* of prakriti (nature) itself, which means that just as through ritual a Hindu reinforces the cosmic rhythm, similarly, the role of culture in Bharatavarsha is to identify and reinforce the natural rhythms in a way that protects nature on the one hand and elevates man on the other, simultaneously. Dr Ganesh says that:

> *Samskara* is neither a natural phenomenon nor is it artificially created; it is a culturing of nature that emphasizes the inner rather than the outward aspects of human life. Every phase of life is celebrated. These rites of passage aim to integrate the mind-speech-body of the individual undergoing the *samskara*. As with everything else, the ultimate objective of *samskara* is self-realization.[12]

While the ultimate goal is, of course, moksha or self-realization, at all intermediate stages of life, this 'sanskarana' or culturing continues. To alight with nature and natural cycles and to protect ecosystems is thus a process of 'culturing'. Culture in Bharatavarsha is a protector of nature. In Sanatana Dharma, culture is complementary to nature.

In literature, this binary unfolds as *loka* and shastra. While shastra infuses the Vedic spirit in all parts of Bharatavarsha, loka (folk) makes sure that regional diversity is protected. But the most beautiful thing is that, just like prakriti and sanskriti, and Prakrita and Sanskrit, the loka and shastra in Indian art, culture, and aesthetics are complementary to each other. Some of the greatest principles of the Upanishads are ensconced in the most popular idioms and phrases accessible to every illiterate man. The literary tradition of Bharatavarsha resulted in the greatest written corpus anywhere in the world, and yet its oral culture, reflected most in its loka sanskriti, contains the same principles, the same themes, and the same universals.

This complementary nature can be seen most obviously in the case of deities. On one hand is the Vedic and Puranic pantheon with Shiva, Vishnu, Parvati, Brahma, Lakshmi, Saraswati, and other gods and goddesses that is the most common and most basic expression of Hindu dharma. On the other hand, there are regional gods and goddesses like Vithoba in Maharashtra, goddess Pampa in Karnataka, Sanmahi in Manipur, and several others all over Bharatavarsha. Understanding the inherent unity of all beings, including all deities, we understood that at some plane of consciousness, they met and became one. That is why it was not hard for us to accept all local and regional expressions of divinity, nor was it hard for any region of India to accept that their deities were the expression of the same force represented in Parashiva or Mahavishnu.

Sanatana Dharma, unlike Christianity or Islam, has never tried to suppress the local and regional expressions of divinity. Local gods and goddesses have always been incorporated into and adopted by the Vedic/Sanskrit culture. On the contrary, Christianity and Islam have made sure that the pagan religions and pagan ways of worship are obliterated wherever Christianity becomes the majority religion after conversions. This is not a historical memory but is a process that goes on currently as we speak. In the Indian states of Mizoram and Nagaland, local gods and goddesses and ways of worship were wiped out in the twentieth century and in many districts and villages this happened much after Independence. And as you read these lines, the same process is going on in Arunachal Pradesh as more and more Arunachali tribes convert to Christianity.

On the other hand, Hindu gods and goddesses communicate with regional gods and goddesses, live with them, marry them, and one appears as the other in some *avatara*. The goddess Pampa in Hampi, Karnataka, is seen as the avatara of goddess Parvati and is wedded to Lord Shiva. Lord Vitthoba is seen as an aspect of Lord Krishna. In Agartala, Tripura, there is a temple dedicated to fourteen gods of Tripura who are also the aspects of various deities of the Vedic pantheon. Instead of eliminating the worship of local gods and goddesses, Sanatana Dharma elevated them and preserved them in various ways.

Marga and *Desa* do not meet each other after originating separately. Their origin is one, and that is why there is an inherent and fundamental sameness between them. They both originate in the same seed of supreme consciousness, and that is why their unity is much more fundamental. In this context, unity is more fundamental, and diversity is emergent, not the other way around. Hence, it would be more apt to say that Bharatavarsha displays diversity in unity and not unity in diversity, for unity of the supreme consciousness is the source of all diversity in nature, gods, languages, cultures, etc. The entire universe is a play of consciousness; every major process of creation is reflective of the descent of consciousness, and this greater unity is reflected in the margiya desiya binary in Bharatavarsha, which is why these binaries in Bharatavarsha have always been complementary instead of conflicting.

This is the reason for the great peace of Sanatana Dharma, where kingdoms ruled without much violence, life was lived with minimum strife, and all life was geared towards the greatest goal of moksha. But the pursuit of that path made sure that the nature of absolute reality was reflected in all the institutions that Sanatana Dharma created for dharma and society. This is a feature of Bharatavarsha that is not appreciated enough. Even China, the only other civilization to compare to India in scale, did not create complementary binaries at this deep a level in society.

The anti-Hindu leadership of independent India harped on the principle of 'unity in diversity', thus reinforcing the Western misunderstanding of Bharatavarsha as a conglomeration of mind-boggling variety and diversity. This is far from the truth. Yes, the diversity is there. Yes, there is also a unity. But that unity is not an artificial patchwork of the empire. That unity is the primary cause of all diversity.

This is why Hindu unity, with its source in the divine, is not destructive but generative of diversity. That unity of Brahman is from where all diversity descends. All that we see and can imagine comes from this fundamental unity. Any attempt at Hindu unity, anchored in its gods, will not reduce diversity but instead protect and increase it.

This was because our great sages had seen the reality from the highest point of view and had realized that opposites can co-sustain instead of conflicting. This is how Hindu society was built: a dynamic balance of opposites. So, let us investigate some of these systems of harmony that Sanatana Dharma created—systems rooted in the greatest unity of all: the realization that all that is, is Brahman.

Chapter 4

A Dynamic Balance of Opposites

'Good becomes evil and evil becomes good by its own fulfillment.'

—Shri Nisargadatta Maharaja

Ardhanarisvara, Edward Moor, c. 1800. This is the greatest symbol of the dynamic balance of opposites that Sanatana Dharma upholds[1]

Purusharthas

Having a deep understanding of the fundamental unity of all creation, the Hindu civilization never tried to kill diversity of expression. Secure in the fundamental unity of all existence, Sanatana Dharma protected diversity in all walks of life. No sect tried to eliminate others. No region tried to impose its culture on others. The Margiya or the Vedic darshana was infused in every pore of this great country, but never was an attempt made to destroy the cultural self-expression of any region. This infusion of the Vedic spirit never meant the suppression of regional identity. Likewise, the celebration of regional diversity did not mean that the universal, the fundamental, and the Sanatana would be forgotten. The dynamic balance of opposites—of margiya and desiya—is what the civilization of Bharatavarsha, ruled by Sanatana Dharma, has always been.

This balance, which itself is dharma, is seen in every aspect of life, including in the pursuit of happiness. Sanatana Dharma built a civilization wedded to the pursuit of happiness. The *Taittiriya Upanishad* grades happiness of many kinds, starting from lower physical pleasures to *brahmananda*—the bliss that one feels upon the realization that one is Brahman. And the Upanishad says that at every stage of consciousness, happiness increases manifold, and in brahmananda it is 10^{20} times of the base unit of happiness, which is a way of saying that the joy of brahmananda is limitless and nothing compares to it.

This is why, while our civilization considered the pursuit of happiness central to life, it was not hedonistic pleasures that it focused upon. Physical pleasures were not neglected but were limited and bound by higher pleasures and higher pursuits. This code was embedded in the four goals of life that were considered necessary for a Hindu to follow. These goals were called the purusharthas, and they are the most famous set of fours in Hindu dharma: dharma, artha, kama, and moksha.

We have already discussed in detail what dharma is, but in the context of purusharthas, some dimensions are worth mentioning. However, before that, one needs to understand artha and kama. Artha is the pursuit of power and money, means by which worldly influence is gained, wealth is gained, and most of the works in society are sustained. Artha is necessary for any society to sustain. No nation, people, or society can hope to function without the pursuit of artha. Even the pursuit of dharma is not possible if artha is neglected, because if artha is neglected and the country becomes poor and weak, then the neighbours will attack and come to rule. Artha is thus a very fundamental pursuit of human life, both on an individual and societal levels.

Kama is also self-descriptive, but more than what most people now think of it, it is the pursuit of pleasure of sexual, emotional, and artistic kind. Human life is incomplete without the pursuit of pleasure. Apart from physical pleasures, we need emotional succour in life, and a healthy society creates a healthy environment for its people in public and private life. And without art, life is reduced to only utility and lower pleasures. Art is what makes life livable, especially for those who have to live far from nature. Cities of the world, from very early times, have been the centres of art for a reason; more the distance from nature, more the need to elevate life through cultural means. Just like dharma is necessary when rta is in imbalance, kala is necessary when harmony with nature or prakriti is in imbalance. Thus, the pursuit of kama is also central to human life. It might not seem as necessary as artha in the shorter run, but in the long-term view, it is very difficult to sustain life without the pursuit of kama either.

Artha and kama are thus absolutely critical to life, but they are not sufficient in themselves. Most of the world today pursues artha and kama, power and pleasure, without any restraint or any other force limiting it. Most of the violence and restlessness exist in the world because artha and kama are unrestrained.

Sanatana Dharma, however, seeks to restrain the pursuits of artha and kama through another purushartha—dharma. For a Hindu, dharma is the guiding force behind the pursuits of artha and kama. Dharma limits and restrains both. Dharma makes sure they do not become uncontrolled. Dharma ensures that an eternal balance is maintained, allowing society to sustain in dynamic equilibrium. *Itihasa* scholar Ami Ganatra says:

> One of the key features of the Indic worldview is its emphasis on the alignment of Dharma, *artha* and *kama*. The pursuit of *artha* and *kama* is not looked down upon. But it is important that Dharma forms the foundation of all actions for the sake of happiness and sustainability.[2]

This can also be understood with the framework of srishti, sthiti, and laya. Shivakumar G.V. writes that the philosophical basis of purusharthas is the srishti, sthiti, and laya framework mentioned in the texts. This framework is also one way to express the process of involution–evolution or ascent and descent of consciousness. The play of consciousness unfolds in a way in which there is creation, sustenance, and then dissolution (srishti, sthiti, and laya). For the world to uphold, all three are necessary. Something in the world always keeps getting created, and something always keeps getting dissolved or destroyed; thus, srishti and laya are necessary. For the system to continue, the patterns that preserve this cycle of creation and destruction have to be sustained, and that is sthiti.

Any imbalance in this process disturbs the whole dynamic. If there is only creation and no dissolution, then the growth becomes cancerous. Creativity that has taken shape in the Western world today is of the cancerous kind. Individuals are encouraged to keep creating new articles based on strange new ideas all the time, as this goes well with a market that needs new products to sell every day. No care is taken of how all that has been created will be dissolved. This cancerous creativity and creation is the reason for many ecological problems in the world today. We keep creating phones, cars, plastic, and chemicals without ever giving a thought to where they will go and sink in nature. Perhaps the greatest symbols of the cancerous growth of the modern world are the garbage dumps that one can see outside every big city in many parts of the world today. Everyone favours 'boosting the economy' by selling as many articles as possible, but nobody thinks of what happens to the packaging or garbage. Similar are the drums of nuclear waste that line so many deserts all over the world today. Nobody knows what to do with the nuclear waste, which is radioactive. It just sits in the desert waiting for a disaster to happen. This is creation or srishti (and also sthiti) in severe imbalance.

On the other hand, the communist and Islamic countries are ruled by ideologies and systems that kill any creativity or anything that is new because, in dogmatic ideologies, creativity is highly resented. As a result, they destroy what is there but are unable to create something new. When communism took over Russia, it kept spending the Russian cultural and resource capital that was created over millennia. They managed to spend it in less than seventy years and collapsed under the weight of their own dead ideology, which was incapable of any srishti, or creation.

When Islam swept like wildfire in West Asia in the seventh and eighth centuries, it got hold of some of the greatest cultural wealth in the world as the first lands it converted outside Arabia, of what are now Iraq, Syria, Iran, and parts of Turkey, were at the crossroads of Europe and Asia and benefitted from the culture and wisdom of both. Thus resulted a brief era, which is mistakenly called the golden age of Islam, in which arts and sciences are supposed to have flourished. But this spark of creativity was soon extinguished as Islamic ideology grew its roots deeper and the spark of creativity shifted elsewhere from West Asia, never to return back there. The 'golden age of Islam' was actually the result of Islamic armies coming to rule the cultural and knowledge wealth of many great empires and civilizations of that day. That wealth lasted for about 100 years under Islamic rule, and Islamic empires greatly benefitted from it, but soon the anti-creative impulse took over. What was old was spent, nothing new was created, and dusk came for the Islamic empires in those areas. This is an example of laya or dissolution in imbalance. Where nothing new is created, dissolution or destruction takes over and the spark of civilization dies.

Sthiti, thus, is necessary for maintaining the dynamics of srishti and laya. And sthiti is dharma. It balances the play of srishti and laya. Dharma makes sure that artha and kama do not become uncontrolled. It makes sure that the pursuit of power, wealth, and pleasure is limited and maintained by the agency of dharma. Dharma works as the thermostat or the negative feedback loop in this case, and whenever it sees a tendency moving away from the golden mean, it brings it back towards the centre. This is why dharma precedes artha and kama. As Dr Ganesh and Hari Ravikumar write: 'Dharma has been given the first position of the four because it is the key to balancing the natural instinct of *kama* and the relentless attempt at *artha*; this balance, when sustained over long years, holds the potential to ultimately attain moksa.'[3]

The texts say that if any conflict arises between the pursuit of dharma on the one hand and artha and kama on the other, then it is the pursuit of dharma that takes precedence. Thus, there is a hierarchy in purusharthas. Dharma has to guide artha and kama and not the other way around. Pursuit of artha without the restraint of dharma leads to a lifestyle which we may call *artha sarvopari* life (with artha dictating dharma and not vice versa). We have already discussed how this primacy of artha over dharma leads to cancerous growth. Pursuit of kama over dharma also leads to a situation where hedonistic pleasures abound and social order collapses. The West today is also caught in that kama imbalance spiral. That is why it is necessary for the pursuits of *artha* and *kama* to be limited by the guidance of dharma, as Shri Ram Swarup writes:

> Broadly speaking, Sanatana dharma has spoken of four aims of man's pursuit (*purusharthas*). The first two, physical well-being and acquisition of wealth, even for their fulfillment, have to accept the guidance of the third, the ethical law, the dharma. Dharma in turn is rooted in the fourth, *moksha*, the principle of liberation in man from the pull of his lower nature. There can be no lasting ethical behavior without cultivating dispassion and a taste for higher life. A Hindu *sannyasin* takes the vow of fearlessness; he takes no offence and offers no injury to anyone.[4]

Shri Ram Swarup talks about a crucial point here: while dharma sustains artha and kama, the idea of moksha is critical for the laws of dharma to sustain. In its quest to keep order, dharma is helped by the fourth purushartha—moksha.

Human life, according to Sanatana Dharma, is a river that is characterized by the flow consisting of artha and kama, which give life direction and speed. But the activity of artha and kama is limited and channelized by the twin banks of dharma and moksha. Moksha is as necessary for the pursuit of artha and kama as is dharma. One can argue why moksha is a necessary purushartha. Why is it not sufficient to have only the other three? And moksha is not the pursuit of everyone, at least in one life. It is true that not everyone is a mumukshu (desirous of moksha) and wants to experience more of life. Even for such a person, moksha is not a purushartha to be dispensed with for a very deep reason. One should uphold dharma because upholding dharma makes it possible for the individual to move towards absolute happiness, the bliss of realizing one's true nature, which is Brahman. Thus, without moksha, dharma does not make sense.

Why should one balance one's lower pleasures if there is no higher pleasure? What is the sense in limiting pleasure if there is no promise of limitless, boundless, and unending pleasure? What is the sense in forgoing power too? The answer is that the pleasure that kama provides and the power that artha provides are limited. While the pleasure that moksha provides is unlimited and the happiness that it provides is of the highest kind. This is why lower pleasures have to be limited and transcended so that the path towards highest pleasure opens up.

From another point of view, moksha provides release from the cycle of life and death. If there is no *moksha*, then the endless cycle of life and death becomes sadistic. Why am I forced to go through birth and death and pain if there is no option of choosing out? And without the idea of *punarjanma*, there is no reason why one should not be a nihilist.

Albert Camus asked the greatest philosophical question that can be asked from one life perspective in *The Myth of Sisyphus* and also in his other literary works: If there is nothing beyond death, then why not live a hedonistic life maximizing physical pleasures until you are in your prime till the age of forty and then commit suicide? For what is the point of holding back from pleasures if there is no other life? And what is the point of continuing the misery if there is no other life? Suicide then becomes a very logical choice. Camus' position is the natural position of a materialistic civilization that believes in only one life.

A worldview built on multiple lives perspective with *moksha* as the way out, on the other hand, automatically goes towards creating a dharmic order in society. Dharma limits artha and kama, and the promise of moksha keeps one's faith in dharma, and the dynamic equilibrium sustains. Thus, dharma and moksha guide artha and kama in a way that balances every urge and every pleasure to its optimum and lets a human being lead a life of balance, which ultimately nudges him towards ultimate knowledge, happiness, and moksha. Shivakumar G.V. writes:

> The modern world recognizes that the *Mahabharata* explores the relation between *Artha/Kama* and Dharma. But modernity does not present these narratives in ways for society to internalize. Worse, it fails to recognize how the pursuit of *Moksha* sustains Dharma. Without the latter, the former exploration loses direction. In its refusal and inability to recognize *Moksha*, the modern world triumphs in the world of *Artha/Kama* with a façade of exploring Dharma.[5]

There is another deeper reason why moksha is a necessary counterpart of dharma. Without moksha, there is no proof of dharma. Let us understand it in the way we have understood dharma and life cycles in this section. Moksha, seen from the perspective of the individual, is the force of laya or involution, where an individual does meditation, turns his focus inwards by concentrating on a mantra, and activates his kundalini. Moksha is the fruit of the ascension of kundalini from muladhara to sahasrara, upon meeting which moksha is attained. As we have discussed before, when a jnani/jivanmukta gets moksha, the bowl of nectar is released, and the entire world is bathed with a new light. When such a jnani speaks on matters pertaining to samsara, he gives the optimum and best of solutions because he is looking at the world through the greatest vantage point conceivable. His solutions are not deliberate exertions but spontaneous outpourings from the point of view of absolute knowledge. Sanatana Dharma created the civilization of Bharatavarsha with the help of these jivanmuktas or jnanis reflecting upon the world from the point of view of Brahman.

So here is another definition of dharma. Dharma is the force of evolution that guides creation by artha and kama with the insight obtained during the process of involution in moksha. This is why, without moksha, dharma would lose its force, because without jivanmuktas certifying dharma from direct experience of ultimate reality, there would be no proof that dharma is right; without jnanis confirming dharmic principles with their apta vakyas, there would be no validity of shabda pramana and no confirmation whether the dharmic principles that are being propounded are correct or not. Dr Ganesh and Hari Ravikumar say: 'Sanatana-dharma upholds the acts of self-realized people who are selfless, inclusive, and competent, who have noble intentions even if their chosen means are not moral in the way a textbook of Normative Ethics defines it.'[6]

It is the constant confirmation of jivanmuktas with their apta vakyas that our texts have gained the status of shabda pramana. And it is the constant guidance of living rishis like Shri Ramana Maharishi, Shri Nisargadatta Maharaja, Shri Ramakarishna Paramhamsa, Shri Neem Karoli Baba, and Amritanandamayi Maa that extreme orthodoxy and dogmatism never evolved in Bharatavarsha and Sanatana Dharma, because our tradition was kept ever updated and ever new with fresh insights from the highest experience that ever is—moksha.

This is how the twin banks of dharma and moksha guide human beings in their pursuit of artha and kama. Without this model of purusharthas and without this goal setting in life, the pursuits of artha and kama would become unrestrained and lose their force after first bouts of creation. Hindu civilization kept things in perpetual balance because the fast-flowing waters of artha and kama were always limited, guided, and channelized by the great banks of dharma and moksha.

Without a darshana of life that encourages individuals to turn inwards and meditate, the accompanying practice or customs become redundant, arbitrary, and finally tyrannical. Thus, Meemansa without Vedanta is nothing but meaningless rituals; samkhya without yoga is an old wives' tale; dharma without moksha is an order for nothing. Similarly, philosophy without practice becomes shallow and vacuous at best, or worse, it becomes dogma, like it became in Christianity and Islam. For a healthy civilization in balance, a civilization guided by

Sanatana Dharma, both are necessary and complementary—the darshana and the practice.

Dr Ganesh and Hari Ravikumar explain it by comparing it to the four parts of the Vedas—*Samhitas*, *Brahmanas*, *Aranyakas*, and *Upanishads*. While Samhitas deal with invocation of the deities with wonder and respect, Brahmanas talk about the actual rituals (*yajnas*) that have to be performed, Aranyakas (written in *aranya* or forest) focus on introspection and meditation, and Upanishads focus completely on *prajna* (wisdom) and self-realization (moksha). 'We also see a connection between these divisions of the Vedas and the four stages of human life—the Samhitas correspond to *brahmacharya*, the Brahmanas correspond to *garhasthya*, the Aranyakas correspond to vanaprastha, and the Upanishads correspond to *sannyasa*.'[7]

Without Upanishads and Aranyakas, the Brahmanas and Samhitas become meaningless, and without Samhitas and Brahmanas, the darshana given in the Upanishads cannot be actualized and realized. While the Samhitas and Brahmanas represent the process of evolution, the Upanishads and the Aranyakas represent the process of involution. Moksha is the lynchpin that upholds the apparatus of dharma, and dharma upholds artha and kama.

We can illustrate this with a beautiful analogy from Hindu temple architecture. Every evolved Hindu temple has a shikhara above the garbha-griha. The shikhara has a kalasha at the top containing navagrahas, and there is a kalasha underground the vigraha of the deity in the garbha-griha, which also has a kalasha with navagrahas. The underground kalasha is the individual consciousness with the power of kundalini to rise through the vertical profile of the temple and through the vigraha of the deity, like kundalini rises in sushumna nadi. Just as this individual consciousness ascends from underground, the universal consciousness descends from the *kalasha* above, and this process of ascent and descent of consciousness is called darshana, which is how we also address our philosophy. Darshana, as we have seen, is the direct witnessing of ultimate truth by yogis in meditation.

But there is another architectural motif in the vertical profile of the Hindu temple that is able to illustrate the necessity of moksha for dharma. The temple shikhara is kept in place by two critical elements in architecture. One, of course, is the solid foundation on which the entire structure stands, and the other is the keystone at the top. The keystone is directly below the kalasha in the shikhara. It is the keystone that holds all the individual stones and pieces of the shikhara in place. It seems counter-intuitive but is a fact to anyone who understands basic architectural principles. Support can also be given from above, and not just from below. If you pull out the keystone, then the structural alignment of the entire shikhara or the superstructure is disturbed, and the temple shikhara collapses under its own weight.[8]

What does this mean for the pair of dharma and moksha? We can think of the foundation of a temple as dharma, that force which upholds the society and the individual from below, creating a firm ground for people to stand. And we can think of moksha as the keystone that holds the structure of Hindu society from above. While dharma upholds from below, moksha supports from above, and this is how the edifice of Sanatana Dharma perpetuates. Without moksha, dharma will not be able to function, and without dharma, there will be no artha and kama.

To take the example of the two kalashas, between the oneness and unity of the individual seed underground and the universal consciousness above, there is all the diversity. Between these two kalashas is the entire visible temple, and we see all kinds of diversity here. But all this diversity of motifs is upheld by the two kalashas or two forces guarding, upholding, and supporting the entire structure. Thus, it is the unity of consciousness or siddhanta that upholds the diversity of structure or abhivyakti.

Let us end our discussion on purusharthas by considering the duration of their utility. As expressed at the start of this section, Sanatana Dharma is all about experiences. The axioms that are central to Sanatana Dharma are also means or props to help us hold on to something, some intermediate truths. As we ascend the states of consciousness through meditation, these props become increasingly less necessary. Even atman and Brahman are props of the ultimate experience of ultimate reality. Similarly, purusharthas too, like every other institution in Sanatana Dharma, are means by which we lead our lives in a way that leads us towards jnana or non-duality of experience. When we reach there, the props stop being necessary. The *Yoga Sutras*, after giving elaborate instructions for the ascent of consciousness, culminate with the sutra that expresses the dissolution of the need for purusharthas after their job is done.

> पुरुषार्थशून्यानां गुणानां प्रतिप्रसवः कैवल्यं।
> स्वरूपप्रतिष्ठा वा चितिशक्तिरिति।।

> Ultimate liberation is when the gunas, devoid of any purpose for the purusa, return to their original [latent] state; in other words, when the power of consciousness is situated in its own essential nature.[9]

Varna and Ashrama

Varnashrama is another important set of fours in Sanatana Dharma. It is actually made up of two sets of fours, *varna* and *ashrama*. For the sake of convenience, let us discuss them one by one. Varna divides the society into four primary groups: Brahmins, Kshatriyas, Vaishyas, and Shudras. Brahmins pursue knowledge, Kshatriyas pursue power, and Vaishyas pursue money, while Shudras are artisans or worksmen. *Jati* is a related concept that sometimes overlaps but at other times it is independent of varna. Jati has always been related to one's profession, language, and region, while varna is the fourfold division of society with members of each varna spread across society and country. In one interpretation, varna is horizontal with a hierarchy amongst the varnas, and jati is horizontal with no particular and recognizable hierarchy between all jatis. Both of them are partially true, as we will see.

This seems to be the natural fourfold division of human society, broadly speaking. It is also a good division of labour since forces pursuing knowledge, power, money, and masses are never concentrated in one source, preventing overarching dictators or totalitarian ideologies. India has seen far fewer dictatorships and tyrannical rulers and kingdoms in the past than any other civilization on earth because power was never allowed to be concentrated in one hand and in one place. If any class became too unbridled, it was limited by the other. This does not mean that there was no tyranny at any point in time in India, but it was far less so than other civilizations, and the reason was the democratic division of power into not just four but many parts. Varna was just one instrument of this decentralization of power; there were many other mechanisms.

This division naturally results in a heterogeneous and non-monolithic society with lots of diversity. And Indic civilization has always been invested in preserving diversity, even if it means a less centralized, less 'united', and less 'equal' society. As we will discuss in the chapter on secularism in the Shatrubodha section, equality and freedom are incompatible values. If any State or civilization chooses to go for more equality, then it means less freedom, and if one goes for more freedom, then it means less equality. The capitalist world today, represented by the 'American model', tilts more in the favour of freedom, while the more socialist European welfare states have gone into the favour of oppressive equality.

Sanatana Dharma, like always, created a dynamic balance between many sets of opposites, like freedom and security, freedom and equality, and also between competition and security. Shatavdhani Dr R. Ganesh and Hari Ravikumar assert this dynamic balance:

> If there is one lesson that history has taught us unequivocally, it is that absolute freedom and perfect equality can never co-exist, given the inherent diversity of individuals. Social inequality is the result when we chase absolute freedom. When we go after perfect equality, personal freedom is destroyed. To avoid these extremes, we have the compromise of dharma. *Varna-dharma* ensures a basic level of equity and *svadharma* ensures a basic level of personal freedom.[10]

The identity created by one's varna and jati provided great security to the individuals. Not that there was no room for personal freedom at all, but the broad goals of life were largely decided by one's circumstances, giving one direction and purpose. In the absence of contemporary college education for vocational training, most professional skills were also learnt within one's family and community. It was a system that greatly prized security of identity. Sidney Low observed:

> There is no doubt that it is the main cause of the fundamental stability and contentment by which Indian society has been braced up for centuries against the shocks of politics and the cataclysms of Nature. It provides every man with his place, his career, his occupation, his circle of friends. It makes him at the outset a member of a corporate body, it protects him through life from the canker of social jealousy and unfulfilled aspirations, it ensures him companionship and a sense of community with others in like case with himself. The caste organization is to the Hindu his club, his trade union, his benefit society, his

> philanthropic society. There are no work houses in India and none are as yet needed.[11]

This does not mean that there was no freedom or competition. To see how this system also yielded freedom, we need to take the examples of business clusters based on caste today in many parts of India.[12] R. Vaidyanathan, in his book *Caste as Social Capital*, shows caste guilds have supported entrepreneurship and encouraged countless start-ups. Along with providing loans to individuals and families starting businesses, they have also protected them from aggressive corporate manoeuvres like hostile takeovers and 'bleed to death' competitive practices. P. Kanagasabapathi, in his seminal work *Indian Models of Economy, Business and Management*, talks about the business clusters of Tamil Nadu and Gujarat, which were mostly community-driven and supported. There was a lot of internal diversity in these 'caste guilds', and in many cases one guild contained many castes with similar professions. It is more correct to say that these were community guilds that sometimes overlapped with caste and sometimes contained more than one caste in one guild.

These community guilds balanced competitive spirit with the basic urge for security in human society. One was free from other castes or guilds encroaching upon the jobs of a particular community, but within the community there was enough scope to compete and win against others. Inside the community, the best man always won. But no community encroached upon the rights of others. Shri Ram Swarup calls this 'communitarian democracy'.

> The contribution of Hindu thought in the social field was great indeed. It taught us how to create a society of more or less self-governing communities; it gave us 'communitarian democracy', the foundation of a true democracy. In this society, no one was rootless, no body belonged to an anonymous mass; everyone

> had a niche, a place where he was not a stranger; as a member of a great community, no one could be pushed around and he had the protection of the community. And yet no community was a law unto itself. Each followed the guidance of dharma. Never was there a society so free from coercive state apparatus. Every one belonged, everyone had security, dignity, a vocation. The world needs this system or something like it—and much advanced thinking is veering round to this view—in order to overcome the rootlessness and the atomization that is becoming man's lot under new forces at work.[13]

It was a balance between competition and social security. Dharma, like always, created a dynamic balance between these two opposites and prevented Hindu society from falling into either extreme. One can see the effects of a society built on the concept of limitless competition in the modern West. While a minuscule minority enjoys the benefits of great competition, most others either suffer greatly or eke out a mundane existence of just scraping by in life, while all the narrative around them exhorts them to 'excel' and 'do the best'. The pitfalls of the other extreme of complete security have always been obvious. Socialist and communist countries tried to do that with no creativity and competition. We can see as a historical fact that there never was an economic, social, and political disaster of the scale that communist countries artificially created because they had completely killed the competitive and hence the entrepreneurial spirit. Sanatana Dharma had found a middle path, and varnashrama dharma was one of the expressions of this middle path. Outside the group, security was encouraged, and inside the group, competition, creativity, and entrepreneurship were favoured, as Dr Coomaraswamy says:

> Given the natural classes, one of the good elements of what is now regarded as democracy was provided by making the castes self-governing; thus it was secured that a man should

> be tried by his peers (whereas, under Industrial Democracy, an artist may be tried by a jury of tradesmen, or a poacher by a bench of squires). Within the caste there existed equality of opportunity for all, and the caste as a body had collective privileges and responsibilities. Society thus organized has much the appearance of what would now be called Guild Socialism.[14]

Sanatana Dharma created a social environment in India that celebrated diversity at a level that was unprecedented. This was because it accepted that different communities would have different value systems, and a one-size-fits-all approach will not be feasible for a large and diverse society like Bharatavarsha. Any Judeo-Christian or Western society today prefers a universal value system in which individuals as well as communities are straitjacketed in one system or the other. Earlier, most of these systems were dominated by overt Judeo-Christian culture; now technology-led enlightenment liberal value system has taken hold. But the formula remains the same—that one set of values should command all.

This leads to constant battles of value systems, each of which claim to be universal. It is not unlike the Christian religious wars of mediaeval Europe when one Christian denomination would declare all others as non-Christian and invalid and would try to impose its own dogma on everyone it could command. However, Hindu culture built a civilization based on multiple value systems because it understood the inherent diversity of human nature. Varna was one contributor to this diversity, but there were many diversifying and diversity-nourishing factors involved. There were hundreds of value systems preserving and celebrating this diversity. It was not a celebration of anarchy, and similar groups tended to band together. The foundational idea was to leave communities alone to manage themselves if they agree to public rules of behaviour. India's orientation towards multiple value systems helped incorporate the immigrant and even the invading populations before the Islamic invasions. This is the reason Parsis still thrive in India, and India is one of the countries where the almost extinct Persian religion of Zoroastrianism still thrives. India's great cultural diversity ensured that we did not just 'tolerate' but celebrate diversity, and multiple value systems were a reason for that.

The point here is that the multiple value system was not a mere thought or institution in Bharatavarsha. It was a cultivated habit. We kept creating and preserving diversity through multiple value systems to achieve great tolerance and peace, and at the same time never missed imbuing every path with the pursuit of the ultimate knowledge, making sure the pole star is never lost from sight and we remain as one, undivided people, united in our pursuit of the four purusharthas, with moksha as the final goal.

Even though today varna and jati are said to be exclusive to Hindu society, a quick analysis of world history shows that this was not so, and the world was broadly divided between these groups. Alvin Toffler, in *Power Shift*, shows that the three main forces behind every power in the world were muscle, money, and mind, broadly overlapping with the three varnas that we just mentioned.[15] It was just that in India this system was taken more systematically and seriously than in other places, which is also the reason that our civilization could create an entire society based on the pursuit of knowledge.

Owing to the heterogeneous and diverse character of Hindu society in Bharatavarsha, many have alleged that India has always been 'divided' and there has been no overarching 'unity' in India. Naipaul, towards the end of the twentieth century, called India a 'million mutinies'. Its 'disunited' character has frustrated anyone who seeks unity, for good or for bad. And this has saved Hindu society from getting swayed over or being taken over by any ideology or group easily, again for good or for bad.

This was the reason that when the formal modes of defence were eliminated during the Islamic invasions, it was these small social groups that saved India from the fury of the Muslim kings. These compact small groups closed down and became self-sufficient. It was the disunity of these self-sufficient groups that prevented any takeover by any centralizing force, even as barbaric and tyrannical as the Delhi Sultanate and the Mughal Empire. K.S. Lal, in his seminal work *Growth of Scheduled Castes and Tribes in India*, says that jati was one of the reasons that Hindu society survived the Hindu holocaust by Islamic invaders. When the official fighter class, or the Kshatriyas, were defeated, every caste would take up the baton and would resist against the Islamic invaders. K.S. Lal attests the ultimate demise of the Mughal Empire to the constant resistance of caste militias.

That it gave Hindus identity, security, and protection against invaders is true. But are there any downsides to varna? Of course there are. There is no system created by humans that does not have faults, and even though in Bharatavarsha institutions and structures were built from the inspiration of jnanis, they had to be implemented in a samsara, which by its very nature is full of faults. So, any social system will also have faults, loopholes, and also some cases of decay. The varnashrama system also suffered from all of these problems, as is natural to any other system, even those based on liberty, equality, and fraternity.

Varnashrama dharma has been the focus of great criticism from outside and also from the Hindu community. One charge against it is that it is based on birth-based distinctions, duties, privileges, and rights, so it locks people in the circumstances of their birth and thus stops all possibility for those individuals and communities who are born with low social status and many social disabilities to uplift themselves and better their circumstances. The first question that arises is this: Is it birth-based or not?

Some scholars say that yes, it is birth-based, and the shastras do indeed support this claim. Many others say that it is entirely karma-based, resting their assertion on a fundamental axiom of Sanatana Dharma: the axiom of karma and punarjanma. The karma theory says that everyone gets the phala of one's karma in the long run of multiple births, and thus the circumstances of one's birth are one's own doing. If karma is an axiom, then this is true. And the foundation of varnashrama dharma rested on the fact that one was born in a place that would do justice to one's aptitude.

Seen from a scientific point of view, is it possible for people to be born largely in groups that do justice to their inner aptitude? Sociobiology says yes. It says that it is not just our genes that influence our culture, but culture also influences genetics. This is called gene-culture co-evolution. And if, for centuries, a group with certain characteristics practices endogamy, cultural differences become more defined and prominent. Cognitive psychologist James Haidt says that 'cultural and genetic evolution are intertwined', and at a certain point in evolutionary history, there was great evolutionary pressure on the human brain to take advantage of learning from culture.

> All human beings today are the products of the co-evolution of a set of genes (which is almost identical across cultures) and a set of cultural elements (which is diverse across cultures, but still constrained by the capacities and predispositions of the human mind).... After a thousand years of inbreeding within caste, castes will diverge slightly on a few genetic traits—for example, shades of skin color—which might in turn lead to a growing cultural association of caste with color rather than just with occupation. In this way genes and cultures co-evolve; they mutually affect each other, and neither process can be studied in isolation for human beings.[16]

This does not pronounce a judgement on the varna system; it does not say whether varna is good or bad. It just lends credence to the varna theory that specific groups devoted to specific pursuits, practicing endogamy for generations, will result in children being born who are more suited to the circumstances of their birth. There can be great group benefits of this system, as well as disadvantages, and even systemic injustices are possible. Just the fact that the system has some 'confirmation in science' does not deny the fact that there are always individuals in any such system who are exceptions and misfits. It does not preclude injustice either. It just says that varna based on birth, aligned with aptitude broadly, is possible.

While this system makes for more efficiency in perfect condition, divides power into many parts, and creates self-sufficient defence units in case of any external attack, there was one more reason that can be considered as the more important reason for the sustenance of the varna system in Bharatavarsha. The varna system was important to Bharatavarsha because it allowed us to dedicate a class purely for the study of the Vedas, which are far from mere texts but are considered as the breath of Brahman.

> The Vedas are sounds emanating from the vibrations of this Great Intelligence, the Great Gnosis. That is why we believe that the mantras of the Vedas originate from the *Parmatman* himself. We must take special care of such sounds to ensure the good of the world. Yes, the Vedic mantras are sequences of sounds that are meant for the good of the world.[17]

Coming back to misfits and exceptions, since everyone is born with a mixed bag of good and bad karma, everyone has to suffer one way or another, and any misalignment in one's inner aptitude or svadharma to one's circumstances of birth is also due to one's own karma. This is what the karma theory says. Does that mean there is no way out of bad circumstances? This is not so, since the theory of karma also says that while one's birth is based on past lives' karma, one's present karma will decide the next births, and thus in this way one's destiny is entirely in one's own control. So yes, varna was birth-based, and yes, birth was a result of karma; therefore, yes, everything is based on karma.

But is this not a fatalistic view of life? Are we supposed to watch others suffer in misery and pain just because their past life's karma led them here? Is this not a justification of others' suffering? Absolutely not, and the theory of karma itself exhorts and encourages us to help others who are stuck in unfortunate circumstances. It tells us that it is the duty of every capable citizen to physically and materially alleviate the condition of his fellow citizens of any class by doing public works for them. 'Dharma is afterlife insurance. But in this life too it is dharma that gives us peace and happiness.'[18]

Thus, a king has to improve the living standards of all of his subjects. Vaishyas are enjoined upon to do public service with the access to money they have. Even individuals with very meagre financial resources are exhorted to do charity as much as they can and whenever they can. Hindu charity, *daana*, is the greatest agency to improve the conditions of our fellow human beings in this very life. Just because someone is suffering from his past life's karma does not mean that he has to be left alone. He has to be helped; the cycle has to be broken; and a new cycle of good karma has to be started.

The theory of karma says that punarjanma and *prarabdha* are to understand the cause of suffering and evil in the world. Karma is to eliminate that suffering as much as possible even in one life. Punarjanma is to understand the cycles that are hidden, that have been continuing since ages and many lives. Karma is to end the bad cycles in this life so that new and good cycles can begin. To recall our discussion on moksha, laya, or involution, happens when one stops identifying with one's actions. This stoppage of identification with one's actions is nothing but the stoppage of cycles that go against rta, and any great suffering or tyranny is against rta. And it is a Hindu's greatest job to restore rta. Dharma is after all, *rtena rtam*, that which restores rta, or the cosmic balance. Thus, the varna theory coupled with the siddhanta of karma did not produce a fatalistic and sadistic outlook in Hindus. Hindu texts and tradition are very clear that it is our duty to alleviate the suffering of individuals and groups even in one life.

The second question that arises is this: Was everyone forced to be part of this system? If someone was not Brahmin, Kshatriya, or Vaishya, was he automatically Shudra? This is clearly wrong. Though this might come as a shock to both the supporters and detractors of varna theory, varnas were not limited to four. There were many more, and a large percentage of Hindu society lived outside the *chaturvarna* system. There are many groups and jatis today that do not fall into any of the four groups of varna. Many are found in 'transition'. The *Dharmashastras* themselves keep warning about '*varnasankara*' or 'mixing of varnas', and still the mixing keeps happening. This leads to 'mixed' and 'in-between' groups, and the shastras wax eloquent on where these groups belong. This is not a situation that exists only today, but even in the times of Manu, the mixing of varnas was quite prevalent. For a better part of Hindu history, most of Hindu society did not live according to the fourfold divisions of varna. Most lived in groups that did not fall into any category of Brahmins, Kshatriyas, Vaishyas, or Shudras. Manu himself acknowledges that due to the mixing of the varnas in many communities, there are at least fifteen varnas.[19]

The third great question that arises about varna is: Was it flexible? Was social mobility possible in this system? Was it possible for people to gain or lose varnas? Any look at ancient and mediaeval literature, at *Itihasa-puranas* and *Dharmashastras* themselves, tells us that yes, it was possible. It was not a free-for-all where you could freely pick and choose your varna. But there was inter-generational mobility in varna and jati. The unit that 'changed varna' was, however, not the individual, but the extended family, or kutumba, and sometimes even the entire community. The *Dharmashastras* themselves attest to this movement where some 'gained' the jati, and some 'lost' it. The *Dharmashastras* are also continuously warning about the mixing of varnas. The entire logic of varna was built on the argument that if endogamy is practiced, then the aptitude of offspring is more likely to match their birth. This necessitates endogamy. But exogamy was as much a fact of Hindu life as endogamy was, and the shastras, Itihasas, and Puranas are all witness to the fact that exogamy happened. The *Dharmashastras* themselves keep talking about categories and sub-categories that kept getting created when there were cross-varna marriages. P.V. Kane attests to the fact that over time these sub-categories had become too many to trace, and the *Dharmashastra* authors abandoned attempts to categorize them all, thus once again attesting to the fact that most of the Hindu society existed outside varnashrama dharma.

The authors of the *Dharmashastras* also assert that varna and jati also changed if the particular vocation that one was born with was not followed for many successive generations, generally five or six. Since many failed to do so, especially during the mediaeval ages, they 'lost' their varna in this way. K.S. Lal also explains how many Kshatriyas 'lost' their varnas, fighting with the Islamic invaders, and became 'tribal' by fleeing to forests and adopting a tribal lifestyle. The numbers of what are now SCs and STs swelled during the mediaeval invasions greatly. Moreover, as Dr M.S. Chaitra proposes in an upcoming paper, the way varna is being read by today's scholars on both sides is deeply coloured with the colonial lens, which has led most to confuse the political and the social on one hand and the contextual with the universal on the other.

Thus, the varna and jati situation on the ground was far more diverse and complex than can be assessed while looking at the texts. The fourfold varna was only for a minority of communities in India, and most of the society remained outside it. The fourfold system was mostly considered necessary for the highly specialized pursuit of spiritual knowledge, defence, and international and national commerce. This does not mean that only Brahmins were allowed to study, only Kshatriyas were allowed to fight, and only Vaishyas engaged in commerce. Agriculture and commerce were second nature to almost every family except very few, and more than 99 per cent of the population engaged in agriculture and small businesses. Similarly, almost all classes and communities contributed soldiers to any war. And almost every community had their own rulers and own kings. Education was allowed to all but was organized locally by every community. Only Vedic education was confined to Brahmins, but the essence of *dharma* was taken to every nook and corner of India with the help of Itihasas, Puranas, natya and katha pravachan parampara of India. There was a great democracy of knowledge in this.

There is another argument that says that in practice, things were never as clinical as the texts seem to portray. Even in the classical Hindu era, things were not entirely run according to the varna system, as we already saw that most of the society did not come under the four varnas. One beautiful example is the great Sanskrit play called *the Mrichhakatika*, or *The Little Clay Cart*, by Shudraka, who is a Kshatriya. The hero of the play, Charudatta, is a Brahmin who engages in business, is enamoured with and marries a courtesan, while already married himself. He is aided in his adventures by his Brahmin friend. We see almost every varna rule flouted in this single story. The same is true of many cases throughout the Itihasas and Puranas.

The fourth question about varna is this: What about untouchability and many jatis losing social prestige so much so that they lost all self-respect? Did this happen? It does not need research to prove that. The evidence is everywhere. Some communities did lose dignity, with many of them getting locked in pathetic social circumstances with very few opportunities of uplifting them from those conditions. How did this happen, one might ask? There are various reasons that cannot be dwelt in detail here due to the shortage of space. But in short, one reason was the mediaeval invasions and the resulting distortions in Hindu social order leading to many breakdowns on many levels. This might have resulted in entire communities getting the short end of the stick. Sanatana Dharma always remains fresh by constantly updating and adapting to new circumstances while keeping the universals alive. But during the mediaeval ages, many of these processes of reform were prevented, leading to ossification and rigidity in social order.

Moreover, during times of great distress, the defensive instincts of a society kick in, and creative impulses take a back seat. Security, especially of women, becomes the top priority, and freedom takes a back seat. The falling status of women and their education in the *Dharmashastras* over the ages is an indicator of this imbalance towards security a little too much, due to great and unprecedented danger to Hindu women. And as we discussed, any system that banks too much on security and stability starts dying off slowly, with social rigidity and hierarchy taking over the creative and libertarian spirits. Such a system loses steam over a period of time and breaks down upon a significant challenge to its social order. The Islamic social order was never a challenge to even the most ossified varna system since Hindus of all varnas and jatis were treated horribly by Islamic invaders. However, the market capitalist model that the British brought in opened up new economic and social possibilities for a lot of communities, leading to the disappearance of a system that was already in fast decay.

Does this mean that the system developed faults only due to external disturbances and there was nothing wrong with them originally? This is not so, and any system has its own drawbacks, and the varna system must have its own. Systems built on freedom, while giving hope of success to everyone, also result in life-sapping competition and also great inequality like today's United States. Systems built on equality, while taking benefits to everyone, result in the curtailing of individual freedom and injustice to many who can excel in a competitive society. Similarly, systems built on division of labour can lurch towards positions where the divisions become too rigid, and compartments become too watertight. There are many signs in India's history that this too must have happened at some point in time in Indian history. This is why many bhakti saints, like Shri Ramanujacharya, Shri Namdev, Chaitanya Mahaprabhu, Shri Basavanna, and others, advocated transcending the rigidity of birth identities. Dr Raghavan says:

> The system of dharma shastras that hold forth on a variety of topics of individual and community life is an important institution for the maintenance of dharma. However, since the determination of dharma is highly sensitive to time and context, cheat sheets can quickly become outdated. If not updated, they may turn out to be counterproductive. However, the process of updation requires dharmisthas who are well-established in the sensibility of dharma and can call it out unbiasedly.[20]

The fifth question about the varna system is that it let Brahmins monopolize knowledge and did not let other communities study. Is there any truth in that? Despite some Smritis seeming to suggest that, India's history and vast literary culture say that this was not so. Some Smritis do explicitly forbid some communities from studying the Vedas, but the prohibition was not about knowledge in general but only regarding the study of the Vedas and only about its practice in performing yajna. All other subjects were freely studied by all other jatis and varnas. Shri Dharampal's work in modern India when the British arrived in India proves this point beyond any doubt. And as far as the Vedic knowledge is concerned, only the preservation of Vedic sounds was considered the duty of only Brahmins; the knowledge contained in the Vedas was freely available to anyone who wanted to truly seek.

> We need only one class of people charged with the mission of keeping the sound of the Vedas alive in the world. The ideas contained in them for spiritual uplift are open to all. The songs of non-Brahmin saints like Appar and Nammazhvar are replete with Vedic and Vedantic thoughts.[21]

For this purpose, vehicles of mass dissemination of the paths of attaining ultimate knowledge were created. One of those vehicles was the *Natyashastra* and the tradition of dance and drama. It is the stated goal of the *Natyashastra* to take the knowledge of the Vedas to everyone: 'As the Vedas are not to be listened to by those born as Shudras, be pleased to create another Veda which will belong to all the Varnas.'[22] The *Natyashastra* is also called the fifth Veda, and the Veda that was created to take the knowledge of the Vedas to those who are not able to partake of the knowledge directly through performing yajnas. If Sanatana Dharma had wanted to create a monopoly of knowledge, then why would it create the *Natyashastra*?

There are many texts that claim to be the *pancham* Veda, or the fifth Veda, in India. The Mahabharata is an Itihasa text, and it is also claimed as a pancham Veda. The purpose of the Itihasas too is to take the knowledge of the Vedas to those who are not able to perform the yajna themselves. The Ramayana is also said to contain all the knowledge of the Vedas in capsule form, and it is written in a form of story that can be conveyed to the masses. To further democratize knowledge dissemination, both the Ramayana and the Mahabharata were adapted for reenacting in various mediums such as stage plays, poetry, or songs sung by roaming bards. There was absolutely no bar on who these actors were. No one was bothered about the jati or varna of the roaming bard. If anything, they were most probably not

Brahmins. They sang and talked about these great epics in the manner they liked, and in the language they preferred, making any sort of monopoly impossible.

Additionally, there are hundreds of authorized or recognized Ramayanas and many versions of various episodes of the Mahabharata. If the Hindu culture were an intolerant culture like Christianity, then it would convene a council of priests and declare all except one version of the Ramayana and the Mahabharata to be wrong and heretical. The fact that the multiple versions of these great epics were allowed tells us about the anti-monopolistic character of the Indic knowledge system.

Ayurveda is also called the fifth Veda. It is a discipline, and yet it is called the fifth Veda, for it is a life science and instructs not just on medicine or food, but on an entire lifestyle and thus qualifies to be a text akin to the Vedas in its orientation towards pure knowledge. It also shows that the very idea of pancham Veda was kept fluid, to convey the sense that though the Vedas were to be respected highly, it was not impossible to attain the highest form of knowledge outside the Vedas.

The very existence and birth of the Hindu temple as an institution was to take the knowledge of the Vedas to those who are not directly capable of performing the yajna. The Hindu temple is built in the image of a *yajna vedi*. The temple *vimana* is imagined as the fire of a fire altar of a yajna vedi. Stella Kramrisch says: '*The Sulva-sutras* contained in *the Kalpa-sutras*, represent the rules and give proportionate measurement for laying out and piling up the Vedic altar. On them basically rests the building of the Hindu temple.'[23]

Thus, there was no monopoly of knowledge. Only the rights of performing yajnas were guarded, but the dissemination of the same knowledge was not at all prohibited and in fact encouraged by various institutions and mechanisms.

But like Swami Vivekananda maintained, in no other culture will you find sacred texts like the Vedas which give themselves secondary importance. Our texts are so beautiful and so deep that they have built-in mechanisms to prevent mindless orthodoxies from forming. While later Smritis do restrict the knowledge of the Vedas to certain communities, we find *the Shukla Yajur Veda* declaring:

यथेमां वाचं कल्याणीमावदानी जनेभ्यः।
ब्रह्मराजन्याभ्यां शूद्राय चार्याय च स्वाय चारणाय।।

> May I speak the Sacred Word to the masses of the people (*janebhya*), to the *Brahmana*, the *Kshatriya*, the *Sudra*, and the *Arya*, and to our own men and the strangers. This includes all people.[24]

This does not mean that later texts have no use or relevance. It just means that different times pick up different strands from our texts, strands that are perfect for the condition and need of the society then. Right now, we need strands to unite. Swami Vivekananda also felt the same in his times, and for that he quoted the relevant parts of the texts. And that is the very nature of our great shastras. They are forever yielding and forever relevant. They produce what is necessary and relevant for a time and place. It is on us to decide what is relevant today and what is not.

The sixth and the most burning question about varna today is this: Is varna applicable now? The answer is a clear no, for most of the society, by the varna logic itself. The *Dharmashastras* say that one loses one's varna by two processes: one, by intermarrying with other varnas, which is not allowed, and two, by not living up to one's own karmic responsibility related to one's varna. And since both have happened in galore, and most individuals are no longer living up to the vocation or varna dharma of one's birth, the system is not applicable anymore. This is what Gandhi also believed. While upholding the logic of the system in its prime, he accepted that in contemporary times it was not applicable. This seems to be a correct conclusion.

Thus, as things stand today, varna is not applicable to most of the society, except in the cases of temple *archakas*, where both Brahmin and non-Brahmin priests follow hereditary vocations and the *charya* (lifestyle) related to it. We should respect and support those temple archakas who still maintain their own *varna* duties while we accept that the rest of Hindus (around 99 per cent) are now of mixed varnas who shall follow *samanya* Hindu dharma.

One of the most common lists of features that make up samanya dharma for Hindus include: meditation, brilliance, faith, honour, truth, freedom from anger, detachment, courage, etc. What is most important is that in many such lists enumerated by various Hindu texts, meditation is always mentioned as an integral part of samanya dharma. In contemporary times, meditation has become an integral part of practicing samanya dharma. The *Mahanirvana Tantra*, a seventeenth-century Shakta text, starts out by saying that the varnashrama dharma is decayed in Kali Yuga and most do not follow the Smritis. This does not mean that dharma has ceased to exist; it just means that now dharma is being propagated and perpetuated by different means and institutions, the most potent of which is the guru-shishya parampara in which the guru initiates the disciple in meditation. And in meditation there is no class, varna, or jati. The *Yoga Sutras* say:

> जातिदेशकालसमयानवच्छिन्नाः सार्वभौमा महाव्रतम्॥
>
> [These yamas] are considered the great vow. They are not exempted by one's class, place, time, or circumstance. They are universal.[25]

Without sadhana or meditation, the theoretical knowledge of the scriptures becomes almost useless, as there is no experience of the truths that are being spoken of in the texts. Sanatana Dharma is primarily experiential in nature, as this section started out by stressing that without experience, textual knowledge gives the impression to the seeker that he knows, but in actuality, in the absence of the experience, he does not know. As a result, he develops an illusion of knowledge without having real knowledge, and this situation is highly resented in a primarily experiential civilization like ours. Commentators of the *Yoga Sutras* confirm the necessity of experience:

> Hariharananda [commenting on the *Yoga Sutras*] qualifies this by noting that although from the scripture one may learn that life is suffering and that the soul is different from the body, and although one may also arrive at these truths by the process of inference and logic, such theoretical knowledge does not actually prevent one from experiencing this suffering, nor, for that matter, does it give one direct perception of the soul. Therefore, in an immediate sort of way, one is hardly better off than an ignorant person who does not know these things. But when scripture and inference are coupled with meditation and insight, or wisdom, then one can come to the point of actual realized insight rather than theoretical knowledge. It is from such actual lucidity that the cessation of suffering and perception of the self … arise. The path of yoga, as always, stresses direct experience over other forms of knowledge.[26]

Turning our gaze to an important principle: just because varna no more holds in most of the society, does that mean that Hindu dharma/Sanatana Dharma is also no more? Many textual literalists seem to think so. This is very far from the truth. One can consider that Sanatana Dharma is dead only when one equates it completely to varnashrama dharma. This is not so and never has been. Sanatana Dharma refuses to be located in any physical institution completely because if it is possible to locate Sanatana Dharma completely in some physical system, then it is also possible to destroy it. But Sanatana Dharma is indestructible because it survives the destruction of all its physical or concrete institutions and still goes on. That is the strength of the greatest dharma and greatest civilization that was ever created on earth. When one system dies, another takes its place, but the eternal tradition goes on.

Ashrama

The varna system is based on the narrative of duties and responsibilities, but any narrative of duties decays when individuals and groups forget their duties but keep protecting their rights and privileges. But dharma is a dynamic balance of opposites in all cases, and just because it created a system of negotiating with differences of birth, it also created a system leading to the elimination of all differences.

In the original design, the varna system had an inbuilt mechanism to prevent this decay (from duties to rights) from happening. This system was not just complementary but an integral part of the varna system: it was the system of ashramas, and it was the ashramas that made varna complete and functional. The second part of varnashrama dharma is ashrama. Ashramas, like purusharthas, are four: *brahmacharya*, *grihastha*, *vanaprastha*, and *sannyasa*.

Brahmacharya is the age of childhood when we are supposed to devote our time to studies and live a frugal life, which helps our consciousness become focused and thus more conducive to learning. Brahmacharya is not a stage of indulgence, and one lives frugally and without indulgence in this ashrama. Upon entering youth, one enters into grihastha ashrama, engages in artha and kama, gets married, has children, earns wealth, and gains power in society and for the family. But when one's children grow up and get married, one has to enter vanaprastha, which means withdrawing from active decision-making in family and social life and devoting more time to spiritual activities like japa, *tapa*, and *satsanga* (company of great saints). While entering grihastha from brahmacharya, one expands into artha and kama; when one enters vanaprastha from grihastha, one has to do the opposite and start withdrawing from the desire to gain artha and kama in life. Starting to withdraw desires is the significant feature of vanaprastha. At last comes sannyasa, where all worldly desires are supposed to be abandoned and all life should be devoted to the pursuit of moksha.

Thus, while brahmacharya and grihastha are ashramas equivalent to the process of evolution or srishti, when one gains in knowledge, power, and money and expands in samsara, the other two ashramas of vanaprastha and sannyasa correspond to the process of involution and laya, where one withdraws from samsara, turns inwards, and increasingly becomes interested in moksha and not artha or kama. Dr Ganesh explains the inherent reason behind vanaprastha beautifully:

> Retirement from active social life and moving away from materialistic pursuits was the next stage. A person in this stage was expected to employ his wisdom and experience to mentor younger people from the two earlier life-stages when they sought for guidance. In the past, the retired individual departed to the forests and spent his time in contemplation. The guidelines for this stage are given under four basic practices—1. Constantly reflecting upon what separates *vastu*-tantra from *kartr*-tantra, discerning the eternal from the ephemeral; 2. Gradually giving up the desire for physical pleasures and expectation of heavenly joys; 3. Cultivating the six-fold wealth of: a. control of the sense organs, b. control of the body, c. withdrawal of the mind from the external world, d. forbearance in the face of ups and downs in life, e. sincerity and devotion towards the words of the learned, and f. intense focus; and 4. Developing a sustained interest in *moksa*, which is the experience of Bliss devoid of any trace of sorrow.[27]

Varna cannot function without ashrama. It is the necessary half of varna. People forget about ashrama when they talk about varna. While varna navigated with the differences of birth, ashrama took care to equalize everyone in this life itself. One system worked on the differentiation of birth, and the other told us that all are one; all are equal, as all is Brahman.

It was also a tacit acknowledgement of Hindu darshana that while society was full of differences, there were no differences at the higher stages of consciousness, for ultimately all is Brahman. This is why Hindu texts themselves keep stressing that ultimately there is no difference between one and the other, that all is one. The texts have been explicit in expressing this truth about varna too. The *Avadhuta Gita*, one of the most purely non-dual texts, proclaims this ultimate truth:

> वेदा न लोका न सुरा न यज्ञा वर्णाश्रमो नैव कुलं न जातिः।
> न धूममार्गो न च दीप्तिमार्गो ब्रह्मैकरूपं परमार्थतत्त्वम्।।
>
> There are no Vedas, no worlds, no gods, no sacrifices. There is certainly no caste, no stage in life, no family, no birth. There is neither the path of smoke nor the path of light. There is only the highest Truth, the homogeneous Brahman.[28]

In another verse:

> महदादि जगत्सर्वं न किंचित्प्रतिभाति मे।
> ब्रह्मैव केवलं सर्वं कथं वर्णाश्रमस्थितिः।।
>
> The whole universe, beginning with the principle of cosmic intelligence, is not in the least manifest to me. All is indeed Brahman alone. How can there be any existence in caste or stage of life for me?[29]

The *Avadhuta Gita* is one of the most sublime texts on advaita or non-dualism. It is written in extremely lyrical verses that take one to the discussion of the ultimate truth or reality at once. These verses are clearly expressing the central truth of advaita that if there is no one else in this cosmos then how can social differences or differentiations be ultimately real and last forever? Another great non-dualist text is the *Ashtavakra Gita*, which expresses the same truth:

> न त्वं विप्रादि को वर्णों नाश्रमी नाक्षगोचरः।
> असंगोसि निराकारो विश्वसाक्षी सुखी भव।।
>
> You do not belong to the Brahmin or any other caste or to any *Ashrama*. You are not perceived by the eyes. Unattached, formless and witness of all are you. Be happy.[30]

This does not mean that these saints favoured discarding all social order. They did not. They were just making sure that our society as a whole did not lose sight of the ultimate truth. They were ensuring that we never forget that all the social order exists too for the purpose of moksha. Like we discussed above, without the goal of moksha, the path of dharma becomes meaningless. These jnanis wanted to tell us that unity was the ultimate truth and not diversity. They were telling us that if the social differences in our mind become bigger than the underlying unity then we are losing our path. Any system built on either equality or differences of birth is ultimately a prop so that its individuals can realize the ultimate truth. If that purpose is not being fulfilled, then the entire point of the system becomes obsolete.

And the ashrama was that institution that never let us forget that the goal was always moksha; that while traversing through the three ashramas of brahmacharya, grihastha, and vanaprastha, ultimately one has to get to sannyasa, where all differences become null and void. From the yardstick that we have been using in this section, while varna was the force of evolution or srishti and sthiti, which created and maintained all the differences, ashrama was the force of involution or laya, which dissolved all social differences into one quest of moksha.

Thus, while varna was the process of differentiation, ashrama was the process of equalization. And without the equalizing force of ashrama, varna would not make any sense.

Just like without the peg of moksha, rules of dharma become meaningless and arbitrary; thus, without ashrama or the process of involution, varna becomes a tyrannical order with no goal apart from sustaining itself. This truth was stressed again and again to indicate that we should not cling to institutions that have decayed beyond their prime and have stopped being the vehicles of self-realization or moksha.

Can social order not exist without an overarching spiritual goal? It can, like it does in all monotheistic societies and like it does in the West, but without the idea of the spiritual goal of moksha, dharma would stop being meaningful, and without the authority of dharma, artha and kama, the two purusharthas would fall out of balance. This state of imbalance is what the West and Islamic world today suffer from, and this state of imbalance also set into the Hindu social system when the processes of involution (reflected in ashramas) disappeared, leading to differences of birth and differentiation becoming an end in itself.

The fault set in when individuals stopped entering vanaprastha. Individuals, too fond of their rights, which they achieved in the first two stages of their life, started clinging too much to them, forgetting that all that they have gained, they are also supposed to let go of even while they are alive. That just like they plunged into life upon entering grihastha, so they have to start winding up when they enter vanaprastha. Vanaprastha is where the involution begins. And when that did not happen, the rot started setting in with communities and individuals protecting their rights but no longer wanting to perform their duties. This is why we see some individuals still defending their caste privileges after generations of having lost any right to claim them (having long foregone the duties incumbent upon them).

This is not something that happened only in the past. One such process is happening as we speak and is the cause of the rot of another great institution that Sanatana Dharma created, the Hindu family. In the joint family tradition, the older generation is not undergoing vanaprastha, thus not vacating the space for the younger generation, making the entire system too suffocating and too full of internal strife. This strife is inevitable if vanaprastha does not happen, as the older generation clings to their rights but abandons their duties, forgetting that this is the time to let go of their desires and not to embrace them. This results in disaster for the family: 'Unfulfilled desires turn into anger. Anger that is appeased then gets aggravated by a new desire.'[31]

Younger generations either suffocate in this system or opt out of it entirely by living in nuclear families or even without marriage in big cities, turning their backs on a system that, in their memory, was nothing but petty tyranny.

So, what does Hindu society do today?

The beautiful thing about ashrama is that while varna cannot exist without ashrama, ashrama can exist without dharma. Today everyone can lead a life of samanya Hindu dharma with focused study in childhood and go about the world in a balanced dharmic way during their grihastha ashrama. When their children grow up, they can move towards vanaprastha by giving up desires and rights and turning their senses and attention inwards through japa, tapa, satsanga, and meditation. And when the involution is sufficiently involved, they can turn their back on samsara and finally delve into sannyasa.

This will preserve the institution of family and make space for the younger generation. By giving youth more ownership, they can be encouraged to preserve dharma and the institutions that uphold dharma. Along with following purusharthas and ashrama dharma, one should develop the habit of meditation so that the infirmities of the mind are regularly cleansed. The desire for moksha will infuse dharma in one's life, and that will make dharma *drishti* arise. Dr Ganesh says:

> [T]he greatest dharma is attaining self-knowledge and awakening the self, which happens by walking the path of the Vedas—by regulating the breathing; by working hard for purifying the self; by listening to the scriptures, contemplating and analyzing what has been learnt, and sustaining that elevated spirit of awareness throughout; and by the knowledge attained from studying with a teacher. If *samanya*-dharma is likened to a flower then self-awareness is indeed the fruit.[32]

To see this in the light of the title of this chapter, varnashrama dharma was the dynamic balance of opposites, where varna in its evolutionary and differentiating power was limited by *ashrama* with its involutionary and equalizing force. When ashrama dharma became weak, the dynamic balance was disturbed, and the system went into deep imbalance, stressing too much on differences. By bringing ashrama dharma back into our lives with force, this imbalance can be corrected, and the dynamic balance of opposites can be restored. Does this mean that varnashrama dharma will be restored? It might be, and it might not be. Sanatana Dharma gives birth to institutions as time needs and also dissolves them of its own will when the time so comes. It is also greatly capable of generating new institutions whenever the time and conditions so arise. We should not worry about what form the Hindu social order will take in the future. That is not our duty. Our duty is to follow samanya dharma diligently and to keep cleansing our minds of all ignorance and impurities by following ashrama dharma and by doing meditation. If we serve dharma by doing just that, dharma will present institutions, apparatuses, and mechanisms to save itself and us.

In the end, everything is about the ascent and descent of consciousness. If we just take *sankalpa* to ascend, the deities and the gurus of this great tradition will take ten steps forward and help us. Remember that the shakti does not stay neutral. It actively helps anyone who takes the sankalpa to rise, and it is the rise of prajna or wisdom inside us during meditation that establishes dharma in samsara. So let us take this sankalpa to rise, as individuals in our sadhana and collectively as Hindus, for establishing dharma in Bharatavarsha and the world.

But what if there is trouble in arriving at the level of 'collective' that is necessary for Hindus to succeed, flourish, and propagate Sanatana Dharma in the world? What if there is a conflict between two Hindu groups? Two Hindu identities? Two kartavyas or dharmas? What shall we do then? What takes precedence? We will have no difficulty in choosing what shall be done in case of any conflict or situation if we have a clear pyramid of priorities in our minds. It turns out that jivanmuktas, rishis, and avataras in this great country have already thought over this conundrum and presented a pyramid of priorities for us. Let us next discuss the Pyramid of Svayambodha.

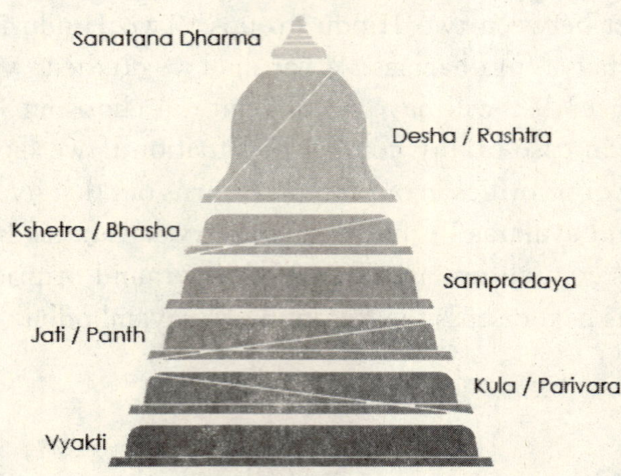

Fig. 1 The Pyramid of Svayambodha

Chapter 5

We, the Hindus

'Discard all dharmas and seek refuge only in me. I will free you from all sins.'

—Shri Krishna, the Bhagavada Gita

Arjuna and Lord Krishna on the Battlefield of Kurukshetra, The British Museum, c. 1830. The greatest boon for a Hindu is to perpetually fight to protect dharma[1]

Who Are We? The Svayambodha of Hindus

Who are we? This was the question we started this section with. That we are Hindu is obvious to anyone who has picked up this book to read. But what does it mean to be a Hindu? This is the question that we grappled with in the present section. We explored some of the fundamental axioms, practices, and experiences that are part of being a Hindu. We learnt that dharma is to protect and re-establish rta, the natural order of things. We learnt about how Hindu society is motivated to balance the natural order of things with the concept of pancha rnas and kartavyabodha. We discussed how the theories of karma and punarjanma are central to Hindu cosmology and worldview, and we also discussed the axiomatic props of atman and Brahman and how they are central to a Hindu universe. Atman is the element that never dies. It is the goal of human life to realize through meditation that atman is Brahman.

We delved into the beautiful story of the ascent and descent of consciousness; how the world is a play of consciousness; how the Brahman, the Supreme Consciousness, descends and becomes many and results in samsara; and how we can realize our true nature that is Brahman by meditating in what is called the ascent of consciousness. This process is reflected in many ways and many dimensions in koshas, chakras, vak, etc. It is also reflected in the way the world evolves into diversity through the process of evolution and how we can turn our senses and the mind inwards to realize the oneness of all through the process of involution.

We also realized that the slogan of 'Unity in Diversity' is fundamentally wrong and opposite of what the truth is. The Hindu does not artificially try to unite diverse elements. He realizes the fundamental unity of nature, cosmos, knowledge, and being. And it is this vision of underlying, inherent, and fundamental unity that generates, nurtures, and celebrates diversity of expression.

The Hindu paradigm is that of Diversity in Unity, with unity being the fundamental element, not diversity. It is on this fundamental truth that the Hindu social philosophy is based upon.

What was the most important learning for us was the fact that our jnanis and jivanmuktas who attained moksha through this process of involution were the ones who advised and guided the Hindu worldview and Sanatana Dharma through the insights gained during meditation. Their word, *apta vakya*, has been the greatest and never-faulting source of guidance for Hindu social practices and institutions. The self-realized saint, a Ramana Maharishi, or a Ramakrishna Paramhamsa, stands at the top of the pyramid in Hindu schemes of things. It is the word of these jivanmuktas that validates shabda pramana. It is the word of these jnanis that lays the foundation of Hindu institutions and practices.

The Hindu worldview, descending from the wisdom of jivanmuktas, gives Hindus some broad goals in life, in the form of purusharthas—dharma, artha, kama, and moksha. A civilization of perpetual balance, we never neglected samsara but took care that the pursuit of artha and kama was overseen by the order of dharma and the goal of moksha. Another set of four ashramas—brahmacharya, grihastha, vanaprastha, and sannyasa—tells us that no matter how different the circumstances of our birth and work lives are, we all have to abandon all desires, turn inwards, and move towards attaining moksha by taking sannyasa. This ensures that while artha and kama are taken care of, dharma and moksha remain supreme and guiding forces. By maintaining both worldly and spiritual desires in balance, Sanatana Dharma has been a dynamic balance of opposites. We also understood that in today's world, samanya dharma remains critical for Hindus.

In this journey, we realized that Hindu dharma is about practices and experiences and not about dogma. We understood how all textual evidence is just a confirmation of experience and not vice versa. The Vedas and Upanishads themselves express this truth.[2] Hindus have always been clear, due to the constant guidance of jnanis and jivanmuktas, that the ultimate reality cannot be expressed in any human language or in any other medium. Ultimate truth, knowledge, and happiness are matters of experience only, and that is why everyone has to experience them himself. It is impossible to describe ultimate reality completely truthfully, and any description will be a failed attempt. That is why Hindu dharma maintains that truth cannot be encoded in a dogma. And this is the reason that Hindu dharma is not a matter of dogma or belief. We will see in the Shatrubodha section the nature of those sects that consider dogma to be primary and not experiences.

The inner experience of ultimate reality invests our jnanis with the greatest wisdom, which then goes into designing rituals that help others ascend to higher states of consciousness by meditation. This direct experience of Brahman is the foundation behind the primary practices, customs, and rituals of Hindu dharma. That is why, by practicing these rituals, the workings of rta, or satya, become evident to us and align our inner nature with our surroundings more closely so that ultimately we can move towards realizing the satya, the ultimate truth, for ourselves. This is the Hindu way of life. In short, it is what it means to be a Hindu. This is about the experience of being Hindu. But aren't there any geographical and other concrete markers that make us Hindu? It turns out that yes, there are. In concrete terms:

- We, the Hindus, are the indigenous inhabitants of Bharatavarsha that extends from the mountains to the sea, as the texts explain. This great and sacred land of Bharatavarsha is thus the *punyabhumi* of Hindus. Shri Radha Kumud Mookerjee, in his wonderful work *The Fundamental Unity of India*, proves it beyond doubt through our texts and practices that the sacred land of Bharatavarsha is central to the Hindu imagination and existence.

- Sanskrit is our *devabhasha*, the divine language, which is closest to reality due to its origin in the chitta bhumis of yogis and jnanis during meditation. Sanskrit is a vehicle of self-realization as it gives us props in the form of names and mantras of deities that help us realize the ultimate truth. It is also what binds all Hindus in one sutra.
- Our dharma is rightly called Sanatana Dharma since it is not man-made. It is the order inherent in nature. Dharma is that which protects the order of rta-satya. And since it always has been, it is called the 'Sanatana Dharma' or the 'Eternal Tradition'.
- Our identity is Hindu, and Hindu dharma is synonymous with Sanatana Dharma. It is immaterial whether the word 'Hindu' is indigenous or the distortion of the word *Sindhu* by outsiders, but it amply conveys the meaning of Svayambodha that needs to be conveyed, and hence it is the most sacred, important, and critical identity Hindus have.

Now let us move towards defining the Pyramid of Svayambodha. It is the pyramid of priorities that helps us in negotiating and solving an internal conflict when an external enemy is at the gates. Figure 1 illustrates the Pyramid of Svayambodha.

The Svayambodha Pyramid of Priorities

Sanatana Dharma nurtured diversity, for that is how evolution unfolds. In the course of our history, that diversity helped us in having multiple identities, multiple value systems, and maximum but optimum balance of freedom and security. This diversity also let multiple identities flourish. Hindu society found security, prosperity, and freedom in multiple groups and communities. It is a matter of great pride that this diversity was nurtured instead of being crushed by Sanatana Dharma.

But what Hindus should not forget is that this diversity was always nurtured on a fundamental unity of being, the source of which was the realization that all that is, is Brahman. Hindu institutions and identities were created by keeping in mind the incredibly diverse nature of human beings and so that no great violence is done against svabhava of individual beings. But they were also infused with the Vedic or margiya spirit, so that at the individual level, all that diversity aids the realization of the underlying unity, and at the social level, it leads to the sustenance of the greatest identity—that of Sanatana Dharma. Any diversity is uplifting if this underlying unity is not forgotten. But if this underlying unity is forgotten, then diversity can become counterproductive and even destructive, as external enemies divide us into hundreds of splinters and destroy us, one individual, one community, at a time.

Hindu diversity is a means to understand Hindu unity. But if means become ends, then the entire edifice becomes counterproductive. The texts explain about *vishesha* dharmas not so that they become the most important priority for us. They explain the vishesha dharmas so that these dharmas can serve the greatest dharma that ever is—Sanatana Dharma. We were organized in small units like families, not so that they become an end in themselves and not so that we keep supporting our family even at the cost of the destruction of society, dharma, and planet. We were organized in small units, like families, so that we could serve Sanatana Dharma in both individual and then group capacity, in the form of blood-related family. We were organized in jatis and varnas so that these units could defend Sanatana Dharma by becoming self-sufficient when formal mechanisms of defence were down and when the larger structures of management and governance disappeared, and the society was left to fend for itself. We were not organized in jatis and varnas, so that we destroy Sanatana Dharma everywhere else while serving our own jati and varna, considering it supreme. We were exhorted to serve Bharatavarsha so that we could serve Sanatana Dharma and not for any other motive.

Every single identity that a Hindu has—individual, family, clan, community, jati, varna, and *desha*—they all exist to serve Sanatana Dharma. The authority of every single one of these identities to command its followers comes from its service to Sanatana Dharma. If any of these units or identities fails to serve Sanatana Dharma, then their authority, validity, and utility stand null and void. Everything and everyone exist so they can uphold dharma—Sanatana Dharma—so in turn, Sanatana Dharma can uphold them. The moment this order is disturbed and any lower identity or unit, may it be any varna, jati, kutumba, *kshetra*, or *vyakti*, violates or stands against Sanatana Dharma, then such an identity has to be discarded, and such a group or unit has to be opposed until the Sanatana order, with dharma at the top of the order of priorities, is restored.

Losing this order of priorities with Sanatana Dharma at the top is disastrous both internally and against external enemies. Without the overarching authority of Sanatana Dharma, nationalism becomes fascist and xenophobic; varna and jati become closed, redundant, and oppressive; family descends into petty tyranny; the individual descends into the quagmire of never-ending desires. It is Sanatana Dharma that elevates each of these units and identities into vehicles of transformation and prosperity. Without Sanatana Dharma, they become meaningless and even counterproductive.

Against external enemies, to lose this order of priorities is lethal. There are ample examples of this during the mediaeval ages and more so during the era of British colonialism, when the sub-identity of Hindus became more important to them than their Sanatana/Hindu identity. After independence, under the influence of divisive electoral democracy, which encouraged a divided Hindu majority and a united monotheistic minority, this became a severe problem. Jatis and communities started thinking of themselves as the entire world, forgetting that their existence got legitimacy from Sanatana Dharma, and without Sanatana Dharma, there was no meaning and authority to them. What used to be the source of our strength became a bane to Hindu society, dharma, and civilization.

This confusion of the order of priorities is ancient. We have forgotten our priorities again and again, and this is why our jivanmuktas encoded our tradition, practices, and texts with stories and examples clearing this order of priority of dharma for Hindus. We can call this order of priority the Pyramid of Svayambodha. And none other than Shri Krishna makes this pyramid of priorities clear when Arjuna develops confusion between his various dharmas.

In the poignant Vishada Yoga chapter of the Bhagavada Gita, Arjuna faces a deep and searing dilemma that melts his otherwise iron resolve. Being a great warrior, he always knew what war meant; having seen the evil of Duryodhana and his brothers, he knew that he would have to kill his friends, family, and gurus so that dharma can win. And yet, when he actually has to do it, even a great warrior like him develops doubt. He forgets the order of priorities of dharma. He is always for dharma, but in this battlefield of Kurukshetra, in order to protect Sanatana Dharma, he has to violate every other dharma that he had ever known, and it is the weight of having to break all these dharmas under which his heart sinks, and lamenting, he collapses in inaction. The verses that express his consternation on having to violate so many dharmas of his own are worth quoting. Full of real and actual pain on having to make extremely tough decisions, they represent the conundrum of many of us today. Arjuna says he is fully aware that Duryodhana is evil and cannot see the sin that he will incur for killing his own brothers, but Arjuna can, so how can he do the same? He then goes on to explain the consequences of killing one's own kin:

कुलक्षये प्रणश्यन्ति कुलधर्माः सनातनाः।
धर्मे नष्टे कुलं कृत्स्नमधर्मोऽभिभवत्युत।।

When the family line is destroyed, the traditional family dharma is also destroyed. When dharma is destroyed, evil overwhelms the entire family line.

अधर्माभिभवात्कृष्ण प्रदुष्यन्ति कुलस्त्रियः।
स्त्रीषु दुष्टासु वार्ष्णेय जायते वर्णसङ्करः।।

O Krishna! When evil arises, the women of the family become corrupted. O descendant of the Vrishnis! When the women are corrupted, hybrid castes are born.

सङ्करो नरकायैव कुलघ्नानां कुलस्य च।
पतन्ति पितरो ह्येषां लुप्तपिण्डोदकक्रियाः।।

Hybrid castes ensure that the family line and those who destroyed the family line, both go to hell. Because their ancestors fall and are deprived of offerings of funereal cakes and drink.

दोषैरेतैः कुलघ्नानां वर्णसङ्करकारकैः।
उत्साद्यन्ते जातिधर्माः कुलधर्माश्च शाश्वताः।।

From the sins of those who destroy the family line and from hybrid castes being generated, the ancient dharma of the castes and the dharma of the family are both destroyed.[3]

At the start of Chapter 2, he laments again:

अर्जुन उवाच कथं भीष्ममहं संख्ये द्रोणं च मधुसूदन।
इषुभिः प्रतियोत्स्यामि पूजार्हावरिसूदन।।

Arjuna said: 'O Madhusudana! How will I use arrows to fight in this war against Bhishma and Drona? O slayer of enemies! They are deserving of worship.'[4]

Arjuna is arguing that killing the males of his own family will result in women being widowed and left without spouses. That results in them having to resort to marrying males from other kula, jati, or varna, which leads to the *varnasankara* or mixing of varna and jati, and the resulting offspring will be of mixed varnas, thus leading to a loss of kula, jati, and varna dharma. The dilemma that Arjuna is in is valid; the pain that he feels in violating his kula, jati, and varna dharmas is real. In a society in which varnashrama dharma was largely alive and most individuals were born in places where their aptitudes were realized, the concern for violating the kula, jati, and varna dharmas of Arjuna was very real. He is also shocked at the prospect of killing his own gurus, like Bhishma and Dronacharya, who should be worshipped.

Arjuna is not developing cold feet for lack of courage. Courage was something he had in great abundance. His concern is only dharmic. He is worried that through his actions, dharma will be violated. He also accepts that dharma is going to get violated in any case as Duryodhana is bent upon doing it. He just does not want to be a part, an instrument, of destroying dharma by violating his kula, jati, and varna dharmas.

Before coming to the battlefield, Arjuna agrees with Krishna and vows that he has to fight for dharma because dharma is in danger. But in the battlefield, he realizes that for fighting for dharma itself he has to violate many other dharmas. The deep pain that Arjuna feels has to be appreciated more. The dilemma that he is in has to be analysed more deeply, for many of us find ourselves in many such dilemmas and will continue to do so, especially when Sanatana Dharma is in danger from many sides today.

The fight for dharma is not easy. It involves sacrifices at every single step. These sacrifices are not limited to giving up possessions and rights. Sometimes they also involve giving up duties. For serving a greater dharma, we might have to abandon the duties that are incumbent upon us in fulfilling the lower dharmas. And that is most painful for anyone who closely follows dharma. To let go of rights is easy for a dharmic Hindu, but to let go of duties is painful. But that is a sacrifice that every Hindu warrior always has to make in the fight for Sanatana Dharma. Countless soldiers leave their families in pain and poverty when a higher calling of protecting their country summons them. Countless individuals favoured getting executed in the mediaeval era and depriving their sons and daughters of a healthy childhood, for they were asked to give up Sanatana Dharma in favour of Islam, and that was something they could not do. Countless archakas in temples left even their wives and children to die horrible deaths at the hands of the Islamic barbarians because their duty was to save the vigraha of the deity they were worshipping their whole lives.

None of this is easy and creates great emotional stress in those who have to make these sacrifices. Blood relations are the most natural and biological bonds that one has, and to either ignore them or to go against them for upholding dharma is the most difficult and the greatest choice that every Hindu has to make. This is the choice that rattles Arjuna. The pain of having to destroy everything he loved and cared for while growing up, including his gurus, fills him with great pain and sorrow.

The fault of Arjuna is that in deep sorrow over having to violate many lower dharmas, he fails to see that Sanatana Dharma itself is at stake, and when Sanatana Dharma is at stake, all other dharmas cease to be important because Sanatana Dharma always has the highest priority.

The response of Krishna and what follows is very interesting and is spread out in the rest of the Bhagavada Gita in seventeen chapters. He does not contradict Arjuna and thus accepts that if Arjuna kills his family members, what he says will follow, and kula, jati, and varna dharmas will get violated. Even then he exhorts him to fight and do exactly what Arjuna was refraining from doing. What does this mean? Does this mean that Krishna is against varna and other dharmas? Does he favour an individualistic paradigm in which one need not follow any dharma, including that of kula and kutumba?

This is clearly not the truth, since in the Bhagavada Gita and all through the Mahabharata, Krishna instructs to follow all dharmas that the shastras command. Inside the Gita itself, he upholds chaturvarna or varnashrama dharma. But then why the contradictory advice to Arjuna to violate them by telling him to fight?

We see contradiction only if the pyramid of priorities is not clear to us. But to Krishna, everything is clear. He can clearly see that all lower dharmas exist and are valid. But when the highest dharma is at stake, all of them stand null and void in that case. And there is no contradiction in violating those lower dharmas if that is done to save and fight for the greatest dharma in any case—Sanatana Dharma. By both upholding lower dharmas and by telling Arjuna to violate them if necessary to serve Sanatana Dharma, Shri Krishna is telling us very clearly the pyramid of priorities for a Hindu.

In the Shrimad Bhagavad Gita, Shri Krishna has given us a template to navigate through dharma *sankata*, which is to choose between two dharmas when there is a clash between them. By telling Arjuna to choose Sanatana Dharma over every other dharma and duty of his, he has made the pyramid of priorities very clear.

Does that mean that, to serve higher dharma, one necessarily has to incur paap or sin by violating lower dharmas? Does it mean that one who serves Sanatana Dharma is doomed in any case? That is absolutely not the case, and Shri Krishna himself assures us that those who have to violate or forgo lower dharmas for serving Sanatana Dharma are exempt from all the sins. In the last chapter of the Gita, Shri Krishna comes around to this and gives *abhaya* or clean chit to any servant of Sanatana Dharma from any paap that he may have incurred for relinquishing his lower duties:

सर्वधर्मान्परित्यज्य मामेकं शरणं व्रज।
अहं त्वा सर्वपापेभ्यो मोक्षयिष्यामि मा शुचः।।

Discard all dharmas and seek refuge only in me. I will free you from all sins. Do not sorrow.[5]

In this verse, towards the end of his exposition, Shri Krishna very clearly says that there is no need to fall into sorrow or worry about the sins that Arjuna will incur by not following the lower dharmas, because as Brahman himself, Krishna is telling him that in the service of Sanatana Dharma, one incurs no paap for not following one's lower duties. Not only has he made the pyramid of priorities clear, but he has also assured that the Hindu warriors do not incur any paap by choosing Sanatana Dharma over any other dharma of theirs, be it desha, varna, jati, kshetra, or kutumba.

Shri Krishna has made clear that if we ever find Sanatana Dharma itself in danger, and if we think that it is our duty to fight for and protect dharma, then for us the only identity that matters is Hindu (Sanatani); all other identities become immaterial, as for a soldier the only thing that matters is victory. And when Sanatana Dharma today is in danger from not one but multiple quarters, it is indeed the duty for all Hindu warriors to abandon all identities and take up only one—Hindu.

What is perhaps the most amusing aspect of the Shrimad Bhagavad Gita is that Shri Krishna exhorts Arjuna to get up and fight by giving him the *upadesha* about ultimate knowledge, the Brahman. Why tell him that everyone is Brahman when the motive is to encourage him to take up arms and kill the enemies in front? Shri Krishna's method here does not just seem arbitrary but also counterproductive. But his upadesha is far from arbitrary or counterproductive. It is very contextual and meaningful.

Arjuna develops confusion over his duty because he mistakes the institutions and mechanisms that exist to serve dharma as dharma itself. In short, he takes the medium to be the goal and the means to be the end. He forgets that all lower dharmas exist to serve the highest dharma itself, and the highest dharma, the Sanatana Dharma, exists so that a society based on the pursuit of *atmajnana* and *atmabodha* can be created. All the differences and divisions of the world are sustained in dynamic balance by the vision of underlying unity. But if that overarching goal is forgotten, if the pole star of moksha disappears, if the vision of the unity of Brahman is lost, then the edifice of dharma can no longer sustain; when this happens, then differences become primary, mechanisms or means appear as goals, and the whole exercise is no longer dharmic. This is the reason that Shri Krishna gave Arjuna the upadesha about atman and Brahman and how they are one and how Brahman is the cause and the end of everything.

And this confusion is not rare. Hindus, like any other dharmic people, have suffered from this confusion and found themselves in this dilemma again and again. Hindu individuals have been convinced again and again by the leftists that they should pay attention to career and life and not to the 'communal fight of some political Hindus'. Hindu communities have been convinced by the politicians that their jati is the highest unit and an end in itself and that the fight between Islamists and other Hindu groups is not their fight and they should not pay any attention to it. Hindus living in Hindu-majority states have been convinced by the de-Hinduizing narrative of decades that the plight of the Hindus living in Indian states where Hindus are a minority is not their problem.

Hindus have been convinced by their enemies that they are just individuals and, at best, members of their caste and nothing more, and that any force that tries to unite Hindus is a conspiracy of evil Hindutvaites. And enemies of Hindus are greatly skilled at direct and indirect war. In order to keep Hindus divided, they collaborate with even those Hindus who have a comprehensive but peripheral understanding of the texts and who become unwitting collaborators in the game of dividing Hindus. These unwitting collaborators are well versed in textual reading of scriptures, and they constantly keep telling Hindus that they are nothing but their jatis and their communities, and it is Hindu texts themselves that command them to defend these divisions of jatis and communities at all costs, even if that cost is the very loss of Sanatana Dharma. These literalists are very well read, and they produce text after text that order Hindus to maintain caste and community distinctions at any cost. But they conveniently forget to mention every single instance when Hindu texts order Hindus to forget all distinctions and fight for Sanatana Dharma above all. They also do not divulge that a society can sustain nuanced social divisions only in the absence of great external enemies.

These unwitting collaborators do a great disservice to the cause of Sanatana Dharma, for they mislead many dharmic warriors by confusing them about who is the enemy and who is the insider. By telling Hindus that it is more important to fight another Hindu group rather than the monotheistic ideologies that are trying to destroy Sanatana Dharma, they do a great disservice to both Svayambodha and Shatrubodha of Hindus. Their knowledge of many texts and their command over Sanskrit mislead many and lead them astray from the path of battle for dharma, but Shri Krishna has already warned against such folks and their 'flowery language' in the Shrimad Bhagavad Gita itself:

यामिमां पुष्पितां वाचं प्रवदन्त्यविपश्चितः।
वेदवादरताः पार्थ नान्यदस्तीति वादिनः।।

O Partha! Those who are ignorant say these flowery words, praising the Vedas and claiming there is nothing else.[6]

This shloka proves that folks who mistake means for an end have always existed, even in the times of Shri Krishna. These confused Hindus thought that the texts, which are means to attain supreme knowledge, are more important than supreme knowledge itself. They are neither ignorant nor evil. But they have inverted the cause and caused paradigm, having lost all sight of the goal of Hindu life, that is, moksha or supreme knowledge. Shri Ram Swarup has also commented on this feature of many Hindu literalists:

> Here, no active evil is involved and probably the speaker means well. But he speaks words wiser than he knows and deeper than he feels. This lends to his speech a quality which though unintended is quite jarring. He speaks without authority. Socrates was very sensitive to this impurity of speech. He found that the poets, legislators and philosophers spoke not foolishly but over-wisely. They spoke what they did not understand, what was unsupported by their experience and life. This is a very common impurity. People speak words of wisdom without being wise; they speak brave words without being brave. They speak of intensities they do not feel; they speak words they do not understand. They are inauthentic. Shri Krishna warns against flowery language, *puspitam vacam* and also against those given to quoting from the scriptures thoughtlessly, *vedavadaratah*. The talent for quotation is a poor substitute for the understanding of the heart.[7]

Shri Ram Swarup is telling about a common fault that many Hindus develop if they are not acutely aware that Sanatana Dharma is all about experiences and practices and not about dogmas. Even the most well-meaning of Hindus lose their path and become misled if they read the texts without having the experience of an accompanying meditational practice to understand the true meaning of the words written in them. Without meditation and deep sadhana, it is most likely that they miss the wood for the trees and take the means to be the end.

This is the reason that our texts themselves are littered with verse after verse that tell us that these social distinctions mean nothing at a higher level, and if an emergent situation so demands that they be forgotten, even if temporarily, so that the external enemy of Sanatana Dharma can be fought and defeated, then we must not be shy in doing so.

There are many instances in the shastras which make this pyramid of priorities very clear. In the Ramayana, Vibhishana 'betrays' not only his brother, his kula, jati and varna but also his desha, in order to serve Sanatana Dharma. He is able to perceive with his awakened prajna that his desha led by his adharmic brother Ravana is not serving Sanatana Dharma, and it is Shri Rama and his cause by serving which dharma is served. And this is what he does. He does not care about any of his lower identities. He does not care about his own individual reputation. All he cares about is how to serve Sanatana Dharma and that is why he helps Shri Rama, while ignoring all his lower identities and lower kartavyas. He has utmost clarity that he is not accruing any *paap* (sin), by ditching his lower kartavyas, for he knows that to serve the highest of all dharmas, doing that is necessary.

This pyramid of priorities was clear to ancient Hindus. Chanakya in *Niti Sara*, makes this pyramid very clear:

> त्यजेदेकं कुलस्यार्थे ग्रामस्यार्थे कुलं त्यजेत्।
> ग्रामं जनपदस्यार्थे आत्मार्थे पृथिवीं त्यजेत्।।
>
> Discard one for the sake of the family; for the sake of the village, discard the family; discard the village for the sake of the country; for the sake of the Atman, discard the world.[8]

Chanakya is saying that an individual can be forsaken for the family, family for village, village for country and country for atman or self-realization. Here, self or atman does not denote the petty individual but refers to the atman that is Brahman.

And so, for the sake of Sanatana Dharma, which nourishes and perpetuates a society which is geared towards encouraging individuals to have atmajnana, all lower identities including kula, jati, kshetra, and desha can be sacrificed if the need so arises. This verse from *Chanakya Niti* actually appears in the Mahabharata too. Thus, the Mahabharata itself clears pyramid of priorities to resolve *dharma sankata*.[9]

Once again, the call is not to forsake all diversity or identities, but to know which to choose if there is a clash of identities. That is what the pyramid of priorities stands for.

The goal is to protect Sanatana Dharma, which protects a society wedded to the pursuit of ultimate happiness and ultimate knowledge.

The goal is to stay united, as one, in front of an external enemy and understand that it is the unity, sourced in the Brahman, that is the cause of all diversity.

We have arrived at the midpoint of our journey in this book. Like Arjuna, all of us who think Sanatana Dharma is worth saving find ourselves in the intellectual battlefield of ideas.

We are now secure in the knowledge of who we, the Hindus, are: We are a society that is committed to the pursuit of the eternal and unheeding happiness. Hence, to have Svayambodha is to know that a dharmic society is based upon the pursuit of atmabodha, which is gained by meditation and the grace of gurus.

We know the pyramid of priorities. We know which identity and duty to choose over which whenever there is a clash. We know that Sanatana Dharma is always the top priority. We know what to do when there is an emergency, with an enemy at the gates and within them.

Armed with this knowledge of Svayambodha, let us now proceed, my dear Hindus, to gain Shatrubodha.

SECTION B

SHATRUBODHA

In section A, we discussed what it means to be a Hindu in practice and experience. Now we proceed to know the civilizational enemies or *shatrus* of Sanatana Dharma. Whether we like it or not, the truth is that Hindu society is under siege from all sides, and Sanatana Dharma is in danger. The enemies are very intelligent, and while fighting with full force themselves, they have significantly reduced the fighting capability of Hindus by deluding them with distortions and lies. As a result, most Hindus either look away from the battle of existence that Sanatana Dharma is fighting, or some actively aid the enemy narrative and agenda. But Hindu society has great internal strength. Sanatana Dharma has many hidden powers. But as Professor Kapil Kapoor puts it, 'Hindus suffer from the Hanuman syndrome.'[1] They keep forgetting their powers, and someone has to remind them that they are extremely powerful and capable. Once the *smriti* of their own strength is thus awakened, they become a formidable force for dharma, protecting Hindus as well as others who seek the protection of Sanatana Dharma. In this section, we will learn about Shatrubodha—how to identify the ideological and civilizational enemy and how to fight it at the level of ideas. One should be clear that this fight is not with individuals but with ideas and ideologies that encourage the individuals to fight. We shall take Shatrubodha in that spirit.

Chapter 6

Enemies of Sanatana Dharma

'Hindu society is under siege.'
—Sita Ram Goel

Temple Destruction. Midjourney, Inc., 20 Mar. 2025. An AI generated image of Hindu temple being destroyed by Islamic invaders[1]

Who Is a Shatru?

For survival we need Shatrubodha, which means to 'know the enemy'. Speaking in civilizational terms, the most important question of this book is: Who is the enemy of Hindu civilization, and what to do to protect Sanatana Dharma and Hindu society from this enemy?

For a Hindu, an enemy is an ideological and institutional force that aims to destroy Hindu dharma, society, and civilization. This enemy cannot be an individual, although many individuals can embody and represent the enemy force at any given time, but it is critical to understand that individuals are not the enemies. The enemy of Hindu civilization is a political ideology like Marxism, a religious fundamentalism like Islamism or Christian evangelism, or a destructive ideological fashion like wokeism or militant liberalism. Its characteristic as an enemy is decided by its will to destroy Hindu society.

Forty-two years ago, one of the greatest historians and Hindu thinkers of the twentieth century, Shri Sita Ram Goel tried warning Hindu society by writing a book by the name of *Hindu Society under Siege*, claiming that we are under siege from five forces or five kinds of imperialisms, and let alone putting up a fight to survive and defeat the invaders, we are not even aware of the siege.

For defeating the shatru, you need to first have Shatrubodha. The first rule of defence is that we shall be aware that we are under attack.

The bad news is that forty-two years after Sita Ram Goel sounded the warning, there is still not a critical number of Hindus who realize that the Hindu society is under siege and who have proper Shatrubodha.

The good news is that we have made a lot of progress, and since the warning, the number of Hindus having acute Shatrubodha has increased by a factor of many magnitudes. Significant progress has already been achieved, mainly due to the work of the great civilizational warriors like Shri Sita Ram Goel, but much needs to be done.

In *Hindu Society under Siege*, Sita Ram Goel stresses the role of Hindu society in saving Hindu dharma and civilization. The most critical intervention that contemporary Hindus can make is to save Hindu society, as culture lives through society and survives only when society keeps practicing its own dharma and keeps perpetuating and protecting its culture. Most of the ancient world cultures collapsed since their societies converted to either Christianity or Islam. Sita Ram Goel warns us that the same fate might await us in the future if we do not make efforts to save Hindu society.

> Hindu culture can meet the same frightful fate if there were no Hindu society to sustain it. This is the point which is not always remembered even by those who take pride in Hindu culture. There are many Hindus who cherish the great spiritual traditions of Hinduism and its scriptures like the Gita and the Upanishads in which that tradition is enshrined. But they do not cherish with an equal enthusiasm the Hindu society which has honored and preserved these traditions and scriptures down the ages.[2]

Dharma sustains when societies proclaiming it live on. Dharma is not just preserved by preserving the texts or darshana. Dharma is practice. It lives on if the practices embodying it live on. Conversely, dharma dies in a certain region if dharmic practices are abandoned by its former followers. Greek philosophy is still taught in all the universities of the world. Greek scriptures or epics are still extant, and tonnes of doctorates are done on them all over the world every year, and yet Greek tradition is no more because Greek society, bearing Greek tradition, abandoned its ancestral dharma and all the cultural moorings and accepted Christianity. Sanatana Dharma can meet the same fate if Hindu society bearing it breaks down and starts converting to Christianity or Islam, as Sita Ram Goel warned.

> There are many Hindus who proclaim with great confidence that Sanatana Dharma that is Hinduism can never die. This is true in a sense. There will always be individuals in non-Hindu societies who will recover the mystique of Sanatana Dharma through their efforts at self-discovery. But Sanatana Dharma will surely suffer an eclipse and no more inform mankind at large with its message, if there is no Hindu society to sustain it.[3]

The first stage to win a war is to recognize that we are in a state of war. Hindu society is under siege, and we are in a state of war. This is the fact that Hindus need to accept first. Once we have accepted this, we are forced to ponder upon the fact that what are the forces that besiege it? Sita Ram Goel talks about five forces that besiege Hindu society in an attempt to destroy it eventually. More than forty years later these forces still besiege Hindu society, ultimately wanting to destroy Sanatana Dharma in its homeland, Bharatavarsha.

Four of these five forces, according to Sita Ram Goel, are: Islamism, Christianism, Macaulayism, and communism. The fifth force, modernism, is not named directly by him but is indicated throughout the book.

Of these, the first two are known as prophetic monotheistic religions. We will go deeper into the terms later, but these religions are fundamentally different from dharmic sects like Sanatana Dharma. They believe in worshipping only one form or idea of god, and the idea of a mediator—the Prophet—is central to them. An important feature that distinguishes them from dharmic traditions like Sanatana Dharma is their stress on belief or dogma as the primary and only criterion of judgement, as Sanjay Dixit says:

> The fundamental difference between the Sanatana and the Abrahamic world view is that of different frameworks in which these systems operate. The Sanatana system in its essence is an experiential framework that creates a knowledge system, whereas the Abrahamic systems belong to a belief framework.[4]

Traits of prophetic monotheistic religions will be discussed in subsequent chapters. Here we shall discuss how these religions came to besiege Hindu society and dharma. Before that we need to discuss the idea of the Sanatana umbrella, an idea that ensured that peace was maximized in Bharatavarsha and a code was developed to incorporate diverse cultures and ways of life on one hand and to also weave them into the Sanatana idea on the other.

The Sanatana Umbrella

India has absorbed a large number of immigrants and invaders into its society and made them their own with almost zero violence. Sanatana Dharma and the Hindu social system had great capacity to absorb a foreign group of individuals into its own society by letting them practice their own rules and customs and integrating them with the wider Hindu society by establishing the Sanatana umbrella and its universal rules. The greatest and the most universal umbrella that the world ever saw was not Pax Britannica; rather, it was what we can call the Pax Sanatanica—the common Sanatana umbrella that Sanatana Dharma created in which every dharmic sect had the abhaya (freedom from fear) to be what it wanted to be.

This Pax Sanatanica meant that all traditional sects in Bharatavarsha would be allowed to function as they wanted with the only condition of respecting the universal Sanatana customs. These customs were discussed in the Svayambodha section, but an important feature of Hindu society was that it did not believe in imposing one's own tradition, practices, and customs on others. Pax Sanatanica meant that the act of war would never be extended to civilians and remained confined to kings and soldiers. And even with them there were many rules that minimized violence and barbarity. It worked even in the case of foreign invaders like the Shakas, the Huns, and other non-monotheistic invaders. The animosity between kings and soldiers was never carried over to their followers. The soldiers and stragglers who came with the invading armies found a ready home in Bharatavarsha. They were accepted with open arms by Hindus. This openness was embedded deep in the Hindu social system, which allowed maximum diversity as well as maximum integration at the same time due to its highly modular character.

Sanatana umbrella ensured that after the fight of the Kshatriyas was over, the invaders would be treated with kindness and humanity and would be allowed to follow their customs, practices, and rituals as they wanted. Pax Sanatanica meant that even the immigrants and invaders could live on this land as if it was theirs, once the war was over, provided they did not violate the fundamental Sanatana customs and practices. India's culture of multiple value systems allowed this to happen. One could live as a different community with different customs and practices, including diverse food habits. If they only behaved in a publicly sanctioned manner in public spaces, they were left alone to organize their own laws as they wished. This encouraged even the invaders to settle down peacefully as they seldom had to change their core values and cultures. Hindu society accepted them with all their customs and practices, minus the ones that violated Sanatana Dharma.

Islam breaks Pax Sanatanica

The first aberration in this great universal culture was Islam. For the first time, we encountered an invader that was not only barbaric and brutal, but it was like oil in water, unwilling to merge with the local culture and native society at any cost. Instead, it wanted to dominate and destroy Hindu dharma so completely that not a single sign of it remains. Pakistan today is such an example, which used to be a part of Bharatavarsha until a few decades ago and now is a cultural desert where very few signs that it was once part of Pax Sanatanica remain.

Pakistan is what Bharatavarsha would become if Islam wins.

Not only did Islam and Muslims refuse Pax Sanatanica, but they tried to destroy the Sanatana umbrella and everything that it sheltered. No other invader before Islam and Muslims had done this to Bharatavarsha. These invaders were not just after the wealth of native Hindus or the land of Bharatavarsha. Of course they wanted that too, but it was not their primary goal. They were after our dharma. They wanted to convert Hindus to Islam at the point of the sword and did so wherever they could.

Absolutely refusing to be a part of Pax Sanatanica, they violated the most fundamental customs and traditions of the Hindus. For example, the invading Islamic armies attacked during the night, killed unarmed civilians, molested, violated, and sold Hindu women and children as sex slaves in international markets; killed Brahmins and priests; massacred and ate sacred cows; and destroyed Hindu temples.[5]

For the first time, Hindus found with shock that somebody would refuse the benevolence, freedom, and peace of Pax Sanatanica and would try to destroy it instead. A new and unprecedented enemy had arrived on the scene of this great land of Bharatavarsha, something that this land had never before encountered. The Sanatana umbrella lay shattered. After the Delhi Sultanate was established in India, Islamic rule continued in India for at least 500 years in one form or another. This long period of 500 years was the bloodiest chapter in the history of humankind. The following words of Will Durant are now famous among Hindus but are still worth quoting:

> The Islamic conquest of India is probably the bloodiest story in history. It is a discouraging tale, for its evident moral is that civilization is a precious good, whose delicate complex of order and freedom, culture and peace, can at any moment be overthrown by barbarians invading from without or multiplying within. The Hindus had allowed their strength to be wasted in internal

> division and war; they had adopted religions like Buddhism and Jainism, which unnerved them for the tasks of life; they had failed to organize their forces for the protection of their frontiers and their capitals, their wealth and their freedom, from the hordes of Scythians, Huns, Afghans and Turks hovering about India's boundaries and waiting for national weakness to let them in.[6]

Hindu kingdoms were invaded continuously, and all that Hindus held dear—temples, cows, Brahmins, and knowledge—was destroyed ruthlessly. Not a single year went by in this long and tortuous history when genocide of Hindus was not carried on in one or the other part of the country. Many cities and regions were completely depopulated of Hindus many times in this long and difficult era; so complete was their genocide. These facts of history are recorded by Islamic historians themselves. Sita Ram Goel quotes the Muslim author of *Tarik-i-Wassaf*, who is proud of the achievements of Islamic armies:

> The vein of the zeal of religion beat high for the subjection of infidelity and destruction of idols. The Mohammadan forces began to kill and slaughter, on the right and the left unmercifully, throughout the impure land, for the sake of Islam, and blood flowed in torrents. They plundered gold and silver to an extent greater than can be conceived, and an immense number of precious stones as well as a great variety of cloths. They took captive a great number of handsome and elegant maidens and children of both sexes, more than pen can enumerate. In short, the Mohammadan army brought the country to utter ruin and destroyed the lives of the inhabitants and plundered the cities, and captured their offsprings, so that many temples were deserted and the idols were broken and trodden under foot, the largest of which was Somnat. The fragments were conveyed to Delhi and the entrance of the Jami Masjid was paved with them so that people might remember and talk of this brilliant victory. Praise be to Allah the lord of the worlds.[7]

This does not mean that the Islamic invasion of India was a sorry tale of Hindu loss and Islamic victory. Within a hundred years of Prophet Muhammad's death, Islam had spread like wildfire and dominated in one continuous stretch from Spain in the West to India's borders. It was only India that they could not defeat instantly. Islam took around 500 years to enter India proper. Until the Delhi Sultanate was established by Mahmud Ghauri in the thirteenth century, Islam and Muslims were seen as a barbaric interlude in Indian history. They were known as brutally violent invaders who hit and ran, never able to stay. The Arabs exhausted themselves completely in Sindh and Multan. The Persians almost never attempted an invasion. It was the Turks, after many waves, who ultimately succeeded in India. We were the only civilization that did not collapse like a house of cards against the invading Islamic armies. We were the ones who survived. Historian Ram Gopal Mishra writes:

> The early successes of Islam, he writes, were against religions which had lost their hold on the minds of the people. But in India the Hindu way of life, symbolized by high moral values of tolerance, truthfulness and justice was very much the part and parcel of the multitudes mental and material being. These eternal and moral values of life which constitute the core of Hinduism were to sustain it in the next five centuries of Muslim and another two centuries of British rule.[8]

Even after the establishment of the Sultanate, every inch of Islamic rule in India was contested, and not a year passed by without Hindus reversing Islamic gains or giving the invaders a deep fight. Not a city went uncontested. Not a village was a walkover. When they could not defend, they fled as a tactical retreat, but only to once again attack in guerilla warfare and in concentrated army attacks whenever that was possible. First the brave soldiers, the great kshatriyas of this country, fought. When they were all killed in battle, the rest of the society joined in: men, women, and teenagers; priests, businessmen, and artisans. Not a single Hindu community, not a single Hindu family in this great land of Bharatavarsha surrendered without fighting. Veteran historian K.S. Lal writes:

> As we put the record straight, we find that the small and scattered class of trained and traditional Hindu warriors, mostly Rajputs, stood exhausted by the time of the Mughal invasion, having fought the earlier invaders at every step for well-nigh eight centuries—from the middle of the seventh to the end of the fifteenth. The leadership of Hindu resistance to Muslim rule thereafter was provided by what are termed the Backward Castes and the Dalits in present-day India. These classes had fought earlier under the leadership of Rajput Rajas and Zamindars. Now onwards they took up the leadership on themselves, and battled with the Mughal regime till the latter stood shattered by the middle of the eighteenth century. It is a different story that in the process the Backward Castes and the Dalits suffered grievously and found themselves in a bad shape by the time the Islamic nightmare was over.[9]

Every single community, region, and family that survives today in India as Hindu has made an immense contribution to save Sanatana Dharma in this great land. They have made ultimate sacrifices for defending Sanatana Dharma, and the reason that we are all Hindu is that every single Hindu fought as much as he could. That is the only reason Islamic armies did not have a walkover in Bharatavarsha. As K.S. Lal writes, it was due to the Islamic invasions that many of these castes fell into hard times and were relegated to the status of 'low castes' after living in jungles and remote areas for so long.[10] Every Hindu is indebted to them, and we should help them regain a dignified status today and make them aware of their glorious and chivalrous Hindu past.

Even though every Hindu region and community fought bravely, there were some defeats, some lands that were largely lost to conversions to Islam because the Muslims would convert Hindus at the point of the sword whenever they conquered a town or a kingdom. This great land of Bharatavarsha started having pockets of Muslims, or followers of Islam, who did not at all want to integrate themselves with the native culture. If Hindus revered the cow, Muslims ate it. If Hindus built temples, Muslims destroyed them. If Hindus respected Brahmins, Muslims cut their heads off. If Hindus never attacked civilians, civilian Hindus, women, and children were the first targets of Islamic armies.

Pax Sanatanica stood violated. Broadly, it still held as Bharatavarsha was still a Hindu-majority land, but there were many holes in it as some non-universal elements and barbaric principles and practices found their way into the daily lives of Indians as we watched the new converts violate some of the most fundamental principles of Sanatana customs.

These converts to Islam became the new missionaries of Islam in India. Swami Vivekananda, pondering on the problem of decreasing Hindu population in his own time, believed that Hindus have to start de-converting those who had converted to Islam and Christianity under force, and he made a pertinent observation regarding the conversion of Hindus:

> Besides, we shall otherwise decrease in numbers. When the Mohammedans first came, we are said—I think on the authority of Ferishta, the oldest Mohammedan historian—to have been six hundred millions of Hindus. Now we are about two hundred millions. And then every man going out of the Hindu pale is not only a man less, but an enemy the more.[11]

The new converts became the swords and shields of Islam for reasons discussed later in the book. Not only were those converts the residue of Islam in India, as Sita Ram Goel said, but they were also the active agents of an ideology that was alien to native

Hindu culture and civilization.[12] This active and devout Muslim society is what is referred to as the residue of Islamic imperialism in India.

The Muslim society of India is not a neutral spectator of political and cultural trends in this country. It has been continuously trying to further the imperialistic design of Islamic armies in India much after the era of Islamic rule is over in India. Sita Ram Goel says that this residue of Islamic imperialism thinks that India and Hindus were living in ignorance and worshipping demons before Islam came to India, and it is the Muslim armies that brought the only true religion—Islam—to India.[13] Since the conquest and conversion of Hindus and Bharatavarsha could not be completed in the mediaeval era, it is the sacred duty of Indian Muslims today to further this agenda.

Muslims think that it is their destiny to rule the world. As India was the only country that remained a non-Muslim majority after hundreds of years of Islamic rule, they feel that Hindus cheated them from their destiny. They have the same attitude towards the Judeo-Christian West. In the seventeenth century, the Ottoman Empire was at its peak, and the world looked as if it would keel over to Islam, and the whole world would become Muslim. But at this point Christendom finally surged ahead. Christian West had taken a quantum leap when it stumbled upon the new world and its resources, which fuelled the Enlightenment, the scientific revolution, and the industrial revolution in Europe. The age of colonialism cemented the supremacy of the West on Islam. The Islamic world today feels that they have been cheated of their destiny by the Christian West.[14]

In India, this feeling is all too palpable because India is one of the few 'failures' of Islam. India is one of the few places where Islam ruled for more than 500 years but still could not convert the majority to Islam. While Arabs could only enter India, the Turks established the Sultanate in Delhi. It was the Mughals who carried forward the Islamic dream of global conquest, with Aurangzeb making the final push to realize the dream. However, at that point, Hindu powers, like the Marathas, and the British intervened, resulting in the 'loss' of the 'ruling status' of Muslims. That is why the dream of Islamic re-conquest is deeply ingrained in Indian Muslims, which continues to be a cause of social strife.

Christianity Joins Islam in Violating Sanatana Umbrella

The second great imperialism to hit India's shores was another prophetic monotheistic religion—Christianity. Christianity predates Islam, but in India they arrived in reverse order. We did not know of Christianity until the late fifteenth and early sixteenth centuries when the Portuguese invaders came to India's western shores. There were some Christian refugees, like Syrian Christians, who came to Kerala before, but they were too few to register on India's psyche, and also the Christian theology was not developed completely by then. That Islam reached India first, followed by Christianity, had some curious impact on Hindus' psyche and influenced how we look at the others.

The behaviour of these Portuguese Christian invaders was not very different from their Islamic predecessors. Their wrath broke upon Goa, parts of which they had come to rule. They also destroyed Hindu temples, broke vigrahas of Hindu deities, used them as target practice in the Elephanta Caves, killed Brahmins, and cut off their *shikhas*, converting Hindus by force. An almost complete ethnic cleansing of Hindus occurred in the three areas of present-day Goa that were invaded in the early sixteenth centuries: Salcette, Tiswadi, and Bardez.

Christian opinion of Hindu society and Sanatana Dharma was almost exactly the same as the opinion of the Islamic invaders. Christians thought that Hindus were 'living in sin', by which they meant that they were worshipping their own 'false gods' and not the only true Christian God. This might seem very strange to Hindu ears, but Christianity believes that every deity in the world is a 'false god' or a devil, and only the Christian God is the true God with a capital 'G'. Not only this, but the Bible is also very clear that worshipping 'false gods' is a great sin, and it is the sacred duty of the Christians, lay and clergy, to stop non-Christians from worshipping 'false gods' and convert them by force or by fraud.

> Christian religion … like Islam … is an extremely exclusive religion. Christianity too claims for itself a monopoly of truth and virtue, swears by the only true God, the only true Saviour or the only Son of the only true God, the only true Revelation, the only true way of worship, and so on. It too has to its discredit a long and unrelieved record of wanton destruction of ancient religions and cultures and a large-scale killing of heathens. The annals of Europe, Asia Minor, North Africa, and America, particularly Central and South America, provide harrowing details of this destruction and bloodshed.[15]

The only thing different about Christian invaders was that they came from the sea route and not the land route, and their military strength was very limited compared to their Islamic predecessors in India. Most of the Portuguese invasions also remained limited to very small enclaves on the coast, which were important as trade posts but otherwise less populated and geographically a little isolated from most of the power and population centres of Bharatavarsha. The wider Hindu society remained mostly ignorant of the Christian invaders.

The Portuguese were extremely barbaric, and not only did they carry out genocide of Hindus in the areas they ruled, but they also instituted the Inquisition for those converted Hindus whom they did not trust much. While they killed Hindus who did not convert, they did not spare those who had converted, either. These neo-converts were considered not Christian enough, and thus they were punished by the Christian religious tribunal called the Inquisition. Many of them were brutally killed. A Goan historian of Portuguese descent J.C. Barreto Miranda says:

> The cruelties which in the name of the religion of peace and love this tribunal practised in Europe, were carried to even greater excesses in India, where the Inquisitors, surrounded by luxuries which could stand comparison with the real magnificence of the great potentates of Asia, saw with pride the Archbishop as well as the viceroy submitted to their power. Every word of theirs was a sentence to death and at their slightest nod were moved to terror the vast population spread over the Asiatic regions, whose lives fluctuated in their hands, and who, on the most frivolous pretext could be clapped for all time in the deepest dungeons or strangled or offered as food for the flames of the pyre.[16]

But despite this, the Portuguese Christian power was not great enough to rattle any mainstream kingdom inside India, Hindu or Muslim, and thus they remained a fringe power. European Christian presence in India remained pretty small until the British entered the scene.

The next wave of invaders in India was that of the British. These were also extremely devout Christians (albeit of a different sect—Anglicans) and believed, like other Christian sects, that Hindus were the superstitious worshippers of the devil. But they were far more sophisticated, and their design to conquer, subvert, and convert India was far more insidious than their predecessors. The British learnt from the mistakes of other monotheistic invaders in India, recognizing that Hindus were very hard to defeat by brute force. Almost four centuries of Islamic invasions had barely converted one-fifth of the country, and around two centuries of Christian invasions resulted in just a handful of enclaves hardly even noticed in the main power centres of India. The British would take a very different route to destroy Hindu dharma in India.

Cultural Christianity Fools Hindus

The British went for indirect conversion tactics. They set about changing India's culture by replacing Sanatana ideas with cultural Christianity. Using the authority of the State that they had captured, they went for the physical and mental colonization of Hindus. They were as or even more particular about converting Hindus to Christianity, but they adopted a long-term strategy to do so. They decided to subvert some of the most basic and fundamental institutions of India, thereby severing Hindus from their roots, leading to their deracination and de-Hinduization over centuries and eventually leading to their conversion in the far future. And they succeeded in establishing Christian institutions in India, making sure that long after the end of British colonialism at a concrete level, the mental colonization of Hindus would continue and even increase in pace.

By subverting India's education and health systems, along with introducing Christian-conducive polity and economy, they set in motion long-term processes, the effect of which we are witnessing fully only in the last three or four decades. While Islamic and Christian imperialism had arrived in India before the British, the seeds of the other three forces besieging Hindu society—communism, Macaulayism, and modernism—were sown during the British re-engineering of some of the most basic institutions of India.

By destroying the indigenous education system by replacing it with English education, the British set in motion the process of the deracination of Hindus, which created a class that is Hindu only by birth but Christian in ideas and manners, just like Thomas Babbington Macaulay wanted. This class of Hindus would oppose any indigenous demand for decolonization of Hindu institutions and reclamation of Hindu culture. These Hindus would act as the first line of defence of cultural Christianity in India and would make sure that the mental colonization of Hindus would never stop and lead them to a place where they are so de-Hinduized that they can convert at the first approach of a Christian sect.

For example, English education created deracinated Hindus who were ashamed of their own culture and learnt to be non-Hindu in appearance and thoughts in public and relegate their Hindu identity only to the privacy of their homes. This schizophrenic Hindu behaviour became useful when, upon independence, it was suggested that the Indian Constitution and State should not promote Hindu dharma or culture, and independent India should be based on the idea of 'secularism' instead.

Cultural Christianity paved the path for secularism in India.

Even before independence, the call for an impossible 'common platform' with Muslims was readily accepted by Hindus since they had no problem in de-Hinduizing public space and shedding any public campaign of its Hindu identity while Muslims were never ready to do this. English education instituted by the British became responsible for the secular Indian state, which is blocking all attempts to re-Hinduize Hindu political and public space in contemporary times. The very taxonomy of the academic disciplines that the British instituted in higher education in India made sure that it would result in the conversion of Hindus to Christianity in the future.

The British were notorious for dividing Hindus into various factions and uniting minorities into significant blocks to prevent Hindus from ever rising. They used English education to further this policy of division. They divided north and south India on one hand with the concocted theory of the Aryan invasion, and on the other hand, created multiple fault lines within Hindu society based on caste, claiming that the 'higher castes' were invaders who came from outside and started ruling over what later became the 'lower castes'. A third fault line was created between the tribal communities of India and the rest of the Hindus by using the word 'indigenous' for the tribals. The word 'indigenous' means native to a certain place, and by using that word for only the tribal communities of India, it was indicated that the rest of the Hindus, amounting to more than 80 per cent of the Hindu population, are outsiders and invaders. These Indian tribes were declared 'indigenous' on the line of the aboriginal Australian communities, which were truly the original inhabitants of Australia who were replaced by Christian Europeans with a horrible genocide of their people and ethnocide of their culture and religion. This Christian crime was superimposed on Hindu society with no fault of its own, by the use of the word 'indigenous'.

In academics, sociology was defined as the subject that is applied when one studies one's own society, and anthropology was defined as the discipline that one used to study the other. By implementing anthropology on the tribal communities of Hindus, it was tacitly declared that tribals were not Hindus, thus preparing further ground for their conversion to Christianity.

Education, however, was far from the only tool of the Christian imperialists. The economic model imposed on India ensured the fragmentation of its social and family systems while encouraging mindless consumerism and individualism. The model of polity that they encouraged was developed in the Christian West. This model made sure that it focused on a narrative of rights rather than the narrative of duties. Every institutional change introduced by the British would target one major Hindu institution, aiming to break all Hindu walls of defence so that at last a Hindu is left as a culture-less, clueless, hapless individual, ready to be sold any new idea that was forced down his throat, an idea like conversion to Christianity.

While education targeted dharma directly, medicine and economy targeted Hindu lifestyle and social systems, and the Western-style polity targeted the worldview of Hindus anchored in kartavyabodha, thus every 'modern' institution aimed to destroy at least one Hindu wall of defence.

These walls of defences were the multiple identities of a Hindu, which makes it almost impossible for an alien and hostile power to convert a Hindu to its brand of religion or ideology. The various identities act like various walls of defence and to break them all at once is extremely hard. If one identity breaks down, the others make sure the Hindu/ Sanatana core remains secure. And to break them all at once is almost impossible. The British understood this deeply and established institutions that aimed to break core Hindu institutions and identities over a period of decades and centuries. On the other hand, the institutions that they could not distort, like jati and varna, were made to descend into petty infighting, and in this way, what was Hindus' strength was turned into their weakness.

The indirect tactics of conversion that the British used did not mean that they did not attempt the conversion of Hindus directly. Wherever possible, they released Christian missionaries upon native societies like plague, resulting in their conversion. In the tribal areas of India, and particularly in the northeastern parts of India, the British actively pursued the policy of conversion, as is evident by large-scale conversions that had already happened in Nagaland, Mizoram, and Meghalaya at the time of Indian independence.

In the rest of India too, the British Empire released Christian missionaries on unsuspecting Hindu society, who thought of them as Christian 'holy men', just like the Hindu saints. The good Hindu habit of trusting any 'saint-like' personality was turned into a lethal gullibility and exploited to the detriment of the Hindu society.

Multiple Christian sects were let loose on Hindu society, every one of which set upon converting the 'heathen Hindus', 'living in sin'. Coupled with other institutions that the British introduced, the Christian missionaries became ubiquitous. They collaborated with educationists and set up schools and hospitals all over India. At the centre of all such 'mission schools' and 'mission hospitals' was a church of a particular Christian sect.

Christianity, both cultural and deeply religious, started becoming the central idea around which new and 'modern' Indian institutions were created.

The network of these churches was so far and wide that they would reach many tribes, districts, and far-off places before the administration could. The last village of India that got electricity post-independence is in Manipur, and the report published about that village shows the picture of the village with a church in the background. The Church had reached where electricity had not.[17] While early Christian missions rode into India riding on the back of the British Crown, in the later stages of the British Raj, it was the State that piggybacked various Christian missions that had already reached every nook and cranny of this country. Arun Shourie conclusively proves this dual British strategy in his brilliant work *Missionaries in India*.

> The work of the Church was not done by the missionaries alone, the religiously 'neutral administrators' did a good bit of it. Correspondingly, the work of the Empire was not done by the administrators alone, the missionaries did a good bit of it. And that contribution was acknowledged by ruler after ruler.[18]

The British State in India and the Christian missions existed in mutually beneficial collaboration with each other. Somewhere the Crown led the Church, and somewhere the Church led the Crown. Christianity was introduced in India as a colonial enterprise.

Christianity still remains a colonial enterprise in India. It advances the religion, culture, lifestyle, morality, ethics, and economy of the erstwhile European Christian colonizers of India.

In independent India, the makers of the Indian Constitution and the dominant political party were convinced to declare India a secular state, which *de facto* meant an anti-Hindu, pro-Christian, and pro-Islamic state. It is true that the word 'secular' was added to the Indian Constitution during the Emergency, but even at its inception, secularism was espoused as the inspiring principle on the basis of which the Indian State would be constituted.

This ensured that while the Indian State prohibited the teaching of Hindu dharma to its citizens, the Church and the Ummah would be given a free run to open churches, missions, mosques, and *madrassahs* all over the country in the name of minority rights and would paint the country in anti-Hindu colours. The Indian State, in its apathy, adopted a stance of 'enlightened neutralism', which meant leaving the country to whichever power is most hungry for violent conquest. This meant that the Church and Christian sects had a free run in India, and combined with the access to global wealth, Christianity became the most formidable force in independent India, marshalling billions of dollars to its conversion drive. Later chapters will discuss how they destroyed Andhra Pradesh in a span of just two decades by making rivers of money flow in exchange for conversion to Christianity.

The residues of Christian imperialism in India proved to be the most dangerous of all since it marshalled the wealth of the entire Western civilization and the global network of Christianity to complete the process of conversion of Bharatavarsha, a process that began with the arrival of the Portuguese Christian missionaries in India. It also facilitated all other imperialisms plaguing India, including Marxism, Macaulayism, modernism, and even Islamism.

Secular Monotheisms Besiege India

While Macaulayism was a force directly set up by the British, it is English education (a product of Macaulayism) that made sure that the other two forces besieging Hindu society would find fertile ground here.

Communism/Marxism/socialism is the fourth great force that besieges Hindu society, aiming at the destruction and breakdown of Hindu culture and Sanatana Dharma. Communism is another mutation of Christianity minus God, or, as Bertrand Russell put it, 'a Christian heresy'.[19]

Communism is State-espoused atheism where the State prohibits and punishes any practice of religion. It believes that society is divided into two classes, the rich and the poor, and it claims that the communist rule is the rule of the poor over the rich, the downtrodden over the powerful, and the marginalized over the mainstream. In order to safeguard the interests of the marginalized and the poor, a political party inspired by communist ideology needs to capture the State and then abolish all institutions and democratic mechanisms that might allow any other non-communist power or party to come to power. In short, it is the dictatorship of one political party, led by one supreme leader.

Everything in a communist country is controlled by the State; the State, in turn, is controlled by the Party, and Party by the Supreme Leader. Thus, the most important branches of a State, like judiciary, legislature, and executive, are controlled by the communist party and are not independent. The very idea of distribution of power is non-existent in communism, and all power is concentrated in the hands of one supreme leader, like Stalin was for Russia, Mao was for China, and like Kim Jong Un is for North Korea.

Just like various arms of the State, the economy too is not free, and there is no concept of a free market. Trade and business are controlled, once again, by the communist party. All form of art, including dance, drama, music, painting, sculpture, and architecture, are also controlled by the State, with everything serving one single idea—communism, one single party—the Communist Party, and one single leader—the supreme leader. Even private lives are controlled by the State and Soviet Union, where the largest communist experiment was carried out, would even choose spouses for its members in many cases. This extreme coercion with violence is justified by the communist 'pursuit of equality'. Historian of communism, Richard Pipes writes:

> Communism failed and is bound to fail for at least two reasons: one, that to enforce equality, its principal objective, it is necessary to create a coercive apparatus that demands privileges and thereby negates equality; and two, that ethnic and territorial loyalties, when in conflict with class allegiances, everywhere and at all times overwhelm them, dissolving Communism in nationalism, which is why socialism so easily combines with 'Fascism'.[20]

Communism is very similar to prophetic monotheism because, like Christianity and Islam, it also destroys all opposing ideas and concentrates all power and authority in one single source. One idea, one party, one leader, and extreme intolerance for any dissent or opposition are the features of a communist society. Summing up, communism entails State-espoused atheism and State-controlled economy, polity, education, medicine, and pretty much every other aspect of life. Wherever communism grabs State power, it unleashes unimaginable tyranny of torture and coercion on its own citizens, for it claims to be the only correct ideology, and thus any individual found to be differing from the only correct ideology is bound to be wrong and has to be punished. In communist Russia, common citizens were put in concentration camps and made to do forced labour just because their opinions differed from the communist party. These camps were brutal, and millions died of murder, starvation, and exhaustion. All of this was done in the name of 'equality'. When the communist party, like the Christian church, claimed sole possession of truth, everyone else who differed was wrong. Like dogmatic monotheistic religions, people were punished for their 'wrong beliefs', as Anne Applebaum brilliantly observes in her book *Gulag: A History*: 'From the very earliest days of the new Soviet state . . . people were to be sentenced not for what they had done, but for who they were.'[21]

Like Christianity and Islam, communism too has its missionaries whose job is to spread communism all over the world. They have an ideology of world conquest, and they do not believe in national boundaries. In fact, they want to bring down and dissolve national boundaries so that a pan-communist supra-State can be created. It is not very different from the goals and designs of Christianity and Islam, which want to build pan-Christian and pan-Islamic states. That is why in the pre-90s era, when communism was at its zenith, communist thinkers argued that it is the sacred duty of communist countries to fund subversion activities in other non-communist countries. Communists thought of nationalism as an artificial construct created by the rich and the powerful to fool the poor and the marginalized. Hence it was their duty to fight against any form of 'nationalism'.

The Soviet Union funded a vast network of spies who founded Soviet-funded communist parties all over the world by recruiting local people. These communist parties functioned as the fifth column, or the foreign branch of the Soviet Communist Party. The communists would try to foment communist rebellions by destabilizing native governments, subverting their own State, and working to break down and destroy their own culture, society, and dharma. This was not an unorganized activity. Soviet Union had a department called Agitprop (Agitation and Propaganda) Ministry, and the very mandate of this department was to spread communist propaganda all over the world.[22] Agitprop members would run propaganda against the majority community of a country to destabilize them and, in the resulting chaos, capture the State.[23] This is what happened in China and many other countries that became communist later. They had a huge budget allocated to fund subversion activities all over the world.

Most of the publishing houses and press houses in India until the 1990s were owned by the leftists, and they constructed any narrative that they wanted in society at the drop of a hat. They controlled the inflow and outflow of information and were the engineers of public opinion through their propaganda machinery. Even today their hold on India's narratives is supreme, and this is why most popular narratives are anti-Hindu in nature. But India was a hotbed of communist activities much before independence. The history of the communist party in India is a long tale of national subversion. The party came into existence in 1925 and wanted to overthrow the British government in a violent revolution like the one that happened in the Soviet Union. That is why they were tolerated by the Hindu nationalists. Most Hindus thought of them initially just as aggressive revolutionaries, and that is why they were given space in the Indian freedom struggle. But communists hated Hindu nationalists more because nationalism is their arch enemy.

The communists got their golden chance in India during the Second World War when Hindu nationalists were agitating to drive the British out of India, while the communists supported the British colonialists, as Britain and the Soviet Union were fighting on the same side. The Communist Party of India, essentially a puppet of the Soviet Union, vehemently opposed the Quit India Movement. The British took this as an opportunity to take the wind out of Hindu nationalists by jailing them on the pretext of protests against the Crown. Meanwhile, the communists roamed free, as they supported the British Raj. Arun Shourie, in *The Only Fatherland*, quotes numerous documents to prove how the communists in India collaborated with the British Empire, motivated by their alliance with the Soviet Union.[24] During the Quit India Movement, the communists gained a significant influence over Indian politics, swaying public opinion to some degree. The British even encouraged Hindu nationalists to interact with communists in jail, hoping to stave off the edge of their Hindu nationalism and superficially influence some of them.

This was a clear sign that the British did everything to prevent any revival of Hindu dharma and culture. Winston Churchill let Pakistan overrun many parts of Kashmir and Gilgit-Baltistan because he did not want a strong Hindu India. The British obviously preferred Christianity over Islam but favoured Islam over Hindus. This was due to their hatred of Hindus, whom they considered superstitious brutes, but it was also motivated by a fear that a 'pagan power' would rise and give the Christian domination of the world a significant challenge. Hindu nationalism was thus the number one enemy of Christianity and Islam as well as communism. The communists hated Hindu dharma because they knew that until India remained a Hindu majority, it would never give in to a godless atheist ideology like communism.

The Communist Party of India was an open supporter of the idea of Pakistan since the creation of an Islamic state at the border of India would mean a perpetual irritant to India and would decrease the power of Hindu nationalists by many degrees. In order to subvert and divide the nation in two parts, the communist party directed many of its members to join the Congress party and support the demand for Pakistan, thus making Congress policy leftist and anti-Hindu before India even became independent.

Upon Indian independence in 1947, the communists were not able to capture the State at the centre, but in the subsequent years they got a toehold only in the states of West Bengal and

Kerala. But communist ideas had a huge indirect influence on the mindset of the constitution makers and also the Congress party. Jawaharlal Nehru was heavily influenced by socialist and communist ideas. He steered the country towards the communist camp despite claiming neutrality on international forums. In his indicting criticism of Jawaharlal Nehru, *Genesis and Growth of Nehruism*, Sita Ram Goel writes that he was always an inveterate communist:

> Pandit Nehru has done a lot of writing and speaking and … whatever we have before us establishes beyond a shadow of doubt that the man is a communist in terms of the Soviet definition. He has been and remains an admirer not only of the Soviet socio-political and economic system but also of the Marxist-Leninist-Stalinist ideology.[25]

Communist influence increased many times when Indira Gandhi virtually sold out India's educational and media institutions to the communists in exchange for political support for her by the Communist Party of India. Her reason to hand over the country to communists on a platter was more than ideological because, just like her father, she had deep sympathies with the Soviet Union and communism. In fact, it was during her tenure as Prime Minister of India that the communists strengthened their grip on Indian academia, media, and many other institutions. A former KGB clerk Vasili Mitrokhin defected from Russia and published accounts of how the KGB, the Soviet secret service, had thoroughly infiltrated India in the explosive book *The Mitrokhin Archives*. 'After the elections of February 1967, the KGB claimed … that it was able to influence 30 to 40 percent of the new parliament.'[26] Indira Gandhi gave a free ticket to KGB operatives in the Indian government, including the prime minister's office, leading the co-author of Vasili Mitrokhin to write: 'It seemed like the entire country was for sale.'[27]

Arun Shourie in *Eminent Historians* tells the story of how communism made a complete conquest of the Indian education system during the reign of Indira Gandhi. And the primary goal of the communists, who took over Indian education institutions, was to destroy the confidence of the Hindus in their own past, heritage, and culture and make them self-hating defeatists:

> These intellectuals and their patrons have worked a diabolic inversion: the inclusive religion, the pluralist spiritual search of our people and land, they have projected as intolerant, narrow-minded, obscurantist; and the exclusivist, totalitarian, revelatory religions and ideologies—Islam, Christianity, Marxism-Leninism—they have made out to be the epitomes of tolerance, open-mindedness, democracy, secularism! This has been their real crime.[28]

Indian textbooks, secular in nature, became Hindu-hating vehicles and still are. All Hindu heroes were declared as brigands or small-time goons, while all Islamic invaders and mass murderers were whitewashed as beacons of peace and tolerance. Hindu dharma was declared as a font of injustice, superstition, and discrimination, while Islam was extolled as the beacon of equality. Hindus were taught how their dharma is the root cause of every contemporary problem and how Islam and Christianity are equal and equalizing religions. Sita Ram Goel says:

> The first and foremost target of Communism is Sanatana Dharma enshrined in Hindu literature and made living by a long line of saints, mystics and bhaktas. Communism ridicules all this wealth of unrivalled spiritual splendour as a conglomeration of sterile superstition, obnoxious obscurantism and puerile priestcraft; Next, Communism makes an aggressive move towards Hindu *Dharmashastras* which have their source in Sanatana Dharma and which lay down the moral and social principles by which a wholesome social and individual life is

> sustained. Communism denounces these *Dharmashastras* as repositories of primitive prescriptions, Machiavellian morality, caste oppression, untouchability, degradation of women, Brahmin domination, lack of social responsibility, and what not; Thirdly, Communism ... condemns all ... [Hindu] philosophies as Brahminical conspiracies to suppress the Lokayata, the only scientific philosophy pulsating with a revolutionary principle.[29]

This Hindu hatred was institutionalized as the education policy in India, the only country for Hindus in the world. And it was all thanks to communism and the communist takeover of India's education system during the tenure of Dr Nurul Hasan as education minister, under the prime ministership of Indira Gandhi. This was a win-win situation for the Muslim leadership of India since they got their wish of tarnishing the glorious Hindu past of India and instead got to criticize and downplay the greatness of Hindu heroes. They also got the chance to whitewash Islamic invaders as great and benign kings, who were connoisseurs of art and very secular in outlook. Communism gave them the cover to engage in anti-Hindu and pro-Islamist scholarship, all in the name of secularism and liberalism. They fulfilled their goal and did not even receive the blame for it.

Education, however, was far from the only sphere of influence for communism and its anti-Hindu policies. The *Mitrokhin Archives* tells us how many of our political leaders and parties were functioning as spies of the Soviet Union, which had many high-ranking politicians and officials in the Indian government and Congress party in its pay, including having spies in the prime minister's office. The communists oppose all nationalist policies and forces by default and by design.

Contrary to the global scenario where Christianity, Islam, and communism are at loggerheads with each other, in India they are united in their goal, which is the destruction of Hindu society.

Sita Ram Goel describes in his scathing critique of secularism, *India's Secularism*, how all five enemies of Hindu society used the banner of secularism to gather together and pose a united front against anything Hindu.

One can see the signs of this collaboration everywhere in India. Most of the Maoist-infested red corridor of India is also a hotbed of violent Christian conversion activities. Manipur suffers from communist insurrection among many other problems, and Christian conversion is inextricably linked to it. Tripura suffers from the same tragedy. This unholy alliance of the left, Islam, and Christianity is also cemented due to a historical reason. The Soviet Union created institutional mechanisms all over the world to subvert nationalism in every country and capture power whenever possible. This necessitated a huge global network of spies, financial channels for funding their subversion activities, and the academic and media cover to hide reality from the larger population. This network of academia, media, mafia, and global finance suddenly ran out of money and purpose when the Soviet Union collapsed in the 1990s. Lakhs upon lakhs of communists in the pay of the Soviet Union were suddenly out of purpose and out of a job. They had the network, they had the manpower, but they lacked finance and purpose.

Both of these were provided to them by Islam and Christianity. This represents the alliance of the left with Islam on one hand, and the left with Christianity on the other. Robert Spencer traces this unusual friendship between the left and Islam very well in his book *Unholy Alliance*. But, in India, the alliance between the left and the Church is much deeper and more sinister. In India, all three of these forces come together to create a united front with the other two forces besieging Hindu society—Macaulayism and modernism. The most significant legacy of communist imperialism in India is the army of former communist peddlers, who are now mercenaries and ready to sell their service to the highest bidder. Islamic lobbies, as well as the Church, happen to be their greatest buyers in India, as all three of them have the common enemy in Hindu society and Sanatana Dharma.

Sita Ram Goel talks about four enemies of Hindu society, four forces that are besieging us, and the fifth one he indicates in his prose but does not classify as a separate threat. He considers 'modernists' to be a part of the Macaulayites:

> The Hindu who is thus addicted to Macaulayism lives in a world of his own which has hardly any contact with the traditional Hindu society. He looks forward to the day when India will become a society like societies in the West where the rate of growth, the gross national product and the standard of living are the only criteria of progress. He is tolerant towards religion to the extent that it remains a matter of private indulgence and does not interfere with the smooth unfoldment of the socio-political scene. Personally for him, religion is irrelevant, though some of its rituals and festivities can occasionally add some colour to life. For the rest, religion is so much obscurantism, primitive superstition and, in the Indian context at present, a creator of communal riots.[30]

This modern Hindu has bought into the economic miracle of the West and has accepted the worldview that the West has created. He thinks that India should be remade into the image of the West, and all that matters is material prosperity. Such a Hindu maintains that there is no place for dharma in public, and it should not be involved in State affairs. He has bought completely into the Enlightenment paradigm of secularism, wanting to keep religion and State separate. When Shri Sita Ram Goel was writing, modernists had not become the dominant faction of Indian intellectuals, but things have changed a lot in the last forty-two years, and now modernism has emerged as a great force that also lays siege to Hindu society and culture. That is the reason they are classified in this book as one of the great forces that are laying siege to Hindu society.

The modernists go by different tags and names. Some of them still use the old leftist umbrella and argue for an atheist worldview where everything Hindu is regressive and oppressive and has to be abandoned. Some still go by Nehruvian secularism and believe that all public spaces in India should be cleansed of Hindu identity and Hindu dharma should strictly be a matter of personal choice in the privacy of home. However, there are various newer strains of them, including the group known as 'woke', which refers to those who are aware of what they believe to be systemic injustice ubiquitous in traditional, and particularly Hindu, social systems and philosophy. These folks are on the extreme left of the political spectrum in the West, and they generally rally around the LGBTQ rights. They are joined by feminists and other radical activists in India, as all of them consider Hindu society as their major enemy.

It is this ragtag group that is most insidiously anti-Hindu in popular culture. Woke ideology is an import from the West, and there are two principles on which it mostly operates. The first principle is that of radical equality. This group thinks that everyone should be equal to everyone else, and they see any difference in someone's resources and standards as due to some inherent injustice in the system. They believe in a world where there is no space for inequality of any kind, and everyone should be made equal by the State. The second principle on which they operate is the idea of agency, which means that everything in life depends on one's choice, even what gender they are.

These ideas first germinated during the Enlightenment and reached their extreme conclusion in the woke revolution. The West has a habit of stretching any idea to the extreme, and after reaching absurd limits, it starts the journey to the other extreme. In the absence of dharma, which is an eternal thermostat and perpetually aims for balance, Western civilization is rudderless, swinging like a pendulum from one extreme to another. For example, not long ago, in 1952, English courts were physically punishing homosexuals. Alan Turing, the father of modern computers, was forced to castrate himself because he was homosexual. Due to the trauma he went through upon carrying out the court's sentence, he committed suicide a few days later. There are severe punishments for homosexuality in the Bible: 'If a man lies with a man as with a woman, both of them have committed an abomination; they shall surely be put to death; their blood is upon them.'[31]

This is why the homosexuals were targeted and punished during the Christian heyday. The Enlightenment brought some moderation to these punishments but started the trend in the opposite direction to the point where now the LGBTQ lobbies are forcing schools to show children the dance of drag queens, and children are being forcibly taken away by the State for gender change operations. In the words of Mark Tully, in the case of sex, the West has gone from 'constipation to diarrhoea'.

All of these forces together lay siege to Hindu society. While Christian missionaries and Islamic *mullahs* target Hindus for conversion, leftists dominate academics and media, forcing Hindu kids to go through a de-Hinduizing training where they grow up hating everything about their past and develop an inferiority complex so deep that they want to abandon their identity as quickly as possible, becoming a weak imitation of the West. They also provide the academic and institutional skills and networks that are used to further the Islamic and Christian agenda. The Macaulayites obviously dominate the education system of India, and they also act as mercenaries to further Christian and Islamic agendas. The woke/extreme liberal/leftist faction pushes anti-Hinduism in soft culture through various means: an ad that makes fun of Hindu customs; an ad that extols 'Love Jihad'; a movie that shows Hindu dharma as oppressive and redundant, while presenting Christianity and Islam as progressive; a TV serial that shows the Hindu family as a den of moral corruption and systemic oppression, while showing how Christianity looks after the poor in Christian hospitals and schools; a work of fiction that portrays Shri Rama as evil and Ravana as good; a webpage that portrays every Hindu hero as evil and every Islamic monster as a hero; and a trend among Instagrammers to display crosses as fashion icons.

The main thrust of this modernist brigade is to push against the fundamental institutions of Sanatana Dharma and Hindu society, like family, marriage, temples, festivals, etc., so that the last lines of defence of Hindus against the onslaught of global forces like Christianity and Islam are down and Hindus are ready for the final act of conversion.

Any Hindu wanting to save Sanatana Dharma and Hindu society has to understand the complex battleground of dharma vs religion in which Sanatana Dharma is fighting against the forces of Christianity, Islam, communism, leftism, secularism, liberalism, and modernism. These ideas and institutions are the enemies of Hindu society, and that is what we need to fight against. In this chapter we mainly discussed who the enemies are, but it is equally important to know what they are, how they operate, what their primary beliefs are, and what their specific plans are about Sanatana Dharma, Hindu society, and Bharatavarsha. Let us discuss in the next chapter the fundamentals of prophetic monotheism, i.e., Islam and Christianity.

Chapter 7

Fundamentals of Prophetic Monotheism

'For those who wish to be intolerant, monotheism provides very powerful weapons.'

—Catherine Nixey

The Slave Market, Otto Pilny, 1910. A scene from the Arab-Turkish slave market, where non-Muslim slave women are sold like cattle in open[1]

Hindu society is under siege from many forces, but two of the oldest and most powerful are the religious ideologies of Islam and Christianity, collectively known as prophetic monotheism. This chapter will discuss the fundamental traits of prophetic monotheism.[2]

The Idea of 'One True God'

The most peculiar concept of prophetic monotheism is their idea of God. God with a capital 'G' is an invention of Judeo-Christianity. No dharmic tradition all over the world outside the prophetic monotheistic realm had this idea before, and nor does it have any equivalent today.[3] The Christian idea of God is that of an extraterrestrial being who is male and who is so superior to all other beings (deities in pagan traditions) that he is the Only God. Every other heavenly being is an angel or demon, but there is only One God. Christians and Muslims believe that not just one god, but only one form (or idea) of god is permissible for worship and prayers. This one form is the one true God, which is Yahweh in the case of Christianity and Allah in the case of Islam. This is the meaning of monotheism: to worship one form of god. Sita Ram Goel writes:

> The first proposition of Monotheism is that the creator and controller of the Cosmos is the One God who is unique, who does not manifest himself in different forms, and who does not permit the worship of any god or goddess other than himself. There is no element outside or inside the Cosmos which is of the same substance as the One God, or is his part, or is pervaded by him. Therefore, to worship any other gods or goddesses or to regard any part of the Cosmos as divine is a serious crime against the One God.[4]

All other deities and even forms of deities except the one true God are declared as 'false gods', demons, and devils. The

Bible and the Quran are both quite strict about this principle and recommend strict punishments for any of their followers who break this principle. Their sense of superiority vis-à-vis indigenous natural religions and dharmic sects comes from the fact that they think worship of one form of god is the supreme virtue and worshipping more than one form or more than one deity is one of the worst possible crimes that humans can commit.

Those who worship more than one form of the divine, like Hindus, are called 'idolaters', and idolatry is the worst crime in the book of any monotheist. Worshipping any other god than the one true God is compared to infidelity in monotheistic sects. Monotheists consider it their sacred duty to eliminate 'polytheism' from the world, and that is why they destroy Hindu temples and break vigrahas of pagan, dharmic deities. The entire mediaeval history of Islamic destruction of Hindu temples is a result of the monotheistic hatred of the worship of any other deity other than the one recommended in their holy book.

The word 'monotheism' means the worship of one god, and the word 'polytheism' is also coined in opposition to monotheism, which means in the restricted Christian understanding the 'worship of many gods'.

Pagan sects and dharmic traditions like Sanatana Dharma have no parallel idea to the Christian idea of 'God'. Hindus worship various deities, all of whom are part of the same divinity, but there is no universal hierarchical system where one deity is the supreme god, and all others are subordinate to him. Every Hindu sect has a mythology centred on one deity who is, of course, supreme inside his or her own mythology, but there are parallel sects that consider another deity to be supreme. In fact, every deity has a manifestation which is considered the equivalent of Brahman, or the supreme consciousness. Thus, while the *Vishnu Purana* considers Mahavishnu to be the equivalent of Brahman, the *Shiva Purana* considers Parashiva to be that, and the *Devi Mahatmya Purana* considers the Goddess to be the supreme deity. And the mythologies of various sects cross over in polite continuums. On the contrary, all three monotheistic religions of Judaism, Christianity, and Islam have always been fighting with each other violently.

Another important point to consider is that in Sanatana Dharma, the idea of Brahman, Mahavishnu, Parashiva, or Tripurasundari is not that of an individual being that is omniscient, omnipotent, and omnipresent like the Christian God. The Brahman of Sanatana Dharma is supreme consciousness. In its purest form it has no attributes and no desire to create the world. It just exists. It is just knowingness, as Shri Nisargadatta Maharaja describes.[5] This state of being is called the non-dual state. This 'knowingness' cannot be called 'god'. In the words of Shri Ram Swarup, in Hindu dharma we do not have the idea of one true God, but we have the concept of 'god alone is'. In the case of Indian spirituality, 'god' is supreme consciousness, which pervades the entire universe and every living being as well as the non-living entities in it.

> Indian spirituality proclaimed that the true Godhead was beyond number and count; that it had many manifestations which did not exclude or repel each other but included each other and went together in friendship; that it was approached in different ways and through many symbols; that it resided in the heart of its devotees. Here there were no chosen peoples, no exclusive prophethoods, no privileged churches and fraternities and ummahs. The message was subversive of all religions based on exclusive claims.[6]

In Hindu dharma, the creator and the creation are not separate from each other. The Brahman is one in its purest existence as the supreme consciousness, but it is the same Brahman that becomes many when it creates the universe. Thus, Brahman is not just the creator but also the creation, as every living and non-living being in the universe is a reflection of the Brahman itself. Moksha is nothing but the realization by an individual that he is not the individual but Brahman himself. Any individual can become the supreme consciousness through sadhana or meditation. We all are supreme consciousness itself. It is just that we have forgotten our true nature, and it is through meditation that we realize it and 'become god', or the supreme consciousness. Just like human beings can realize their true form as Brahman himself, deities are also the forms of the Brahman only. On various different planes of consciousness and existence, they have different forms, shapes, and powers.

Even in those pagan traditions that do not have a cosmology as well developed as Hindu dharma, there is no idea of God, only the idea of deities, which represent many aspects of nature and other planes of existence. There is a deep cosmic unity in existence in Sanatana Dharma and all dharmic traditions. The idea of false gods does not exist because when everything is Brahman only, there is no scope for it being false. There is no scope for strife or violence either. If there is no other, and just one unending, blissful Brahman, then whom will he fight against?

This idea does not exist in Christianity. 'Becoming god' is an impossibility, and even thinking about it is a great crime. There is only one true God, and by the same corollary, there are multiple 'false gods'. And while in Sanatana Dharma, the point is pressed home again and again that Shiva is Vishnu and Vishnu is Shiva; in prophetic monotheism, the greatest crime is to confuse a 'false god' with the one true God. The Biblical God Yahweh himself keeps punishing his own followers whenever they lose their true path and start worshipping the 'false gods'. Yahweh describes himself in the Bible as a 'jealous God' who instantly flies into rage when he sees that his followers are worshipping other 'false gods'.[7] He is truly a tribal deity who is trying to become universal through violent conquests. Greco-Roman pagans who first encountered this 'jealous Christian God' found his character and habits to be extremely distasteful.

> Many Roman and Greek intellectuals had shown profound distaste for such an involved deity. The idea that a divine being was watching every move of every human being was, to these observers, not a sign of great love but a 'monstrous' absurdity. The Christian God in their writings was frequently described as a prurient busybody, a peculiar 'nuisance' who was 'restless, shamelessly curious, being present at man's every act'. Why was He so interested in the every doing of mere mortals? Even before Christianity, sophisticated Roman thinkers had poured scorn on such an idea. As Pliny the Elder had put it: 'that [a] supreme being, whate'er it be, pays heed to man's affairs is a ridiculous notion. Can we believe that it would not be defied by so gloomy and so multifarious a duty?' Didn't a god have better things to do?[8]

Practising Hindus should have the same attitude towards the Christian God when missionaries try to sell him to Hindus based on pure logic. The monotheistic god is also very warlike and violent and wants a complete conquest of all other nations and peoples on earth. It is the nature of the god that decides how the followers will be, and it is no wonder that the history of Christianity and Islam has been full of violent conquests of others. The nature of the monotheistic god is very different from the nature of the divine in Hindu tradition. Shri Ram Swarup says:

> The God of both teaches them to persecute religions other than their own; both are dogmatic, fundamentalist and theological; both lack Yoga or a proper science or discipline of inner exploration; both seek outward expansion; both are aggressively self-righteous; and both by nature know no true theory of peaceful co-existence.[9]

Violence or strife with others is not incidental to Islam and Christianity. The very nature of their god is such that they will inevitably come into conflict with others; his nature is outward-looking, seeking expansion, devoid of any inner dimension, and extremely dogmatic without any means to balance the dogma with any practice.

Prophetism: The Concept of Surrogate Spirituality

The principle of one true God or monotheism is inextricably tied to the idea of the prophet or prophetism. The two concepts are corollaries of each other. The prophet is the mediator between the one true God and his followers. Jesus is the mediator between Yahweh and Christians, and Prophet Muhammad is the mediator between Allah and Muslims. The nature of the monotheistic god is such that he can never directly communicate with any of his followers, either through vision or speech. Muslims cannot see, hear, or communicate with Allah directly by any means. The only way they can do that is through the prophet. Thus, the prophet here becomes even more important than the one true God, because without the prophet, the god does not have his followers, and the followers do not have their god. Shri Ram Swarup says:

> The theory of a single God had a necessary adjunct in the theory of a single Prophet or a Saviour or Interpreter. The two theories have a family likeness and go together. In fact, as the Semitic God was becoming one, he was also becoming exclusive in his communication. Even when he had a chosen people, these people had no direct approach to Him. He told them that He will send them a prophet and 'will tell him what to say and he will tell the people everything I command. He will speak in my name and I shall punish anyone who refuses to obey him.' In due course, the intermediary became more than a medium. In Christianity, he became the Saviour; in Islam, he became the

> Intercessor and also the last Prophet through whom God ever spoke. Claims began to be made on the behalf, claims almost as tall as for the God he represented. In fact, the God tended to become redundant and the intermediary took his place, who in turn was re-presented by his own nominees.[10]

These two interdependent concepts—prophetism and monotheism—are central and indispensable to the religious category we know as prophetic monotheism. All three existing religions of this category—Judaism, Christianity, and Islam—are monotheistic and have the concept of prophet as the intermediary, or the mediator, without whom god's word cannot be conveyed to his followers. This is how prophetic monotheism derives its name.

Of these, Christianity and Islam are basically personality cults based on the personality of the prophets they are centred upon with a very elaborate theory of God to support their claim to prophetism.

The only proof that the prophet is a prophet is that God has ordained him to be so. And the only proof that God exists is that the prophet says so. The Bible says: 'No one knows the Son (Jesus) except the Father (Yahweh), and no one knows the Father except the Son and anyone to whom the Son chooses to reveal him.'[11] In this circular logic, one can very clearly see that the prophet here is even more important than the god. Koenraad Elst writes on the overwhelming importance of prophets in prophetic monotheism:

> At the centre of the Judaeo-Christian tradition stands an institution which we moderns tend to consider as irrational par excellence: the belief that the Creator of the Universe is a person, with personal traits and whims, who communicates messages to us through privileged channels called prophets. This irrational belief mixes up the eternal and the temporal, the metaphysical and the phenomenal. Moreover, it is the foundation of exclusivist claims on divine revelation: it divides mankind

> in those who are in touch with the privileged messengers and those who aren't.[12]

Judaism, the first great monotheistic religion, out of which Christianity was born, had a concept of recurring prophets. Prophets would come from time to time. But Christianity introduced the idea of the 'seal of prophecy'. It meant that Jesus is the 'last prophet' and that no more prophets will come after him. The teachings of Jesus Christ represented the final truth that was revealed by Yahweh to his followers through Jesus.

This was a revolutionary innovation in prophetic monotheism since, with one stroke, it declared that Jesus had the latest and the final version of truth and that there is no possibility of any change or correction to this version of 'truth' since there is no possibility of any prophet coming after him. This concept made all of humankind dependent upon the truth that Jesus claimed to have brought to earth. Jesus as the 'last prophet' became not just central to Christianity but he became the overwhelming personality that outshone God himself. That is why Shri Ram Swarup calls these monotheisms 'religions of proxy', because they cannot work without the intermediary, or the proxy, that is the prophet. 'Here everything takes place through proxy, through an intermediary. Here man knows God through a proxy; and probably God too knows man through the same proxy. The proxy is the favoured individual, a privileged mediator.'[13]

Between Yahweh, the God, and Jesus, the prophet, everything is settled, and 'truth' cannot be found outside this duo. Christian theology makes it inevitable that the one true God communicates only through a proxy, which is the prophet. Sita Ram Goel says:

> The One God remains outside the Cosmos while man remains inside it. Therefore, direct contact between the two is inconceivable. Thus finding man groping in the dark, the One God takes pity on him and, in order to convey his

> commandments to man, he sends his prophets from time to time. Every commandment of the One God revealed by each prophet is unprecedented; it had never been heard before. In this process of history, the One God at last sends his perfect prophet through whose mouth a comprehensive and complete code of commandments of the One God is received by man. This prophet is called the Last Prophet who pronounces the final commandments of the One God, to which nothing can be added and from which nothing can be subtracted. In the revelations by the Last Prophet, the whole truth is incorporated.[14]

However, this sole claim on truth was to be short-lived because, like most other things, Islam copied and one-upped Christianity even in this aspect. Prophet Muhammad claimed that it was not Jesus but he who was the last prophet. It was with him that the God (Allah) had sent his last and final word, and it was with him that the tradition of prophetism ends. His word represents the final and most complete version of truth revealed by God.

Needless to say, these dogmatic ideas lead to violence. And this is what the history of the world has been too. Christianity committed horrible genocides and destroyed native cultures, religions, traditions, and cultures en masse wherever it went. Sita Ram Goel, in his scathing critique of Christianity, *Jesus Christ: An Artifice for Aggression*, says:

> Historians of Christianity saw the Jesus of the gospels inspiring theocratic states which extinguished all human freedoms, church hierarchies which killed and burnt at the stake millions of men and women after denouncing them as heretics and witches, and military missions which massacred whole populations and wiped out whole civilizations in course of the holy wars waged against the heathens in Europe, America, Asia, Africa and the Oceania.[15]

To a Hindu, these ideas seem so alien that they are almost incomprehensible. How can truth be even expressible in any human language? And how can a human institution claim monopoly of truth? Sanatana Dharma maintains that it is impossible for anyone to tell anyone else about absolute truth. It is inexpressible in any human language or any material or intellectual means. The Svayambodha section discussed that India's theory of language itself says that the highest truth remains at *para* level, which is beyond any human language or material means. No one can reach that level with language or linguistics. It is only a matter of experience, and this experience can be accessed in deep sessions of meditation. One can never know truth via proxy.

In the vision of Advaita, there can be no proxies because nothing else exists in the universe but only the supreme consciousness, the divine godhead whom we know as Brahman, Parashiva, Mahavishnu, etc. Sanatana Dharma maintains that it is that one supreme consciousness, the Brahman, which has become many by forgetting its true nature, and thus we all are nothing but the forgotten forms of the same supreme consciousness. In short, we all are 'god', if we want to use that term, and have forgotten our *satya svarupa*, our truest form. When we get to know ourselves, our truest selves, through meditation, we realize that we are nothing but supreme consciousness itself. This state of 'knowingness' is called moksha or nirvana. This realization is so deep in the Indic milieu that one finds this principle repeated not just all over the shastras but also in the folk culture. A very famous *bhajana* '*Ud Jayega Hans Akela*', by a twentieth-century artist Kumar Gandharva goes like this:

> *Guru ki karni Guru jayega … Chele ki karni chela … Ud Jayega Hans akela.*[16]

> Guru will pay for his own karma; *shishya* will pay for his own and in the end the atman will leave this body and will be all alone.

The glory of the guru in Hindu tradition is supreme. No relation is considered to be higher and purer than the relation between the guru and the shishya. The path of moksha is shown to the shishya by the guru only, but even a guru cannot nullify the karma of his shishya, and even a guru cannot himself walk the path of moksha on behalf of the shishya. That the shishya has to do himself. There is no outsourcing here, and not even the greatest of the authorities—the guru—can 'get' moksha for the shishya. He can only show the path and be there at every stage, but the path has to be walked by the shishya himself. 'Sanatana dharma cannot be a proxy religion. It teaches that one cannot live on truths seen by others. It teaches you direct and personal perception of truth. The voices and visions of one man cannot become standard or authority for all.'[17] Here, in pursuit of the highest goal and highest truth of moksha, it is the individual agency that is supreme. No one can do it for someone else. Everyone has to do it himself. There is no outsourcing of karma in Hindu tradition and Sanatana Dharma. We pay for our own karmas, and we have to do all the action that is necessary to achieve moksha.

Prophetic monotheism has no use for this deep spiritual theory and praxis. Instead, it has the concept of proxies or intermediaries whom they call prophets. As both the claims of prophetism and monotheism are exclusive, these two religions are not just fighting with others but also against each other for the sole claim on truth for the past 1,400 years. Due to their exclusive claims, these sects declare every other religion and tradition as false. Both Islam and Christianity claim to be the one true religion, and it is the idea of prophetism that is at the centre of it. Koenraad Elst, in *Psychology of Prophetism*, claims that Biblical prophets might be psychologically sick. Quoting various Christological researchers, he shows how most Biblical prophets suffered from classical traits of egomaniacs who have grand delusions about their own greatness. They start imagining that they are so special that God speaks to them, and they imagine themselves to be the centre of apocalyptic movements. Needing no other proof other than their own mental delusions, they go on a rampage, destroying everything in their path.

> Prophetism has caused innumerable hardships without giving anything valuable in return. Not one of the valuable things in the cultures dominated by it can be traced to their prophetic-monotheistic component. Its source has more often than not been mental darkness. Today, there is no justification for keeping humanity in the mental prison of prophetism any longer.[18]

The Church (in the case of Christianity) and the Ummah (the brotherhood in the case of Islam) are the institutional equivalents of prophetism. The Christians speak about the Church as a singular body, a unity, and an agent with a will and desire of its own. The Church is spoken of in singular as the highest body with the highest authority. Hindus have no parallel institution to 'the Church'. The Hindu temple also has an agency of its own, but every temple has a different individual consciousness, although they all lead the devotee towards the same path eventually. But the Hindus cannot speak of 'the Temple' as the Christians speak of 'the Church' and the Muslims speak of 'the Ummah'. This is because for Hindus, dharma is not just institutions and organizations. Dharma is in practices and experiences and customs. A Hindu will easily take guidance from any jnani, but a Christian cannot even take the word of the most knowledgeable person as truth, as truth is the monopoly of the Church. The Church is the overarching body in Christianity that decides everything, from what the central beliefs of Christianity are to what one can do in Church or at home. Origen, an early church father, said that 'nothing which is at variance with the tradition of the apostles and of the church is to be accepted as true'.[19]

One Life Metaphysics

Another important belief of prophetic monotheism is the belief in only one life. For a Hindu, reincarnation or punarjanma is an axiomatic truth. Entire Hindu cosmology stands on the concept of reincarnation. But prophetic monotheism believes that there is only one life, and after death one goes to either heaven or hell depending upon what his belief was. In Christianity, all non-Christians necessarily go to hell, and only Christians can go to heaven. In Islam, the same concept exists.

Christianity in particular believes in the concept of resurrection and not reincarnation. While Hindu cosmology talks about the unending cycle of life, death, and rebirth, with moksha as the way out, Christianity distorts this pagan concept. Reincarnation was not unknown to the Greeks, and in almost all pagan cosmologies, we can find evidence of the knowledge of reincarnation. Greece, Rome, and Egypt were the cultures that surrounded the birthplace of Christianity, and all three places were aware of reincarnation. There were elaborate myths structured around the concept. Christianity took one myth surrounding reincarnation from Egypt and distorted it. The resulting bastardization is the dogma of Resurrection. While reincarnation is of the ego or atman, Resurrection is a unique event in history in which Jesus rose from the dead not only in spirit but also in flesh and bone. This bodily Resurrection is a central dogma in Christianity.

Christian theology evolved over centuries and adapted to the events and incidents that it encountered. Jesus was originally just a run-of-the-mill Jewish prophet who revolted against the Roman Empire and was given a death sentence by hanging on the cross, which was the standard way of punishing the rebels in the Roman Empire. His followers had to make sense of his death, and 100 years after his death, imaginary tales were concocted to create a theology around it. It was said that Jesus died for the sins of his followers, and this was his supreme sacrifice for those who believed in him. But he could not die, as he was the Son of God, so it was claimed that he rose along with his body in what was the event of Resurrection and then rose and went back to heaven to live with God, the Father, and this event was called Ascension. All of these are central dogmas in Christianity, and every Christian has to believe in them. This is how the Resurrection became a central belief of Christianity. These differences in the Christian vs Hindu/pagan worldview create many binaries, like Resurrection vs reincarnation, salvation vs moksha, etc., and they have a deep impact on their respective societies.

In Hindu culture, moksha is not a gift given to the chosen people by an exclusive god. Moksha is something everyone has to get for himself. Nobody can do it for others. What it means is that the individual has his destiny completely under his control. He can choose to get out of the cycle of birth and death by doing meditation under the guidance of a guru and achieve moksha. It is this individual agency and control that is missing in prophetic monotheism.

Monotheism does not have the concept of moksha. It has the belief of salvation. And salvation is not something one can do oneself at all. There is no individual agency in Christian and Muslim salvation. Salvation has to be done by someone else, and that someone else is none other than the prophet. In fact, the only thing a person has to 'do' is to have 'correct belief'. Action has zero importance in monotheism. All that matters is 'correct belief', and correct belief is nothing apart from the belief in the dogma of Christianity and Islam.

In fact, not just salvation, even sin is committed by someone else on the poor common man's behalf. Adam did the original sin, and Jesus 'repented' and 'atoned' for that. The dogma of 'original sin' is tied inextricably to 'atonement'. Adam sinned, and Jesus saved on behalf of all Christians to come. Both sinning and saving had nothing to do with the individual action of common Christians. For a Christian born after Christ, there really is no choice. Both the sinning and saving had been done in the past. The only thing he has to do is to declare his acceptance of the Christian dogma and the myths of original sin and atonement by Jesus. In such a one-life worldview, there can be no moksha, only 'salvation', which is gifted by a capricious god.

It is not hard to see that compared to a follower of a dharmic sect like Hindu dharma, Christians and Muslims are at the complete mercy of the intercessionary powers of their prophets. One can only hope to 'believe' in Christianity and hope that in the end Jesus will choose to send one to heaven and not hell. This worldview, originating from one-life metaphysics, has a serious impact on world history, culture, and ecology. One-life metaphysics leads to extremes of behaviour. In contrast, the theory of karma-phala-siddhanta makes one very responsible in all conditions, even when one is alone without anyone watching, because the fear of incurring 'bad karma' is always lurking in one's mind. But in a monotheistic worldview where one's actions have nothing to do with the consequences that depend entirely on one's belief, there is extreme irresponsibility about one's actions.

Killing infidels in jihad, or heathens in Crusades, was so easy for Islamic jihadis and Christian crusaders because there was no fear of incurring bad karma for killing someone or engaging in violence against someone for no reason other than that they had a 'wrong belief'. Once they were assured heaven on the basis of their belief and belief only, no violence or depraved behaviour was unthinkable. Just like sinning and saving were outsourced to the prophets, so was responsibility. The only thing one had to do, like signing a paper, was to have 'correct belief' in the one true religion. To a conscientious individual, this outsourcing is a terrible thing, but for criminals and scoundrels, it is a clean chit that they could use to just 'wash away their sins' instantly.

The first Christian Roman emperor, Constantine, did just that—outsource repentance of his sins to Jesus. It is said that Constantine was always a despicable man. Before he converted to Christianity, he had done unimaginable acts of cruelty to his own family members. Suspecting that his wife had an affair with his son, he had his wife slowly boiled to death in his own bath. But then he wanted to 'feel good' and wanted to 'wash away his sins'. The pagan gods, of course, did not comply, for what he did was despicable, and it was not something that could be washed off. But Christianity was ready to convert a scoundrel like Constantine by promising him that his 'sins would be washed away instantly' and the only thing he had to do in return was to 'convert to Christianity', the only true religion, and then force everyone under him to convert too. We are running a little ahead of our story, but the outsourcing of sinning and repentance was a brilliant invention of Christianity. It encouraged the most hardened criminals, and still does, to convert to Christianity. In turn they had to provide their services to persecute non-Christians and promote Christianity, which they easily did being what they were.

On the front of ecology too, one-life metaphysics had a very bad effect. The Bible says there is just one life, and the world is created for the consumption of god's chosen people. This is why any kind of exploitation is alright in Christianity, because animals and plants are born for exploitation. In the post-Renaissance world, this highly irresponsible Christian worldview became global when Christian conquistadors invaded and conquered new countries and continents, destroying local flora and fauna in a never-ending orgy of destruction of nature. Having no view of many lives, and no understanding of pancha rnas and particularly bhuta rna, led to ecologically irresponsible behaviour in the Judeo-Christian Western world and Islamic world. While a

Hindu is responsible to all creatures in the universe, including insects, for a Christian, nature exists solely for the consumption of man. Sita Ram Goel says:

> As a consequence of the One God remaining outside, whatever there is in the Cosmos is material and man has unhindered right to use it all. Therefore, with the decline of Christianity in the Western countries, there erupted a volcano of materialism and consumerism. The natural resources began to be ruthlessly exploited. The incurable epidemic of consumerism which is pushing the world towards destruction today, had its seed in the Monotheism of Christianity.[20]

This attitude did not subside when Christianity declined in the West. When atheism became prominent, it rejected some claims of Christianity, but not all. Mainly it rejected the salvationary powers of Christianity but did not re-establish the concepts of reincarnation and multiple-lives value systems that existed in the pre-Christian pagan Europe. It was also almost impossible for them to revive those pagan concepts because they were not mere concepts for pagans and rested on long-established rituals and practices. Unable to revive the old, Enlightenment Europe continued with one-life metaphysics and made it even more destructive and irresponsible.

For if there is just one life and if one is in a position to enjoy the material benefits of life as much as possible—mainly food and sex—then why not do that? If there is nothing after death, then why care how the future is going to look? If nothing continues beyond death, then why care if the planet will remain livable after one's death or not? This is the argument of most 'development evangelists' like Hans Rosling, who think that no sustainable vision of the future should stop luxuries in present time, even if it means destruction in the future.

Socially speaking, one-life metaphysics discourages individuals from taking up responsibilities and duties. They think that having family and kids is an unjust burden on themselves and an unnecessary hurdle in their pursuit of pleasure. This leads to widespread nihilism, irresponsible social behaviour, and the breakdown of family and ancient traditions. Eventually, a life full of hedonistic pursuits and devoid of meaning results in a pandemic of depression. The modern West is currently facing this pandemic, and depression is becoming more common in all regions that are adopting the modern lifestyle.

The ecological crisis that is upon us today is also a direct result of one-life metaphysics, rooted in the Christian worldview. The Bible gives man dominion over nature, and the one-life metaphysics removes all fear of retribution. 'Everything that lives and moves about will be food for you. Just as I gave you the green plants, I now give you everything.'[21]

It is this Christian worldview that has resulted in the current ecological crisis in the world. On the other hand, a dharmic worldview supported with multiple-lives metaphysics and karmic theory will bring up responsible individuals who will care for both nature and culture. A pancha rna worldview takes care of nature as well as culture. Any traditional society like Sanatana Dharma treats man as one species among many. His speciality comes only from his ability to reflect upon oneself, to meditate, and to contemplate the deepest secrets of the universe. We have seen how deeply ecological the Hindu point of view is. But the Biblical worldview makes one treat nature as a resource to be exploited. This sense of entitlement has resulted in unsustainable use of nature, and the ideology of conquest has resulted in rampant destruction of ecology and ecosystems.

Judgement Day, Heaven, and Hell

Concepts of heaven and hell are not exclusive to prophetic monotheistic religions but also exist in Sanatana Dharma. The Puranas too mention hells and heavens—of various kinds—but they are not permanent.[22] Heaven is a reward for good karma, and hell is a punishment for bad karma. However, since no action is infinite, its reward or punishment also cannot be infinite, and consequently, any stay in heaven or hell is temporary. After going through the punishment or reward of one's acts, one is back in the cycle of life and death. The only permanent way out is to get moksha. In that path, heaven is far from the highest reward. It is actually an impediment, as it is said to neutralize one's good karma. One who does not accept heaven keeps climbing to the higher states of consciousness and ultimately gets moksha.

In prophetic monotheism, judgement is not based upon one's actions. People are judged for their belief. Belief here means belief in 'Christian truth'. Any failure to believe in the Christian truth is considered an unimaginable sin of infinite proportions. Infinite sin can only incur infinite punishment, and that is what the Christian hell is for. Anyone who denies either Christianity or Islam is committing the gravest sin possible and is thus consigned to everlasting hell.[23] This hell has no end, and sinners (non-believers) are punished for eternity. Descriptions of hell in the writings of Christian scholars are nothing short of those in modern horror movies, full of blood and gore. Unbelievers are boiled or skinned alive, and when there is no more skin, they are given fresh skin, and the process continues. This is just one of the many tortures described in the eternal hell of Christianity.

Heaven too is permanent in Christian theology. The idea behind the concept of permanent heaven and hell is related to Judgement Day. It is believed that on Judgement Day, Prophet Jesus will come and judge all that were ever born, and while he will put good Christians in everlasting heaven, non-Christians will all be in everlasting hell. This 'second coming' of Jesus is said to usher in the 'Kingdom of God' or the 'Kingdom of Heaven on Earth'. It is only possible after the Judgement Day. Islam believes that on the day of *Qayamat*, when the world ends, Prophet Muhammad will send Muslims to *Jannat* (heaven) and non-Muslims to *jahandum* (hell). Both of them are everlasting. Shri Ram Swarup, in his magisterial study of the Muslim mind, *Understanding Islam through Hadith*, traces the inspiration of Muslim behaviour in Islamic law Shariat, which is based on collections of eyewitness accounts of the prophet, collectively called Hadith:

> After the believers and the unbelievers are sifted and sent to their respective abodes, the chapter is closed forever. Allah would admit the inmates of Paradise into Paradise and the inmates of Hell into Hell. Then the Announcer would stand between them and say: O inmates of Paradise, there are no death for you. O inmates of Hell, there are no death for you. You would live forever therein (6829).[24]

The reward for an unthinking, completely believing Christian is life in an everlasting heaven where he will undergo the same material pleasures as he can have on earth, but in unlimited quantity and forever. Descriptions of heaven in Christianity and jannat in Islam are quite imaginative, and one should read them in detail. Descriptions of jahandum are also equally scary. Shri Ram Swarup quotes the related Hadith: 'In caloric heat, the fire we know here on earth is only one-seventieth part of the Fire of Hell (6811).There would be among them those to whom Fire will reach up to their ankles, to some up to their knees, to some up to their waists, and to some up to their collar-bones (6816).'[25] The extraordinary barbarity and brutality of the imagination that conceived everlasting torture is beyond the mind of a Hindu. But that is what motivates and scares believing Christians and Muslims. Even from the point of view of one-life metaphysics, eternal hell seems an indescribably barbaric idea.

But can someone redeem oneself? It turns out that yes, there is a concept of redemption in Christianity. But it is not available to non-Christians. It is only for Christians who have sinned but have also come back to 'faith', which is Christianity. To these repentant Christians, redemption is available. Redemption is possible only when there is acceptance of the Christian claim of 'truth'. Without this show of belief and faith in Christianity, redemption is impossible. Since non-believers go to hell just for their lack of belief, it is impossible that any amount of torture can nullify their lack of belief. This makes redemption impossible for them, and thus they are consigned to eternal hell. The exclusive claims of Christianity necessitate an extremely barbaric and intolerant worldview.

Linear View of Time

Christianity prides itself on being a 'historical religion' since it began at a certain time in history. Islam begins on the date when Prophet Muhammad receives the Quran in revelation. Thus, they both have a specific beginning in history, and that is why they have a linear view of time. Christians believe that God created the universe in the past and that every event that ever happened was leading up to the great moment when Christianity began. After the death of Christ, believing Christians are waiting for the Last Judgement when Jesus comes again, ends the existence of life on earth, and begins the Kingdom of Heaven where Christians will experience everlasting pleasures in heaven. Islam has a parallel theology.

The Christian worldview sees time as an arrow, as the universe was claimed by Christian scholars to have begun around 6,000 years ago, and every event that happened before the birth of Christ was just leading towards his birth and the advent of Christianity. Christianity is thus seen as a unique and unprecedented event in history, in this linear view of time. This view had many consequences. Every event before and after the birth of Christ was interpreted with a Christian lens. The resulting distortion affected not just pre-Christian but post-Christian history too. While the world before Christ was waiting for his rebirth, the world after Christ is waiting for his 'second coming', or the Judgement Day.

When this worldview abandoned its overtly Christian moorings during the Enlightenment, it did not go back to the circular view of time that used to exist in the pagan cultures. While Christianity asked to wait for Christ's second coming for the Kingdom of Heaven to arrive on earth, the Enlightenment philosophers claimed that heaven on earth can arrive without the second coming or the Judgement Day. The reason their movement itself is called Enlightenment with a capital 'E' is because they claimed that any salvation or absolution can be achieved materialistically on this earth with the new-found resources that colonial Christian conquistadors had found in the new world.

The Industrial Revolution was based on this philosophy of maximizing the material pleasures of human beings on this earth with the help of science and technology. Christianity had already taught its followers to view the pagan past as the Age of Darkness and the Christian future as the Age of Light. Secular Enlightenment just eliminated the goal from this future by deleting the Christian *telos* (goal) of Judgement Day and made progress eternal and goalless. In other words, while the goal of Christian 'progress' was to progress towards the Judgement Day and stop at heaven, the goal of material 'Enlightenment' was to keep progressing for its own sake without any full stop in the future. The Christian arrow of time used to stop at Judgement Day. The Enlightenment arrow of time shot into an infinite future with finite resources.

On the contrary, the Hindu view of time is circular and believes that cycles come and go, and sometimes good becomes dominant and sometimes bad. Yugas go in cycles: Krita (Sata) Yuga becomes Treta Yuga, Treta Yuga becomes Dwapara Yuga, Dwapara Yuga becomes Kali Yuga, and after Kali Yuga, the cycle starts again, and the Krita Yuga or Sata Yuga comes again. This does not mean that everything will be repeated exactly as it is, but the sense conveyed is that there are cycles, and time is circular.

This view changes the entire perspective of man. What is behind you is also ahead in a circle, and thus not everything in the past is dark, and not everything in the future is bright. Civilizations rise and fall. Regress is as common as progress. This attitude is also conducive to the karmic view where one's karma begets results in the next birth, which leads to more karma and then rebirth. A cycle commences, and the only way to break that cycle is to attain moksha, which is liberation from the cycle of life and death. Moksha is beyond time, as Brahman is not subject to time. Just as time and space were born with the Big Bang, and thus the question 'What existed before the Big Bang?' is irrelevant, similarly, 'What happens after moksha?' is meaningless, as there is nothing beyond moksha.

While Christianity is self-consciously plotted on a timescale, any natural religion[26] like Sanatana Dharma is beyond time. Because Christianity and Islam have a linear view of time, they also take pride in their 'historicity'. Rajiv Malhotra calls them 'historical religions', which means that these religions claim a specific beginning in history. Their central dogma revolves around this historical event. Rajiv Malhotra says:

> The Judeo-Christian traditions, in contrast, depend on the historical revelations of prophets who speak of the collective destiny of whole peoples and of humankind. The human condition stems from an act of disobedience or 'sin', beginning with the 'original sin' of Adam and Eve, the forbears of all humanity. Every individual is born a sinner.[27]

Followers of Christianity and Islam think the Hindus are inferior because Sanatana Dharma does not have a particular beginning in a particular time, and it is not even a religion because it does not have a specific beginning. While for a Hindu, what is inferior is to have a beginning in time, because anything that begins also has an end. The arrogance of 'being historical' is deep in Christianity and Islam, and it is because they are both personality cults, and the dates when they began are related to the lives of the prophets or persons at the centre of these personality cults.

Divided Time, Place, and Humanity

Prophetic monotheism believes in a strict division of time. The time before the advent of Christianity is the Age of Ignorance, because the Bible containing 'knowledge' had not been revealed by then. The age after Christianity is known as the Age of Knowledge or Age of Light since the prophet has revealed the 'only true knowledge' in the Bible. Islam maintains that the time before Islam was revealed to Prophet Muhammad is the Age of *Jahiliya* (the Age of Ignorance), and the time after that is known as the Age of *Ilm* (the Age of Knowledge). This shows us the attitude of monotheism towards everything ancient and traditional.

The world is also divided into *Darl-ul-Islam*, the abode of Islam and peace, and *Dar-ul-Harb*, the land of perpetual war, as any non-Muslim land, like India, has to be fought and converted to Islam. It is the sacred duty of all Muslims to turn all Dar-ul-Harbs into Dar-ul-Islams. Christianity also believes that the sphere of Christendom has to be increased, and the 'good news' (by which they mean only the Bible and the Christian religion) has to be taken to everyone forcefully. Both the sects believe that the entire world was meant to be their property and is bestowed on them, the chosen people, by their exclusive and partisan god. Thus, it is their right to fight and take away others' lands in the name of Jesus Christ or Prophet Muhammad, because they dearly believe the earth was their own land.

Similarly, humanity is also divided into two groups, the 'in-group' and the 'out-group'. For Christianity, all Christians are in-group, and all non-Christians are out-group. All Muslims for Islam are in-group, and all non-Muslims are out-group. As Sita Ram Goel says:

> Two events take place after the advent of the Last Prophet. Firstly, the history of mankind gets divided into two periods. The period before the coming of the Last Prophet, becomes the period of darkness or ignorance, and the period thereafter the period of light or knowledge. No mode of worship or cultural heritage or social custom of the earlier period remains valid, and a complete destruction of whatever prevailed earlier is considered conducive to salvation of mankind. Secondly, after the coming of the Last Prophet, mankind is divided into two groups. One group is that which professes complete faith in the Last Prophet and begins to follow the path shown by him. The other group is that which professes doubts regarding the Last Prophet or repudiates him. The first group becomes dear to the One God, and the second invites his wrath. The One God commands the first group to wage ceaseless *jihad* against the second group, and either make that group submit to the Last Prophet or annihilate it altogether.[28]

Prophetic monotheism has the concept of 'one true god' but no vision of a united humanity. This does not mean that dharmic traditions do not have the idea of a social or political 'other'. They do as they should because just as this book proposes, one cannot defend one's sociopolitical and cultural formations if one does not have an idea of boundaries and what is 'in-group' and what is 'out-group'. But at the same time, we should all be aware that ultimately we are all part of the same supreme consciousness, and no being in the universe is outside its realm. Prophetic monotheistic religions, however, have no concept of an *advaitic* unity, and thus internal human divisions seem supreme to them, and they tend to transpose petty human politics onto the character of their god. This is why the monotheistic god is angry, jealous, and cruel, and humanity stands ripped apart in irreconcilable and mutually hostile camps.

This division of humanity between 'believers' and 'non-believers' is so extreme that moral and ethical rules exist only for the 'in-group' and not for the 'out-group'. Islamic law is very clear that believers and non-believers are to be treated very differently, and all ethical laws of charity, compassion, and brotherhood are for Muslims only; non-Muslims are not to be covered by any humane laws. Non-believers are so dehumanized that the believers think that they are sub-humans. Shri Ram Swarup illuminates this inhuman division, which is central to the imagination of any believing Christian or Muslim:

> Paganism has multiple Gods but believes in one humanity; Semitic religions have one God but at least two humanities: believers on one hand and unbelievers or infidels or heathens on the other. The division is not just social, or racial, or cultural; it is metaphysical. Believers owe nothing to infidels, not even ordinary ethical behavior. The Quran requires that Muslims 'are vehement against misbelievers, but kind amongst themselves'.[29,30]

Conversion: Why Prophetic Monotheism Is Dangerous for Others

One of the most central concepts and institutions of prophetic monotheism is conversion. Judaism, the oldest religion of this kind, does not seek converts anymore. In the ancient times it converted, but only the 'chosen people' of Israel. It did not convert non-Israelites. Christianity changed all of this when it brought a revolutionary new concept: the idea that Christians can and should convert anyone to Christianity, irrespective of ethnicity, nationality, and religion.

From the point of view of dharmic traditions like Sanatana Dharma, this is the single most dangerous invention ever made. This is because the agency of conversion makes it possible that Christianity grows at a great pace and can completely destroy a pagan religion by converting every last one of its followers to Christianity. This is what Christianity did in Europe in the first millennium, and in North Africa and West Asia. In the second millennium, it first converted North America and South America at gunpoint and then proceeded to convert Central and Southern Africa to Christianity in the eighteenth and nineteenth centuries. As the pope declared in 1999, the focus of the third millennium is on Asia, and most centrally on converting India and Hindus.[31] And he had the audacity to say this in India, about India, on the occasion of Deepawali: 'Just as the first millennium saw the cross firmly planted in the soil of Europe, and the second in that of America and Africa, so may the third Christian millennium witness a great harvest of faith on this vast and vital continent.'[32]

The pope was actually indicating to his forward soldiers, the missionaries of thousands of Christian sects, to redouble their energies to convert India and China. Hindus did not even understand what was being said properly because they did not have the agency and tool of conversion, but every Christian all over the world understood the call of the pope, which was no less than a call for war. That is why conversion is the most lethal invention of Christianity.

Judaism had a hatred of all the religions that came before it. Its god, Yahweh, was jealous, cruel, and partisan. Early Jews carried an unjustified superiority complex and hated the followers of other religions. But as they did not seek converts outside Israel, their mental perversions were their own. It is Christianity that made these perversions global by inventing the concept of conversion or proselytization. It did not just start accepting converts; it aggressively went to convert the most disaffected sections of Roman society of that time, like criminals, slaves, and other such classes. At the same time, they were targeting the elites and succeeded in converting the Roman emperor Constantine to Christianity, which turned the tide in its favour. Very soon, Christianity became the dominant religion of Rome and Greece through forceful conversions and the wholesale destruction of the classical pagan religions of these regions.

While Judaism introduced most of the central concepts of prophetic monotheism, Christianity became global by an aggressive conversion agenda, and Islam added one more layer of orthodoxy to it by keeping the Quran strictly as the law book. Thus, their spiritual book was also their law book, and there was no distinction between civil law and religious law. Along with all the tenets of prophetic monotheism and with the conversion agenda of Christianity, Islam also had a very strict legal system in which Islamic law Shariat ruled every aspect of life. This is the reason that Islam is the most aggressive of all mutations of prophetic monotheism.

There is a deep reason why conversion or proselytization is so central to the prophetic monotheistic religions. They have no inner dimension where an individual following them can take an inward journey and change oneself from within. There is no scope for inner growth, and hence the urge to grow, to change, is turned outwards towards what they consider as 'enemies', which is all those who do not subscribe to their brand of religious ideology. Shri Ram Swarup says:

> In India's spiritual tradition, a faulty vision (*prajna-aparadha*) is considered a great poisoner ... in the absence of a true science of interiority, Christianity took to an ideology of physical and outward expansion. It holds good for Islam too. They both have faced an inner problem—the problem of an undeveloped spirituality. This has constituted danger to the rest of the humanity as well.[33]

Christianity also believes that it is the sacred duty of Christians to convert every single person on earth to Christianity, as the Last Judgement is dependent on it.

> Jesus Christ has bequeathed to his Church all unbelievers as its inheritance and all parts of the earth as its possession. At the same time, he has forfeited the life, liberty, honor and property of all unbelievers in favor of the faithful. It is obligatory on the Church to convert all unbelievers, by all means at its disposal at any time and place. The world should thus be prepared for the Second Coming of Christ which is always imminent, though the exact time is unrevealed. Christ will finally conquer all unbelievers and establish his Kingdom over all nations for a thousand years.[34]

At the start of the twentieth century, when the British Empire was at its height but when already the beginnings of the end could be seen, various Christian churches, missionaries, and theologians agreed that the European military power might not last forever, and thus it was very critical that the Church become completely independent in its agenda of world conversion. Many meetings were held in the United States of Christian missionaries and theologians from many sects across the world who met and agreed that the only way for Christianity to survive was to embrace wholeheartedly the agenda of world conversion, or the absolute conversion of the entire world. Douglas Clyde Macintosh writes in 1914, on the eve of the First World War:

> If the Christian propaganda is justifiable at all, it is not this world-evangelization that we must chiefly think of, or regard as the end; the end is world-Christianization, ultimately, and proximately, world-conversion. Except for the sake of world-conversion, world-evangelization is meaningless. Except upon the basis of world-conversion, world-Christianization is impossible.[35]

The author is responding to say that evangelization (which means introducing the offer of Christianity) to everyone is not enough, and conversion (which is the actual conversion) is necessary, and thus Christians cannot wait for centuries to let individuals accept the message of Jesus Christ; they have to hurry it by whatever means possible. And he is supported by the Bible, which says that the 'final command' of Jesus was: 'All power is given unto me in heaven and in earth. Go ye therefore, and teach all nations, baptizing them in the name of the Father, and of the Son, and of the Holy Ghost. Teaching them to observe all things whatsoever I have command you.'[36]

Jesus commands Christians to convert all non-Christian individuals, groups, and countries to Christianity in the Bible. The colonial, missionary, and predatory nature of Christianity cannot be any clearer. This missionary drive for the conversion of every single non-Christian to Christianity is inevitable in a religion where there are professional missionaries whose job is to convert non-Christians. For if they stop converting, they are out of a job, and thus to exist and continue their lifestyle and privileges, which they get as a missionary, they need to keep converting the entire world and keep finding newer and newer people to convert.

It is not unlike a virus, which has to find a new host body to survive. Once it infects a body, that body is mostly doomed to death, and as soon as the host dies, the virus tries to find a new body to infect and continue its life cycle. It is critical that viruses are not considered living beings, but they have the inbuilt mechanism to propagate themselves without being alive. One can say that the similarity with a prophetic monotheistic religion is very uncanny here.

It also has a lot of similarities with the modern economy. For a modern economy to exist and to be sustainable, it always needs to grow. Any stop in growth means death. It is a very monotheistic idea, and it is not surprising that it comes from a Judeo-Christian cultural background. The entire thrust of modern corporate is to keep finding newer and newer markets to sell their products after 'saturation' arrives in one market. This is the very same urge that is at the core of Christianity: the urge to grow at the expense of others. It is also a wonderful way to embed proselytization in the very design of one's own religion, because conversion of others is critical to existing as a Christian, and thus, just to exist and continue as Christians, they need to convert or fund conversion activities. Islam also believes in the same theory and practice.

Hindus, just by being Hindus, are directly in the path of Muslims going to jannat. That is why it is incumbent upon Muslims to convert Hindus. This is the reason that no Hindu can afford to be ignorant about Islam or Christianity.

For we may not be interested in Islam, but Islam is interested in us.

And so is Christianity. 'Jesus loves you,' the Church says, and this sentence means that since he 'loves someone', that 'someone' has to convert to Christianity. And the Church will not leave someone alone until he converts to Christianity. Jesus Christ here sounds like a stalker who will not relent until his unrequited love is reciprocated back through conversion to Christianity.

For you may not love Jesus, but Jesus loves you and will not relent until you love him back.

The goal of converting the entire globe is central to the existence of Christianity and Islam. For the sake of their own religion, they need to convert us, and thus Hindus cannot afford to remain ignorant about the nature of Islam and Christianity. Conversion or proselytization is a sufficient reason for a Hindu to be interested in Christianity and Islam. We need to know them, for they want to convert us.

Islam aggressively seeks the conversion of others, but it never allows Muslims to leave Islam. You can accept Islam but can never leave it. Leaving Islam is punishable by death according to the Islamic law Shariat. Islam has no exit doors.

'Once a Muslim, always a Muslim' is not just a convention; it is a law followed in Islam. Combined with the conversion agenda, this rule of no exit makes sure that the numbers of Islam always increase as it keeps gaining more and more Muslims through conversion and a higher rate of reproduction but never loses Muslims to other religions, as the act of leaving Islam is brutally punished by death.

To sum up some beliefs of the three monotheistic religions, Judaism is monotheistic and prophetic, but it does not have the concept of the last prophet or the 'seal of prophecy'. It also does not seek converts anymore, and hence its beliefs are its own without much impact upon the outer world. But for the ancient Jews, the Bible was also the law book. Old Jewish laws were thus not very different from Islamic law.

Christianity came upon the scene and made some fundamental changes to the belief system it had imbibed from Christianity. First, it universalized Christianity by opening it up for conversion to everyone. Judaism converted only the Israelites but not the Romans or Greeks. Christianity opened conversions up to Romans, Greeks, and, by extension, everyone else in the world, becoming 'universal' or 'catholic'. This was the single most revolutionary innovation of prophetic monotheism, where Christianity's conversion drive became a global pandemic. With the conversion of the Roman emperor to Christianity, it got hold of the resources of one of the largest empires of those times. Christianity introduced the missionary element to prophetic monotheism. Until Judaism, the ideas of monotheism, prophetism, and iconoclasm were limited to Israel and the Jews, but now these ideas were threatening all the established traditional dharmas and pagan religions all over the world. However, the New Testament did not declare itself a law book, and scope was left to create secular and canon laws in later stages.

Islam was the last and the most potent combination of prophetic monotheistic ideas since it was not just prophetic, monotheistic, and iconoclastic, but it was also missionary and sought converts. But it was one step further in fundamentalism and orthodoxy, as its holy book also doubled up as the law book, and thus it was much easier in Islam to institute religious law in every sphere of life. It also had no separation of religion and State, as Prophet Muhammad was also a military commander, and thus religious, military, and civil authorities were all combined in him and, after him, in the institution of the Caliph.

Iconoclasm

An important feature of all prophetic monotheistic religions is iconoclasm. The word means 'destruction of images and icons of "false" gods and goddesses, which are considered heretical'. If a sect believes that there is only one true god, with there being only one prophet to whom the god conveys 'final truth' and every other god or form is a 'false god', some natural derivations are inevitable. Add to this cocktail of faith the belief of Judgement Day and the incumbent duty upon all believers to convert everyone else in the world to their religion. And you have an inevitable consequence—iconoclasm. Shri Ram Swarup writes: 'They (monotheists) have believed that demolishing the images on an altar, particularly in the temples of their neighbors, is the best way of worshipping their God and it is the service most acceptable to him. The impeccable hostility towards "other" Gods is the most important part of their *sadhana*.'[37]

Iconoclasm was central to Judaism too. The Old Testament is full of iconoclastic verses. Jews were also iconoclasts and destroyed all the icons of all gods other than Yahweh inside Israel. They were not doing something against their religion because Judaism commanded in the Bible that they shall destroy the 'idols' of other gods, and being dogmatic people, they followed these injunctions of the Bible literally. 'Thou shalt not bow down to their gods, nor serve them, nor do after their works: but thou shalt utterly overthrow them, and quite break down their images.'[38]

Christianity was also iconoclastic, and its tales of iconoclasm are told in detail by various authors, including Catherine Nixey. When Christianity took over Greco-Roman culture, the pagan religions in this region suffered an unprecedented loss. Its gods and goddesses were banned, their temples and icons brutally destroyed. The same story was repeated all over North Africa and Western Europe. Shri Ram Swarup says that iconoclasm is not one aspect of monotheism, but they are the two sides of the same coin:

> Semitic My-Godism described as Monotheism has another dimension: Iconoclasm. In fact, the two are two sides of the same coin. When worshippers of the Semitic God came into Contact with their neighbours, it was not clear what they abhorred more, their Gods or their idols. In point of fact, they made no such fine distinction. Trained as they were, they made war on both indiscriminately.[39]

When Christianity reached the New World, the native religions of the Americas were destroyed, and the icons of the Mayan, Aztec, Inca, and other gods and goddesses were brutally destroyed in a fit of iconoclastic rage. The same process was repeated wherever Christianity went. Its record of iconoclasm is no better than that of Islam. 'Christianity and Islam have engaged in large-scale destruction of temples of others through the centuries. Both have thought that to serve their God they have to demolish the temples of their infidel neighbors and demolish the images of their Gods.'[40]

Islamic iconoclasm is a well-known fact. Islam began as a great iconoclastic religion with Prophet Muhammad himself destroying more than 300 icons of Arabian gods and goddesses upon his occupation of Mecca. Ever since Islamic armies left the sands of Arabia, Islamic soldiers have been destroying temples and others' places of worship as their sacred duty, because 'idolatry' is a great sin in Islam, and *kaffirs* are accused of great idolatry. It is considered the sacred duty of Muslims to forcibly stop the idolaters, like Hindus, from worshipping 'false gods' and walking on the 'path of the devil' by destroying their 'dens of ignorance and idolatry'. They followed the same pattern of iconoclasm that they had started in Arabia, as Sita Ram Goel states in his magisterial study, *Hindu Temples: What Happened to Them*:

> It is, however, recorded history that the armies of Islam did everywhere what had been done in Arabia, as they advanced into Iran, Khorasan, Transoxiana, Seistan, Afghanistan and India. Hundreds of thousands of Fire Temples of the Zoroastrians, Buddhist monasteries and Hindu temples disappeared or yielded place to mosques, ziarats and dargahs. Modern archaeology, has reconstructed what happened along the trail of Islamic invasion of all these ancient lands.[41]

The record of Islamic iconoclasm in India is unmatched. This history of the destruction of Hindu temples is told with glee by Islamic historians themselves, as destroying the '*butkhaanas*' (temples) of 'idol worshippers' was a religious duty for Muslims. Muslim historians tell this story without any sense of regret but with a sense of great pride that the religious duty that is incumbent upon every Muslim is being fulfilled by the Islamic invaders in India and elsewhere. Islamic kings themselves were proud of their destruction of temples and others' places of worship. Mahmud Ghazni is praised in *Tabqat-i-Nasiri* for destroying Hindu temples like this:

> He was endowed with great virtues and vast abilities, and the same predominant star was in the ascendant at his birth as

> appeared at the dawn of Islam itself. When Sultan Mahmud ascended the throne of sovereignty his illustrious deeds became manifest unto all mankind within the pale of Islam when he converted so many thousands of idol-temples into masjids and captured many of the cities of Hindustan. He led an army to Naharwala of Gujarat, and brought away Manat, the idol from Somnath, and had it broken into four parts, one of which was cast before the centre of the great masjid at Ghaznin, the second before the gateway of the Sultans palace, and the third and fourth were sent to Makkah and Madinah respectively. Mahmud's coins struck at Lahore in the seventh year of his reign describe him as the right hand of the Caliph and the breaker of idols.[42]

It was the history of the destruction of Hindu temples by Islamic invaders and the rape and pillage that spread in the wake of it that led Will Durant to issue the statement that the history of the Islamic invasion of India is the bloodiest chapter in the history of mankind. Islamic iconoclasm became a little better known in India due to the Ram Janmabhoomi movement. In the run-up to the movement, Sita Ram Goel collected a group of historians and archaeologists who gathered evidence, mainly from archaeological, epigraphical, and literary sources, to create a preliminary list of Hindu temples that were destroyed by the Islamic invaders. The number obviously runs in multiples of lakhs, as thousands upon thousands of temples were destroyed in every single district. The group came up with a preliminary list of around 2,000 temples, but Sita Ram Goel calls it the tip of an iceberg, hinting at the actual number of temples that were lost due to the destruction that the Islamic invaders heaped upon India. It is impossible to even summarize the sad history of the destruction of Hindu temples by faithful Muslims. In the end, it would be pertinent to see what the modus operandi was whenever Islamic invaders destroyed Hindu temples, as described by Sita Ram Goel in detail:

> 1. The idols were mutilated or smashed or burnt or melted down if they were made of precious metals; 2. Sculptures in relief on walls and pillars were disfigured or scraped away or torn down; 3. Idols of stone and inferior metals or their pieces were taken away, sometimes by cartloads, to be thrown down before the main mosque in (a) the metropolis of the ruling Muslim sultan and (b) the holy cities of Islam, particularly Mecca, Medina and Baghdad; 4. There were instances of idols being turned into lavatory seats or handed over to butchers to be used as weights while selling meat; 5. Brahmin priests and other holy men in and around the temple were molested or murdered; 6. Sacred vessels and scriptures used in worship were defiled and scattered or burnt; 7. Temples were damaged or despoiled or demolished or burnt down or converted into mosques with some structural alterations or entire mosques were raised on the same sites mostly with temple materials; 8. Cows were slaughtered on the temple sites so that Hindus could not use them again.[43]

This is perhaps the sorriest tale in the history of arts and culture. It breaks the heart of a Hindu who visits these temples all over India, in his own country, only to find that almost every single one of the ancient temples has been destroyed by the Islamic invaders. He is unable to grasp the magnitude of the tragedy as he shifts his eyes from one *murti* to another and finds that every single one of them is desecrated. Some of the most beautiful vigrahas are beheaded. Goddesses are the special target of the fury of the Islamic invader, and the breasts are extraordinarily mutilated. Lakhs upon lakhs of vigrahas in a temple, every single one of them destroyed. Lakhs upon lakhs of temples in Bharatavarsha, and almost every single one of them destroyed. Iconoclasm is no aberration in Islam; it is its central tenet. If Islamists ever come to power in India, all Hindu temples will not be a week's purchase.

Belief vs Action

Mohammed Ali Johar, one of the two Ali brothers, was a 'freedom activist' in pre-independence India who was also a fundamentalist Islamist. He was far from a terrorist or an extremist in the sense that we understand today, and yet he made a comment on Mahatma Gandhi that should send a chill down the spine of Hindus and tell them exactly what the nature of Islam is. Commenting on Gandhi, Mohammed Ali said:

> However pure Gandhiji's character may be, he must appear to me from the point of view of religion inferior to any Mussalman, even though he be without character. Yes, according to my religion and creed, I do hold an adulterous and a fallen Mussalman to be better than Mahatma Gandhi.[44]

Fanaticism and barbarism of the comment aside, Mohammed Ali is stating a fundamental concept of Islam here in very clear terms. From the point of view of a good Muslim, the worst Muslim man is better than the best Hindu man. The pyramid of a Muslim man's priorities in life is being made very clear here. No matter how good a Hindu is, he will always remain inferior to the worst of Muslims, for he is a kaffir (the hated non-Muslim), and until he accepts the one true religion of Islam, he cannot be absolved of his sin of being born as a Hindu. Ali Johar's statement was not an individual opinion. He was just voicing the belief of Islam and Muslims. The Quran, the holy book of Islam and Muslims, confirms this:

> Do not marry polytheistic women until they believe; for a believing slave-woman is better than a free polytheist, even though she may look pleasant to you. And do not marry your women to polytheistic men until they believe, for a believing slave-man is better than a free polytheist, even though he may look pleasant to you.[45] (Quran 2:221)

Harsh Narain, one of the greatest Hindu scholars on Islam, said: 'The Quran teaches that a Muslim slave is better than an idolater, howsoever good the latter appear to the Muslims.'[46] Because for them, individual action means nothing. All that is important is what someone believes in. To be more specific, all that matters to them is what religion someone believes in. Shri Ram Swarup also stresses how dogma is central to the prophetic monotheistic religion of Islam, as he gleaned from the Islamic law books of Hadith:

> In religions where theology is supreme, moral action occupies a secondary place. A man is justified by faith; he is already one of God's elect or damned long before he is even born. Muhammad anticipates Luther and Calvin by a thousand years, 'None amongst you would attain salvation purely because of his deeds,' Muhammad says (6760). 'Observe moderation' in your doings, he advises; but if you fail, 'try to do as much as you can do and be happy for none would be able to get into paradise because of his deeds alone' (6770). It is not God's grace that wins salvation but either the atoning death of His only son or the intercessory power of His last Prophet.[47]

This pyramid of hierarchies is very clear to Muslims. Their Shatrubodha is their Svayambodha, as they cannot conceive of themselves without a conception of the other, and due to this it is easy for them to have a clear Shatrubodha. And in that Islamic pyramid of Shatrubodha, the best of the Hindus occupy the lowest rungs of priorities, lower than the worst Muslim. Harsh Narain talks about the status of Hindus in the Islamic list of priorities:

> Are idolaters unclean in body, in faith, or in both? According to Imam Malik as also to Hasan BaSari, idolaters' body is unclean, so that, if an idolater put his hand into water, the water would become unclean. On the contrary, according to the Hanafites,

> idolaters are unclean in faith. And there is a third school, led by Anwar Shah Kashmiri, according to whom idolaters are unclean in body and faith both. He claims that even Imam Abu Hanifah subscribes to this view when he rules: 'If a Kafir falls into a well, all its water will have to be drawn out, even though he is pulled out of the well alive.'[48]

The non-Muslim idolater is at the bottom of the pyramid for believing Muslims. He is the filthiest of all creatures and is dirty in every sense of the word. Hindus are considered the 'worst of the idolaters' since they worship 'everything'. Even then history was such that while all other opponents of Islam got destroyed in a matter of a few years or decades, Hindus kept standing even after centuries of Islamic rule and came out as majority inhabitants of the Indian subcontinent in 1947. This increases the hatred of the Hindu even more in the hearts of fanatical Islamic believers. Ayatollah Khomeini, one of the most fanatical Shia leaders and thinkers ever to be born, said this about the 'unclean idolaters':

> Eleven things are unclean: urine, excrement, sperm, blood, a dog, a pig, bones, a non-Muslim man and woman, wine, beer, perspiration of the camel that eats filth. The whole body of a non-Muslim is unclean, even his hair, his nails, and all secretions of his body. A child below the age of puberty is unclean if his parents and grandparents are not Muslims.[49]

The meta-principle behind this is of central concern to us here: In Islam, actions are completely inconsequential; belief is not just necessary; it is also sufficient. It is so because no amount of good action will nullify the lack of belief in Islam here. No matter how many good actions a Hindu does, he cannot become better than a Muslim because his belief is incorrect as he has not accepted Islam. Conversely, no number of evil actions on the part of a Muslim will make him worse than a Hindu, for his belief is correct as he is a Muslim. Action here is not less important but completely inconsequential since no amount of action can nullify lack of belief. Consequently, the only thing that is important in prophetic monotheism is blind belief. That is why these religions are so dogmatic.

This is the most fundamental difference between a prophetic monotheistic religion on one hand and a dharmic tradition on the other. Belief vs action is the difference between religion and dharma. Dharma stands upon action, while religion stands upon belief.

This dependence on belief or dogma was not an invention of Islam, like most other things. It was an invention of Christianity. One of the most central concepts of Christianity is the idea of 'original sin', and the highest Christian authority of the Vatican says:

> By his sin Adam, as the first man, lost the original holiness and justice he had received from God, not only for himself but for all humans. Adam and Eve transmitted to their descendants human nature wounded by their own first sin and hence deprived of original holiness and justice; this deprivation is called 'original sin'. As a result of original sin, human nature is weakened in its powers, subject to ignorance, suffering and the domination of death, and inclined to sin (this inclination is called 'concupiscence').[50]

The theory is: since man has been corrupted due to the 'original sin', he has to atone for this ancestral crime. But he cannot do this himself. Someone else has to 'atone' for him. This someone else is none other than the Son of God, Jesus Christ. Christian theology claims that Jesus Christ atoned for the sins of his followers, the Christians. Just like 'original sin' was outsourced to Adam, its 'atonement' was also outsourced to Jesus Christ. While Adam sinned for man, Jesus atoned for him. Man, in this entire process, was completely helpless, without any agency or control over his actions. Sinning and repenting were both out of his hands. They were professional matters to be handled only by 'divine experts' like the Church. Just like we outsource jobs today, Christianity outsourced both sin and repentance millennia ago. In effect, it invented outsourcing, just like it invented marketing.

This outsourcing was not accidental to Christianity but central to its design. If the Church were to preserve its role as the mediator between Christians and God (being the vehicle of Jesus Christ), it could not leave repentance and redemption to individuals. If individuals could repent and redeem themselves, what was the necessity of the Church, and by extension, what was the necessity of Jesus himself? One could reach God on his own. But as discussed above, prophetic monotheistic religions cannot do without mediators. While he lived, Jesus Christ was the mediator and held supreme power. After his death, his powers passed on to an institution—the Church. The Church was in institution what Jesus was in person—a mediator. To keep power centralized under the Church, it was made impossible for individuals to do repentance or redemption on their own. Even for such a deeply personal act as repentance, it was the Church who did it for them. This forced outsourcing of sinning and repenting to the Church made the Church supremely powerful.

But none of this would work until action was rendered inconsequential and dogma took its place. For if action could redeem someone, then once again everything would be decentralized since action is in the control of individuals and not only of the Church. The Church made dogma or belief centrally important and rendered action completely unimportant. Since dogma meant only the Christian dogma and belief meant only the belief in Christianity, this act made the Church supremely powerful by giving all agency of 'repentance' by 'belief in Christ' to the Church itself and not to the individual.

Another element of Christian belief was that Jesus had atoned for the sins of not only the followers of his own time but for all time to come. It ridiculously means that Jesus did not only atone for the sins of the past but also for the future. All those born after the 'atonement' would also be redeemed of their sins, but only if they believed in Christ. In other words, people could continue to commit sin and every kind of crime. They would be redeemed if only they believe in Christ. This means that if a person goes and commits murder and right away converts to Christianity after the murder, then he has great chances of going to heaven. Any crime that any potential convert commits is already 'atoned' by Jesus Christ, that is, only if he completes his promise of conversion to Christianity.

From this point on in history, the entire concept of sin and remorse was altered. Before the advent of Christianity, man was judged on the basis of his actions. Christianity started judging on the basis of belief. Hence, a man who did good deeds all his life but did not believe in Christ would still be considered evil and burn in hell forever. On the other hand, a person who committed all sorts of crimes in his life but believed in Christ would go to heaven. His sins would be forgiven, as his belief in Christ would wash away his crimes.

Action was rendered completely inconsequential. Belief became not just necessary but also sufficient.

This stress on 'belief' and total disregard of action, practices, and experiences by Christians caught the eyes of the pagan Greek observers too. Galen, the great Greek physician, believed that debates solved many problems, but with Christians, he found that debates did not work as they did not at all bank their logic on either experience or rational logic. Catherine Nixey quotes Galen's disappointment where he records the peculiarity of Christians' overwhelming stress on belief and only belief:

> There was, however, one group of people who even the great Galen found himself unable to convince. This was a group

> who did not form their beliefs by basing them on experiments or on observations, but on faith alone—and who, worse still, were actually proud of this fact. These peculiar people were for Galen the epitome of intellectual dogmatism. When he wished to adequately convey the blockheadedness of another group of physicians, Galen used these people as an analogy to express the depths of his irritation. They were the Christians.[51]

Islam just followed Christianity in this. Dogma is necessary and sufficient in Islam. Actions are inconsequential. To believe in the message of Prophet Muhammad is necessary, and it makes little difference whether one is a good person or not. That is the reason why Mahatma Gandhi was worse than the worst Muslim for Mohammed Ali Johar.

This is the most critical difference between prophetic monotheism, like Islam and Christianity, on one hand, and dharmic traditions like Sanatana Dharma on the other. The binary of belief vs action, dogma vs practices, and beliefs vs customs represents the distinction between religion vs dharma or religion vs tradition.[52]

People of the Book

One of the most distinctive and important features of prophetic monotheistic religions like Islam and Christianity is that they call themselves 'People of the Book'. This is a term that is incomprehensible to a Hindu. Why would some people be called 'People of the Book' and why would others not be that? The Hindu gets even more bewildered when he gets to know that Hindus are not considered People of the Book and only Christians, Muslims, and Jews are included in this term! Hindu dharma has created the greatest body of literature that ever existed in any tradition all over the world in the entire history of mankind, and yet the followers of a desert religion with hardly any literary history are included in the definition of the People of the Book, and Hindus are not. It is natural for a Hindu to get flabbergasted and not understand the dogma of the People of the Book. It is something so counter-intuitive and distant from his experience of life that it becomes completely incomprehensible for him. So let us try to understand what this concept means.[53]

The monotheists (all three) believe that truth is not something to be attained by practice. Rather, it is something that has been revealed by the 'only true god' to his 'chosen believers' through the intermediary, the prophet, at a certain point in time in history. This 'truth' is expressible in human language, as is evident from its 'revelation' to the prophets by their only god. Unlike dharmic traditions, where truth is inexpressible in any human language, including Sanskrit, the monotheistic traditions believe the opposite. They think that it is perfectly possible for truth to be expressed in human language. To Jews it was expressed in Hebrew, to Christians in Aramaic, and to Muslims in Arabic. The dogma is that the 'truth' was revealed to a prophet once in history and is recorded in a particular book.

The Bible is the record of the Judeo-Christian dogma in human language in book form. Similarly, the Quran is the record of the Islamic dogma. For each of these three monotheistic sects, this 'book' is the final 'word of God', which is unchangeable and incontrovertible. For Jews and Christians, all that is ever to be known is there in the Bible, and humans need not read any other book. For Muslims, all that ever needs to be known is in the Quran, and humans need not go to any other source to find 'truth'. From the Christian point of view, if someone has read every other book in the world but not 'the Book', that is, the Bible, then he has read nothing and he knows nothing. Vice versa, if he has read the Bible and accepts its dogma and claims, then even if he knows nothing else, it is okay since he has read the only book that ever should be read. Muslims have the same attitude towards the Quran. For them it is not just another book; it is 'the Book' with a capital 'B'.

This is why they refer to themselves as the 'People of the Book'. No matter how many books Hindus have, none of them is 'The Book' that contains the 'Word of God' directly (as per the monotheistic point of view). And while Jews, Christians, and Muslims have rival claims to truth, they accept that all three of them are 'People of the Book' since god's word was revealed to them directly through prophets, even though every sect claims that the other two sects distorted the 'word of god' later. They consider the three sects as better than the horrible 'idolaters' like Hindus, the rank polytheists like pagans who worship 'false gods', do not have a beginning in time, do not have the concept of prophets, and do not have 'revelation' or 'word of god'.

Hindus in this way are at the bottom of the monotheist pyramid. They are the worst kinds of idolaters who idolize 'anyone' and 'anything'. Most influential Islamic schools of jurisprudence allow only two options to Hindus in an Islamic State: conversion to Islam or death. Hindus were subjected to unending genocide because of this 'law' in Islam. However, since killing all of the Hindus was a technical impossibility due to their great number, another school of jurisprudence was applied in some parts of India, and Hindus were allowed to exist as Hindus for the time being, but with serious disabilities.

They had to pay a tax for staying Hindu. This tax was apart from all other taxes that the State usually extracts from its subjects. It is the sacred duty of every Islamic ruler to convert his non-Muslim subjects to Islam in his kingdom by force or by any other means. However, not all non-Muslims are treated equally. Greater respect is given to the dogmatic sister religions of Christianity and Judaism, which are considered 'People of the Book' and hence better than rank idolaters and polytheists like Hindus. The People of the Book can stay non-Muslim and practice their own religion in private if they pay a certain tax. This tax is known as *jizyah*.

Hindus did not have this luxury. Under most Islamic schools of jurisprudence, including the one that should have been technically applied in India, Hindus had only two options: conversion to Islam or death. However, due to the sheer impossibility of killing crores of Hindus, another Islamic school of jurisprudence was applied in India, and jizyah tax was applied on them. This tax of 'being Hindu', jizyah, is nothing but protection money that Islamic rulers took from their Hindu subjects in return for 'protecting' them from their own Islamic tyranny. It is not very different from the 'protection money' that the mafia in any contemporary city like Mumbai takes from the shopkeepers and anyone who wishes to function in a great city. Jizyah is recommended by the Quran:

> Those who do not believe in Allah and the Last Day—even though they were given the scriptures, and who do not hold as unlawful that which Allah and His Messenger have declared to be unlawful, and who do not follow the true religion—fight against them until they pay tribute out of their hand and are utterly subdued.[54]

Jizyah had many goals. Firstly, it was a means to reconcile reality with Islamic dogma. In other words, when it was impossible to either convert or kill all non-Muslims in an area, an explanation, a way out, had to be concocted to explain the discrepancy between the theory and reality, and jizyah was that way out. Secondly, jizyah was a means to encourage non-Muslims to convert to Islam. It was a 'punishment for unbelief'.[55] Non-Muslims had to pay a heavy tax of jizyah in order to stay non-Muslim. But if they converted to Islam, they could stop paying jizyah and start staking claim to war booty, which is called *ghanimat* in Islamic law.[56] Narain says that it was a fiscal means to motivate conversions to Islam: 'The long-term policy behind it appears to be to compel or motivate the Dhimmi-s slowly to turn to Islam and embrace it. They were let live in the hope of their conversion in course of time. It is thereby a camouflaged engine of repression.'[57]

Thirdly, it was meant to humiliate non-Muslims and Hindus for 'being Hindu' so much so that ultimately they relent and convert to Islam, and thus put an end to the incessant humiliations due to their own dharmic practices and due to their 'lack of faith in Islam'. There were many disabilities imposed on Hindus under jizyah. Fiscal loss was not the only one. Hindus could not prevent Muslims from forcefully entering their private meetings, even their homes. They had to dress in an inferior manner and had to bear the badge of being a 'third-class subject of the Islamic State' on their dress. One should remember that Hitler also forced Jews to wear a distinctive badge to declare their Jewish origin. This led to the easy identification of Jews when massacres of Jews by Germans started. In India, this was a daily fact of life for Hindus under jizyah.

Hindus could not bear arms, of course, and could not ride horses or other pack animals. They could not wear jewellery or practise their customs and practices in public or in Muslim presence. They could not cremate their dead near Muslims and even had to mourn their dead in private. Jizyah was the instrument of the Islamic State to render Hindus non-citizens. The rules to pay jizyah also included elaborate rules to humiliate the Hindus who were paying this tax. The *qazi* (Islamic cleric) of Alauddin Khilji recommended to him: 'If the *jizyah*-collector asks a Hindu for silver, the latter should offer gold in all humility. If the collector wishes to spit into his mouth, the latter should open his mouth without demur, so as to enable the former to spit into it.'[58]

How long would a population bear financial burdens as well as the burden of constant and unending social humiliation of this abject kind? It is not the 'promise of equality of Islam' that encouraged many Hindus to convert to Islam, as many leftists claim.

It was the extremely back-breaking nature of the jizyah tax that finally convinced many Hindus to convert to Islam so that they could end their status as the perpetually humiliated third-class non-citizens in their own country.

Lastly, jizyah was imposed to destroy and obliterate all traces of the religion or dharmic tradition that prevailed in a certain country where Islamic rule had come to be established. Because under jizyah, Hindus could not build any new temples or repair the old ones, this law led to the unprecedented damage to the Hindu temples of Bharatavarsha. Temples, like any other building, need constant repair, and in the absence of any such repair for centuries, a majority of Hindu temples fell under irreparable damage and decay. Hindus could not even repair the temples damaged by the Islamic invaders and other Muslims. This law stayed even in the case of any temple damaged after the implementation of jizyah, meaning that if in an Islamic State within India, any Muslim damaged a temple or a vigraha, then the Hindus were not allowed to repair it and could just helplessly watch it getting desecrated, destroyed, and damaged. This clause of jizyah ensured that the temple ecosystem of Bharatavarsha would suffer a permanent setback.

Non-Muslims: Squatters on Muslim Lands

> The Muslim psyche is of a peculiar making, vis-a-vis its attitude towards non-Muslims. According to the Prophet, every child is born in Islam, but its parents make it a non-Muslim. The Quran declares the Muslims to be the best community and raised up to guide and govern humanity as vice-regents of God on earth, and Islam to be the chosen religion destined to triumph over all other religions. The Quran also says that the earth belongs to Allah. 'He causes it to be inherited by whom of His servants He will.' On the basis of it all the Prophet rules that all land belongs to God or himself, the natural corollary being that all

> land belongs, through God and the Prophet, to the Muslims. In their bid to conquer Spain, a contingent of the Arabs under Tariq landed on its shores and Tariq burnt the ship which carried them. On the soldiers' protest as to how they would return to their homeland, Tariq burst out, in Iqbal's words: That is, 'All land belongs to us, because it belongs to our God.' This serves to vouchsafe to the Muslims the moral right to grab lands in *Jihad* from non-Muslims. Indeed, as Ibn Taymiyyah, the 14th-century Muslim jurist-theologian, would have it, *Jihad* simply restores lands to the Muslims, who enjoy a kind of Divine right over these.[59]

The above lines by Harsh Narain excellently summarize the psyche of Muslims vis-à-vis the land and property of non-Muslims. Hindus believe Islam to be 1,400 years old. This would be confirmed by most objective historians, but this is not what the Muslims believe. They believe that every child is born Muslim because the oldest religion is actually Islam. Allah had sent his message before anyone else, but his message was distorted by Jews and Christians and hence he sent his best and last prophet, Prophet Muhammad, to correct and finalize his revelation.

On the basis of this absurd claim, Muslims argue that theirs is the oldest religion, and that Prophet Muhammad just corrected and purified the message sent by Allah earlier. This makes Islam the oldest religion and every other religion an imposter. It also makes the followers of other religions, even before the advent of Islam, *mushrik*, or those who have 'quit Islam'. Quitting Islam is a cardinal sin in Islam and is punishable by death. This is also one of the reasons that killing non-Muslims in jihad is legal tender for Islamic fighters. They are the ones who 'betrayed the final Word of God' and thus are the scoundrels of the worst kind. To treat them harshly is only a religious thing to do for a good Muslim. This logic also dictates that when someone converts to Islam, he is not converting but 'reconverting' as everyone is originally a Muslim.

V.S. Naipaul, in his travels in Indonesia, met an Islamic revolutionary who was converting a new couple to Islam and was reiterating the same principle: 'We welcome you back to Islam. Back to Islam, because in our belief everyone was born as a Muslim, without sin. You have come back to Islam because you have opened your heart to the truth. In everything submitting yourself to the will of God. Islam means submission.'[60]

Just like the Muslim claim of Islam being the oldest religion, they also believe that all earth with all its flora and fauna was bequeathed to Muslims by Allah. Thus, all land legally belongs to Muslims. This makes every non-Muslim an illegal occupier of Muslim lands. We, the Hindus, along with all other non-Muslims, are thus illegal squatters on Muslim lands. This is why it is quite 'legal' for Muslims to dislodge us from the land that was bestowed on them by their beloved Allah. Absurd as it may seem, belief is everything in Islam. Belief is law too. Their belief becomes their law, and they believe that Hindus have no right to their ancestral property or anything earned by them since everything on earth already belongs to Muslims. Thus, any land that Muslims gain in jihad is not an 'unjust' grabbing of non-Muslim lands. It is the 'recapture' of originally Muslim lands on which non-Muslims had come to squat.

While this is the underlying belief, Muslim society also knows how to navigate through modern law, as in non-Muslim countries they have to live under 'secular law'. However, even in this case, Islamic law has inbuilt strategies to continue grabbing non-Muslim lands. Land acquisition for Islam, like conversion to Islam, is a one-way process. Just like the rule of 'once a Muslim, always a Muslim' works in the case of individual conversion to Islam, once a land comes under Muslim control, it is forever to be under Muslim control. This right of Muslims on a certain piece of land is called *waqf*. To take care of the 'legal rights of Muslims', there is a Waqf Board in India, and it oversees that any land that Muslims take, legally or illegally, has to be forever under Muslim control. Just like conversion, land too is converted to a 'waqf land' in Islam and never can revert to non-Muslim control.

Entire India is considered waqf land in another version of Islamic belief, since India was once ruled by Islamic kings. It unfortunately went back to the 'hated idolaters', and thus it has to be 'recaptured' by faithful and good Muslims, as India is legally Muslim land. This is what they believe. And this is the psyche of Islam and Muslims. As everything in Islam is dogma, this dogmatic belief that all land belongs to Islam is fanatically followed by believing Muslims. Like most other dogmas, this too is not an invention of Islam, and long before Islam, Christianity had perfected the art of claiming antiquity for itself.

Contrary to what barbarian Christian monks wrote about the pagan Roman Empire, it was religiously a very tolerant place. In the pre-Christian world, every sect worshipped its own deities, had their own ways of worship but did not disrespect or dishonour others' deities and traditions. Religious fanaticism was an invention of Judaism and Christianity. The Roman Empire was not just respectful of others' deities; it was proud to say that in the empire everyone was free to worship any deity they liked.

Jews and Christians were the only 'sects' that were objected to by the Roman pagans. But why? Because Judaism and Christianity were not natural religions and Jews and Christians were seen by the pagan Romans as very odd and strange people. Jews were the first people and first sect whose followers would openly say that all other deities were 'false deities' and worshipping them was 'sin'. Roman pagans were shocked to hear that a deity could be a 'false deity' or 'false god'. They could understand that Jews were different, and they did not bother, for they were very tolerant of diversity. What they could not understand was why the Jews could not reciprocate the diversity of the Roman pagan milieu, and why they abused Roman gods, customs, and practices. In later times, Christians were seen with the same suspicion. Christians were mostly seen as just another Jewish sect from the strange, deity-abusing land of Israel.

This is why the Romans asked the Jews to prove their validity as established tradition and old religion. Romans, like any pagan sect, respected antiquity, and any custom or practice that was continued for thousands of years was worthy of respect and protection. They asked the Jews, how old is their 'tradition'? S.N. Balgangadhara and Divya Jhingran capture the reply of the Jews to the Roman question of proving antiquity:

> The Jews appear to have met this charge in two ways: Firstly, by showing that the Jews were a people with a history; and secondly, by laying claims to great antiquity. They argued that they were more ancient than the Ancients themselves. They claimed that Greek legislators had actually plagiarized the Mosaic Law and Heraclitus stole his theory of opposites from Moses 'like a thief'.[61]

Just like Muslims claim that Islam is the original religion and that other religions stole from it, here, Jews too claimed antiquity by arguing that theirs was an ancient sect and it was actually the pagan Greeks who stole from Judaism and not the other way around. The Jews played a trick against the pagan Greeks. They just showed how Moses was older than Homer (one of many Greek poets) and thus claimed antiquity, and by claiming antiquity, they argued that their deity-abusing sect was also an established and old 'custom' and 'practice' back in Israel.

The Romans accepted the deity-abusing sect of the Jews as Jews made them believe that this was the 'tradition' in Israel, and Romans accepted and respected any sect that could show that it was a time-honoured tradition. Romans would never go against any practice that existed for centuries. They were right to have this attitude with most other pagan sects (natural religions) because they all shared a common culture and common idea of respecting the traditions of others. But they made a critical mistake in accepting a monotheistic religion that believed in destroying every other natural religion, thus starting the beginning of the end of Roman paganism. We have evidence of what went on in the minds of the Greco-Romans while negotiating with the Jews and Christians. It is enlightening to read the thought process of the second-century CE pagan Greek philosopher Celsus, who was a great opponent of Judaism and Christianity and yet accepted their right to do as they pleased, something which was never reciprocated by either Jews or Christians:

> The Jews became an individual nation, and made laws according to the custom of their country; and they maintain these laws among themselves at the present day, and observe a worship which may be very peculiar but is at least traditional. In this respect they behave like the rest of mankind, because each nation follows its traditional customs, whatever kind may happen to be established … and it is impious to abandon the customs which have existed in the locality from the beginning.[62]

The high culture of Greece is very evident here. First, Celsus is respecting any nation's right to self-determination in case of customs and practices. No matter how weird they seem to Celsus as a Greek, he is willing to respect them since it is a different 'nation'. This was despite the fact that Celsus had a very low opinion of Jews and thought that the Bible was 'utter trash'. Second, he does not like or prefer anyone abandoning their ancient tradition, customs, and practices, no matter what they are. Continuing traditional practices is a great value for him, even if those practices are alien and disgusting.

The third point is very critical, as it shows that if we fail to identify the ideological enemy and if we do not have good enough Shatrubodha, it leads to our own demise. Celsus accepts the claims of the Jews that they are more ancient than the Greeks and accepts them as a 'tradition', ignoring all the evidence that they are a completely new sect that is not traditional at all and that aims to destroy others' customs and practices. Celsus knows that this Jewish 'tradition' actually destroys all other established traditions and natural religions, and that is why accepting this new religion will lead to the destruction of all other original and true traditions and pagan religions. But he fails to see the danger and practices tolerance with an intolerant sect, ultimately leading to the death of the tolerant sect itself. The Shatrubodha point to remember here is that one should practice tolerance only with a tolerant sect or group. Tolerating intolerant sects destroys tolerance itself.

No open society can afford to entertain an ideology that is not open. No tolerant culture can tolerate an intolerant sect. No free society can allow an ideology that aims to destroy all freedom.

The Jews, in order to get their deity-abusing dogma accepted as a valid 'sect', had to claim that it was their practice back home in Israel, the origin place of Jews and Judaism. And by claiming that their religion was much older than the Greco-Roman pagan sects, they established antiquity and at the same time hoped to be accepted as a 'tradition' by the pagan Romans. And Romans did accept that.

In hindsight it was the most serious mistake in the history of humankind. Had they not accepted Jews in the Roman Empire, there would be no Christians in the Roman Empire, and their peculiar and deity-abusing sect would have died its natural death. Without Judaism or Christianity, Islam could never have been born, and the world would be free of prophetic monotheism altogether. But this did not happen, as we all know.

The Christian story was different altogether. They did not have the luxury of claiming antiquity like Jews because Jesus Christ was not just born in front of Romans; he was also killed by the Romans for rebelling against the Roman Empire. It was impossible for Christians to claim antiquity if they considered

Jesus Christ to be their cult leader. And while Jews abused others' deities and customs, Christians abused Jews too, along with every other Roman pagan tradition. So, the Christians were thought to be without any 'tradition' or without any way of worship. They were quite frequently referred to as 'atheists' in early Greco-Roman accounts.

Christians were the first atheists.

This might sound counter-intuitive now but was very logical to Roman pagans in the second century CE. The world had only witnessed traditional dharmas like Sanatana Dharma before Judaism and Christianity entered the scene. In the sense in which Christianity was a 'religion', the world was quite unaware of it. With no established practices or customs of their own, and the habit of abusing all pagan gods and refusing to offer sacrifice to them, they were called 'atheists' by ancient pagan Romans. The Christians were so strange that they were known as 'people without deities', or 'without customs, rituals, and rites', or 'atheists', in other words. Porphyry, a Greek philosopher of the third and fourth centuries CE, remarks on Christians:

> How can men fail to be in every way impious and atheistical, who have apostatized from those ancestral gods by whom every nation and every state is sustained? ... (They have not adhered) to the God who is honored among the Jews according to their customary rites, but (have) cut out for themselves a new kind of track ... that keeps neither the ways of the Greeks nor those of the Jews.[63]

Christians had to prove their validity as a valid religious sect without having any antiquity or any traditional practice. They found a way out by claiming that one does not need to be traditional in order to be religious, and religion does not necessarily have to be transmitted through generations as an ancestral practice, but it can be invented anew as in it can be 'revealed' suddenly by God to his set of 'chosen people'.

Christians said that their 'philosophy' was older than the Greeks and other pagans and that Christianity was 'the first, most ancient, and most primitive of all religions'. Instead of proving their customs or practices very old (which they could not since they did not have any), they proved that their philosophy, or 'belief or dogma' was the most ancient, and hence they were the oldest of all sects. We have seen that for Christianity, 'belief' was all that mattered, and since in their minds their 'belief' or 'dogma' was the most ancient, they were also the bearers of the most ancient sect. This claim was repeated by one Christian author after another, and gradually people started to believe in it.

This is how Judaism, Christianity, and Islam turned the pagan/dharmic/Hindu question on its head: When accused of coming late to the scene of 'religious tradition', they claimed that their dogma was the most ancient, and hence it is the pagans and Hindus who were the usurpers of tradition, not them. It was a remarkable feat of skullduggery, but the monotheists were adept at it from the very beginning. For Hindus, this history is relevant because it shows how important dogma is to the monotheists. In all these 'disputes', practice was not something the Jews and Christians were even remotely concerned with.

Heresy, Inquisition, and Misogyny

Any system that is just based on blind belief is bound to have the concept of sin defined in the terms of lack of belief. Heresy—the lack of belief or the loss of belief—is a central concept in prophetic monotheism and is considered a great sin. At first, Christianity was on a winning spree in Europe, and all one needed to 'convert' to Christianity was to renounce the old gods and embrace 'Jesus Christ as the savior'. But once all of Europe was converted to Christianity, more severe demands were put on Christians. They had to 'prove' their faith in Christianity, and whoever failed to 'prove faith' was punished horribly. Those who were found guilty of not having 'enough belief in Christ' were tortured and killed brutally by the Church. Entire tribunals were set to find out 'heretics' (those with false or rescinded belief in Christianity) and punish them. Christian monks of the Dominican, Jesuit, and other orders were sent to every corner of Christendom to seek out heretics and punish them to make an example out of them. This chapter in the history of Christendom is known as the Inquisition. The foundation of the Inquisition was, of course, the Bible: 'He who blasphemes the name of the Lord shall be put to death.'[64]

Inquisition turned an established custom of law upside down. Normally, under any system of law, the accused is assumed not guilty or innocent until the crime is proved. The Inquisition turned this custom on its head and declared that whomever the Christian Church accuses of heresy was guilty until proven innocent. Any such accused could be punished at the will of the holy inquisitor, who was none other than a high-ranking Church official. This inquisitor was answerable to no one but only to the pope, and he was the judge, jury, and executioner all rolled into one. If there ever was a kangaroo court, the Christian Inquisition was one. The Church sent these inquisitors to every corner of Europe and hunted any dissenter out and killed them brutally. A 'trial' was held to prove that the accused was indeed a heretic. Helen Ellerbe writes about the farce that this trial used to be:

> Despite an ostensible trial, inquisitional procedure left no possibility for the suspected to prove his or her innocence; the process resulted in the condemnation of anyone even suspected of heresy. The accused was denied the right of counsel. No particulars were given as to the time or place of the suspected heresies, or to what kind of heresies were suspected. A suspected friendship with a convicted heretic was also a crime.[65]

This is often the only way to support a dogmatic faith, a blind belief. As it has no truth in it, violence becomes necessary to defend this falsehood. That is why Christian monks justified extreme violence when they destroyed pagan Greece, as one of the Christian monks St Shenoute said: 'There is no crime for those who have Christ.'[66] Until Europe had many pagans, the focus was to convert the pagan non-Christians, but as soon as no more pagans were left in Europe, the Church turned on its own, the Christians, for the Christians themselves started discovering that Christianity's claims were false and started abandoning it. To stop this massive bleeding of Christianity when it met truth and reality check, the Inquisition was instituted, which used unimaginable torture to force any dissenter to stay quiet, and soon they started burning heretics alive.

> The harshest sentence of burning at the stake was given to those who either failed in their previous penance, relapsed into heresy, or who would not confess to any crime. Although the Church had begun killing heretics in the late fourth century and again in 1022 CE at Orleans, papal statutes of 1231 now insisted that heretics suffer death by fire.[67]

Can a Hindu imagine a Shankaracharya or the head of any other Matha issuing orders to kill Hindus because they are not Hindu enough? A Hindu cannot imagine this. Hindu dharma is based on experiences and practices and not blind belief or dogma, and thus any fundamentalism is weeded out by any wise man, someone whose prajna is awakened. On the other hand, any religion that focuses only on dogma and not on action is bound to descend to this level. Today we see that Islamists exhort Islamist lobbies to kill any non-Muslim or a Muslim who is accused of heresy in public. We are witness to many lynchings in public on the accusation of blasphemy even today and even in 'peaceful secular nations' like Bangladesh.[68]

Christianity in mediaeval Europe was more 'methodical' and consequently far more 'sadistic'. In mob lynching, the agony of the victim lasts for a few minutes and maybe an hour or so, but the Christian missionaries and Church priests and monks who became inquisitors were far more sadistic. They could not just let the victims be killed in a mob lynching. They were also more given to 'law and order' and the 'rule of law', and just so they could kill the non-Christians and heretics at will, they changed the law. The accused had to 'confess' that he had indeed 'left Christianity' or committed a sin that was forbidden in the Bible. If he did not confess right away, then he was tortured horribly to force him to confess under torture. Before finally killing a victim, who was accused of 'heresy' or just for not being a Christian, he would be sometimes tortured for days and for weeks. Mediaeval chroniclers themselves have left many accounts of this torture, initiated, encouraged, and sanctioned by the pope and the Church. Helen Ellerbe recounts:

> Thus, with license granted by the Pope himself, inquisitors were free to explore the depths of horror and cruelty. Dressed as black-robed fiends with black cowls over their heads, inquisitors extracted confessions from nearly anyone. The Inquisition invented every conceivable device to inflict pain by slowly dismembering and dislocating the body. Many of these devices were inscribed with the motto 'Glory be only to God'. The rack, the hoist and water tortures were the most common. Victims were rubbed with lard or grease and slowly roasted alive. Ovens built to kill people, made infamous in twentieth-century Nazi Germany, were first used by the Christian Inquisition in Eastern Europe. Victims were thrown into a pit full of snakes and buried alive. One particularly gruesome torture involved turning a large dish full of mice upside down on the victim's naked stomach. A fire was then lit on top of the dish causing the mice to panic and burrow into the stomach. Should a victim withstand such pain without

> confession, he or she would be burned alive at the stake, often in mass public burnings, called auto-da-fe.[69]

Thousands of men and women were burnt alive by the Church for they were not 'Christian enough'. This is not just a part of European history. India and Hindus too suffered from the Christian Inquisition. The Inquisition reached Indian shores too with the arrival of Christianity. The Portuguese started the Goan Inquisition in 1560 CE, and it lasted until 1812 CE. More than 17,000 Indian converts to Christianity were thus tried for not being 'Christian enough', and seventy-two were burnt alive by the Goan Church. It seems laughable to a Hindu that a religion that just arrived and converted would also start killing those same converts for not being Christian enough, but the beliefs of prophetic monotheism are strange enough.

In India, however, the direct genocide of Hindus was limited to the Portuguese enclaves and mostly in Goa. The rest of India survived the genocide by Christian powers because Portugal was limited to a handful of enclaves on the Indian coast, and Spain never reached India, two of the most genocidal Christian countries. India was subjected to the tyranny of the British, whose method of conversion was most often indirect. This is also the reason that Christianity is seen as a 'good religion' in India, as the Church is very clever in hiding its genocidal history, and gullible Hindus are ready to believe whatever the Church says because they consider it to be just another dharma, under the illusion of sarva-dharma-samabhava.

There is another chapter of Christian Inquisition that should be mentioned in brief here: 'The Genocide and Destruction of Native Americans.' Most of the 'Americans' today are not really Americans but Europeans who settled in North and South America after the genocide of more than 95 per cent of the pagan natives who lived there. The Christian Inquisition reached the Americas after Columbus 'discovered' the Americas for European Christians so that he could 'convert the heathen Indians to our Holy Faith'.[70] As soon as the Americas were 'discovered' by Europeans, the Church started calling for 'saving the native pagans from hell' by 'converting them to Christianity', and if they refused to do so, they were killed. A Christian jurist of those times, Encisco, writing in 1509, says:

> The king has every right to send his men to the Indies to demand their territory from these idolaters because he had received it from the pope. If the Indians refuse, he may quite legally fight them, kill them and enslave them, just as Joshua enslaved the inhabitants of the country of Canaan.[71]

The Bible awards Israel to the Jews after the genocide of its inhabitants by Israelites. No wonder that the Christians took inspiration from the genocide of other communities when they 'discovered the Americas'. Columbus had stumbled upon the Americas in search of India, and when they found that the natives were 'not Christians', the Christian missionaries tried to convert them all by force and started killing anyone who was not willing to. David E. Stannard, in his heart-rending study of the genocide of native pagan Americans at the hands of European Christian missionaries, *American Holocaust*, tells us how almost entire populations of most of the countries of the Americas were wiped out by direct genocide, starvation, and deliberately introduced diseases from Europe:

> Within no more than a handful of generations following their first encounters with Europeans, the vast majority of the Western Hemisphere's native peoples had been exterminated . . . The destruction of the Indians of the Americas was, far and away, the most massive act of genocide in the history of the world. That is why, as one historian aptly has said, far from

> the heroic and romantic heraldry that customarily is used to symbolize the European settlement of the Americas, the emblem most congruent with reality would be a pyramid of skulls.[72]

The genocide of pagan natives was so complete that most of what we now call Caribbean countries lost their entire populations with not even a single individual surviving. Almost all Caribbean countries today are entirely populated by forced indentured labourers from Africa, but the Native Americans have been completely destroyed in the genocide by European Christians. We have discussed above how Muslims consider the whole world to be their property, and they think that it is actually non-Muslims who are the squatters on the original Islamic lands. This feature too has been copied by them from the worthier predecessor of Islam—that is none other than Christianity.

The Church always claimed the entire earth to be its own property. Thus colonialism was simply a step to get back its lands from the 'illegal non-Christian usurpers'. This is why in 1492, Pope Alexander VI 'divided the world' into two parts between two Christian countries, Spain and Portugal, for conquest, loot, and genocide. When Columbus reached the Americas, he and his Christian soldiers started molesting and killing the native indigenous people. But before they did all that, they would first read out the 'legal order' by which they were allowed to do so by the decree of the Church and the Christian crown of Spain. The letter went like this:

> I certify to you that, with the help of God, we shall powerfully enter into your country and shall make war against you in all ways and manners that we can, and shall subject you to the yoke and obedience of the Church and of Their Highnesses. We shall take you and your wives and your children, and shall make slaves of them, and as such shall sell and dispose of them as Their Highnesses may command. And we shall take your

> goods, and shall do you all the mischief and damage that we can, as to vassals who do not obey and refuse to receive their lord and resist and contradict him.[73]

If there ever was a declaration of genocide, this is it. The behaviour of Christianity and Islam towards their minorities is a tale that is well known, and the minorities everywhere have been horribly persecuted and met with genocide and repeated massacres. When Europe became secular, protection of minorities became an important article of faith there; however, this article is thoughtlessly applied to pagan majority countries like India, forgetting that it is the prophetic monotheists who persecute the minorities and not the other way around.

Misogyny is another gift of prophetic monotheism to humanity. Hatred against women existed all over the world in sporadic form, but it is the Bible that codified and institutionalized hatred of women. Women were considered second-class citizens in Christendom because the Bible considered women the cause of the fall of Adam. Eve, the first woman and the temptress of Adam, was created as an afterthought by Yahweh, from the rib of Adam, to keep him entertained. Even the New Testament is full of hatred for women: 'It is a good thing for a man to have nothing to do with a woman.'[74] This view was supported by most Christian saints, monks, priests, and scholars. St Peter, one of the twelve apostles, thought that the woman was 'the weaker vessel'.[75] St Clement of Alexandria believed that 'every woman should be filled with shame by the thought that she is a woman'.[76] And Father Tertullian thought that women were 'devil's gateways'.[77]

Europe burnt with bonfires of heretics and 'witches' as women were always the first target of the Church, as they were never trusted enough in Christianity. Being the cause of the 'Fall of Adam', they were considered the reason mankind was a sinner. The Christian hatred for women burst out most prominently in the witch trials of the mediaeval era when women were accused of being 'worshippers of the devil', 'consorts of the devil', sorceresses, and witches and were accused of every kind of evil just for practicing some alternative medicine for home use. They were the particular target of the Church because while men were forced to completely let go of their 'pagan past and practices', the women at home continued many practices that were pagan in nature. This enraged the Church to no limit, and it decided to weed out paganism at home by burning those women at stake who were accused of 'witchcraft'. In 1484, Pope Innocent VIII ordered the inquisitors to prosecute and kill women who were accused as witches.[78] The torture of women was even more inhuman, and the process of 'interrogation' by Christian monks working as inquisitors was often worse than death, as described by historian Walter Nigg: '[S]he was stripped naked and the executioner shaved off all her body hair in order to seek in the hidden places of the body the sign which the devil imprinted on his cohorts. Warts, freckles, and birthmarks were considered certain tokens of amorous relations with Satan.'[79]

Even children were not spared. Girls as young as nine and a half years old were tried for witchcraft, and all the atrocities described above were performed on them.[80] Children younger than that were tortured to elicit testimony against their parents and were forced to watch the Christian inquisitors burn them alive on a stake at public squares.[81] More than 60,000 women were burnt alive after being falsely accused of 'being witches'.[82]

Another important feature of prophetic monotheism is that individuals are given no agency or choice. They are just units in the machinery of their religion but not independent individuals with will. In Islam, a Muslim is not an individual. He is only part of a group, a unit to be utilized in the service of Islam. He behaves as if he has no individuality, as if he is only a unit of a group and nothing more. This is because the Islamic law Shariat does not allow any scope for individuality. Islam intervenes in every aspect of human life. It is a 'total system'.

In Islam, every instruction is law, as their holy book, the Quran, is also the law book. Islamic law intervenes and dictates the behaviour of an individual even in such personal things as sex and relationships.

Theoretically speaking, individuality is not allowed in Islam. There is no clash of identities, as there is just one identity—Muslim. This is true to various degrees about Christianity too. This is the reason that individual lives are given so little importance in prophetic monotheistic religions. A rabidly Islamist State like Pakistan easily sacrifices ordinary Muslims for the cause of Islam because for them, individuals are not individuals but units, and as long as the overall graph keeps increasing and the Muslim population keeps growing, individuals can be sacrificed in the cause of Islam.

This is the reason that a large majority of the Islamic community chooses to live in absolute squalor so they can serve Islam by living in close ghettoes, giving them street credit. In some villages of Bihar and Bengal, many Islamic villages have pathetic living conditions, but the inhabitants are satisfied since in those conditions, 'Islam is not in danger'. Only Islam and its concerns are real. Everything else is an illusion. That is why Muslims belong mostly to a type with very little individuality of their own. Christianity is not different, and when it was at its zenith of power in Europe, it treated individuals only as units in the service of Christianity, as is recorded by many pagan Roman officials:

> Romans often found the Christians offensively irritating in court—not without reason, if the acts of the martyrs are to be believed. The Christians spat, metaphorically and literally, in the face of Roman legal process. In one famous trial, a martyr named Sanctus responded to every question with: 'I am a Christian.' A Christian author records the event with great approbation. 'With such determination did he stand up to their onslaughts that he would not tell them his own name, race, and birthplace,

> or whether he was a slave or free; to every question he replied in Latin, "I am a Christian." This he proclaimed over and over again, instead of name, birthplace, nationality and everything else, and not another word did the heathen hear from him.' The 'heathen' were less approving of this behaviour and the presiding governor promptly had him tortured some more.[83]

The fanaticism was so high in these radical Christians that they were willing to obliterate all of their identities in service of a religion of world conquest that had imperial and colonial ambitions. This is not the same as the Svayambodha pyramid of identities because here the lower identities are never allowed to exist; they are all obliterated, and only one, the Christian identity, remains. There is no co-existence of both unity and diversity, only a violent and political unity in their Christian identity.

Monotheistic Cocktail: Akhenaten, Zarathustra, and Moses

This book began with Kalicharan's question: What is it that differentiates Muslim behaviour from Hindu behaviour, or how are Muslims and Christians able to unite on an abstract idea while Hindus cannot. To answer this question, we need to delve a little deeper into some aspects of ancient history and the cultures surrounding the Mediterranean and the Persian Gulf. Let us investigate the beginnings of Judeo-Christianity, where it all began. The answer to Kalicharan's question is hidden in the beginnings of Judaism, somewhere between the geography and history of Egypt and Israel.

Egypt during 1353–36 BCE was ruled by one of the most idiosyncratic, eccentric, and self-important rulers. His name was Akhenaten, and he brought a traumatic revolution to his country, the kind of which was unprecedented in history and particularly in a great civilization like Egypt. He abandoned the natural religion of Egypt and introduced what can be considered as the world's first proto-monotheism based on the cult of Aten, an aspect of the Sun god. He declared that Aten was the only true god and adopted his cult as the state religion. Aten was the disc of the Sun god of Egypt and thus one aspect of one god. But that one aspect was turned by Akhenaten into the only religious cult allowed by his court. But he did not just invent a new cult surrounding an obscure god. He tried to eliminate all other traditional sects and eliminate the worship of all other gods. He banned the worship of all other gods, destroyed their temples, and suppressed their followers. He basically centralized religiosity and made everything flow through him to take absolute control of the lives of Egyptians. He was the first one in recorded history to realize that the best way to colonize someone is to control their religious/dharmic lives.

Akhenaten also declared that only he was allowed to worship Aten and that all devotion to God Aten should go through him. He commanded that the respect and devotion that the Egyptians directed towards various deities and towards Aten should now be directed to him. Thus, anticipating Prophet Jesus and Prophet Muhammad by thousands of years, he became the indispensable mediator between God and his followers. All spirituality and religiosity had to be centralized in him and directed by him. But there are more parallels with monotheism in Akhenaten's new religion. One of the speeches that he gave to declare his new religion still survives. It is illuminating to read these words uttered almost 3,500 years ago:

> The temples of the gods fallen to ruin, their bodies do not endure. Since the time of the ancestors, it is the wise man that knows these things. Behold, I, the king, am speaking so that I might inform you concerning the appearances of the gods. I know their temples, and I am versed in the writings, specifically, the inventory of their primeval bodies. And I have watched as they [the gods] have ceased their appearances, one after the

> other. All of them have stopped, except the god who gave birth to himself. And no one knows the mystery of how he performs his tasks. This god goes where he pleases and no one else knows his going. I approach him, the things which he has made. How exalted they are.[84]

Here Akhenaten is saying that gods are ineffective or non-existent and any worship of them is just superstition. This has always been so, but people had been fooled, and it is Akhenaten who has realized the truth and is trying to establish the right belief. This narrative is starkly similar to the narrative of Christian missionaries against pagan and Hindu deities. Akhenaten is alleging that the other gods are 'false gods' and the only god worthy of worship is the god that he approves of—Aten, and that worship to him cannot be independent and can only go through him, Akhenaten, Aten God's sole representative on earth. This is virtually the claim of Jesus and the Church for Christianity against paganism. This is the claim of Islam and Prophet Muhammad against Hindu gods. Missionaries and mullahs also declare that Hindu gods are 'false gods' and they should not be worshipped as they do not come to the 'aid of Hindus when they are attacked by invaders and missionaries'; hence they are mere 'idols' and nothing else.

We have already discussed how this view is very superficial and materialistic. It ignores the other subtler dimensions of existence, the greater planes of consciousness on which deities and gods operate. The monotheists can never see the koshas (sheaths) above the annamaya kosha. The missionaries can never listen to words that are uttered in vak above the level of vaikhari. They can never grasp reality that is beyond the mind, and we know that deities exist only on these higher planes of consciousness, whether we take the framework of kosha or vak. The monotheists also do not understand that the gods do not disappear anywhere. It is only the human beings who lose access to them. And any time this access is gained again, the gods appear again. That is the call of Shri Ram Swarup to Hindus that they should help the pagans all over the world, including the Egyptians, to help wake up the paths to access their ancient gods.[85]

Coming back to our story, Akhenaten virtually produced a template of prophetic monotheism for posterity to follow. In his own times, however, his endeavours did not make much impact in Egypt itself. It was still a largely dharmic society from a Hindu point of view because the Egyptians threw away the barbaric religion of Akhenaten and his own authority as soon as he was dead. His idols were taken out while the old icons of old gods were reinstated. All of his injunctions and changes were reversed. All of his laws were reverted back to the pure pagan stage before him with one change. The pharaohs were trusted even less now, and the authority to represent the divinity was more democratized, and everyone started arguing for more personal means to access the deities and the divine. The world's first attempt at prophetic monotheism was defeated.

But every society has devas and asuras, and the asuras within the Egyptian society had noticed the ideological package to exert imperial and colonial control that Akhenaten had created. The prophetic monotheistic cat was out of the bag. It was none other than Moses, the most important prophet of Judaism, who had noticed the prophetic monotheistic ideology of Akhenaten. And he would make good use of it.

Jews had a tradition of prophets who kept coming in their history from time to time, but one of the most important Jewish prophets (also accepted by Christianity) is Moses. Moses was born in Egypt and lived most of his life there, living under the rule of the pagan Egyptian pharaohs. Most scholars agree that Moses lived around 1391–1271 BCE. Thus, either Moses was a contemporary of Pharaoh Akhenaten or he came just on the heels of his disastrous reign. In any case, Moses was privy to the horror story of attempted monotheism that Akhenaten had tried. And it is very significant that it is under Moses that the Jewish tradition gets a new definition and life. Some of the most defining characteristics of prophetic monotheism as seen in Judaism, including their status as the 'People of the Book', wedded to a dogma, were created during the times of Moses.

In the centuries preceding Moses' birth, due to an internal disturbance, some Israelis had migrated to live in Egypt. It was in this Israeli migrant community in Egypt that Moses was born. The political conditions of Egypt during those times were not good, and the society was in turmoil. As the population of Israelis was growing, they were increasingly seen as an untrustworthy minority that would side with the enemy whenever any external attack happened. This was not an unfounded doubt about the Jews, as even at this early stage, they suffered from a superiority complex where they felt that they had a special relationship with God and they were his favoured children while others worshipped 'false gods'. Henry Chadwick attests to the notoriety of the Jews in the ancient pagan world:

> In the ancient world everyone knew at least three things about the Jews: they would not be associated either directly or indirectly with any pagan cult (which seemed antisocial), they refused to eat not only meat that had been offered in sacrifice to the gods but also all pork (which seemed ridiculous), and they circumcised their male infants (which seemed repulsive).[86]

They were primed to notice and admire Akhenaten's attempt at monotheism.

This behaviour increased the doubt in the minds of the Egyptian Pharaohs that the Jews would side with the enemy when an invasion occurs. The hatred that the Jews showed for the indigenous and majority pagans of Egypt who had given them shelter did not go a long way in creating trust between them and the Egyptian State.

When things became bad and the State grew insecure, it is not unthinkable that Jews would be punished on charges of treason. There is a Biblical myth that one Egyptian pharaoh ordered all newborn Jewish babies to be killed to control their population. This could be a story that the Jewish historians later concocted, but what cannot be denied is that there were tensions between the indigenous Egyptian pagan community on one hand and the immigrant monotheistic Jewish community on the other.

It is said that Moses survived the order to kill all babies because he was helped by the local pagans. He is said to have been adopted in the Egyptian royal palace as a foundling. He survived and grew up into a young man in Egypt in this atmosphere of tension between the two communities. The Biblical story says that one day he got enraged upon an Egyptian slave owner who was beating an Israeli (Jew) and killed that slave owner. In order to escape the Egyptian punishment, he fled to Israel. It is in Israel that he was reintroduced to his Jewish roots. The Biblical story goes that the Jewish god Yahweh appeared to him as a burning bush and ordered him to bring back the Israelites from Egypt and settle them in Israel. Moses went back and departed from Egypt with the Israelites after many tribulations. On their way back, while Moses was on Mount Sinai, the Ten Commandments were revealed to him by Yahweh. The Ten Commandments are the most important instructions to Christians and Jews and constitute the foundation of Judeo-Christian behaviour. Moses instructed his followers to live by the Ten Commandments. But Moses remained for a long time at Mount Sinai, and during his absence some of his followers created the image of a golden calf and worshipped it, fearing that Moses was dead and that they were leaderless.

When Moses came back with the Ten Commandments and saw that his followers were worshipping some other god, he got furious and punished the culprits. Then he made them enter a sacred contract with Yahweh where they promised that they would be Yahweh's exclusive followers and Yahweh would favour them too as his chosen people. They would not worship any other god and follow the leadership of the priesthood, which was headed by Moses' brother Aaron, and they would always worship and pray to Yahweh with the help of the Tabernacle, the mobile shrine or tent that the travellers could take with them everywhere. This is how the 'chosen people' enter into an exclusive contract with a god who speaks only to certain people and limits revelation to not those who deserve it but to those who satisfy his ego.

This is just a story until we unravel some of its details, which are important to Hindus. First of all, the Israelites or the Jews whom Moses was leading out of Egypt already had some idea of a monotheistic god because Abraham, the first Jewish prophet and ancestor of the Jews, is said to have entered into a contract with a god (Yahweh) who was different than other gods. So, the Jews whom Moses was leading were not just any common group. They were very distinct. History before them had never known any such group outside Israel. These Jews or Israelites had a superiority complex regarding their god (Yahweh). They hated Egyptian gods and ways of life, and this led Egyptians to mistrust them. Moses had to lead this group of Israelites out of Egypt and guide them until they reached Israel. This was easier said than done because Moses had a few challenges.

The most important task of Moses was to keep the Israelites rooted in their new religion until they reached Israel. This was very difficult since, to keep a group connected to its roots, the idea of a sacred land is most necessary, and that is something the Israelites did not have. Egypt was a land sacred to the Egyptians, but not to the Israelites, since their new and peculiar religion centred on a 'jealous god Yahweh' prohibited them from growing roots in any place they lived, other than Israel. Their monotheistic religion prevented them from growing roots in Egypt by not letting them respect and adopt indigenous gods, customs, rituals, and practices. It made them perpetual foreigners.

The problem became severe during their journey back to Israel. 'False gods' have always been the greatest threat to any monotheistic sect, and even at this early stage of monotheism, worshipping 'false gods' was a very clear and present danger. This was a problem even when the Israelites lived in Egypt. It was going to be a greater problem when they were travelling under harsh desert conditions, when faith in Yahweh would become weak and when the dream of the 'promised land' where 'rivers of milk and honey' flowed was just a dream. And we saw that when Moses went on Mount Sinai, in his absence, his followers once again 'descended' into idol worship of 'false gods'.

In short, the intellectual idea of monotheism was so unnatural that constant efforts had to be made to keep monotheism alive. But this was very difficult in the absence of a 'sacred land' and in the absence of active icon worship. Icon worship of a particular deity is the second most important factor in keeping a social group rooted. The sacred motherland and sacred deities, the two most critical factors in keeping a group united and rooted, were not available to Moses and his followers. He had to invent something new. Moses came up with a brilliant solution consisting of two elements.

The first idea was an abstract substitute of the sacred land. Moses did not want his followers to grow roots in Egypt. Instead, he wanted them to become loyal to a land that was far away and that they had never seen. This land existed only in the imagination of the Israelites until they reached there. But many 'bad things' like 'worship of false gods' could happen during the journey. This is why Moses came up with a brilliant substitute. This substitute was the idea of the Ten Commandments—ten instructions that were so short they could be remembered and carried in the mind itself. They could also be written on clay or stone tablets and carried easily.

The concrete agencies of a sacred land and an icon of a god were replaced with the abstract idea of the Ten Commandments. Practices, customs, and traditions centred in the deities of the land were substituted by an abstract dogma centred in the 'Ten Commandments'. This is a paradigm shift in the identity politics of humankind. For the first time we witness a group of people identifying with an abstract and mobile dogma of identity rather than with the concrete markers of land and practices rooted in local gods.

The Ten Commandments make the paradigm shift, from a concrete to a mobile foundation of identity, possible. Later on, the idea of the Ten Commandments becomes more and more abstract as more text, instructions, and chapters keep getting added to it. This mass of instructions becomes too big and becomes a 'book'. This is not just any normal book, which were in millions even in the ancient pagan world. It is 'the Book'. The Book of identity, which demarcates the chosen people of God from others, which defines the 'in-group' of monotheists who worship one true God and differentiates them from the 'out-group', the group of ordinary normal pagans who worship so many false gods. Later on, those who followed this mobile idea of identity centred in the Book started getting called the People of the Book. Henry Chadwick writes:

> Judaism was the religion of a book in a way that no other ancient religion was. The reconstruction of Israelite society after the catastrophe of the Babylonian deportation had been firmly based on the Law of Moses. There were no more prophets to proclaim the mediate word of God. God's revelation to his people was in writing, and needed to be interpreted by learned scribes and 'lawyers', so that the original documents were supplemented by exegetical tradition in the rabbinical schools.[87]

We see that something of the proto-Church was already in the making. If a group is called People of the Book, and that book is the only one that cannot be verified by any experience, then it needs an organization like the Church or a body that does the interpretation for its followers. To define book with a capital 'B' and thus claim its exclusivity is a particularly monotheistic idea, and that idea originated with Moses and his journey back home to Israel along with his followers.

Later, when the Israelites arrived in Israel, this idea did not become defunct but was kept alive, and gradually it became a central part of a dogma since even though Jews got their land in Israel, the abstract idea of the Book proved to be useful to keep them uniform and united. It became handy in the course of their history too since the Jews were displaced many times in history. In the absence of a sacred homeland and any particular land that they could call their own, the abstract and portable idea of the Book was a very handy technique to keep their identity unique and intact. It is this feature that kept their distinct Jewish identity alive over three millennia, making it possible for them to create Israel again in 1948 CE. The creation of Israel itself is an illustrative case of how an abstract dogma of the Book helps keep its followers united even though separated by millennia over half of the world.

The 'Book' was how they made religion mobile.

But the idea of the Book (or the Ten Commandments) was not the only element in Moses' solution. Another was the element of the Tabernacle—the mobile shrine. In the absence of a permanent place of worship, they came up with the mobile idea of a shrine, which could be folded and carried with them wherever they went. This element gave them great strength. While the idea of the Ten Commandments or the Book kept their identity intact, the daily rituals organized around the Tabernacle heightened that sense of identity and oneness with their fellow Israelites.

While the Book provided the dogma, the Tabernacle provided the practice. The Jewish religion was complete. It was untethered from place and gods. It was mobile and ready to be exported.

The Tabernacle was how they made the temple mobile.

One crucial element was missing, which was to be contributed more than 1,000 years later by Christianity. Moses' job was to take the Israelites to Israel and make them settle there. So, the mobile idea was used in the period of exile, or 'exodus', and when they were scattered by the invaders like Nebuchadnezzar. But this monotheistic idea was mostly confined to Israel and Israelites. But Christianity, the monotheistic successor of Judaism, opened up conversions to people of all ethnicities and nationalities instead of keeping it limited to the people of Israel. Paul himself was not an Israeli but a Roman citizen:

> Paul was a Christian, perhaps indeed the first Christian, but he was also a Roman. That was new. Even if the occasional Jew gained Roman citizenship, Jews weren't Romans. As a religion, Judaism was ethnic, which gave Jews some privileged exemptions unavailable to any other Roman subjects, but it also meant they were perpetually aliens. In contrast, Christianity was not ethnic. Although Christian leaders were intent on separating themselves physically and ideologically from the Jewish communities out of which they'd grown, they also accepted newcomers to their congregations without regard for ethnic origin or social class. In the socially stratified world of antiquity, the egalitarianism of Christianity was unusual and, to many, appealing.[88]

Thus, even though Christianity hated pagan polytheists as or even more than the Jews did, it added one element that made it possible for it to become a global religion in the coming centuries. It opened up conversions to non-Israeli people too. Everyone could become a Christian, and thus, even though Christians hated the local and indigenous gods, customs, and rituals, one could join them and adopt the superiority complex of Christianity by converting to the neo-revolutionary sect. Christianity remained exclusivist, but one could buy one's way into it by converting to it, by abandoning the ways of their ancestors. And in this way, it became 'universal'. This 'universality' brought more mobility to the idea of prophetic monotheism, making it easier for individuals across the globe to identify with it and to 'convert' to it.

Before Christianity could improve on Judaism, there were some more influences on it from the East. Around the sixth century BCE, ancient Persia saw the rise of a religion called Zoroastrianism centred around the personality of Zarathustra or Zoroaster who is a prophet-like figure who mediated between the Zoroastrian god Ahura Mazda and his followers. He is said to be the first proper prophet in history. Even though he was pre-empted by Akhenaten in ideology, Zarathustra encoded his ideology in a Book called Zend Avesta, the sacred scriptures of the Zoroastrians.

Zoroastrianism shows many features of proto-Christianity: the prophet-like figure of Zarathustra, the deep belief in heaven and hell, and the almost infallible figure of the devil. When the Persian kings attacked Israel, their army and court must have introduced the Zarathustrian idea of dualism and prophethood, centred in a Book. They must also have introduced the idea of a clear distinction between heaven and hell and the almost complete omniscience of the devil. Zarathustra, like Prophet Jesus and Prophet Muhammad, came from the desert, what is now Sistan in Iran.

The monotheistic zeitgeist was complete. What started with Akhenaten, utilized by Moses, and inspired by Zarathustra was finished with final touches by Paul of Christianity.

Prophetic monotheism, in its most lethal avatar in Christianity, was both abstract and portable. It could be carried anywhere, exported to any group or country. Its followers could survive the loss of a sacred land and concrete markers of identity.

This cognitive shift in the psyche of man, orchestrated by Moses and then completed by Paul, changed the entire history of mankind in the millennia to come. Christianity started destroying natural religions of the world, and soon it was joined in this quest by Islam.

This is also the answer to Kalicharan's question: Why Muslims unite under an abstract idea of religion, defying all concrete markers in the land in which they live, and why can Hindus not understand this psyche, let alone mimic it? Muslims and Christians can unite across the globe because they are the People of the Book and not the people of any sacred land or the followers of any god rooted in the rituals and customs of a land. Like flotsam, they are not attached to any place or civilization. Instead, they are only attached to the idea of monotheism ensconced in the abstract and mobile idea of the People of the Book. They can survive the loss of the holy land, as Judaism and Christianity both did. Israel was claimed back by Jews only in 1948, and until then it was lost to both Christianity and Judaism, which were born there. In fact, they are so unattached to the land they live in that they have no difficulty in working against their own motherland, because their loyalties are to their para-terrestrial religion. Hindus need to understand this psyche of followers of Islam and Christianity and prepare a response based on this central feature of prophetic monotheism.

Dharma Is Not Religion

We have now discussed in some detail what dharma is (like Sanatana Dharma) and what prophetic monotheism is (like Islam or Christianity). It should be clear by now to us that dharma is not religion and religion is not dharma. Dharma and religion are untranslatables, which means that they are two very different categories with very few points of intersection between them. To confuse dharma with religion thus would be a category mistake.

And it is not simply a matter of wrong translation. The very characters of dharma and religion are fundamentally different.

Dharma is centred in practices and experiences, while religion is centred in dogma and belief. Dharma maintains that god alone is the entire universe, and every animate and inanimate object is a part of it, while religion says that there is one true god while all other gods are false gods. Dharma says that man can become divine by the practice of meditation, while religion says that for man to imagine becoming God is the greatest sin. Dharma says that man is the reflection of the Brahman, or the Supreme Consciousness, and through meditation this true nature of man can be realized, while religion says that man is an eternal sinner and can never redeem himself. Dharma says that every individual has to realize and experience the truth for himself, while religion says that man is helpless, both in sinning and redeeming, and that even these intimately personal quests have to be outsourced to the Church or the Ummah. Dharma maintains that a deity or a guru can show one the path, but moksha has to be realized by every individual himself, while religion maintains that the agency of a mediator like the prophet or the Church is indispensable, and it is impossible to arrive at truth if the authority of the prophet is rejected. Dharma maintains that it is the message that leads individuals on the path of moksha that is important and not the messengers, while religion elevates the messenger (the prophet) to the highest pedestal and makes the mediator the most important personality around which the religious cult moves. Dharma teaches real spirituality, which is accessible to every person on earth, while religion preaches surrogate spirituality, which is available only to those who buy the dogma of the Church or the Ummah. Dharma maintains continuity between nature and culture, while religion believes that it is the job of culture to make a complete conquest of nature. Dharma maintains that man is superior to other creatures only in his ability to realize his true nature through meditation, and otherwise he is just one species among millions; religion claims that god's chosen people can use nature and every creature in it as they want. Dharma maintains that the highest goal of human life is moksha, and the state of moksha is nothing but a state of unending bliss, which itself is Brahman or supreme consciousness, while religion maintains that the highest goal of human life is to go to heaven, where one can have the same material pleasures in limitless quantity that one has on earth. Dharma maintains that one can attain moksha through many paths, while religion maintains that there is only one path towards 'salvation', which is redemption by a human institution like the Church. Dharma maintains that Brahman is devoid of any form and yet every form comes from it, while religion claims that any depiction of any 'form' as 'god' is a crime. Dharma does not differentiate between men and women, as both are part of the same consciousness, and hence it has many gods and goddesses, while religion thinks woman is an evil temptress who was created as an afterthought from the rib of Adam to entertain him when he is bored. Dharma maintains that the creation and creator are one, and thus Brahman is everything and everyone at any time, while religion claims that it is insulting for the male, jealous god to come down to his own creation after he has created it, and it falls upon his representatives on earth, like the Church and the Ummah, to run the human affairs. Dharma sustains, while religion destroys.

Chapter 8

Hindu View of Prophetic Monotheism

'But the god of the ecstasies of non-yogic bhumi or kama bhumi is very different. He has strong likes and dislikes and has cruel preferences. He has his favorite people, churches and ummahs, and his implacable enemies. He is also very egoistic and self-regarding; he can brook no other god or gods. He insists that all gods other than himself are false and should not be worshiped. He is a "jealous god", as he describes himself in the Bible."

—Shri Ram Swarup

The Slave Market, J.L. Gerome, 27 Mar. 2017. A white non-Muslim girl being sold in an open market, with prospective Muslim buyers checking whether she has full teeth or not[1]

Monotheism from the Lens of Pancha Rnas

Having seen some of the most important features of prophetic monotheism and contrasting them against dharmic traditions, the time has come now to analyse them through a very deeply dharmic scale. This scale is the concept of pancha rnas. It is the most fundamental Hindu framework that guides the model code of conduct based on kartavyabodha. And as dharma is all about experiences and practices, let us analyse and judge monotheism from the Hindu point of view by putting monotheistic religions through the prism of pancha rnas.

What happens when a traditional person converts to a prophetic monotheistic religion? To go out of the fold of any dharmic tradition is a momentous act, and modern constitutions might make it seem like a small personal choice, but in reality, conversion is a groundbreaking event in the life of the individual who is converting and also in the life of his family and larger society. To take a step out of Sanatana Dharma and into a religion like Islam and Christianity is a great step. Any individual who does so breaks many unwritten contracts that he had been following in his traditional society. One may say these are simply arbitrary human rules, but they are not. Let us analyse what happens when the sacred contract with nature and culture that an individual has in a traditional society is broken.

The first contract that a Hindu or a pagan breaks when he converts to Christianity or Islam is the deva rna. If the gods of a particular land continue to be worshipped, it is very difficult to colonize it permanently. After the political power of the colonial entity ends, colonialism also ends. This is how Mongol, Scythian, and Hun colonialism in India and elsewhere ended. Once their political power was gone, pretty much everything was gone. Today if one does not read history, one would not even know that Mongols, Huns, and Scythians ever visited their country. But if the colonial subjects are converted to the religion of the colonizer, then colonization becomes embedded deep into their culture, and the colonial subjects become almost permanently colonized. Almost every single country and nation that Christianity and Islam ruled and managed to convert is heavily colonized even today. Christianity and Islam destroy the indigenous dharma and tradition of a community and convert them in order to permanently colonize them. These Christians and Muslims are living embodiments of Christian and Islamic imperialism.

Islam and Christianity directly violate deva rna. And that is why a Hindu convert to either Islam or Christianity stops worshipping old gods, disrupting the millennia-old tradition, disrupting ancient continuity, severing the cultural thread that connects his present and future to his past.[2] To accept the kartavyabodha of being a Hindu and accept one's own share of *rnanubandha* is a great sankalpa. To convert and refuse to honour those *anubandhas* (contract) is a great vikalpa, the antithesis of sankalpa. This is not something only new converts to Christianity or Islam have to do. Breaking the sacred contract of deva rna is the very nature of Christianity. It is an integral part of becoming a Christian. The code is given in the Bible itself. The instruction against 'idol worship' is well known and is repeated through both the Old Testament and the New Testament.

> You shall have no other gods before me. You shall not make for yourself a carved image, or any likeness of anything that is in heaven above, or that is in the earth beneath, or that is in the water under the earth.[3] (Bible, Exodus 20:3–4)
>
> And you shall overthrow their altars, and break their pillars, and burn their groves with fire; and you shall hew down the graven images of their gods, and destroy the names of them out of that place.[4] (Bible, Deuteronomy 12:3)

Most Hindus today who convert to Christianity do not understand what conversion actually means. This ignorance is due to their lack of exposure to a monotheistic society. For whatever reason they convert, they first think that Christianity is just another sect like various Hindu sects and Jesus is just another god or deity that people worship, and how does it hurt if they start worshipping Jesus, another god? Although some exclusive demands of Christianity start from the beginning, they are generally shrouded in moral and ethical cloaks to fool the targets. It is only upon conversion that the new convert realizes that he has to start giving up most of his old lifestyle bit by bit, as Christianity has exclusive demands on every aspect of his life. At first a cross appears in his house shrine; then it takes centre stage; after a while other deities start disappearing on the constant demands of the pastor, who tells them that they are 'false gods' or 'demons', and eventually only Jesus remains. But the Hindu victim is clueless of all this when the Church starts approaching him for conversion.

However, they can learn from history. They can learn from the experience of the pagans of Europe when Christianity became the official religion of the Roman Empire and started destroying all aspects of pagan life, and the first object of the Christian ire was, of course, the temples dedicated to the 'false gods' whom Romans and Greeks worshipped. Iconoclasm starts with Jews who destroyed the 'idols' of 'false gods'. All the old deities of Canaan (Israel) and Egypt were declared by the Jews to be demons and devils, and any new convert to Judaism was told to stop worshipping them. The same attitude was adopted by Christianity, where the new converts in the Roman Empire first stopped worshipping the old gods and then helped in the destruction of their icons and their temples.

Fanatic and intolerant Christian 'saints' like St Augustine mocked the 'tolerance of pagans' who let Christians practice Christianity in the pagan Roman Empire and firmly believed that Christians should never tolerate the 'false religion of pagans'. He thought that it was the sacred duty of Christians to force non-Christians to convert to Christianity.[5] And iconoclasm was an integral part of Christian proselytization; if the pagans worshipped 'false gods', then the logical conclusion was that their temples needed to be destroyed. Another superstitious Christian Bishop Theophilus, before destroying and looting the greatest pagan temple of Serapis, in Alexandria, Egypt, said: 'The cross is that which closed the temples of the idols and opened the churches and crowns them. The cross is that which has confounded the demons and made them flee in terror.'[6]

Just like Mahmud of Ghazni would destroy the most exquisite Hindu temples of Mathura, having no appreciation of arts and aesthetics, so did the barbaric and fanatic Christians destroy lakhs upon lakhs of pagan temples all over what are now the modern countries of Italy, Greece, Turkey, Egypt, Syria, Israel, etc. Fanatical Theophilus was waiting for the day when Christians would become a sizeable minority in Serapis, where he was the bishop. As soon as that was achieved, he gathered his band of fanatical Christians and led them to destroy the temple of Serapis, which was famed to be the most beautiful building of Alexandria.

> Theophilus's righteous followers began to tear at those famous artworks, the lifelike statues and the gold-plated walls.... The soldier struck Serapis's face with a double-headed axe. The god's great ivory profile, blackened by centuries of smoke, shattered. The watching Christians roared with delight and then, emboldened, surged round to complete the job. Serapis's head was wrenched from its neck; the feet and hands were chopped off with axes, dragged apart with ropes, then, for good measure, burned... The giant torso of the god was saved for a more public humiliation: it was taken into the amphitheatre and burned in front of a great crowd.[7]

And just like Islamic invaders would build mosques over destroyed Hindu temples in India, Christians would build aesthetically atrocious churches over the ruins of pagan temples so that no pagan could ever recreate a temple at the site of the church. They did so at theTemple of Serapis in Alexandria, as they did everywhere else. In Greece, the destruction was far greater, for the pagan civilization being destroyed by Christianity was also far greater. Thousands upon thousands of temples were destroyed, looted, and the 'idols of the false Greek deities' were melted and taken away by reveling Christian priests and leaders. Sita Ram Goel says: 'The history of Christianity in the Roman Empire is not an obscure subject. The careers of many Christian emperors, popes, patriarchs, bishops, saints, and monks are proof that the contest between paganism and Christianity was decided not by philosophical cajoleries but by brute physical force.'[8]

There were some common patterns to the Christian destruction of the pagan temples. Not just the temples were destroyed but everything that pagans held sacred: priests, scholars, women, and sacred rites were defiled by fanatical Christians who stayed true to the Biblical order of destroying pagan ways of life and worship. One common practice was to build churches over the pagan temples so that pagans were never able to reclaim their sites.[9] Another common practice was to use the pieces of sculptures of the deities as footstones and in other insulting ways to perpetually keep insulting the 'false gods'. Christian destruction of the pagan Greek world is heartrending, as Nixey puts it:

> In a spasm of destruction never seen before—and one that appalled many non-Christians watching it—during the fourth and fifth centuries, the Christian Church demolished, vandalized and melted down a simply staggering quantity of art. Classical statues were knocked from their plinths, defaced, defiled and torn limb from limb. Temples were razed to their foundations and burned to the ground. A temple widely considered to be the most magnificent in the entire empire was levelled. Many of the Parthenon sculptures were attacked, faces were mutilated,

> hands and limbs were hacked off and gods were decapitated. Some of the finest statues on the whole building were almost certainly smashed off then ground into rubble that was then used to build churches.[10]

Throughout the length and breadth of the Roman Empire, countless temples were destroyed by Christian fanatics. Palmyra, a great ancient city, was a Greek outpost in the Syrian desert, full of exquisite pagan temples with high ceilings, elegant pillars, exquisite sculptures, and stupendous architecture. Many great temples graced the town, but the greatest was dedicated to the goddess Athena, for pagans of antiquity were great worshippers of the feminine. Athena was the goddess of wisdom, much like goddess Saraswati, and was deeply respected by pagans of the ancient world. But when Christians became the majority in this place, they destroyed this beautiful temple in an act that was so barbaric it defies imagination. But it is natural since misogyny, or hatred of women, is inherent in the Biblical worldview. When women as human beings were hated, it was no wonder that women as deities were hated even more. It defies imagination how these barbarian Christian 'monks' could so brutally destroy the exquisite sculpture of Greek goddess Athena in her great temple in Palmyra.

> When the men entered the temple they took a weapon and smashed the back of Athena's head with a single blow so hard that it decapitated the goddess. The head fell to the floor, slicing off that nose, crushing the once-smooth cheeks. Athena's eyes, untouched, looked out over a now-disfigured face. Mere decapitation wasn't enough. More blows fell, scalping Athena, striking the helmet from the goddess's head, smashing it into pieces. Further blows followed. The statue fell from its pedestal, then the arms and shoulders were chopped off. The body was left on its front in the dirt; the nearby altar was sliced off just above its base. Only then does it seem that these men—these

> Christians—felt satisfied that their work was done. They melted out once again into the desert. Behind them the temple fell silent. The votive lamps, no longer tended, went out. On the floor, the head of Athena slowly started to be covered by the sands of the Syrian desert. The 'triumph' of Christianity had begun.[11]

Christianity today presents itself as a force of 'love' and 'peace', but neither of these values were practiced with non-Christians at any point in time, and wherever Christianity came to power, it was followed with the holocaust of the pagans who refused to convert, followed by an orgy of destruction of pagan temples by devout Christians. This is because the hatred and destruction of the gods and temples of other religious and dharmic traditions is at the root of Christianity. It is a central and not a peripheral practice. The Bible is full of commands to destroy 'idols' and 'temples'.

Violating deva rna is a central requirement for becoming a Christian and also a Muslim because, one and a half millennia after fanatical Christians destroyed the temple of Athena in Palmyra, the poor town of Palmyra had to suffer the brunt of another monotheistic religion and another iconoclastic cult. In May 2015, ISIS, the Islamic terrorist organization of West Asia, invaded Palmyra, which by then was a ruined town, only visited for its ancient ruins, and destroyed whatever sculptures of the 'false gods' and 'pagan deities' had been spared by mistake by their Christian predecessors hundreds of years ago.[12] Interestingly, they destroyed the reconstructed sculpture of the Goddess Athena once again. Goddesses and women are special targets of the iconoclastic fury of a prophetic monotheistic religion.

Islam, as the above example proves, has been no less zealous in this record than Christianity, and the trail of death and destruction that it left in its wake of conquests in India is called by the great world historian Will Durant as the bloodiest tale in history.

The Muslim destruction of Hindu temples is a heartrending part of India's past. Mahmud of Ghazni was a typical Islamic invader whose goal was to destroy Hindu temples, kill Brahmins and cows, and then convert Hindus to Islam at the point of the sword. His attack and destruction of Mathura is infamous. Mathura, at that time, had thousands of Hindu temples, all of which were heartlessly destroyed by Ghazni:

> The Sultan then departed from the environs of the city, in which was a temple of the Hindus. The name of this place was Maharatul Hind. On both sides of the city there were a thousand houses, to which idol temples were attached, all strengthened from top to bottom by rivets of iron, and all made of masonry work. In the middle of the city there was a temple larger and firmer than the rest, which can neither be described nor painted. The Sultan thus wrote respecting it: If any should wish to construct a building equal to this, he would not be able to do it without expending a hundred thousand red dinars, and it would occupy two hundred years even though the most experienced and able workmen were employed. The Sultan gave orders that all the temples should be burnt with naptha and fire, and leveled with the ground.[13]

When Hindus demanded to rebuild the Shri Rama temple in Ayodhya, monotheists the world over started portraying Hindus as bloodthirsty monsters attacking poor minorities and their religious places. As most of the media and academia were leftist then, it fell upon the shoulders of a small group of historians led by the indefatigable Sita Ram Goel to present the history of the destruction of Hindu temples to Hindu masses. In a magisterial study in two volumes edited by Sita Ram Goel, titled *Hindu Temples: What Happened to Them*, many great historians and scholars came together to present the argument and evidence that tells the story of the destruction of countless Hindu temples by Islamic invaders. Based on history written by Islamic historians themselves, he conclusively proves that 'almost all Muslim rulers destroyed or desecrated Hindu temples whenever and wherever they could'.[14]

This destruction was comprehensive in time and space. There was no time when the Islamic invaders and rulers in India did not destroy Hindu temples, and there was no place where the destruction did not take place. Temples were destroyed even in remote places like the coastal towns of Odisha, the far reaches of upper Assam, and deep south in Tamil Nadu.

> In most cases the destruction of temples was followed by erection of mosques, madrasas and khanqahs etc., on the temple sites and, frequently, with temple materials. Allah was thanked every time for enabling the iconoclast concerned to render service to the religion of Muhammad by means of this pious performance.[15]

Based on the overwhelming evidence from Islamic scholars and historians who were eyewitnesses to the destruction that Islamic kings unleashed on Hindu kingdoms, Sita Ram Goel has come up with some patterns that were common to the destruction. Destruction of a temple was not a standalone act of vandalism. Brahmins and cows were butchered inside the temples to 'defile them'. Books and libraries were burnt in bonfires that burnt for days, and scholars, even minors, were beheaded in the temple premises for they followed 'false religion' and 'false gods'. Most importantly, important care was taken to insult the desecrated vigrahas of deities by using them in toilets and footstones in Islamic cities.

> The idols were mutilated or smashed or burnt or melted down if they were made of precious metals. Sculptures in relief on walls and pillars were disfigured or scraped away or torn down. Idols of stone and inferior metals or their pieces were taken

> away, sometimes by cartloads, to be thrown down before the main mosque in (a) the metropolis of the ruling Muslim sultan and (b) the holy cities of Islam, particularly Mecca, Medina and Baghdad. There were instances of idols being turned into lavatory seats or handed over to butchers to be used as weights while selling meat. Brahmin priests and other holy men in and around the temple were molested or murdered. Sacred vessels and scriptures used in worship were defiled and scattered or burnt. Temples were damaged or despoiled or demolished or burnt down or converted into mosques with some structural alterations or entire mosques were raised on the same sites mostly with temple materials. Cows were slaughtered on the temple sites so that Hindus could not use them again.[16]

The 'humiliation' and 'insult' are not something incidental or peripheral to the iconoclastic behaviour of Islam and Christianity. It is considered important to insult and terrorize the 'pagan' and the 'kaffir' so that he eventually converts to the monotheistic sect, being unable to bear insult to his lifestyle and deities. Islamic historians proudly proclaim how the 'hated idols of the false gods' were humiliated. Indian archaeology is a living proof of this. At so many forts and palaces in India, one can still see the parts of the destroyed Hindu temples being used as footstones, intending to humiliate the Hindus.[17] This phenomenon is far from limited to India; Islam, Christianity, and Judaism even went to the extent of writing manuals of how to insult 'accursed pagan deities', as Nixey narrates:

> Statues, the very seat of the demons themselves, suffered some of the most vicious attacks. It was not enough merely to take a statue down; the demon within it had to be humiliated, disgraced, tortured, dismembered and thus neutralized. A Jewish tractate known as *the Avodah Zarah* provided detailed instructions on how to properly mistreat a statue. One can desecrate a statue, it advised, by 'cutting off the tip of its ear or nose or finger, by battering

> it—even although its bulk be not diminished—it is desecrated'. Merely taking the statue down, or spitting at it, or dragging it about, or throwing dirt upon it, was not, the treatise warned, sufficient—though the resourceful Christian might indulge in all of these as an added humiliation to the demon within.[18]

Whenever a Hindu converts to either Islam or Christianity, he has to start believing in the dogma that these religions propound, and this dogma says that all Hindu deities are demons, 'false gods', and not only is it the duty of the new convert to stop worshipping them but it is also his sacred duty to help weed out the 'false practice' of 'false religions' whenever he can. One should remember what Swami Vivekananda said: A convert from Hindu dharma is not just one Hindu less, but one enemy more. Once again, it is not about the individual, but about the ideology that inspires him. The same individual who was once caring for and nourishing great art and culture before conversion starts destroying them after converting to a prophetic monotheistic religion. So, it is not something inside the individual, but the dogma he has started following that encourages him to destroy Hindu temples.

This becomes clearer when we analyse the nature of the monotheistic gods of Christianity and Islam, which the new convert has to start believing in. The high culture of dharmic deities instantly collapses in the mind of the individual who converts, and he instead has to forcibly buy into the idea of the monotheistic god. The devas disappear from the mind, and the jealous, violent, and cruel god appears. Illuminating the history of the people in West Asia who converted to Islam, Shri Ram Swarup talks about the cultural decline related to humanity's idea of deities and the divine:

> The greatest decline was in the concept of their Godhead which was at the root of all other kinds of degradation. Their new God

> was 'one', it was male; it was exclusive and intolerant; it took pride in refusing 'partnership' with 'other' Gods—whatever that may mean. It was also different from their accustomed Gods in another important sense: their traditional Gods spoke to them directly, but the new one dealt with them through an intermediary.[19]

Shri Ram Swarup illustrates the decline in the concept of godhead when a person converts to Islam, and at the same time, he also defines the very nature of the monotheistic god. The breaking of the deva rna is thus a great loss to the native and indigenous culture, arts, sciences, and ways of life.

Islam and Christianity also violate rishi rna. For Christianity and Islam, the entirety of knowledge is contained inside the Bible and the Quran, respectively, and any book or knowledge outside their 'Book' is considered an inspiration of the devil. To support this theory, it becomes not just important but necessary for Christianity to reject any knowledge outside the Bible as inspired from the 'devil'. The same is true of Islam and the Quran. Thus, it becomes imperative for Christianity and Islam to not just reject but also destroy the knowledge systems of all ancient dharmic and pagan traditions.

This is why Islamic invaders burnt the great libraries of ancient India—Nalanda, Vikramshila, and Takshashila were all destroyed by Islamic invaders because for them any knowledge outside of the Quran was sin and liable to be destroyed. Naturally the scholars and saints who propagated these knowledge systems were seen as sinners and killed along with the burning of their libraries, ashrams, and monasteries. Sanatana Dharma survived due to its inner resilience, but Buddhism in India was wiped out by the Islamic invaders, as it was mostly located in the monasteries and depended on the State largesse. The destruction of Nalanda by Islamic invaders was considered in Islamic countries a great and commendable act in the service of Allah since a 'den of idolatry' had been exterminated and books and 'scholars of devil worshippers' were destroyed. Dr Ambedkar records:

> The Musalman invaders sacked the Buddhist Universities of Nalanda, Vikramasila, Jagaddala, Odantapuri to name only a few. They razed to the ground Buddhist monasteries with which the country was studded. The Monks fled away in thousands to Nepal, Tibet and other places outside India. A very large number were killed outright by the Muslim commanders. How the Buddhist priesthood perished by the sword of the Muslim invaders has been recorded by the Muslim historians themselves.[20]

The great library of Nalanda was also burnt after the university was destroyed. It is said that the library burnt for days on end; there were so many books in it. The Islamic invaders replicated this macabre dance of death all over India. All the great Hindu and Buddhist libraries met an ignominious death at the hands of the barbarian Islamic invaders. While for any civilized person this seems like an unimaginable crime, to a devout Islamic king it was a charitable act since he was just destroying the 'dens of ignorance' as the 'books of kaffir Hindus' contained not just ignorance but also great evil, and by destroying Hindu books, the Islamic invaders were doing good.

Even in this, Islam was not a pioneer. Christianity had paved the way long ago. Christianity's firm belief that the Bible contained all that was there to know made them resent the knowledge of ancient Greco-Roman scholars. Christian monks often destroyed ancient manuscripts and overwrote them with Biblical verses in a breathtaking case of cultural destruction. It is actually the advent of Christianity that heralded the onset of the Dark Ages in Europe, as all knowledge centres were destroyed, pagan scholars persecuted, and libraries burnt.

> Books—which were often stored in temples—suffered terribly. The remains of the greatest library in the ancient world, a

> library that had once held perhaps 700,000 volumes, were destroyed in this way by Christians. It was over a millennium before any other library would even come close to its holdings. Works by censured philosophers were forbidden and bonfires blazed across the empire as outlawed books went up in flames.[21]

Throughout the length and breadth of the Roman Empire, libraries went up in flames as Christianity came to rule. Pagan scholars, philosophers, and intellectuals looked helplessly as the books they had cherished and libraries they had built their whole lives went up in flames as Christians burnt them after destroying the pagan temples. The 'unchristian books' were the devil's work, so of course they had to be burnt. It is Christianity that gave the world the culture of book burning and book banning: '[T]he burning of books was part of the advent and imposition of Christianity.'[22] Twenty-eight public libraries were burnt by Christians only in the city of Rome.[23] Persecution of free thinkers and philosophers was an invention of Christianity, and historians record that in Antioch, 'philosophers ... were variously tortured, burned alive and beheaded'[24] by devout and faithful Christians. And it was not an orthodox minority that burnt all these books and killed all the philosophers. Some of the greatest 'saints' of Christianity, like St Augustine, St John Chrysostom, and St Cyril, were directly involved in book burnings and the killing of pagan intellectuals and priests. And it was all authorized by the Church.[25] Early Christian literature asked Christians to 'stay clear of all pagan books'.

Greek science was considered evil magic inspired by Satan. The ancient Greeks had made great advancements in many branches of science and were on the verge of many great discoveries when Christianity overtook the Roman Empire, destroyed Roman and Greek science, and plunged Europe into the Dark Ages. About 2,000 years before Newton, Archimedes had come very close to discovering calculus. His formulas and derivations, had they survived, would have led to the discovery of calculus very early in the first millennium CE. But, as Christian barbarism would have it, the manuscripts containing his mathematics were scraped off by Christian monks and overwritten with Biblical verses. Greek philosophers were considered 'dangerous' with their 'diverse views on religion' with many ways to reach the divine. The Christians did not just hate knowledge, but in the words of pagan philosopher and scientist Celsus, they 'celebrated ignorance'. He accused Christians of 'actively targeting idiocy in their recruitment'.[26] If one were to mark a single incident that banished Europe to the Dark Ages, it would be the brutal mob lynching of the pagan female librarian of Alexandria, Hypatia, by none other than the faithful Christians, led by one of the most 'venerable Christians saints' St Cyril:

> One day in March ad 415, Hypatia set out from her home to go for her daily ride through the city. Suddenly, she found her way blocked by a 'multitude of believers in God'. They ordered her to get down from her chariot. Knowing what had recently happened to her friend Orestes, she must have realized as she climbed down that her situation was a serious one. She cannot possibly have realized quite how serious. As soon as she stood on the street, the parabalani, under the guidance of a Church magistrate called Peter—'a perfect believer in all respects in Jesus Christ'—surged round and seized 'the pagan woman'. They then dragged Alexandria's greatest living mathematician through the streets to a church. Once inside, they ripped the clothes from her body and, using broken pieces of pottery as blades, flayed her skin from her flesh. Some say that, while she still gasped for breath, they gouged out her eyes. Once she was dead, they tore her body into pieces and threw what was left of the 'luminous child of reason' onto a pyre and burned her.[27]

Hypatia was one of the greatest scholars of the ancient world, extremely erudite, beautiful, law-abiding, respecting freedom of expression and thought, and believing in a plural world. All of these were great crimes in the book of devout and orthodox Christians who hated knowledge and promoted stupidity and ignorance. Christianity and Islam both fail horribly on the scale of rishi rna. And if a Hindu converts to either Christianity or Islam, he commits a great crime against knowledge seeking and knowledge tradition itself. To become a Christian, or a Muslim, is to automatically break the rishi rna—the debt of the saint-scholars of Bharatavarsha and any other ancient pagan civilization.

How do Christianity and Islam look if you measure them on the scale of the third great rna of the Hindu universe, pitra rna? To pay pitra rna is to respect and worship the ancestors, and it is a great crime in Christianity and Islam. Ancestor worship is the clearest sign of respecting the past, and the past we know is a time of ignorance for both Islam and Christianity. On the other hand, Christianity or Islam is the clearest sign of a break from the past. Hindu dharma builds on the past. Christianity declares the past as darkness to be forgotten. Hindus worship the ancestors. Christianity and Islam assign them to hell. Thus, prophetic monotheism violates pitra rna directly. Christianity was always a revolutionary religion that sought a complete break from the past. To worship anyone else other than the 'one true God', Yahweh, is equivalent to worshipping a 'false god', so ancestor worship is also worship of the false gods. The Bible has a deep disrespect of ancestors:

> For the living know that they will die, but the dead know nothing, and they have no more reward, for the memory of them is forgotten. Their love and their hate and their envy have already perished, and forever they have no more share in all that is done under the sun.[28]

Christians believed that pagans worshipped the ancestors only so that they could magically summon their souls to do their chores, and in the Christian universe, apart from Jesus, only demons came down to help human beings. They also hated soothsayers (fortune tellers) as the Church did not want its followers to get confused about the Judgement Day. Any pagan tradition that connected them with their pagan past or a possible pagan future was a threat to the Church, and hence it tried to eliminate all ancestor worship.

This is not something that happened in a distant past in a far-off land. It is happening today in India and also to Hindus. In India's northeastern states of Meghalaya, Mizoram, Nagaland, and Arunachal Pradesh, the Church has forced the converted tribes to abandon ancestor worship because now they have 'found the true religion'. As most of the aspects of the lives of these tribes were intimately connected to their ancestors, this anti-ancestor clause of Christianity has resulted in a painful break from the past that manifests in identity loss, alienation, and a civilizational dejection that has led to many social problems like substance abuse and depression.

Islam too is as abhorrent of any ancestor worship like Christianity. This is common to any revolutionary religion that is not a natural tradition of the land. As a new ideology that has never been heard before, it can only gain followers by encouraging individuals to break away from their past and their culture completely. This is what Islam did too in order to gain new followers. And to make sure that Islam is completely opposed to the 'pagan traditions' of the land, it made sure that ancestors were looked down upon instead of being respected. According to Islam, anyone who did not believe in Islam will end up in hell. Even those who were born before the advent of Islam are consigned to hell for no fault of their own. All ancestors are therefore included in the list of the inhabitants of hell. According to a hadith, a Muslim once asked the prophet where his dead father was: in heaven or in hell, to which the prophet is reported to have said, 'My father and your father are in Hell.'[29] The Quran itself claims that it is not in the hands of the prophet to judge who goes to heaven and who goes to hell; only Allah can judge that. Since no one who had not accepted Islam could go to heaven, all ancestors of the prophet and everyone else must also be in hell. 'It is not for the Prophet and those who have believed to ask forgiveness for the polytheists, even if they were relatives, after it has become clear to them that they are companions of Hellfire.'[30]

This was a technical matter, and in that the prophet could not make an exception for even his own family. Everyone who was born in the past and had no means of knowing about the 'one true religion', 'one true god', and the 'only prophet' was also consigned to the everlasting fire of hell without a fault of his own. The Bible also says: 'And many of those who sleep in the dust of the earth shall awake, some to everlasting life, and some to shame and everlasting contempt.'[31] If ancestor worship were allowed, then non-Christians would also be able to go to heaven, which is directly contradictory to Christian eschatology. This is how deep a break from the past Islam and Christianity are. To follow Islam and Christianity is to break the sacred bond of pitra rna. And to convert to Islam or Christianity is an even more violent act, psychologically speaking, for the person has to start living his life in exactly the opposite way from how he lived before conversion. V.S. Naipaul, one of the greatest literary observers and commentators on Islam, said:

> Islam is in its origins an Arab religion. Everyone not an Arab who is a Muslim is a convert. Islam is not simply a matter of conscience or private belief. It makes imperial demands. A convert's worldview alters. His holy places are in Arab lands; his sacred language is Arabic. His idea of history alters. He rejects his own; he becomes, whether he likes it or not, a part of the Arab story. The convert has to turn away from everything that is his. The disturbance for societies is immense, and even

> after a thousand years can remain unresolved; the turning away has to be done again and again. People develop fantasies about who and what they are; and in the Islam of converted countries there is an element of neurosis and nihilism. These countries can be easily set on the boil.[32]

Prophetic monotheistic religions do not respect the nru rna or the manushya rna either, the fourth sacred contract that a Hindu has to respect. While a Hindu always is in contract with his fellow society and human beings, Christianity is a contract between the 'only true god' and his 'chosen people'. There is no need for human beings to enter into any contract with fellow human beings. All the brotherhood exists only within the 'in-group', and the larger humanity is brutally othered in both Christian and Islamic worldviews. In fact, because Christianity grows through conversion, it always encouraged individuals of a non-Christian pagan society to revolt from their own religion and society. A new radical sect grows not by inspiring brotherhood and faith in fellow human beings but by fomenting violence and animosity within various individuals of a group, by exploiting the inner fault lines of that group, and by making one individual rebel against others. Jesus Christ was very clear that this was his goal, as becomes obvious from these verses.

> For I have come to turn a man against his father, a daughter against her mother, a daughter-in-law against her mother-in-law—a man's enemies will be the members of his own household. Anyone who loves their father or mother more than me is not worthy of me; anyone who loves their son or daughter more than me is not worthy of me. Whoever does not take up their cross and follow me is not worthy of me.[33]

Jesus makes it very clear that he does not believe in familial harmony, and he does not hesitate to break families apart for the benefit of Christianity. Loyalty to him and his new cult was more important for him than any family relations. He incited family members to revolt against their own families in order to join the new cult of Christianity. Without this, a cult that disrespects all the laws of the land, including its religion, would not have grown. Breaking the manushya rna thus is an integral part of becoming Christian. The same is true about Islam. Some of the most hardened outcasts of society of the times of Prophet Muhammad had joined Islam because it offered them a chance to exploit and oppress their contemporaries. It is true even about a monotheistic atheist cult like communism. In the communist Soviet Union, the Communist Party encouraged members of society to spy on each other and report anyone who did anything against the party to the authorities. This created an atmosphere of perpetual surveillance state in the Soviet Union, where everyone was spying on each other. No one dared speak his mind openly because anyone could be a spy.

The Communist Party, however, wanted to take the surveillance to another stage. It would encourage even family members to spy on each other. As a result, wives reported that their husbands were 'mumbling anti-party sentiments in sleep', leading to the arrest of the husband and a promotion or socio-political perk that was awarded to the wife for her 'loyalty' to the Communist Party, even against her own husband. The Russian society reached this stage after extreme physical and mental stress. Most of society was being starved to death and would do anything to get more resources from the State. Sometimes a neighbour would report the 'anti-party activities' of the next-door neighbour so that he could get the better apartment of his neighbour, which would be assigned to them if the former occupant got arrested for 'anti-party activities'. In a very famous case, a twelve-year-old boy, Pavel, who reported the 'anti-party activities' of his father to the party and got him arrested, was hailed as the model party worker and celebrated in highly publicized campaigns to encourage others to do the same.

The Christian surveillance state was no less brutal and employed these psy-ops on its victims and new converts. The concept of a godfather and godmother is to keep perpetual surveillance on the newly born kid whose parents are not trusted to give him a 'proper Christian upbringing'. When biological parents could not be trusted, the Church provided Christian parents with godfathers and godmothers to make sure that Christianity was not compromised while upbringing the child. This is how deeply Christianity intruded in the personal lives of its followers. During the Inquisition, the new converts to Christianity were not allowed to shut their doors on Fridays and Saturdays to make sure they were not following their old religion (Judaism and Islam). Christianity always fed the zealousness of the new converts by encouraging them to report the 'pagan activities' of their families and neighbours.

Christianity in itself is a rebellion against manushya rna, because far from protecting the family, it leads to the breakdown of family. In India, as Christianity is increasing its numbers in many states of India, it is at its most lethal, family-breaking potential currently. Innocent Hindu girls are converted by their Christian boyfriends, and then their hearts are filled with hatred for Hindu dharma, leading to either the destruction of family or to the conversion of the entire family to Christianity. This is because Christianity thrives on social strife and creates social tensions if there are not any so that it can grow by converting vulnerable individuals.

The fifth of the rnas, bhuta rna, is the most critical rna from the point of view of ecology and sustainability. And both Christianity and Islam break this rna completely. It is the debt of nature on human beings. We are indebted to the flora, fauna, and the larger ecosystem that sustains us through our lives. In an all-encompassing view, Sanatana Dharma does not neglect nature and its role in sustaining life. This is remarkable if you contrast this with either the approach of the prophetic monotheistic religions or all modern ideologies, including the narrative of human rights. We know that our world is going through a great crisis of climate change. Ecosystems are collapsing right, left, and centre; the planet is heating beyond the sustainable point, and the world is heading towards multiple crises. Direct correlation of this tragic state of being is with the modern lifestyle that we have adopted. But the roots of this modern debacle are not just in the Enlightenment but go back to the Judeo-Christian value system rooted in the Bible. Helen Ellerbe tells us how Christianity distanced humanity from nature:

> Christianity has distanced humanity from nature. As people came to perceive God as a singular supremacy detached from the physical world, they lost their reverence for nature. In Christian eyes, the physical world became the realm of the devil. A society that had once celebrated nature through seasonal festivals began to commemorate biblical events bearing no connection to the earth. Holidays lost much of their celebratory spirit and took on a tone of penance and sorrow. Time, once thought to be cyclical like the seasons, was now perceived to be linear. In their rejection of the cyclical nature of life, orthodox Christians came to focus more upon death than upon life.[34]

Nature was declared evil by Christianity as it was a tree and a fruit that had tempted Adam and led to the fall of humanity. The Greek god of nature, Pan, was taken as the prototype to depict Satan. Thomas Aquinas, one of the greatest Christian 'saints', declared that animals have no souls and the only reason they exist is to satiate the hunger of man.[35] In the mediaeval era, the Church believed that animals were the vehicles of Satan, and thus countless animals were 'tried' and 'tortured' by Christian inquisitors. Trees were hated by the Church too, especially because the pagans worshipped trees, just like Hindus do today. One military general of the Christian king of Gaul (contemporary France) decreed in 789 CE: 'With regard to trees, and rocks and springs, wherever ignorant people put lights or make other observances, we give notice to everyone that this is a most evil practice, execrable to God, and wherever they are found, they are to be taken away and destroyed.'[36]

After Christianity became the State religion in the Roman Empire, the fanatical Christians started destroying temples and killing pagan priests and philosophers, but they did not stop at just that. The superstitious Christians also started destroying all the sacred groves of the pagans, as pagans, just like Hindus, worshipped divinity in all forms, including in the form of a tree, a mountain, a river, or a spring, and since every part of nature could not be instantly destroyed, the fury of the early Christians broke upon the sacred groves or gardens that were built as shrines or around temples of pagan deities. 'The sacred groves of the old gods for example, those tranquil natural shrines like the one Pliny had so admired, were set about with axes and their ancient trees hacked down.'[37]

A very revered Christian 'saint' Benedict, who is said to be the founder of Christian monasticism, destroyed sacred groves wherever he went. He went around in France 'pulling down the idols and destroying the groves on the mountain ... and gave himself no rest until he had uprooted the last remnant of heathenism in those parts'.[38] This most 'revered' Christian saint is responsible for large-scale ecological destruction in France. Justo L. Gonzalez confirms: 'Benedict moved to the small community of Monte Cassino, a place so remote that there still was a sacred grove, and the local inhabitants continued celebrating ancient pagan worship. Benedict and his followers cut the grove, overturned the pagan altar, and built a monastic foundation in that very place.'[39] Imagine the comprehensiveness of Christian barbarity, where their 'saints' discovered even the extremely remote natural heavens and destroyed everything natural there, just so that the 'accursed, evil pagans' could not continue worshipping nature and would instead start worshipping the unnatural, artificial, and constructed god of the Bible.

'Saint' Augustine approved the wholesale destruction of nature in the destruction of sacred groves across all of Christendom and especially in North Africa. He said that the destruction of the groves and temples was 'clear proof of our not honoring, but rather abhorring, these things'.[40] The eco-sensitive pagan civilization of North Africa had carefully built and nurtured the sacred groves and the water bodies around them for centuries and millennia. These groves were not just objects of veneration but lifelines of the communities that lived nearby. The Christian destruction of the sacred groves of the Roman Empire, particularly in North Africa, led to desertification and ecological disaster of a scale the region had not seen before. A Hindu, who is taught to protect nature by honouring the bhuta rna, finds it difficult to imagine how someone who goes by the tag of 'saint' can destroy nature so wantonly and cruelly. This destruction was not the result of a few outlier fanatics. The 'saints' who led the destruction of the groves were central to Christianity, and this wanton destruction was very much approved by the Church and sanctioned by the Bible itself: 'And ye shall overthrow their altars, and break their pillars, and burn their groves with fire; and ye shall hew down the graven images of their gods, and destroy the names of them out of that place.'[41]

The Bible itself tells them to destroy the sacred groves by burning them with fire. But the roots of the destruction of earth's ecology are deeper within the Biblical worldview. Scholars trace the root of the current ecological problem to the anthropocentric view of the modern world. We disturbed the balance of nature the moment we put man at the centre of existence as the most important species with all plants and animals for the consumption and use of man. This view is not just modern; it is embedded in the Biblical and Judeo-Christian point of view where the Bible declares that all plants and animals are for man, God's favourite creation, to consume and use at his own convenience. 'Every creature that lives and moves will be food for you; as I gave the green plants, I have given you everything.'[42]

Lynn White traced this connection of today's ecological crisis to the Judeo-Christian worldview, which became universal during the colonial age when the Enlightenment values smuggled some core Christian attitudes as 'universal ideas and institutions' and forcefully made the entire world adopt them.

> Christianity is the most anthropocentric religion the world has seen. As early as the 2nd century both Tertullian and Saint Irenaeus of Lyons were insisting that when God shaped Adam he was foreshadowing the image of the incarnate Christ, the Second Adam. Man shares, in great measure, God's transcendence of nature. Christianity, in absolute contrast to ancient paganism and Asia's religions (except, perhaps, Zorastrianism), not only established a dualism of man and nature but also insisted that it is God's will that man exploit nature for his proper ends. At the level of the common people this worked out in an interesting way. In Antiquity every tree, every spring, every stream, every hill had its own genius loci, its guardian spirit. These spirits were accessible to men, but were very unlike men; centaurs, fauns, and mermaids show their ambivalence. Before one cut a tree, mined a mountain, or dammed a brook, it was important to placate the spirit in charge of that particular situation, and to keep it placated. By destroying pagan animism, Christianity made it possible to exploit nature in a mood of indifference to the feelings of natural objects.[43]

Jews and Christians, the 'chosen people', promised to worship Yahweh, the Judeo-Christian God, exclusively and also to not worship any other god or form of any other deity. Their loyalty was rewarded by their God by giving them exclusive dominion over nature. This attitude survived through the Renaissance and even through the Enlightenment, and it is the Enlightenment, coupled with colonialism, that mainstreamed the anti-ecological stance of the Bible by replacing the eco-sensitive indigenous institutions of traditional societies with Christian-tinted Enlightenment institutions. This resulted in a loss of ecological sense and led to the global ecological crisis.

While Christianity and Islam encourage eco-destructive behaviour by giving dominion of nature to man, dharmic traditions like Sanatana Dharma institutionalize ecological sense by framing customs and rites respecting natural boundaries as holy rituals, enforcing human behaviour that respects nature and preserves ecosystems. Based on the analysis of bhuta rna, we can say that Christianity, Islam, as well as modernity fail on the scale of bhuta rna.

We can thus conclusively say that Christianity and Islam fail on all five counts of the pancha rna worldview, the core framework of Svayambodha for Hindus. It is very clear that Christianity and Islam are not traditions. They are forces that want to destroy dharmic tradition and all its customs and practices by forcing the converts to abandon their duties towards everything they hold dear and sacred and become irresponsible towards the environment and fellow human beings. Any place where monotheism dominates, it will not let the inhabitants complete their rnaubandhas (five sacred contracts of pancha rnas) properly. But is there any other lens, any other Hindu point of view from which monotheism can be seen? There is another deeply Hindu framework from which monotheism has been analysed.

Shri Ram Swarup has used the *yogic chitta bhumis* of Patanjala Yoga *Darshana* and has commented on the non-yogic chitta bhumis and extended them to the nature of prophetic monotheistic gods. It is the most deeply Hindu framework from which prophetic monotheism has been analysed and the most original analysis and turning of the gaze at the shatru.

Monotheism from the Lens of Yogic Chitta Bhumis

To be Hindu is to know the siddhanta of karma-phala-punarjanma and to do sadhana under the guidance of a guru. Sadhana or meditation is central to being a Hindu because Sanatana Dharma banks itself on experience rather than dogma or blind belief. Experience in Sanatana Dharma is not limited to five senses and their extension, the mind. On the contrary, the ancient sages of this great land discovered how to experience the stages of consciousness beyond the six senses, where even the mind disappears and where pure consciousness or knowingness remains.

Dharma is eternal balance. Bharatiya civilization was materially prosperous, but at the same time we never neglected the inner dimension of spirituality and evolved elaborate practices to discover the deepest secrets of life and ask the most pertinent questions: Why do we exist? Why is there something instead of nothing? Why universe? What is the purpose of life? The questions about the universe are questions about oneself too, and in order to know about everything, to gain the highest knowledge, we do not have to foray outside but inside. There is a continuity and oneness between the macro and the micro, and to know the Brahman (Hindu idea of divine), we have to know atman, the self. In the words of Shri Ram Swarup:

> The ancient sages studied man and for that they started with themselves; they turned their gaze inward and found there a vast internal life. Going still deeper, they discovered, beyond their more external being, another life or principle which takes another language to describe it; they found it self-existent, bodiless, pure, luminous and conscious; they found that it is in some way unborn and undying; that it does not come along with the body nor does it die with it; that it is beyond sorrow and decay; that it shines from within and it knows itself as self-evident. They found that it is their very essence, their true Self;

> they called it atman, which is pure, immortal, and untouched by evil. They found that this innermost truth of their being is also the truth of all beings that it is inside as well as outside, that it pervades all; that the atman is also Brahman, that the immanent divine principle is also the transcendental principle and divine ground of all.[44]

Bharatavarsha had a developed vision of the divine because we had a developed vision of the self. That is why we did not run around trying to know every single detail about the universe, although we had fairly developed scientific disciplines too. Understanding that atman is Brahman in its highest form, we set about to know atman and through it to know Brahman, starting from the micro and then grappling with the macro. As the *Kathopanishad* says, '[M]ost men look outward, but some seeking a higher law and life turn their gaze inward and behold the soul face to face.'[45]

While going on this inner journey, we also discovered the roadblocks. Our ancient sages discovered that it was the agency of the chitta that was the major roadblock to knowing the self or the Brahman. It is the chitta that upholds the veil of maya and prevents knowledge from appearing. We set out to overcome the vagaries of the mind; we set upon chitta *shuddhi*. We developed meditational techniques that would first calm the mind and then make it disappear altogether in higher stages. And we wrote texts that detail this process of chitta shuddhi.

The *Yoga Sutras* by Rishi Patanjali is the world's first text that details the process of meditation for chitta shuddhi. The very second sutra declares: योगश्चित्तवृत्तिनिरोधः (Yoga is the cessation of the tendencies of the mind).[46] The *Yoga Sutras* is one of the most wonderful discoveries in human history, where our ancient Hindu sages discovered and recorded the essence of the process of meditation. The text discusses the entire journey an individual takes when practising yoga. Hindus do not 'believe' that Brahman is atman; they know from experience that it is so.

> Yoga gives not only Self-knowledge, *atma-jnana*, it also gives knowledge of God or Gods. The man on the inner journey not only realizes that God or Gods are within him, but he also realizes that he is within them. On this path, one meets many divine figures which are also truths of his own soul. Here, there is no God who hates 'other' Gods; for there are no 'others' here. In a yogic God there is no hatred and no otherness of certain non-yogic Gods. He is in all the Gods and all other Gods are in him; he has also no reason to detest partners, for he does not become less for having them, nor does he cease to be Himself on that account. He realizes Advaita; he realizes that God alone is, which is quite a different thing from saying that there is only one God; he realizes that 'God alone' is not the same thing as a lone God.[47]

Shri Ram Swarup describes beautifully that on the inner journey of yoga, a yogi realizes the oneness of all life. He does not have to believe in the concept of Advaita; rather, he gets to experience it; he witnesses how supreme consciousness, or Brahman, pervades everyone and everything; that not just the living beings but also the inanimate objects form the same continuum of consciousness. He also realizes that the ultimate truth, or the supreme consciousness, cannot be described in words or expressed in any medium. And as he also has access to the siddhanta of the four levels of vak, he knows that the Brahman can only be realized at the level of para, and not in any human language or medium properly. It can only be indicated at. This is why a Hindu who is aware of the fundamentals of Sanatana Dharma can easily tell that any Christian or Islamic claim of presenting the 'final truth' in a human language in a 'Book' is bluff at best and a plain lie at worst. He knows that 'one cannot live another man's truth' and that ultimate truth has to be realized by everyone on his own. A Hindu has no concept of what Shri Ram Swarup calls 'surrogate spirituality'.

The *Yoga Sutras* detail ashtanga yoga or eight stages of meditation: *yama* (restraints), *niyama* (observances), *asana* (posture), *pranayama* (breath control), *pratyahara* (withdrawal of senses), *dharana* (concentration), *dhyana* (meditation), and *samadhi*. When an individual lives through some rules and routine that is conducive to a yogic way of life, when he learns to sit in proper asana for hours at a stretch, when he knows how to control breath (the key to meditation), he then is able to withdraw his senses from samsara, or the outer world, and is able to concentrate and meditate, which then takes him to the highest stage, which is called samadhi, which has no translation in English. Yogic samadhi is the stage where the activity of the mind, or the chitta, ceases, the mind disappears, and knowledge, always present, appears.

This process is commented upon by the greatest of commentators, and it is far out of the scope of the present writer to comment on those processes. Here, the purpose is to attract the attention of the reader towards another side phenomenon of non-yogic samadhis. Yes, they exist. The purpose of all the exposition of yoga and its stages was to bring the reader to the point of samadhi. Shri Ram Swarup stresses in many of his works, including *Hindu View of Christianity and Islam* and *Meditations: Yogas, Gods, Religions*, that Rishi Patanjali has dropped a hint in the *Yoga Sutras* that there are non-yogic samadhis too, which is illuminated more by Vyasa, the great commentator of yoga darshana.

> Vyasa, the great commentator of *Yogadarshana*, does somewhat better. He tells us that mind has five habitual states of planes (*bhumis*): *mudha* (dull or inert), *kshipta* (restless, or probably it is *samkshipta* and means contracted), *vikshipta* (scattered),

> *ekagra* (one-pointed), and *niruddha* (stopped). He makes a further pregnant statement that *samadhi* is natural to mind and it can take place on all *bhumis* (*sarvabhauma*); but he adds a warning that the samadhis of the first three *bhumis* are non-yogic and only the samadhis of the last two *bhumis* are yogic. Only the yogic *samadhi* leads to spiritual development.[48]

Shri Ram Swarup explains how there are different kinds of samadhis and not every samadhi is yogic; not every samadhi will take the seer to the highest level. He says that lower chitta bhumis like *mudha*, *kshipta*, and *vikshipta* are also able to throw up their own characteristic samadhis, and what is most interesting is that these samadhis have their own egogods and desiregods. They have their own *dvesha-dharmas* and *moha-dharmas*. Yoga is a means to access higher reality. Samadhi gives access to higher states of consciousness, and one meets different entities, deities, and gods on this journey. As has been discussed in the Svayambodha section, the entire universe descends from a single source, which we call by various names like Brahman, Parashiva, Mahavishnu, etc. That is why all the deities and higher beings on higher planes of consciousness are also part of the same shakti. Yoga and samadhi take the seer on a tour through this play of consciousness, and he meets various of these gods on his path.

While yogic chitta bhumis yield yogic gods who help and aid the seer in his path towards moksha, non-yogic chitta bhumis and non-yogic samadhi yield ego gods and desire gods who allure the seer away from the path of moksha and lead him towards asuric power, which makes him feel very strong and powerful but which leads to a great fall, as far as the spiritual path is concerned. The god arising from yogic chitta bhumi 'is free, actually and potentially, from all limiting qualities like desire, aversion, hankering, ego and nescience; free from all actions, their consequences, present or future, active or latent. Or in the language of Patanjala Yoga, he is untouched by *klesha-karma-vipaka-aashaya*'.[49] This is not, however, the case with the gods who arise from non-yogic chitta bhumis in non-yogic samadhis; they are egotistical, angry, jealous, covetous, and cruel. These gods have very sharp likes and dislikes; they bestow bounties on chosen people and have other tendencies pertaining to lower stages of consciousness.

> But the god of the ecstasies of non-yogic *bhumi* or *kama bhumi* is very different. He has strong likes and dislikes and has cruel preferences. He has his favorite people, churches and ummahs, and his implacable enemies. He is also very egoistic and self-regarding; he can brook no other god or gods. He insists that all gods other than himself are false and should not be worshiped. He is a 'jealous god', as he describes himself in the Bible.[50]

Shri Ram Swarup gives us a searing insight here, which makes everything about the religious landscape of the world crystal clear. The gods that arise from the non-yogic chitta bhumis like mudha, kshipta, and vikshipta are very much like the God of the Bible and the Quran. Yahweh, the God of the Bible, is self-described as a jealous and an angry god. To a Hindu it would be ridiculous to attribute any quality to the highest godhead like Brahman or Parashiva, let alone a lower quality like jealousy, anger, or quality. But the Biblical God is unashamedly jealous, cruel, and angry. The god of the Quran is no different.

The god of prophetic monotheism is a god arising from a non-yogic chitta bhumi. This explains almost everything about the nature of the Biblical and Quranic God and the nature of Islam and Christianity. The behaviour of monotheistic gods, mediators, and followers can very easily be explained once we understand where their behaviour arises from. All the violence, cruelty, barbarity, and iconoclasm associated with monotheism suddenly become understandable once we understand this idea.

Prophetic monotheism suffers from the problem of undeveloped spirituality as we discussed above. But it is not altogether powerless and not completely unaware of other states of consciousness. The immense power that Islam and Christianity have accrued over centuries is not a complete accident. Their prophets have also tapped into altered states of consciousness, either wilfully or accidentally, and have tasted realms other than the three-dimensional world. But just because someone goes to another state of consciousness does not mean that they have accessed the higher or sattvika states of consciousness. One can also access rajasika and tamasika states during his journey out of the three-dimensional world. The Bhagavada Gita, 'in its last two chapters, discusses various spiritual truths like austerity, faith, duty, knowledge in their triple expression and sharply distinguishes their *sattvika* forms from their *rajasika* and *tamasika* imitations. The same could be said of *samadhis* and their pure and impure forms distinguished.'[51]

It seems very possible that the Biblical God accessed the rajasika and tamasika forms of faith and knowledge, having arisen from a non-yogic chitta bhumi. This is the path breaking insight of Shri Ram Swarup. Taking *purva paksha* to its height, he uses a deeply Hindu lens of the yogic chitta bhumis of the *Yoga Sutras* and analyses prophetic monotheism and its gods from that lens, having arrived at the conclusion that these gods arise from non-yogic chitta bhumis like mudha, kshipta, and vikshipta.

> Jehovah and Allah are non-Yogic Gods, belonging to non-Yogic religions—religions which are more like ideologies than spiritualities. They are self-regarding Gods and embody an intolerant idea. They do not project a too happy psyche, and as their source is not a *dhyana-bhumi* sufficiently deep and pure, they would hardly do for the Gods of developed spiritualities.[52]

This insight will be remembered as a paradigm shift in the history of humankind where a pagan/dharmic/Hindu lens was used by a great Hindu seer and thinker to analyse the nature of Abrahamic or monotheistic god. Shri Ram Swarup has solved many problems with one argument. First, he has returned the gaze successfully. So far, it was Christian, Islamic, and atheist scholars who looked at Hindu dharma and gods from their biased religious lens. While Swami Dayananda returned the gaze, he stopped at a rational and logical analysis of Islam and Christianity, which is brilliant as it is, but is not Hindu at the core, as it does not use Hindu heuristics. Shri Ram Swarup uses a Hindu heuristic model of yogic chitta bhumis in returning the Hindu gaze on Islam and Christianity. And thirdly, he invents a new model of explaining the 'other', while remaining completely within the shastriya or Hindu tradition, as he uses a deeply traditional model, that of chitta bhumis, to achieve his goal.

This will be remembered in the future as one of the greatest insights in the battle between dharma and religion.

He also explains that Christianity and Islam misunderstood some of the deepest traditional or dharmic ideas, like the idea of the oneness, of all life and yet at the same time the plurality of existence, and he also explains why. He says that in yoga, one meets every kind of chitta bhumis, including the kama bhumis and krodha bhumis, but they are seldom presented to the seer unalloyed. They are often mixed with the experience of the higher, more sattvika, purer yogic chitta bhumis and yogic samadhis. Most yogis understand the allures and delusions of non-yogic samadhis and quietly move on to higher states of consciousness. Bhagwan Buddha met many such non-yogic gods and beings in his journey of *nirvana*. The Maya 'demon' that he meets on his journey who allures him with the offer of various kingdoms or various lokas is exactly like the Biblical God who offers 'rivers of milk and honey' to his 'chosen people'.

Buddha, being wiser and sattvika, moved on, like most other Hindu yogis who came before and after him. But the Biblical prophet, like Moses, could not resist the offer of one of these non-yogic gods. The result is prophetic monotheism and the idea of the 'only true god'. Shri Ram Swarup, in his illusion-shattering words, says:

> The 'oneness' attributed to these non-yogic Gods is different from the 'oneness' of a yogic God. The oneness of the latter is like the oneness of the sky which pervades all, which is everywhere and is in all; it contains everything, though it is contained by none; it is Advaita, undifferentiated reality, not the monadity of numbered things. A yogic God is a unity, not a unit, it is compatible with 'other' Gods, includes them, and is manifested by them. The advaitic-God of the Yogas and the *Puranas* is not the monad-God of the Bible and the Quran.[53]

Like the beating Sun clears the clouds of a rainy day, these insightful words of Shri Ram Swarup tell us why Islam and Christianity are not similar to Hindu dharma and Bauddha dharma, why religion is not dharma, and why there can be no *samabhava* or *samanvya* between dharma like Sanatana Dharma on one hand and Islam and Christianity on the other. From a Hindu point of view, Islam and Christianity are guilty of a greater knowledge crime apart from all the violence and barbarity that their followers have wreaked on other societies. They are guilty of 'prajna-aparadha', of promoting and supporting a faulty vision, misleading millions upon millions of individuals the world over for about two millennia.

Apart from all other reasons to fight the Islamic and Christian forces arraigned against Hindu society, the Hindus have a greater reason to do so: to free the world from a deep-seated illusion, the illusion of prophetic monotheism and its non-yogic god.

Why Hindus Did Not Do an Early Purva Paksha of Monotheism?

The groundbreaking insight of Shri Ram Swarup begs a question: why was this not done before in Bharatavarsha? Hindu society has a long tradition of *purva paksha* in which one would thoroughly study and familiarize oneself with the opposite point of view before criticizing it. All the logicians and proponents of different points of view in Vedanta and other systems of philosophy would do a thorough purva paksha of any point of view they sought to refute. The question that arises is that did we do a purva paksha of Islam, especially in the mediaeval era when the attacks were happening? And if not, then why not? Why did we abandon our tradition of studying the opponent upon the advent of Islam?

One of the first great purva pakshas of Islam was done only in the nineteenth century by Swami Dayananda, who did a thorough study of the claims of Islam, Christianity, and their theology. Adopting a rationalist and logical point of view, he demolished all the claims of the opponents thoroughly. He also did a thorough critique of Christianity from the same point of view. In the south, H.H. Chattampi Swamikal did a purva paksha of Christianity in the late nineteenth century. Swami Vivekananda was one of the most significant critics of Christianity and Islam who came after Swami Dayananda. He is not perpetually in criticism and also seeks to accommodate and appreciate but makes the Hindu point of view very clear and rejects some of the most fundamental tenets of monotheism. He was followed by the brilliant Shri Aurobindo Ghosh, who combined the yogic and the rationalist lens to make a searing critique of monotheism.

But it is fundamentally in the school of Voice of India, with two great savants of Shri Ram Swarup and Shri Sita Ram Goel, that the purva paksha of Christianity becomes complete. These two great scholars lay bare every single aspect of these two monotheisms and also their sister ideologies and truly 'reverse the gaze'. Through a series of books, they warn Hindu society of all its dangers and give them solutions about its defense. A host of scholars like Dr Koenraad Elst, Padma Bhushan Shri Vamadeva Shastri (aka David Frawley), Shrikant Talageri, N.S. Rajaram, Arun Shourie, Harsh Narain, Ishwar Sharan, etc., add to the greatest compendium of Shatrubodha ever created in the history of Bharatavarsha.

It is the Voice of India School which makes it a single-point agenda to make Hindus aware of all the existential dangers their culture, dharma, and civilization are facing. Their work also created a host of scholars who are now carrying forward the Shatrubodha tradition of Hindu dharma. The Voice of India School is followed by the brilliant critique of Indology and Western history writing by Rajiv Malhotra, who exposes the designs of seemingly innocuous institutions that are passed off as universal in history but in actuality are very much the products of time and space and are tools of Western (Judeo-Christian) conquest and search for power. The awareness that Rajiv Malhotra spreads adds to the growing renaissance that was created by the Voice of India School and a host of other younger scholars who come up with criticism of monotheistic ideologies. But that is not the point here.

The question that arises is this: When India had a great tradition of purva paksha in its history, then why did we miss criticizing Islam while it had arrived at our gates in the eighth century itself and had established its rule in the thirteenth century? This question has been asked a few times, and the absence of any great Shatrubodha tradition before Swami Vivekananda and Swami Dayananda is taken as a 'proof' that Hindus are incapable of having Shatrubodha. But is it true? We have already seen that when Hindus get to it, they can do a brilliant analysis of their shatru and develop a great tradition of Shatrubodha, as the Voice of India School did. But why did we not do it in the mediaeval ages, is the question.

One reason the Hindus did not do purva paksha of Islam is because the carriers of Islam came to India bearing swords and daggers, and far from debating with Hindu scholars, they beheaded them, destroyed everything Hindus loved, and engaged in a continuous genocide wherever they went. It is not too far-fetched to think that doing purva paksha is a little difficult with no head on your shoulders. Even then there must have been some places and some periods of time when an Islamic attack was away for at least one decade or so. So, was there not enough time and motivation to create a critique?

It seems that Hindu commentators did not consider Islamic attackers to have a theory that was worth refuting. They were all about blood and violence. But that was not the only reason for not countering them. Their behaviour was not only barbaric; their religion seemed to have no darshana (philosophy), only beliefs and dogmas. Their behaviour seemed barbaric and just reactionary with no core or theory of its own. They existed, it seemed, only to negate whatever Hindus did and created. They had an anti-philosophy. Hindu society before this instance had never encountered such an enemy. Every other invader had respected Hindu darshana, temples, rituals, and sacred customs. This apocalyptic Islamic invasion seemed so different. So apart from being taken aback by such inhuman barbarity, Hindu society also considered Islam to have no philosophy worth refuting.

The Sufis came on the trail of the Islamic invaders, but they also aroused very little interest in our acharyas and shastriya tradition, for the Sufis copied Vedantic vocabulary without developing any serious praxis to actualize the darshana contained in the words. By copying Vedantic vocabulary, they once again offered very little to critique or even arouse interest in Hindu acharyas. As Sanjay Dixit says, most of the Sufis who came to India were just Islamic spies who helped Islamic invaders get inside information on Hindu kingdoms and helped pave the way for the destruction of Hindu heartlands.

What Islam offered as theology was nothing more than a collection of law books, the hadith, or the Islamic schools of jurisprudence. So, it was rightly understood as a matter of legal concern and was not considered fit for study by the great acharyas as it offered pretty much nothing in the case of philosophy, let alone spirituality. The Quran was not any different, as it was also a law book. Moreover, any interpretation of the Quran was punished by death by Islamic invaders and the mullahs, and hence it must have scared off others from commenting upon it. The concept of God and other related questions were dealt with by the Sufis, but as said above, they just copied Vedantic vocabulary; hence it invoked very little response in Hindu society.

Islam needed a very novel treatment. It is understandable that the Hindus did not work on it until the age of Islamic rule in India was over. To give Islam a proper purva paksha treatment, Hindus needed to rewire many habits, do cross-disciplinary studies, and needed to invent new categories where law marries philosophy and spirituality. First of all, the very category of 'religion' or '*mazhab*', as Islam was called, was very different from dharma and how dharma was understood in Bharatavarsha. We have already seen how dharma is not religion and how religion is full of dogma, blind belief, and only theory with no practice of inner evolution. It was very difficult for Hindus to understand the category of 'mazhab/religion' as they had no exposure to it before. Hindus could not understand how the most sacred book of Muslims, the Quran, was a law book. To Hindus, many texts were sacred, and they held the Vedas, the Upanishads, and the Bhagavada Gita as the most sublime of sacred literature. But they were very far from being law books. Even the Smritis or the Dharmashastras are far from being mandatory law books like the Quran.

Hindus could understand that Muslims glorified Prophet Muhammad as their role model, but they could not understand that Muslims tried to copy the prophet in the most mundane of matters too, like in washing hands and that too literally. Hindus too considered Shri Rama to be *maryada purushottama*, the best of men, but they were least bothered with what Shri Rama ate, how he dressed, or how he washed his hands. Shri Rama was and is a model of conduct in terms of larger ethics and morality, but nobody is bothered to even think of the mundane matters like how Rama ate or hunted. Moreover, while Hindus followed Shri Rama in one context, they followed Shri Krishna in another and someone else and so on. There was no single model of conduct. There was no single Rama *katha* either, as there were many versions of the Ramayana, and they too kept getting 'edited' according to local taste and need. And one's conscience, or *antah karana*, was always a judge or arbiter in case of any dilemma.

The Hindu could not understand how a universal model of conduct could be created on the basis of the literal interpretation of what one person did in his life hundreds of years ago, without any variations based on time, place, and necessity. Hindus could not understand that common sense and conscience had no role to play in the 'universal law' that Islam had created.

Islam, in total, was a very different entity altogether. It produced a category crisis in Hindu society since we did not know where to place it.

Islam mimicked natural traditions and dharma like Sanatana Dharma in some of its outward manifestations, like a 'place of worship' or 'pilgrimage', but any close inspection of it was confusing for Hindus because they seemed to hit a wall on any attempt at deeper analysis. While any discipline in Hindu dharma has avenues leading to higher darshana, higher spirituality, and ways of self-knowledge, Islamic disciplines yielded nothing. It was as if this strange new religion was a mock palace, which mimicked the appearance of a palace from the outside, but none of the windows or doors actually opened when you went close.

It was just a cardboard box with no openings and nothing inside—just a façade.

To have a complete purva paksha of Islam, Hindus needed a long period of stability where they would be able to create new categories of knowledge. This could not happen in India until the age of Islamic invasions and colonial Islamic rule continued in India. Some of the first great critiques of Islam were done only after the arrival of the British in India. The British arrival changed Hindu perspective a little, for they started feeling that Islam was not an aberration but a type. At first it was only a handful of Hindus who encountered the Christian Portuguese in Goa and some other coastal areas of India. There was virtually nothing different between these Christians of Goa and the Muslim invaders of the Middle Ages. But not many Hindus were touched with the new religion of Christianity. As a result, Islam remained an aberration and did not become a type until the British arrived in India.

The religion of the British, Christianity, was just like Islam in its attitude towards Sanatana Dharma and Hindu rituals. It held native customs and Hindu civilization in disgust and sought to replace Hindu dharma with Christianity. This religion too did not have a deeper spiritual vision or understanding of life. And it too mimicked religion very well. It is with the arrival of British Christianity in India that the Hindu perspective changes. The sense that Islam belonged to a type starts taking root in the Hindu mind, and as soon as this happens, it also galvanizes a response. Some of the first critiques of Islam and Christianity, or monotheism, happened during the era of British rule in India. It is not just Swami Dayananda or Swami Vivekananda who critique Christianity but even Mahatma Gandhi counters it sharply. The Hindu mind is awakened, and ground is set for a complete purva paksha of prophetic monotheism by the Voice of India School. The time is also ripe since even after all the atrocities and impoverishment that the British entail during their rule, a respite from constant physical violence is provided to some states and some places, and the Hindu mind gets to work.

There is one more reason behind this. It was because the chronology of the two monotheisms in India was inverted. Islam arrived here first and Christianity later. Christianity was also prophetic and monotheist, but due to its historical development, it developed a rich tradition of sophisticated theology and religious debates. We remember that Christianity did not become imperial just after its birth, unlike Islam, which became imperial in the life of its founder, Prophet Muhammad. Prophet Muhammad had conquered most of the Arabian Peninsula in his life, and within four decades of his death, Islamic armies held sway from Spain in the west to Sindh in the east, and Islam had become an imperialistic religion in less than a century of its birth.

Christianity, on the other hand, remained a minority religion for almost 400 years after its birth. Having to adapt to the disadvantages of the minority status, it developed a tradition of debate. While the sword could not hold sway, the pen was adopted as there was no other option. Also, without having perks of power to offer to its followers, early Church fathers had to delve into intellectual sophistry to justify Christianity to its followers. This evolved into a tradition of Christian apologia that gave the appearance of intellectual sophistication. When the British came to India with all this pseudo-spiritual but highly intellectual tradition of Christian theology and eschatology, the Hindus found them worthier than Islam as a candidate for purva paksha.

That is why it would not be wrong to say that if Christianity had arrived first in India, we would have developed a tradition of purva paksha of prophetic monotheism much earlier. Because as soon as Christianity arrived and established itself in India, our saints, scholars, thinkers, and philosophers set down for purva paksha and did a brilliant job of it. While it remained scattered in the writings and works of most of the pre-independence thinkers, the post-independence school of Voice of India on one hand and the Dharampal school of Gandhian education and ecology on the other did a thorough critique of Islam, Christianity, and the institutions that it had created and imported in India. Later on, they were joined by the school of S.N. Balgangadhara, where they made a critique of Judaism, Christianity, and Islam as a different category than 'tradition' or dharma.

It is just unfortunate that since India continues to suffer from colonial anti-Hindu institutions of knowledge and communication, these schools of purva paksha were killed with silence, letting a cricketcommentator like Ramachandra Guha say that the 'rightists' in India have no intellectual tradition behind them. Voice of India was kept hidden by the left-liberal cabal, which dominated Indian media and academia until the arrival of the internet broke the monopoly and Shatrubodha School swept through the Hindu youth. The arrival of Rajiv Malhotra on the scene made purva paksha tradition more popular and lent it great credibility. He was accompanied by brilliant scholars, historians, and thinkers like Meenakshi Jain, J. Sai Deepak, Sandeep Balakrishna, Vikram Sampath, Sanjeev Sanyal, and others.

Sanatana Dharma is capable of creating even new institutions and developing new attitudes to tackle a new problem that Hindu society faces. There is much evidence of it. One comes from architecture. In ancient times, Hindus preferred to build their temples in temporary material like they still build the theatre stage. It was more ecological and suited the Hindu rhythm of life. Temples, bearing the similar purpose as the yajna vedi, were also constructed and then deconstructed when the purpose was solved. This tradition can still be seen in various Hindu festivals like Ganesha Utsava, where *utsarjana* (establishing the deva) and *visarjana* (seeing him off) are integral parts of the process. But when the Buddhists came on the scene and started dotting the Indian landscape with cave temples, *chaitya viharas*, and Buddha monoliths all over, there was a danger that the posterity would see the Indian past as only Buddhist. This is when Sanatana

Dharma responds and starts creating Hindu temples in more concrete material like stone and brick, and very soon these stone temples dot the entire landscape of India. Thus, we started a new tradition to tackle a new emergency. Sanatana Dharma is entirely capable of coming up with new institutions and attitudes to tackle an emergency.

To conclude our query, yes, Hindus can develop sharp Shatrubodha. Yes, they can create a new tradition from scratch if they have to. They have done so in the past. The job of this generation of Hindus is to mainstream Shatrubodha so that every Hindu knows who he is not and who his ideological enemy is.

Chapter 9

The Long Arc of Christianity

'The Church had devastating impact upon society. As the Church assumed leadership, activity in the fields of medicine, technology, science, education, history, art and commerce all but collapsed. Europe entered the Dark Ages. Although the Church amassed immense wealth during these centuries, most of what defines civilization disappeared.'

—Helen Ellerbe

Anna, daughter of Giovanni Charboniere of La Torre, being tortured by more pious Christians during the Waldensian massacre, Samuel Moreland, 1658[1]

Dharma is not religion. To confuse them is a category mistake. We have understood this from the previous chapters. They also differ in how they think about the 'other'. While the dharmic sects do not believe in destroying other sects at all, religion is very keen to destroy dharma by converting its followers to a religious sect. Therefore, even while dharmic sects think in eternal cyclical time and religions think in limited linear time, the former have short-term strategies while religions like Islam and Christianity think and plan in long arcs. This is due to the monotheistic aspiration of world conquest and domination. Any sect that wants to convert the rest of the world to its brand of religion will have long-term plans. These plans, when executed, become the long arcs of history. Most policy analysts and international relations experts focus on economy, geography, polity, and short-term politics as they should, but most of them ignore the long arcs of history, which are a result of the world conquest goals of Islam and Christianity. To ignore religion's role in world history is a cardinal mistake.

This is the reason that great economists and political scientists like Francis Fukuyama miss the elephant in the room and make predictions as if religion never mattered. However, we have seen that religion (more particularly prophetic monotheism) is one of the major drivers of world history, along with economy, geography, and technology. We ignore it only at our peril. Another reason that most international relations and policy experts from the West do not mention religion as a great criterion is that they are quite aware that the 'neutral', 'international', and 'universal' policies that they recommend are actually very Christian policies at the core, and they know that by posing them as universal, they will be able to further the Judeo-Christian and Western agenda more powerfully and without any opposition.[2]

This necessitates that the Hindu policy and international relations experts see history and policy in long arcs with religion, and particularly prophetic monotheistic religions, as the most critical criterion in the way the world moves forward. The Hindu experts should expose the underlying Christian assumptions of supposedly 'universal' policy theories and recommendations. This chapter is a humble attempt to do that. In this chapter and the next, we will analyse the long arcs of history with certain religions, like Islam and Christianity, at the centre of these arcs. It makes sense to start with Christianity. There are a few ways in which the long arc of Christianity can be shown. The first one is, of course, the fantastic way in which Christianity grabbed state power in the ancient Roman Empire.

Christianity Conquers Roman Empire

It must have been a ridiculous sight for the pagan inhabitants of Rome to see a ragtag band of unkempt 'atheists' daring to abuse Roman gods in Rome and refusing to partake in any public festivity surrounding Roman festivals. Romans were a very tolerant group and incorporated all kinds of religious practices, provided the tolerated group did not insult the ways of the Romans themselves. It was the policy of the empire to tolerate every religious sect[3] and give them a space in the empire. Rome was a melting pot of various cultures that the Roman Empire ruled. So, they were surprised when this new group did not respect that basic minimum rule of toleration and did not reciprocate the tolerance that Romans showed them. What they realized with shock and disgust was that this hatred for the pagan gods was not accidental but dogmatic to the new cult.

This new cult of 'atheists' built around the hatred for pagan gods and ways of life was none other than Christianity.

We are talking about events happening during the second century CE. The Christians followed a belief system that was so dogmatic, fundamentalist, and radical that they openly abused the gods of an empire that ruled them. Clement of Alexandria, an early

Christian 'philosopher' of the second century CE, called pagan gods 'inhuman demons' and 'hostile to the human race'. He had such hatred for them that he told the pagans that 'man is better than these gods of yours, who are but demons'. Thinking that worship of the gods in icons is nothing but superstition, he declared that those images were 'more worthless than any animal'.[4] We have already seen in chapter 8 how deep the hatred and intolerance for the pagan way of life was in the hearts of the early Christians.

Christians in those times were in great minority, and their numbers must have been only in a few thousand in the empire. They were living in Roman-ruled cities under Roman law and benefitted from the policy of religious tolerance of the pagan Roman Empire. Even Henry Chadwick, a believing Christian and a historian of the Church, could not help in expressing the tolerance of the pagan Roman Empire:

> No pagan cult was exclusive of any other.... The Roman government was in practice tolerant of any cult provided that it did not encourage sedition or weaken morality. Indeed, one reason for Roman military success was believed to be the fact that, while other peoples worshipped only their own local deities, the Romans worshipped all deities without exclusiveness and had therefore been rewarded for their piety.[5]

Pagans believed in what the Romans called *pax deorum*, or 'the peace of the gods'. It was not dissimilar to Pax Sanatanica or the Sanatana umbrella that we discussed in the Svayambodha section. Everyone was free to worship any deity that they liked or what was the tradition in his own region, clan, and family. Like the Vedic advice to let good thoughts come from all sides, the pagan philosopher Symmachus summed up the pagan attitude by saying that it is useless for the Church or any other body to become the gatekeepers of 'only one truth'. He said that it is 'not possible to attain to so sublime a mystery by one route alone'.[6]

And yet this tolerance was never reciprocated, and the Christians kept throwing hatred at pagan customs and rituals, even while they were refugees and minorities in the Roman Empire. Fanatical Christian monk, 'Saint' Augustine said, '[T]hat all superstition of pagans and heathens should be annihilated is what God wants, God commands, God proclaims!'[7] The new cult of Christianity became so powerful later that not only did it destroy Roman paganism but it also succeeded all over the world and changed the world beyond recognition.[8] The world has never been the same after the violent Christian intervention.

This journey, from their minority phase of hurling insulting epithets in the streets and getting persecuted for that to ruling the entire world 'in the name of Christ', constitutes the long arc of Christianity, which pagan/dharmic sects like Sanatana Dharma should study if they want to avoid extinction at the hands of an intolerant monotheistic cult like Christianity.

To be honest, Christians were not the first group to act like this, even inside the Roman Empire. The Jews were actually the first to have the concept of 'false gods' and pour scorn on pagan gods and have an utterly ridiculous sense of religious superiority. The Romans tolerated and incorporated every sect but had a hard time incorporating the Jews, as Justo L. Gonzalez says: 'The Roman brand of tolerance could not reconcile what appeared to be the obstinacy of the Jews, who insisted on worshipping only their God, and who threatened rebellion at the smallest challenge to their faith.'[9]

Even then the Romans did not reciprocate the hatred of the Jews. Pagan 'religious' tolerance is infinite and often to its detriment. Since the Jews did not convert, the Romans were secure that their 'atheist disease' would not spread much. However, Christianity was not the same, and Romans failed to notice and tackle the revolutionary mutation that Christianity introduced—opening up conversions to everyone. Prophetic monotheism, which was born in Judaism but remained a national sect, truly became universal in Christianity.

The Shatrubodha point here to remember is that if the Romans had kept a close tab on the internal affairs of the Jews (and their various sects), then perhaps they would have realized the threat that Christianity posed to them. To them it looked like the Christians were just another Jewish sect. To be honest, this was natural for the Romans to believe because Jews believed in many prophets who kept coming again and again in their history. So, when a Jewish rebel, Jesus, led an uprising against the Romans and got killed as a punishment, they thought it was just another Jewish prophet who appeared and then got killed. From their perspective, nothing new had happened. Rebellions in the Roman Empire and prophets among the Jews were very common things.

But they were wrong. While the Romans punished Jesus and promptly forgot it as an inconsequential event, new churnings were happening in Israel and amongst the Jews. The new Christian sect organized a few decades later by Paul introduced the revolutionary change of accepting converts from other races, ethnicities, and nationalities; that is, they universalized conversion, opening it up to Romans and everyone else. This directly threatened the socio-political balance of Roman society inside Rome, for Christians sought conversion of Romans and Greeks in Rome and the Roman Empire itself, threatening the very demography of the great empire.

Christianity was in religion what Romans were in politics. Romans were multi-ethnic and accepted all as their subjects, provided the subjects accepted the Roman suzerainty. Similarly, the Christians accepted everyone from any background, provided they accepted Christ as their saviour and Christianity as their religion. In hope of growing big and fast, they did not neglect the possibility of influencing and grabbing great political centres of power like the Roman Empire. On one hand, Christians would throw scorn on the pagan way of life, and on the other, they would support one Roman official against another in the court, hoping to get a toehold in the internal politics of the Roman court. But Christianity would become a state religion only in the fourth century. In the second and third centuries, Christians kept playing the dual strategy of influencing one or the other party in the Roman court while discrediting and abusing Roman gods on streets.

Christian tendency to abuse pagan gods in public started drawing the attention of the Roman Empire. Jews had always behaved the same, but they were never big in number. Christians, on the other hand, had started getting a significant amount of converts due to their innovative techniques and methods of conversion. When Pliny the Younger went to what is now northern Turkey to administer that province for the Roman Empire, he was worried that the cancer of the new intolerant religion was fast spreading, and not just in cities; Christianity was spreading even in the countryside, and this was a very worrisome trend.

Christianity would cater to the most disaffected communities and individuals of the empire, exploiting the fault lines of the multinational, multi-ethnic Roman Empire. Christians would accept criminals and other anti-social elements of the society, provided just one thing: that they abandon their ancestral religion and accept the new cult of Christianity. This was a very lucrative offer to the underclass of the Roman Empire since it helped them turn the moral tables on Roman society. Earlier they used to occupy the lowest moral rung of the pagan Roman society. But upon their conversions they would start claiming moral high ground without changing their behaviour at all. Instead of being branded as criminals, they were hailed as heroes by their new 'brothers in religion'—Christians. According to Christianity, it did not matter how one behaved in personal life. One could be a murderer, a molester, a tyrant, a traitor, and yet could go to heaven, provided just one thing—right faith. One could commit all sorts of crime and would still end up in heaven if one believed in the right religion, which was Christianity. Henry Chadwick says, 'What was wrong with the State was its old paganism. Change its religion and all would be well.'[10]

Christianity in the second and third centuries CE got more converts in both European and Asian parts of the Roman Empire. As more churches came up, bishops upped the game of insulting the pagan gods and customs and provoking the empire and the authorities more than ever. This achieved the intended outcome. They ran into the crosshairs of the Roman Empire, and some of them, like Ignatius of Antioch and Polycarp of Smyrna, ultimately got death punishment at the hands of the Roman authorities. This was exactly the outcome that the Church was intending. They were fanatic zealots who believed in the martyrdom myths of Christianity and believed that dying 'in the name of Christ' got them instant heaven. Henry Chadwick, the church historian, confirms:

> The conviction that martyrdom granted immediate admission to paradise and conferred a victor's crown, combined with a somber evaluation of the Roman Empire as a political institution, led to a tendency towards acts of provocation on the part of over-enthusiastic believers ... who were especially prone to identify reticence with cowardice and moral compromise.[11]

Far from fearing death, they courted death at the hands of pagan Romans. While most of these agent provocateurs actually believed they got easy heaven by dying at the hands of Romans while serving Christ, their suicide would allow their community to claim religious persecution and gather more and more sympathy amongst the unsuspecting subjects of the Empire. Portraying themselves as victims of a great power, they got the sympathy of various marginalized sections of the society and got ever more converts. Every 'martyrdom' by a crazy Christian resulted in a fresh harvest of converts among the underclass of society. They were, in short, martyrdom hunters. And they created what Rajiv Malhotra calls 'atrocity literature'—which slanders non-Christians, creates more sympathy for Christianity, and encourages more conversions.

Support for Christianity was growing because more and more ethnic and tribal communities living on the outskirts of the Roman Empire were becoming Christian majority. At first Roman governors in these far-flung provinces of the Roman Empire were keen on punishing the Christian 'martyrdom seekers' who insulted pagan gods and damaged their shrines, but very soon the trickle of these 'martyrs' became a flood. Entire communities had now been converted to Christianity, and even inside Rome, the imperial capital, Christians were growing since more and more criminals and disaffected communities were converting to Christianity.[12]

This was not the only way Christianity was gaining influence. On one hand, they were converting the most disaffected sections of Roman society, like convicted criminals, and on the other hand, they had their eyes on the Roman political elite in Roman court. They were gradually approaching Christian nobles and courtiers and more particularly their wives. Christianity reached the home of Roman nobles first through their wives, who started believing the Christian story in a moment of crisis or due to some benefit in court. Once the wife converted, the husband also converted in secret and started influencing the activities of the court to the benefit of Christianity. They would not openly declare that they had converted, but their activities were suspected and pointed out by the pagan governors and priests as they would stop worshipping pagan gods, stop partaking in festivities organized around pagan festivals and gods, and stop partaking in the sacrificial meat that was distributed after ritual sacrifice to Roman gods and goddesses. This is the reason that the Christians were known as 'atheists', and in many Roman records this is the term used for them. A third-century historian Dio notes that Domitilla, the wife of a high-ranking Roman consul, was accused of practicing 'atheism' or Christianity. Henry Chadwick, while talking about the clashes of the early church and the pagan Roman Empire notes that:

> By the end of the second century Christianity was penetrating the upper classes of society, and more than one highly placed personage might wake up to find his wife embarrassing him by disappearing to nocturnal vigils and prayers. Marcia, the concubine of the emperor Commodus (180–92), was a Christian, and was able to gain for the church in Rome a considerable measure of relief.[13]

The modus operandi of Christianity is this: emperors, rulers, and influential government officials are targeted through various means, often by means of love and romantic associations. Once the relationship is established, the Church and Christian lobby become insiders, receiving various benefits. The State is secretly weaponized for Christianity through these romantic associations, and over time, the institutions of the State become too corrupt, allowing a militant ideology like millenarian Christianity to take over. This is how the Roman Empire fell to Christianity. By the second and third centuries, Christianity had started reaching the upper echelons of Roman society and influencing it from within. By this time Roman leaders and the State had started perceiving Christianity as a threat, but only a minor one, more of an irritant. They tried to suppress it by punishing a few of the Christian culprits who vitiated the social climate by spreading religious hatred about pagan gods and goddesses, but it was too little and too late. Christianity had already started finding deep roots in Roman society. Soon the tables were to be turned.

The fourth century had arrived, and the Roman Empire was going through great sociopolitical turmoil. The attacks of the northern tribes had weakened the defences of the empire, particularly the western parts centred around the imperial capital of Rome. The polity of Rome was also under great trouble. The Roman Empire at that time was ruled by a system called tetrarchy in which the empire was ruled by four emperors in four parts of the Empire, ensuring equality and preventing totalitarian dictatorship. However, the dictatorial tendency was strong, and one or the other claimant to the throne was always thinking of becoming the sole emperor.

Constantine was such an emperor. At the turn of the century, he was one of the four emperors ruling significant parts of the Western Roman Empire, including Britain and what is now France. Constantine was prone to barbaric behaviour and hated any 'outsider', which meant any northern tribe outside the boundaries of the classical Roman Empire. He believed in the genocide of all those defeated tribes and had no mercy for them. On the other hand, he had a growing likeness for Christianity and Christians within his empire, for he saw their religion matching his dictatorial and totalitarian vision. Just as he wanted not four but one emperor to rule Rome, so did the Christians want only one true god, Yahweh, to be established. Just as Constantine wanted to destroy all other centres of power, the Christians wanted to ban and destroy all pagan religions. Just as Constantine hated the pagans outside his empire and wanted to destroy them, so did Christianity. Constantine's dictatorial, totalitarian, and barbaric thoughts and goals were matched by the monotheism of Christianity. 'For those who wish to be intolerant, monotheism provides very powerful weapons.'[14]

Constantine started supporting Christians in the areas that he ruled and developed deep relations with them. He started supporting Christian secessionist activities and started using them as spies and a fifth column in the domain of the other three emperors. In most of the Roman Empire, by then, Christianity was partially 'banned' in public spaces as it involved insult of the pagan gods. Constantine's support of Christians strengthened his position inside the empire while all other emperors kept getting weaker and weaker as their domains were hollowed from the inside by Christianity and weakened from outside by foreign attacks. Christianity and the Church were more than willing to play along with the new emperor, hoping he would convert, and eventually he did. In 313, Emperor Constantine declared in the famous Edict of Milan that Christianity was now 'allowed' inside the Roman Empire. Thus, not only was the previous ban lifted, but Christianity was now 'allowed' to preach and convert.

The Edict of Milan is the most unfortunate event for pagans in the history of humankind. By 'allowing' a predatory religious ideology to convert others to their sect, while the pagans had no concept of 'converting' others, Constantine had virtually signed the death warrant of Roman paganism. It was like 'allowing' a lion and goat to eat each other, claiming 'freedom of expression' and 'freedom of religion'. We all know who will eat whom if a lion and goat are 'allowed' to eat each other.

This pattern would be repeated again and again in history. In fact, it has been repeated in hundreds and thousands of cases all over the world in the past 2,000 years when Christianity has asked for the 'right to convert' in the name of 'freedom of religion' and the 'right of choice to choose religion'. In India, this happened when the Indian Constitution was written and Christian sects were allowed in most parts of India, and 'freedom of religion' was granted to Christianity. It is no mystery as to who converted whom in the subsequent years.

In the 313 CE Edict of Milan, Christianity got a free rein to convert pagan masses by any means. Soon after, Emperor Constantine announced that he had converted to Christianity. The conversion of Constantine is one of the most seminal events in the annals of history, and justifiably so, since it changed the entire history of humankind. By providing an intolerant, militant, and monotheistic religious sect of Christianity, the power of one of the most powerful and richest states in history, the Roman Empire, a lethal weapon against religious tolerance and diversity of the world had been created. Christianity did not lose any time, and using its newfound 'freedom', it started converting the masses by hook and crook. The conversion of Emperor Constantine had signalled to the public whose side the emperor was on. This provided great impetus to Christianity, and paganism lost more space every passing year.

Constantine was not losing any time or opportunity to strengthen his hold on the Roman Empire by using Christianity. He had defeated and diminished in status two other emperors of the Roman Empire by 324 CE, and only the Eastern Roman Emperor of that time, Licinius, remained the last challenge in the path of Constantine becoming the sole Roman Emperor. His time came soon. Constantine portrayed Licinius as the 'protector of pagans' and 'persecutor of Christianity', while he proclaimed himself as the 'protector of one true faith—Christianity'. Christians fomented a civil war in which the Christian West was led by Constantine and the 'pagan East' was led by Licinius. In a series of battles in 324 CE, Licinius lost, and Constantine won to the great jubilation of Christianity. Now the persecution of pagans under the barbaric Christian rule had begun. Constantine was also a megalomaniac, and after his victory, he created a new city on the foundation of the pagan Greek city of Byzantium in 330 CE, renamed it Constantinople in his own name, and made it the new capital of the Roman Empire.[15]

> The speed with which toleration slipped into intolerance and then downright suppression shocked non-Christian observers. Not long after Constantine had gained control of the whole empire in ad 324, it is said that he forbade any governors who were still pagan from sacrificing or from worshipping idols, thus disbarring non-Christians from moving into the plum positions in the imperial government.[16]

Laws were passed to ban the building of new pagan temples, and the new Christian State commissioned church building on an unprecedented scale. Christianity did not lose any time and forced Constantine to declare Christianity as the state religion in 332 CE. This further cemented the death of paganism at the hands of Christianity in the Roman Empire. The floodgates of the greatest religious persecution in the history of humankind had just opened. Forced conversions started everywhere, and fanatic and zealous Christians started persecuting pagan religion, increased the intensity of the destruction of pagan temples, and started breaking their icons and killing pagan priests and prominent pagan philosophers in public. It was an unprecedented genocide of pagans and an unparalleled orgy of destruction of ancient knowledge and knowledge systems at the hands of Christianity.

The story of the destruction of the pagan temples by Christianity is not very different from the sad saga of the destruction of Hindu temples at the hands of Islamic invaders in the Middle Ages. They would also destroy the best of art, architecture, and sculpture that the world had ever seen, for they were created 'in ignorance' by 'idolaters' who were 'living in sin'. The Muslim invaders who destroyed Hindu temples thought they were doing Allah's job, and it was the greatest virtue to destroy Hindu temples and vigrahas of Hindu gods. Similarly, the Christians of the Roman Empire destroyed pagan temples and the icons of pagan gods ruthlessly because they thought, and rightly so, that to be a good Christian they needed to destroy the pagan temples, as Nixey explains: 'The Greek and Roman temples, no matter how ancient or beautiful, were the homes of false gods and they had to be destroyed. This was not vandalism: it was God's will. The good Christian had a duty to do nothing less.'[17]

Christians believed and preached that the 'word of god' had finally arrived, and they had put the final truth in their holy book, the Bible. They declared that since the Bible contained 'final knowledge', if anyone was reading or writing new books, then he must certainly be doing Satan's bidding, and so it was the sacred duty of Christians to destroy all the books of pagans and kill all the philosophers. Half a century after Christianity became the state religion of the Roman Empire, the forced conversions, genocides, and ethnic cleansings of pagans continued everywhere where the writ of the Christian Roman Empire ran. By 381 CE, Christianity had become a majority religion in most of the cities of the Roman Empire. It was then that paganism was officially banned by the Church. It was now illegal to be a pagan in the Roman Empire. The death, destruction, and genocide of pagans continued.

The immense tragedy of this turn of events cannot be realized enough. For until 313 CE, Christianity was banned as a religion in Europe, and within seventy years it got itself first unbanned, then weaponized the empire by conspiring with the emperor, and then banned pagans and paganism in their own birthplace. Within a span of seventy years, paganism went from a majority State-protected 'religion' to a banned one in its own homeland. And very soon it would completely die to the point where not a single true traditional pagan would be alive.

Temples destroyed, books burnt, philosophers beheaded, and 'inferior pagan women' molested and lynched in public: this was the new world that Christianity had created. The mob lynching of Hypatia by fanatical Christian crowds, led by 'Saint' Cyril, is considered the onset of the Dark Ages in Europe, when the classical era of knowledge was over, and the dark ages dominated by the Christian world order descended upon the world. The future had never before looked so dark. Ellerbe tries to convey the extent of this darkness upon the future of Europe and the world: 'The Church had devastating impact upon society. As the Church assumed leadership, activity in the fields of medicine, technology, science, education, history, art and commerce all but collapsed. Europe entered the Dark Ages. Although the Church amassed immense wealth during these centuries, most of what defines civilization disappeared.'[18]

As tragic as this story is, Hindus need to understand the long arc in which Christianity plays. Initially it was a small minority, and it played victim, fooling the majority that they were the victims instead of being the perpetrators of epistemic and physical violence. Once this 'persecuted Christianity' got power, it used that same power to persecute pagans at a genocidal scale and destroyed the entire classical civilization with all its knowledge systems, art, and science within a span of seventy short years. While Christianity was in the minority, it played victim and popularized the imagery of Christ as 'lamb', showcasing the victim status of the new religionists. But once it got power, it started projecting Christ as a 'lion', because now the role was reversed, and Christianity and the Church had become the persecutor. From the advent of the new religion in the first half of the first century CE, it took them 350 years, but they eventually won control of the greatest empire in the West by staying persistent in their goal of world domination.

Having a long arc in mind, they bided their time of being out of power, patiently waiting for an opportunity to grab power, and when that opportunity came in the form of the emperor's conversion, they went for the kill without losing time and sealed their victory as permanent by destroying paganism completely and by converting the majority of the European population to Christianity.

Just as it is important for Hindus to perceive rta, the cosmic rhythms of life, it is also equally important for them to understand '*anrta*', or the long arcs of untruths in which monotheistic religions operate. In principle, nothing can be opposite of rta, as all cycles, good or bad, come within it. But any cycle that perpetuates for a long time, but which is against rta, can be called anrta, because it has the potential for great destruction over a long period of time.[19] It does collapse eventually, but when it does, it has already destroyed a lot. These cycles, just by existing for a very long time, mimic rta, but they are not rta. They mimic the dynamism while lacking real dynamism. Monotheistic cycles, being very long but inherently untrue and misaligned with cosmic rhythms, can be called anrta. Let us analyze a few of them.

How Aquinas and Scholastics Digested 'Rationalism' to 'Prove' Christianity

> The Son of God was crucified: I am not ashamed—because it is shameful. The Son of God died: it is immediately credible—because it is silly. He was buried, and rose again: it is certain—because it is impossible.[20]

This is what Tertullian, one of the greatest Christian scholars of the third century CE, thundered about his faith in Christianity. He wrote these words to declare the intensity of his faith in Christianity and at the same time declared that rational logic, reality, or facts were not a criterion in a religion like Christianity. A war was being waged in the early first millennium CE between the rationalist pagan mindset on one hand and the blind belief of Christianity on the other. And unfortunately, Christianity, with all its blind belief and superstition, was winning. There was no rational way to counter the enquiring Greek mind, but Christian fanatics like Tertullian did not need a lot of rationality. Blind belief was all that Christianity needed, being based purely in dogma and not in practices. Early Church fathers understood that there was no need to rationally defend Christianity, and they built upon faith as opposed to reason. Most of the writings of these early Christian scholars are full of declarations of blind and superstitious faith.

But every human cycle comes to a stop after running its course. By the twelfth century, the time of blind faith in Christianity was mostly up. Pagans were all gone by then, either killed or converted to Christianity. Except for some pockets in the northeast, Europe was completely Christian. It is then that the deficit of blind faith started becoming too obvious to a society that had become poor, sick, and barbaric under the totalitarian rule of the Church and the smothering dominance of Christian blind faith. Human limits had been reached. It was time for change.

It is at this juncture that we find a group called the scholastics taking control of the intellectual climate of Europe. The leaders of the scholastics understood that the Age of Faith was over, and the Age of Reason was in the offing. They realized that the future belonged to reason as Europe was bound to rediscover its European pagan roots. Understanding that reason and logic could no longer be banned, they set upon appropriating them for the Church. The goal was to secure the future for Christianity and the power of the Church. No matter what happened, the control of the Church on the world could not be weakened. Thomas Aquinas was one of the most famous of scholastics. He is known as one of the greatest theologians of the Church. It is his vision that changed the future course of the scholastics.

Instead of persecuting and suppressing the 'heathen' desires of Christian scholars for reason and logic, the scholastics decided to use these latest intellectual fashions and trends to Christianity's benefit. Aquinas in particular sought to interpret Aristotelian philosophy through a Christian lens, digesting the pagan Greek philosophy in Christian theology. Before scholastics, Christian theology had little to do with philosophy. Aquinas and the scholastics set out to wed theology and philosophy. For this, entire institutions had to be created to house the scholars, and institutional mechanisms were to be created so that while interacting with ancient Greek philosophy, Christian theology would always have the upper hand.

Not many know that at the foundations of the modern university system is the Christian attempt to 'prove' Christianity through academic and intellectual methods. Church historian Justo L. Gonzalez explains:

> The thirteenth century, which marked the apex of papal power and the birth of the mendicant orders, was also the high point of medieval scholasticism. This theology, which developed in the schools, had its own characteristic methodology. It took root first in monasteries, but in the twelfth-century cathedral schools became the center of theological activity, only to be supplanted, early in the thirteenth century, by universities. From monasteries, which usually existed apart from centers of population, theology moved to cathedral schools, that is, to schools connected with churches that had bishops—and therefore were usually in cities. Then it centered in universities, which were vast associations of scholars gathered in the principal cities.[21]

Gonzalez makes it very clear that when the Church was at its zenith and when monastic orders of Christian monks were taking Christianity to the wider world, it was then that the foundations of the modern university system were laid. Using the method of dialectical reasoning, the scholastic method would involve posing a conventional Christian approach as a question, which would then be taken apart by doubters. Church theologians would then come up with intellectually sophisticated methods to defend the Christian position after figuring in all the queries that could be raised about Christianity. Anselm of Canterbury, who is said to be the forerunner of scholastics, even before Aquinas, had set out to use 'reason' to serve Christian belief or dogma. 'Anselm's significance for the development of scholasticism lies in his desire to apply reason to questions of faith. What he sought in doing this was not to prove something that he did not believe without such proof, but rather to understand more deeply what he already believed.'[22]

It is very clear here that Anselm or other scholastics here were not ready to accept a result that was contrary to their beliefs. Rather, the whole exercise of 'reason' was to make it serve the cause of faith. Only those 'rational' arguments would be used that supported their thesis, and everything else was ignored. Their goal was not the pursuit of truth. Their goal was to 'prove' Christianity from a new methodology that was becoming popular. In a way, most of the humanities today treat research in this way. The problem statement is taken as belief, and then evidence is gathered by quoting text after text to support the original claim, and this is how 'faith' becomes 'rationalized'.

Scholasticism, especially after Thomas Aquinas, became a method 'which applies reason to a truth known by faith, in order to understand it better'.[23] Far from a triumph of rationalist thought, it is the act of using the scholastic method to prove the 'Christian truth'. Obviously not all areas were considered legitimate for this rationalist enquiry. While areas that were considered largely the domain of science were freely subjected to scholastic thought, areas that were considered matters of faith were very carefully guarded.

Aquinas willingly subjected most of the Christian faith to scholastic rationalist enquiry and jettisoned much that was part of it in order to save the core of Christianity. An Augustine or a Tertullian would be angry looking at what Aquinas sacrificed from Christian faith, but had he not done so, Christianity would have collapsed entirely as a religion. He adapted Christianity to weather the next intellectual storm that was to envelop Europe for the next few hundred years. He was preparing Christendom also for the Enlightenment, which was the culmination of the rationalist enquiry. He foresaw the Enlightenment tendencies in the intellectual churnings that were happening all over Europe, and he set out to pre-empt it with a Christian response. As Gonzalez accepts: 'Thomas's significance is ... in his ability to turn a philosophy that many considered a threat into an instrument in the hands of faith.'[24]

Aquinas's most famous book, *Summa Theologica*, is one of the crowning achievements of scholasticism, and it is a text that serves Christianity. The institution in which Aquinas was working later became one of the first universities in Europe—the Pontifical University of Saint Thomas Aquinas. The 'Christian truth' was guarded by the peers who controlled knowledge creation in these universities. Elaborate methods, mirroring the peer review process today, were designed to ensure that only those graduated to powerful academic positions who were true believers in Christianity while exhibiting all the external signs of rationalism.

Aquinas and his scholastics achieved this with three manoeuvers: The first one was not to reject the rationalistic enquiry of his age but to embrace it in 'secular' spheres like science. The second step consisted of taking control of all institutions that provided the outlet of the rationalist urge. The third one was to allow the rationalist enquiry in all 'secular' spheres but not let it question the foundation and fundamentals of the 'Christian truth'. This censuring was ensured by the caucus of professors and scholars who guarded the elite club of university education, ensuring that the crimes of Christianity against pagans and others would remain hidden and its belief system would keep intact.

In the short term, Aquinas' innovations seemed to 'weaken Christian orthodoxy' by allowing 'new ideas' and 'new attitudes', as many unimportant but popular dogmas were abandoned in favour of 'open thinking', but in the long term, the university system created by Aquinas and the scholastics proved to be a great boon to Christianity and its propaganda machine. The vision to have foreseen intellectual waves of the future and to co-opt them can only be the product of a culture that has long arcs of history in mind, and Christianity was and remains such a force that thinks and plans its manoeuvers over millennia.

'Indigenization' of Christianity in India

Another great example of the long arc vision is the 'indigenization' of Christianity in India. 'Indigenization' here has a very technical meaning. It means clothing Christianity in Hindu symbols, language, and mannerisms in order to convert Hindus by deception. This process started much before the British arrival in India but picked up pace during their colonial Christian rule. It is wrong to say that the British did not try to convert Hindus. In the eastern Himalayas, they directly engaged in conversions to make the locals more loyal to the Christian British Crown. In the rest of India, they found Hindus to be too resistant to any Christian missionary activity, and hence they acquired indirect methods of conversion. Having the long arc in mind, they set upon creating institutions and cultivating habits inside Hindus that would make them more conducive to Christian missionaries in centuries to come.

Christian missionaries, much before the British set foot in India, were arguing for methods and mechanisms of conversion that were not direct but deceptive. As Sita Ram Goel writes in his brilliant expose of the insidious Christian conversion activities, *Catholic Ashrams: Sannyasins and Swindlers*, the early Christian missionaries in India lamented that the Hindus were very hard to convert because their resolve for dharma remained very strong. The missionaries then fell upon fraudulent methods of conversion in which they adopted Hindu symbols overtly to fool the population that Christianity is just another sect of Hindu dharma. Under this 'indigenization' or 'inculturation' movement, various Christian sects adopted Hindu terminology as well as dresses, symbols, and habits of Hindus in order to deceive them and convert them to Christianity. Sita Ram Goel says:

> It is obvious, say the mission strategists. Christianity has to drop its alien attire and get clothed in Hindu cultural forms. In short, Christianity has to be presented as an indigenous faith. Christian theology has to be conveyed through categories of Hindu philosophy; Christian worship has to be conducted in the manner and with the materials of Hindu *puja*; Christian sacraments have to sound like Hindu samskaras; Christian Churches have to copy the architecture of Hindu temples; Christian hymns have to be set to Hindu music; Christian themes and personalities have to be presented in styles of Hindu painting; Christian missionaries have to dress and live like Hindu *sannyasins*; Christian mission stations have to look like Hindu ashramas.[25]

The purpose was to mimic Hindu dharma so well that Hindus cannot differentiate between Christianity and other Hindu sects in their overt aspects. We know that mimicking dharma and great sacred traditions was mastered by Christianity ever since its inception. For 'indigenization', most of the institutions of Hindu dharma were to be copied but, of course, repurposed to the nefarious Christian agenda of conversion. Father Bede, a pioneer of 'indigenization', wrote:

> In India we need a Christian Vedanta and a Christian Yoga, that is a system of theology which makes use not only of the terms and concepts but of the whole structure of thought of the Vedanta, as the Greek Fathers used Plato and Aristotle; and a spirituality which will make use not merely of the practices of Hatha Yoga, by which most people understand Yoga, but of the great systems of Karma, Bhakti and *Jnana* Yoga, the way of works or action, of love or devotion, and of knowledge or wisdom, through which the spiritual genius of India has been revealed through the centuries.[26]

Robert de Nobili was one of the greatest proponents of this approach in India. He worked in India in the first half of the seventeenth century, from 1606 CE onwards. He mimicked Hindu symbols, dressed like a Brahmin, called the Bible the 'Yesurveda'—the Veda of Jesus—and preferred Indianizing church architecture. He even went to the limit of wearing the sacred thread and keeping a tuft, thus looking like Brahmins for all practical purposes, but carrying an insidious agenda of conversion of Hindus to Christianity. He called the churches he established 'kovils', as he was working in Tamil Nadu. He composed Christian prayers in Tamil and used Hindu devotional music. He mimicked Hindu samskaras and translated the hymns read during Christian rituals into Tamil and Sanskrit. He called himself and his fellow missionaries 'Brachmans', which sounded very similar to the word 'Brahmin'. All of this fooled Hindus into believing that he was just another leader of just another Hindu sect.

> The Hindus he baptized did not have the faintest notion that they were embracing another faith, least of all Christianity which they despised. The ritual they were required to perform was washing with water from a nearby well, a change of clothes, muttering of mantras coined by De Nobili, and eating of 'prassadam'. They did not suspect that the new names they were given were the names of Christian saints translated into Tamil. All they were told and knew was that they were being initiated by a Brahmin guru into his own '*sampradaya*'. Such initiations were at that time, as they still are, a routine matter for most Hindus.[27]

The efforts of De Nobili did not bring many results in his own lifetime. He converted a little more than a hundred Hindus to Christianity, who promptly reverted back to Hindu dharma as soon as they realized the true purpose of De Nobili. But De Nobili remained unfazed and never relented from his claim that if Christianity wants to succeed in India, then it needs to indigenize and mimic the cultural symbols of Hindu dharma.

His approach did not die with him, and there were some natives, like Brahmabandhab Upadhyaya from Bengal, who converted to Christianity but did not change their name or attire, food, and customs. The movement that was started by De Nobili kept simmering at low heat for centuries until it finally started showing signs of success in the early twentieth century. This was the time when great Hindu saints like Swami Vivekananda, Shri Aurobindo, and others had started the Hindu Renaissance. With rising Hindu resurgence, it was felt necessary by the Church leaders of India and the Vatican to revive the deceptive methods of indigenization of De Nobili. Catholic 'ashrams', as the Christians called their indigenized churches, were opened at many places in India with complete indigenization of the churches.

This indigenization process was not limited to the few churches that were created in these Catholic 'ashrams'. The idea caught on. By India's independence, converts had started coming in some numbers to Christianity through this technique, and so they doubled down on it. Churches in Kerala, Tamil Nadu, and other states like Andhra Pradesh started sporting *deep stambha*, which mimics the deep stambha in a Hindu temple almost completely, with brass coating and all the elements that are necessary, but with just one small cross at the top betraying its true affiliation. Mary was called *Mata Mariam*, churches were called as '*mandirs*', and other overt signs were adopted in many places in India to deceive Hindus into believing that Christianity was not very different from some of their Hindu sects.

And gradually, it started bearing fruit. Hindus started converting to Christianity in many places where conversions were unheard of before. Andhra Pradesh faced, and continues to face, the greatest calamity in its history when it had Christian chief ministers in Y.S.R Reddy and his son Jagan Reddy. Punjab saw a rise in conversions after the Christian-conducive reigns of Captain Amarinder Singh and during the reign of the Aam Aadmi Party.

In all of these places, the techniques are very close to those that were suggested by De Nobili. The Christian converts in these places do not change their names, clothes, or even language. In Punjab, the indigenization is taken to another extreme, where turbaned and bearded Sikhs are now Christian pastors, converting lakhs of Hindus and Sikhs. Most of the Christian pastors in Punjab today have very Hindu names, like pastor Ankit Narula. They speak the local language and eat local food. Until they tell someone, it is impossible to guess their religion. This nativization and indigenization of Christianity is becoming dangerous to Hindu society and the integrity of Hindu civilization.

The point here is that a technique that was invented and perfected almost 400 years ago is only now bearing fruit, but Christianity and the Church kept backing it through centuries, keeping the long arc in mind. An ideology that thinks in millennia banks on long-term investments in institutions. These institutions become vehicles for conversion later on. Hindus should learn to sustain and create institutions and strategy with long arcs in mind so that Sanatana Dharma can keep flourishing for all future.

Civilizational Snipers

Hindu society's struggle with fundamentalist Islam and Christianity, like any civilizational war, has its highs and lows. Sometimes Islam becomes more powerful; sometimes Hindu society seems to be resisting and resurging well. Sometimes Christianity seems to have the upper hand; sometimes Hindus consolidate better and do not relent as easily to conversions. The point is that there are definitely periods of time when Hindu society is not in such bad shape, conversions are not going full swing, and the demographic balance is more or less maintained. This gives a sense of stability to the Hindus, and many of them become complacent that the threat of Christianity has now 'receded', or 'stabilized'. Nothing can be more dangerous to Sanatana Dharma than this delusional attitude of Hindus. It is these illusions of stability that delude Hindus into thinking that the threat is no more and that they might even be winning.

The tide with Islam and Christianity will not be reversed until Hindus start reconverting Christians and Muslims back to Hindu dharma. Without the idea of *shuddhi* or *ghar wapasi*, there is no real stability between the two sides of the war. If Christianity just keeps converting and Islam just keeps growing in numbers, then it is not a matter of 'if', but just a matter of 'when' that Hindu society will be no more, and Hindu dharma will cease to be a practicing dharma. This is not to say that Hindu society will die, but it is not an impossibility if Hindus do not prepare for the civilizational war by understanding the psyche of Islam and Christianity very deeply. This is why Swami Vivekananda believed that Hindus also have to take back converted Muslims and Christians back to the Hindu fold.[28]

Hindus have to understand that the highs and lows do not have the same meaning to them as they do to their opponents in this civilizational war. For Islam, 'highs' meant wholesale destruction of Hindu culture, society, and heritage; mass conversions to Islam; and rapid spread of Islamic culture. 'Lows' on the other hand might mean just a lowering of the intensity of this perpetual war of destruction, or at best just a temporary cessation of the destruction of Hindu society and culture. For Christianity, 'highs' mean control of the Indian state, Indian institutions, and a free pass to Christian missionaries to convert Hindus. 'Lows' on the other hand might just mean all the above activities during 'highs', just at a low intensity.

Ever since its birth, Christianity has been constantly growing. For the first millennium, it remained confined in Europe but made a complete conquest of it, converting all pagans and destroying paganism completely. In the late fifteenth century, it burnt North and South America in an unprecedented orgy of genocide and mass killings, completely Christianizing the two continents by encouraging European settlements and converting the few remaining natives to Christianity. In the nineteenth century, it was Africa's turn, and within a century, African religions were eradicated in a religiocide by Christianity. Sometimes they sprint; sometimes they stroll; but they never backtrack. On the other hand, Hindu society continues to lose piece after piece, and if the current state of affairs continues, it will only be a matter of time before Hindu society is completely absorbed into the Islamic and Christian civilizations.

This is the reason that Hindus cannot become complacent in the period of 'lows' in this civilizational war. This is the reason that Hindus cannot be happy with just maintaining the status quo. Sometimes even great and visionary Hindu leaders feel that their job is done if they are able to maintain the status quo. While it is a matter of great pride for any Hindu leader who achieves this great feat against the onslaught of Islam and Christianity, one needs to understand that this is not enough.

Maintaining the status quo is not enough if one side always keeps growing and the other side always keeps losing. Maintaining the status quo is not enough if Islam and Christianity have inbuilt mechanisms of converting the 'other' into their own branch of 'religion', but Hindu dharma has no agency to counter these lethal tactics. Maintaining the status quo is lethal to the Hindu side when the nature of the enemy is such that as soon as the status quo breaks, even if after hundreds of years, the ancient game of death, destruction, and conversion of Hindu society starts apace once again.

Islam and Christianity agree to a ceasefire to regroup, re-strategize, and attack again. They pickup from where they left off just as a game in suspended animation restarts. Not even a status quo of 400 years is enough when Hindus rule with equanimity and civility in a state like Chhattisgarh, for as soon as this status quo breaks, Christianity and Islam will start picking them up piece by piece.

And in a game of survival, a miss is as good as a mile.

It is not enough to resist and maintain the status quo. Hindus will not win until they make ghar wapasi a central policy of their State, society, and dharmic sects and sampradayas.

We need to understand that Christianity is like a civilizational sniper. It is like that silent enemy sitting at your borders, hidden in plain view, waiting silently for the opportune time. As soon as the time comes, it shoots with clinical precision and achieves its goals. Meanwhile, the prey gets complacent, thinking that the danger has subsided or ended completely, not knowing that the enemy has enough resources, patience, and a long arc vision of history to wait the 'low' out until it is an appropriate time for it to strike.

This is why Hindus cannot rejoice in the fact that Christianity has not become successful in many parts of Uttar Pradesh and Rajasthan by now. This is why Hindus cannot rejoice in the fact that Chhattisgarh and Madhya Pradesh are still largely Hindu states. This is why Hindus cannot become complacent by knowing that Tripura has resisted Christian conversion activities largely by now. For Arunachal Pradesh was also a pristine and a virgin state until the 1980s, when there were scarcely any Christians in the state. Hindus were complacent even then. Just fifty years from then, it is almost a Christian-majority state. The Mizos and Nagas maintained their dharma and respected and revelled in Hindu/dharmic/pagan culture for thousands of years until just 150 years ago. In the span of a century, they were converted to Christianity by the British, and later by all the Christian forces in the world after Indian independence, when India virtually left its northeast to civilizational vultures.

Christianity waits, sniper-like, at the boundaries of Hindu dharma, waiting for centuries to strike at the appropriate time.

Let us take a few of these examples where it has destroyed other dharmic and traditional civilizations with its expertise in civilizational sniping. One of the most striking cases is that of South Korea. The Korean Peninsula today stands divided between two of the most mutually hostile countries in the world—North Korea and South Korea. But things were not always so. During the Second World War, Japan had colonized large parts of Korea, and when the Axis powers lost the war, the Allied powers took over. While the northern part of the undivided Korean country and peninsula was occupied by the Soviet Union and the communist forces, the southern part was occupied by the United States of America and the Western partners of the alliance.

Korea was divided into two countries. While North Korea became communist under the Soviet Union's rule, South Korea became an independent capitalist country, but under heavy military, market, and political influence of the United States of America and the West. The story of North Korea is known to everyone. In short, the communist dictatorship killed free market and all citizen enterprise, destroyed all private property and entrepreneurial skills, created man-made famines due to state interference in agriculture, destroyed all traditional Korean institutions, including education and medicine, and killed lakhs upon lakhs of innocent Koreans directly and indirectly due to real and supposed opposition to the brutal communist dictatorship.[29] The communist destruction of North Korea is one of the greatest human tragedies to have unfolded in the latter half of the twentieth century, apart from the genocide of Hindus in Bangladesh and Kashmir.

This story of the genocide of innocent North Koreans in North Korea by their own government is known to most, if not all, and justly so, since it is an immense human tragedy. However, in the smoke that rises from the communist ruins of North Korea, the world often entirely neglects the destruction of the other half of Korea by a very dangerous prophetic monotheistic cult. The story of the ethnocide of Korean culture by their own State in South Korea is known to very few, although hiding in plain sight.

From 1945 to the dawn of the twenty-first century, the ancient Korean civilization was destroyed by Christianity, in what can only be described as civilizational sniping.

South Korea had scarcely any Christians before 1945, as it was never colonized by any Western power. Some Christian missions were established in its capital and a few more big cities, but they scarcely found any new converts and basically functioned for the European and American merchants who lived and frequented there. However, after the Korean civil war, the United States of America, along with the entire Christian missionary establishment of the West, established itself in the country. It was considered an emergency manoeuver back then, for if the USA had not saved South Korea from the communist advance in the north, then the entire Korean Peninsula would have been won over by communism, and in an age when communism was the greatest threat to the Western world, abandoning South Korea was an unthinkable option. Thus, the USA's presence in South Korea could be explained by geopolitical emergencies, as it is still in international annals.

But dharmic societies forget one crucial geopolitical lesson at their own peril. It is always helpful to the colonial powers if the colonies they are occupying convert to the religion of the colonizer. We shall do well to remember the dictum that the easiest and longest way to colonize a society is to change its religion. Christianity, being fundamentally a colonizing force, goes hand in hand with colonialism. The Church finds it easier to establish itself and convert the natives if the colonizing force is present with its military and political influence, and the colonial powers in turn find it easier to 'pacify' the natives if they are converted by the Church to Christianity.

In fact, conversion is the only real colonialism, for it lasts the longest. As Desmond Tutu once said, 'When the Missionaries arrived, the Africans had the land and the Missionaries had the Bible. They taught how to pray with our eyes closed. When we opened them, they had the land and we had the Bible.'[30] Monotheistic religions are nothing but colonial ideologies masquerading as sacred systems.

This is what happened in South Korea after the Korean civil war ended in 1953 and the DMZ (Demilitarized Zone) was created, just like the LOC (Line of Control) was created between India and Pakistan. DMZ is one of the most heavily militarized borders on earth. The spectre of communist armies invading the south never disappeared for South Korea because North Korea was supported by the communist Soviet Union in its early years and afterwards by communist China. While China adopted market capitalism during the Deng era, they intentionally kept North Korea a closed communist hellhole for the sake of Chinese political interests. It is a sad story that an ancient civilization like Korea was carved up between a horrible communist force in the north and Christian missionary vultures in the south.

The spectre of communist North Korea with its crazy leader justified the continued presence of the US Army and many of its attendant institutions in South Korea, the most prominent being the various churches that descended upon hapless South Koreans who were suffering from not one but many tragedies. The Korean civil war was the result of the Second World War, in which Japan, one of the Axis powers, had invaded and occupied Korea during the war years. It committed many atrocities upon the local Koreans during that time, and the tales of Japanese brutality are still fresh in Korean memory. The Japanese followed the natural religion, or better known as Shinto dharma, which is similar to the local Korean dharma of Sendo (another version of Shinto).

The Church, always quick to exploit any fault line, jumped to exploit the situation as soon as the war was over and claimed that the native Sendo dharma is evil since it 'collaborated' with the invading Japanese. They managed, through the Christian global propaganda machine, to convince people that Japanese military atrocities were actually inspired by Shinto dharma. Since the Korean Sendo tradition was related to the Shinto tradition of Japan, the Church swiftly moved to destroy Sendo dharma in the twentieth century just as it destroyed pagan tradition and natural religions of Europe in the first millennium.

Using their global propaganda channels, the Church sold this lie that Sendo dharma is evil, and Christian missionaries converted the Koreans en masse. Christianity was claimed as the religion of the future, progress, and modernity. Economic success, which was quite unrelated to Christianity, was shown as a feature of the 'future-looking', 'fast-moving' lifestyle that was inseparable from a 'modern religion' like Christianity. The recent arrival of Christianity was used to claim its modernity, and the ancient, timeless origin of Sendo was taken as proof of its backwardness. Of course, the long and ignominious history of the genocide, misogyny, and intolerance of the Church was very carefully hidden.

Christianity thus exploited an extraordinary situation that Korea went through. Due to no fault of its own, Korea was plunged into war. The Second World War was completely a European Christian affair, and the entire world was involved in it because it was the great age of colonialism, and the colonies had no choice but to join the war. East Asia, however, would have remained very far from ground zero because China, Korea, and Japan were not colonized countries, if not for one little detail. Japan itself had joined Germany and Italy in the Second World War and had colonized various parts of the Pacific and East Asia, including the Korean Peninsula and Chinese mainland. Thus Korea found itself under the occupation of an Axis power, Japan. Japan was a strange bedfellow of Germany and Italy, but it joined them because it was humiliated by the USA almost a century ago. Japan was closed to the West and missionaries, but the USA forced Japan to open up and trade with the West by first defeating it militarily. Japan never forgot the humiliation, and when the Second World War started and Germany and Italy were fighting against the USA and Britain, Japan joined Germany to fight the USA. Japan's arena of war was the Pacific, and the first countries that it occupied were Korea and parts of China.

Korea found itself under the brutal Japanese occupation in this way. When Japan started losing in the war, the Soviet communist armies found the excuse to invade Korea from the north, and the Christian Western armies also found it okay to invade Korea from the south in the pretext of saving it. Thus, Korea found itself as the playground of Western Christian powers after the brutal occupation by Japan. Untold atrocities were committed by the communists in Korea during that time, and thus South Korea was 'freed' with the help of Western powers as a 'free', capitalist, 'open' country, with just one caveat. It was not free from Christianity's death embrace. Rather, Christianity and the Church were left free to destroy one of the most ancient natural religions in the world—the Korean Sendo tradition—and replace it with barbaric and superstitious beliefs of dogmatic Christianity. South Korea's 'democratic' and 'free' nature was just a pretext for the Church to carry out conversions without any opposition.

Korea was fresh out of two disasters—Japanese occupation and communist atrocities. This civilizational crisis is something in which Christianity thrives and has become an expert at exploiting any culture or society that is suffering from it. Almost all the Sendo followers of Korea were converted to Christianity in the next three to four decades. Sendo, as a dharmic tradition, is almost dead in Korea now. And it is an utter tragedy of multiple dimensions since Sendo is the original and native tradition and dharma of Korea. Only Buddhists, who had international support, largely survived the conquest of Korea by Christianity.

The sudden death of the ancient Sendo dharma and the sudden spurt of Christianity resulted in nationwide calamity at many levels. Sendo's death meant a violent break from the ancestral tradition in Korea, a devastating violation of pitra rna and deva rna. This resulted in calamities of chronic psychological diseases. Korea today is one of the most endemically depressed countries in the world with some of the highest suicide rates. The cost of living has become so steep that Koreans are not marrying or having kids because it is impossibly costly to do so. The economy too is now stagnant after a few miraculous decades, and the disappearance of meditational practices and rituals from Korean society has resulted in a nihilist, atheist life devoid of hope, spiritual discipline, or order in life.

Atheism has become a pandemic in the country, and around half of Koreans now list themselves as atheists. The loss of belief in their ancient dharma has encouraged them to abandon all rituals. And Christianity has been unable to bring permanent happiness or order to their life. It was able to fool Koreans that it was Christianity that was bringing happiness into their lives while it was the rapid economic boom that brought many material pleasures. However, the situation was exploited by Christianity. But after the brief period of economic euphoria was over, when everyone was benefiting from the financial bonanza, depression set in. Devoid of rituals and ancient customs, nothing is sacred anymore, and the worst form of materialism contributes to the countrywide epidemic of clinical depression and suicide.

The Shatrubodha point to learn here is how Christianity waited for more than 1,000 years for an ancient civilization like Korea to go into multiple crises simultaneously and how it exploited that extremely rare situation to its own benefit and managed to convert Korea to Christianity. An ancient pagan tradition, the Korean civilization, unaware of the monotheistic designs of Christianity, was hit by the sniping Church, which was waiting at the borders, and as a result, ancient Sendo dharma of Korea was destroyed within half a century.

This is how Christianity behaves like a civilizational sniper: waiting patiently at the outskirts of an ancient society for many centuries to strike just at the right time. It is because Christianity always sees history in long arcs and because it has the vision of world conquest. Any religious or dharmic sect that exists, anywhere in the world, is automatically an enemy of Christianity because Christian theology argues that all other sects except Christianity are nothing short of devil worship, and the Bible orders faithful and true Christians to destroy every other sect. This is the reason that Christian missionaries started destroying native pagan religions of the Americas as soon as they set foot on American soil. This is why Vasco de Gama killed Hindus at first sight, for he 'knew' that if they were not Christian, then they were worthy of being eliminated, as that is what the Bible commands.

While hatred and intolerance of non-Christian sects, and the urge to destroy them, are at the core of Christianity, the pagan religions and dharmic sects of the world treat Christianity as just another sect that might be winning in the short term but is never considered an object of concern. This is the pagan well mentality, where they cannot imagine that there are religions like Christianity whose very existence necessitates the destruction of pagan traditions and religions.

That is why the polytheists, like Hindus, cannot be complacent in the 'low' period of Christian activity. The 'low' period has to be spent in reconverting the converted Christians back to our own dharma and creating a strategy to tackle Christianity on a global stage. Ancient dharmic traditions of the world need to have a longer arc of history than monotheistic religions like Christianity, which are civilizational snipers with a far range in time.

This is not a distant threat to Hindus and Bharatavarsha. Hindu society is at even greater risk than Korea was in the Second World War. Korea was beset with untold calamities, and only then did Christianity get a chance to convert it. But in India, Christianity is already present in every nook and corner. Christian churches are extremely well funded and powerful and are working day and night to convert more and more Hindus to Christianity. In fact, Christianity has already done to three Indian states what it did to Korea.

Punjab was a pure Hindu–Sikh state upon India's partition since it was one of the very few states that managed full population transfer. However, Sikh terrorism, its suppression by the Indian government, and the Canadian connection brought international missionary mafia and drug cartels right at the centre of Punjabi society, and it took just around five to seven years of Christian-conducive chief ministers and a mute prime minister controlled by a Christian party president at the centre to convert huge swathes of Punjabi society to Christianity. Amritsar, the very centre of Sikhism, now has around 5 per cent Christians. Jalandhar has one of the largest churches in Asia, and Ludhiana and other cities of Punjab, like Patiala, are fast becoming Christian strongholds. For the first time, Christianity has broken ground deeply in north India and has found itself to be a dominant and fast-growing religion in a major border state in the north. Some reports claim that the Christian population of Punjab is now as much as 15 per cent and nowhere less than 10 per cent. From almost zero to more than 10 per cent in less than a decade is a devastating figure and can create great social disturbances and great destruction of Sikh and Hindu culture and dharma in the state and elsewhere.[31]

Nobody would have believed just a few decades ago that Punjab of all states would fall to Christian missionaries, as it was a Hindu–Sikh stronghold, and Sikh dharma had nothing in common with Christianity. But a combination of terrorism, drugs, and international missionary mafia aided by Pakistan and its intelligence agencies resulted in this disastrous situation. Christian missionaries like Ankit Narula, Bajinder Singh, Raju

Rangila, and many others hold congregations of lakhs of 'converted' and 'to be converted' Hindus and Sikhs, and by usual tricks of 'making a handicapped man walk', a 'dumb boy speak', a 'blind girl see', and by 'driving demons like Shiva and Vishnu out of the poor folks', they convert thousands daily. Needless to say, all these dramas are arranged and belong to a standard Christian conversion toolkit that has been active for 2,000 years.

Christianity, the civilizational sniper, did not lose a moment in striking when the iron was hot, hitting the target where it hurt Hindus and Sikhs the most. Any indigenous dharmic state should have been aware of Christianity's ability to bide time and wait for centuries to strike at the right moment like a sniper. A dharmic society would thwart Christianity's designs and will de-convert Christians back to Sikh dharma and Hindu dharma.

Andhra Pradesh is a similar case where an ancient, deeply Hindu state was converted en masse when the Christian chief minister came to rule under a Christian-led central government. According to many reports, Andhra Pradesh is now around 15 to 20 per cent Christian, and many areas are so completely converted that not a Hindu home is left there while every single home sports a huge cross. Billions of dollars are routed by the Church through 'neutral' NGOs to fund Christian conversions in the countryside of Andhra Pradesh, where land is acquired in a virgin Hindu village with no Christian population, a huge Church is built, complete with all the essential furniture, 'holy essentials' are provided, and Christian priests are appointed with huge salaries. Standard Christian tropes and frauds of preying on vulnerable mothers and depressed family members are employed to start conversion in the area, and out of thin air, the area develops a Christian minority, which is then preferred in jobs and everything else by Christian-first policies, dooming the society for further Christian conversion. Usual missionary tricks are employed to convert the native Hindus to Christianity.

Arun Shourie, in his great expose of Christian conversion activities in India, *Harvesting Our Souls*, says:

> Missionary publications ... are full of targets of detailed plans, of marketing strategies by which the harvest here is to be multiplied: a church to be 'planted' in every village, a Bible to be placed in every pair of hands, lists and characteristics of 'people-groups' which are to be targeted—women, Scheduled Castes, and most of all, tribals; the beliefs and characteristics of each target-group which can be used to enter the group, the beliefs which are liable to be hindrances and how these may be transformed into aids.[32]

With the coming to power of a non-Church-loving government in Andhra Pradesh in 2024, prospects have improved; however, until converted Christians are invited back into Hindu dharma, the problem will not be solved.

We will remember how, in the Roman Empire, everything in the culture of the pagans was left as it was, only their gods were changed. But we must also remember how, as a consequence of their conversion to the closed and dogmatic religion of Christianity, whole Europe was plunged into the Dark Ages. This is also due to another long arc in which Christianity pursues its own missionary activities.

First, they convince a person who is converting to keep everything as it is, including food, language, and culture, and just change the gods. Then gradually one aspect of culture is changed one at a time, and eventually everything changes. In Europe, first they destroyed the religion and the gods of the pagans. Then when Christianity came to power, they destroyed pagan temples, art, literature, and science. And during the Protestant Reformation, they also destroyed the pagan practices that had 'lingered in Christians'. During this Protestant revolution, even the sculptures of angels and the Virgin Mary were destroyed in many churches of Europe. The destruction of paganism was finally complete in the Protestant revolution.

The Church is practicing the same methodology in India. In many states of India, the new converts do not even change their names and continue eating the same food, speaking the same language, and even practicing some of the rituals that are not directly against the Christian belief. Andhra Pradesh, Punjab, and Tamil Nadu are in this stage. Nagaland, Mizoram, and Meghalaya, which have been converted for some decades now, are in advanced stages where most of the old pagan rituals and practices are gone and even the memory of pagan past is receding, leading to more Christianization. In these states, it is the global pop culture that is used to destroy native faiths so that Christianity can grow. Arun Shourie writes:

> An evangelical Internet site exults in how that ministry consciously avoids overturning the beliefs and practices of the target-peoples, how instead it ensures 'deculturisation' over an extended period.... We have not replaced the lotus, 'which is supposed to be the seat of the Indian gods, it reports, we have entrenched the Cross in it!'[33]

Old musical drums that Mizos used in their ceremonies are used in Mizo churches. Nagas wear traditional attire to some of the church services. In Kerala, the Church uses Malayalam to convert and preach, but over a period of time, one by one, the native culture disappears and the Judeo-Christian Western culture is planted. It is inevitable because Christianity is a colonial religion, and colonialism always destroys native culture. Helen Ellerbe talks about the cultural, civilizational, and scientific wasteland that Christianity creates wherever it wins and becomes the majority religion:

> The Christian church has left a legacy, a world view, that permeates every aspect of Western society, both secular

> and religious. It is a legacy that fosters sexism, racism, the intolerance of difference, and the desecration of the natural environment. The Church, throughout much of its history, has demonstrated a disregard for human freedom, dignity, and self-determination. It has attempted to control, contain and confine spirituality, the relationship between an individual and God. As a result, Christianity has helped to create a society in which people are alienated not only from each other but also from the divine.[34]

Arunachal Pradesh is the worst case of neglect by the Indian State, where Jawaharlal Nehru, under the advice of the Christian missionary Verrier Elwin, virtually made Arunachal Pradesh a closed enclave where, in theory, no outsiders were allowed to enter, including the Christian missionaries, but in practice, things were very different. What happened was that the Indian state just turned its eyes away from Arunachal Pradesh and did not even create basic infrastructure of roads, schools, and hospitals while Christianity converted it during this time by providing schools and hospitals and converting the natives in exchange for food, medicine, and education. All this while, the Church had free access to almost all other states in the northeast that share a border with Arunachal Pradesh, and the missionaries sneaked into Arunachal Pradesh from these states and converted the natives. Many Arunachalis were converted while they were travelling to other states. Many converted in return for medicine, money, and education.

The Nagaland Baptist Churches played a great role in the conversion of Arunachal Pradesh. Nagaland is a fully Christian state now, and the biggest business in Nagaland today is the export of Naga missionaries to other tribes of the northeast and other areas of India. Quoting missionary publications, Shourie wrote, more than two decades ago: 'They are trusting God that 10,000 missionaries will be sent from Nagaland.'[35]

The ex-deputy chief minister of Arunachal Pradesh, James Wanglat was phenomenal in converting Arunachal to Christianity during the disastrous reign of Sonia Gandhi at the centre.[36] He himself belonged to a border Naga tribe that lives in Arunachal Pradesh. This tribe converted first through their internal Naga contacts, and then it was these Nagas that sent rapacious Baptist missionaries to every corner of Arunachal Pradesh and converted it from the inside. As these missionaries were 'native Arunachalis', they were not stopped by any law in their movements and had a field day where they converted Arunachali tribes en masse. Admittedly, the number of converted Christians is given to exaggeration, but no one can deny that Christianity is a rampant force in Arunachal Pradesh and is near majority, if not already a majority religion.

A naturally and culturally pristine dharmic state of Arunachal Pradesh was converted to Christianity in a matter of three to four decades. When Hindus object to the Christian missionaries, the clever missionaries say that these tribes of Arunachal Pradesh were never 'Hindu' and only animist or with 'no religion'. This is a very clever trick. Claim that most sects of Hindu dharma are not Hindu and then convert them easily. While northeastern tribes follow various local rituals, they are Hindu in the sense that it is Sanatana Dharma that provided them the umbrella and abhaya so that they could follow any custom they wanted and worship any god they wanted. Christianity, by claiming that they are not Hindu and that they have 'no religion', prepares them for conversion.

Any Hindu who believes in this trope is helping Christian conversion of natives of India. Samuel Johnson once said about pagans and 'heathens': 'The heathens were easily converted, because they had nothing to give up.'[37] In Meghalaya, Mizoram, Nagaland, and Arunachal Pradesh, this is the strategy that the Church adopted. By claiming that the natives had 'no religion', they promptly went ahead to 'give them one'. This is one of many cases where Christianity destroyed an ancient native dharmic tradition and replaced it with Christianity within a matter of decades or just a century. To stop this, a new global alliance has to be made.

Pagans, Hindus, other dharmic sects, and native traditionalists of the world, led by the Hindus, need to come together to fight the onslaught of prophetic monotheism. Hindus and pagans need to create a social, political, and religious strategy to defeat the civilizational sniping of Christianity, and they also need to create a strategy to reverse the gains made by Christianity by making ghar wapasi of the converted Christians back to native traditions like Hindu dharma a central policy.

Summing up the various threads of this chapter, we need to see how all of this history can help Hindus fight adharma in India and the world. India of the twenty-first century has too many frightening parallels to the third and fourth-century Roman Empire. India has to face two of these enemies: Christian missionaries and Islamists, both of whom cry victim while destroying Hindu society through conversions and by changing its demography at a very fast pace. Christianity is destroying Hindu society and Bharatavarsha by converting significant populations across the country, state by state.

More often, the new converts belong to the poorer sections of society, and upon conversion they stop visiting temples, stop taking *prasada* of *archana* or *puja*, and start considering Hindu gods as demons. We are all aware of that household help who suddenly stopped taking prasada of our deities. At first, we are just puzzled and do not ask, but then some day we get to know that she has converted to Christianity because a Church paid the school fee of her child or gave them medicine and wanted her conversion in return. Once the woman follows, the husband follows in a while. In other cases, the man follows for political and social benefits and for simply justifying his own degenerate lifestyle by converting to a religion where all those vices are actually virtues, and then the rest of the family follows.

Just like Christians in ancient Rome were converting people at both the lowest and highest levels of society, in the twenty-first-century Andhra Pradesh, conversions kept happening in the poorer sections of society, like the fishermen community. At the same time, the Church was also targeting the highest echelons, like the rich and landed Reddys, and succeeded in converting some of the most influential Reddys. And when one of them, Y.S.R. Reddy, became the chief minister, it was followed with an avalanche of conversions to Christianity at all levels of society. We know how Christianity destroyed paganism and became a majority religion mainly through state violence once the emperor of the Roman Empire converted. In India, we saw how Andhra Pradesh was devastated with Christian missionary tactics when they suffered under two Christian chief ministers for more than a decade.

Shatrubodha points to keep in mind here is that Christianity targets important individuals in very powerful and influential positions, and once these leaders convert, the followers follow. Most often the trick is to make the sons of powerful non-Christian leaders fall in love with Christian girls, and when these sons become leaders in their own time, Christianity, through the first lady of the State, becomes the unofficial religion of the State; the State gets weaponized, and conversions follow on a mass scale. We all know how India landed itself in the hands of a Christianized State for ten years during the UPA-2 regime. We should also be aware that the wife of Tejaswi Yadav, the son of Lalu Yadav from Bihar, is a Christian named Rachel Godinho. Her name was changed to Rajeshwari Yadav upon marriage to hide a possible controversy, but there is no news of Rachel formally reconverting to Hindu dharma. Tejaswi's own family members, like Sadhu Yadav, expressed extreme displeasure at his marriage to a Christian girl.[38] Tejaswi might become Bihar's chief minister in the future, and the Church will have an insider in the chief minister's office of Bihar. The wife of Udaynidhi Stalin in Tamil Nadu is rumoured to be from a Christian background.[39] And it is no wonder that Udaynidhi Stalin openly talks about 'destroying Sanatana' during elections.[40]

For the Christian conversion agenda to continue, the girl in question need not even be devoutly Christian. But since she becomes the first lady of the chief minister of a particular state, the entire Christian machinery of the world comes to her doorstep with quite innocent proposals like 'helping the poor' with 'medicines', 'hospitals', and 'schools'. When allowed, they continue their insidious activities of conversions to Christianity without hindrance. This has even precedence in ancient Roman history, where Donitilla, the wife of a Roman high-ranking official, converted first, opening the floodgates for conversion activity inside the court and in elite society.

Christianity and its conversion business have emerged as the greatest threat to India's territorial, national, religious, cultural, and civilizational integrity. And if we learn anything from history, we will work towards a state where native traditions like Hindu dharma, Jain dharma, and Sikh dharma are protected from prophetic monotheistic religions like Christianity through active State intervention in favour of Hindu dharma. Otherwise, by constantly dividing and fooling Hindus, Christianity will one day conquer all of India and destroy Sanatana Dharma. This is far from scaremongering. Pagan philosopher Celsus, writing in the second century, more than 100 years before Christianity became a state religion in the Roman Empire, issued warnings to his fellow pagans in panic. Quoting him, Nixey says: 'What is also clear is that Celsus is more than just disdainful. He is worried. Pervading his writing is a clear anxiety that this religion—a religion that he considers stupid, pernicious and vulgar—might spread even further and, in so doing, damage Rome.'[41]

History tells us that it did damage and destroy Rome. Pagans were massacred. Their temples and deities destroyed brutally, and philosophers and priests were beheaded. Another pagan Roman philosopher Pliny, the Younger, worried about the same: 'The "wretched cult" of Christianity has been spreading there and affecting the worship of the old gods. Not only the towns, but villages and rural districts too … are infected.'[42] In India, we see today that Christianity is spreading fast in the villages of Andhra Pradesh, Tamil Nadu, and many other states. The pristine life of these states is being destroyed, and social strife, violence, and destruction of culture are introduced with forceful and state-sponsored Christian conversions. Hindus today have the benefit of studying every religion, culture, and civilization that has been destroyed by Christianity. We have the hindsight of watching Christianity's modus operandi, preparing for all Christian tactics, and stopping its colonial design of conquering India and destroying Sanatana Dharma.

Christianity has reached this stage by fooling Hindu society. It claims perpetual victimhood and creates atrocity literature to slander the majority Hindu community and continues its rampant conversion agenda overtly and covertly. Arun Shourie says: 'Missionary publications and Internet sites are predictably full of gory tales … and the regular Christian publications and sites are full of atrocity-mongering at all times.'[43] It uses billions of dollars at its disposal, which are routed to India through the NGO mafia helped by the human rights lobby. It aims at strategic individuals to either convert important state officials or to marry Christian girls to some of the future political leaders in order to weaponize the State for Christian conversions.

The Shatrubodha point to learn here for Hindus is that even the smallest of concessions to an intolerant ideology results in absolute disaster and puts an end to the very tolerance that led at the first place to 'tolerate' an intolerant ideology.

Hitler did not conduct a coup, unlike the communists all over the world. He came to power by being elected by the majority of Germans. But once he was elected, he destroyed the very democracy that he had used to get elected. After climbing the ladder to power, he destroyed that very ladder so that no other could climb to power and dethrone him. Thus, a thumb rule of tolerance is that one cannot tolerate the intolerant ideologies; otherwise, they will misuse tolerance and destroy it by using it.

Another important thing for Hindus to recognize is that they cannot afford to be uninterested in world affairs. They need to know about everything. For Hindus may not be interested in Christianity, but Christianity is interested in Hindus, and since the reach of the Church is everywhere, Hindus also need to have an interest in everything to compete and then win this war of conversion.

Had the Roman emperors paid attention to the internal Jewish politics, we could have been saved from the monotheist threat. At that time, Jews did not seem to be a big threat since they were very rigid and did not seek converts outside their ethnicity. But the pagan Romans should have known that, since Jews had a habit of producing more and more prophets every few centuries and had many rival sects with small deviations, it was just a matter of time before one of these would produce a mutation that would seek converts outside the ethnic boundaries of Israel becoming a direct threat to the Roman Empire. Had the Romans considered it important to have an opinion on everything and everyone under the sun, they might have nipped the monotheist bud in its origin, and the world would not have had to suffer so much.

Just like that, Hindus need to have an opinion on everything and everyone under the sun in order to dominate the knowledge production in the world, and ultimately, a power that controls knowledge controls the world. First, we should start from India itself and be aware of the Hindus' situation in every single district of India. We shall not think that we are safe since we are living in a Hindu-majority area today. If we continue to neglect the advances of Christianity, our own state, district, and area will also become a Hindu-minority area one day. We have to be aware of any global ideology that plans to destroy Sanatana Dharma, and we need to plan so that their dreams never come true. Any idea of India becoming a *vishwaguru* has to keep this Shatrubodha point in mind.

Chapter 10

The Long Arc of Islam

'Islam has bloody borders.'

—Samuel Huntington

The Bitter Draught of Slavery, Ernest Normand, 1885. A slave trader urging a very old Muslim chief to buy the white Christian slave for his harem. African slaves were used for menial labour in Islamic harems[1]

In the early years of the seventh century, several kings, emperors, and generals across West Asia received a letter from a tribal leader of Arabia. The letter was from Prophet Muhammad, the pre-eminent leader of Islam, a new religion that was just born in the sands of Arabia as an offshoot of prophetic monotheism. This letter declared to the kings of Egypt, Ethiopia, Greece, and Persia about the arrival of Islam that had been sent to god's favourite, Prophet Muhammad, and called upon them to accept the will of the god and submit themselves completely to the authority of the prophet. This god was called Allah in the Arabic language, and it was claimed that not Jesus, but Muhammad was the last prophet.

Some of these kings had heard of some upheavals in the desert sands of Arabia but were hardly perturbed since their empires were big and prosperous, full of great cities like Constantinople, Alexandria, and Persepolis. These countries were centres of civilization, and what is now the Arabian Peninsula was considered a backwater. It was so dry and agriculturally unproductive that it was neglected at best. Except for some coastal areas and some oasis towns, which were necessary for pit stops of the ships and the business caravans, everyone behaved as if Arabia did not exist.

We can imagine the reaction of these leaders and kings upon reading that letter—the tall claims, the absurd demands, and the haughty tone. They must have sniggered at the sheer ridiculousness of the proposition and must have flicked the letter away after a hearty laugh or two. And one couldn't blame them either. Who would have believed that an unknown leader from a non-descript desert tribe, announcing a new religion, was about to give birth to one of the most powerful forces of conquest in human history?

And yet, Alexandria and Persepolis fell to the sword of Islam in the same century. While Constantinople survived as a Christian city for many centuries, the Byzantium Empire completely collapsed in Asia very soon, where most of its richest provinces were located.

In retrospect, we can see how wrong it was to brush that nascent threat from Arabia—Islam—under the carpet.

The purpose of this anecdote is not to portray how correct the prophecies of Islam were, since many other prophecies never came true. The reason behind going into this interesting detail of history is to illustrate the Long Arc of Islam.

Islam sees history in very long arcs—arcs not decades or centuries but millennia long. And this is not a viewpoint adopted in retrospect; rather, it is an action plan executed since the very inception of Islam. Any great dharmic civilization has a duty to keep looking out for such threats and not neglect them. Of course, most of these claims are false. History is witness to more failed messiahs and saviours than the handful who succeeded, but remembering Taleb's principle of black swan events, an anti-fragile society like Sanatana Dharma should have inbuilt mechanisms to single out prophetic monotheistic claimants and counter those that show signs of success.

Let us take the example of Mongol destruction of the Abbasid Caliphate in Baghdad in the thirteenth century and the subsequent rule of the Mongols in Persia (what is now Iran and Iraq). This example will illustrate how Islam sees both victory and loss in long arcs spanning over multiple generations. Any society that wants to resist the march of Islam needs to study these long arcs of Islam and come up with a valid response.

Islam Has Never Lost

Muslims are fond of saying that 'Islam has never lost'. Sadly, except in one case, this is true. But what does that mean? Does that mean that Islamic armies never lost? That their enemies never won against them in battlefield? The answer to this particular question is no. Any student of history will be able to bring up many instances in the past where Islamic armies have lost and lost horribly to their opponents. But the Muslims do not lie when they say Islam has never lost, for they are referring to a very different dimension of Islamic psyche. This psyche considers only one valid criterion to judge victory or loss. And from this criterion, Islam wins, of course, when Islamic armies win, but Islam also wins when Islamic armies lose. We need to delve deeper into this seemingly contradictory statement.

Prophet Muhammad was an incredibly successful war general and saw his armies conquering almost the entire Arabian Peninsula in his life, which is no small achievement in itself. But he could never see his armies and the influence of Islam going out of Arabia and passed away before Islam could break out of the boundaries of Arabia. Very quickly after his death, however, the Islamic armies reached India's gates in the east and knocked at Europe's doors in Spain in the west. This happened because two great empires of those times almost instantly fell against Islam. Persia, one of the greatest empires of Asia of that time, fell within a matter of twenty short years. The Sassanid dynasty ruling Persia was tired of its constant wars with the Byzantine Empire. In just twenty years the empire was gone; Zoroastrianism, their state religion, was declining; and Persia was converting to Islam.

A Shatrubodha point to learn here is that Islamic armies never stopped at political, economic, and social victory. For them a victory was not a victory until it was also a religious victory. Conversions to Islam always followed after the military victory of a Muslim king. This was achieved in many ways. The most favoured and most common way was, of course, forced conversions at the point of the sword. But an equally effective way to convert was the implementation of the jizyah tax.[2] This decided that most non-Muslims under Muslim rule and the yoke of jizyah would eventually convert.

Conversions were the most sacred duty of a Muslim. It was the goal of jihad to bring the light of Islam to all heathens or non-Muslims. The non-Muslims had three options: they could choose to convert to Islam and 'see the light of the one true religion'; they could choose to continue as non-Muslims for some time by paying the back-breaking jizyah tax and agreeing to many crippling restrictions on their religious expression; or, finally, if they did not agree to the above two paths, they could choose death at the hands of the faithful Muslims. This formula is not very different from the war cry of Kashmiri Muslims in 1990s Kashmir, where they threatened Kashmiri Hindus with the slogan: '*Raliv, Galiv or Chaliv*', meaning either convert to Islam, die at the hands of Muslims, or run away to the rest of India.[3] We all know that the genocide of Hindus followed this call in Kashmir, and almost 30,000 Kashmiri Hindus were massacred in cold blood by Islamists. To come back to our story, once Islamic armies win over a place, relentless conversion of non-Muslims takes place. For reasons discussed above, conversion of non-Muslims is incumbent upon Muslims. Many hadith (Islamic law books) support this conversion drive of Islam.

> Narrated Ibn Umar: Allah's Apostle said: 'I have been ordered (by Allah) to fight against the people until they testify that none has the right to be worshipped but Allah and that Muhammad is Allah's Apostle, and offer the prayers perfectly and give the obligatory charity, so if they perform that, then they save their lives and property from me except for Islamic laws and then their reckoning (accounts) will be done by Allah.'[4]
>
> Narrated Abu Huraira: The Verse—'You (true Muslims) are the best of peoples ever raised up for mankind', means, the best of peoples for the people, as you bring them with chains on their necks till they embrace Islam.[5]

Once any individual or group converts to Islam, the process is irreversible. This is another Shatrubodha point to remember. Once in, there is no way out. You can enter Islam, but you can never leave Islam. It is a one-way ticket to one true religion. Islam has no exit doors, only entry ones. Punishment for leaving Islam is death. The Quran says: 'Whoever disbelieves in Allah after his belief . . . except for one who is forced [to renounce his religion] while his heart is secure in faith. But those who [willingly] open their breasts to disbelief, upon them is wrath from Allah, and for them is a great punishment.'[6] (Quran 16:106)

Basing themselves on the Quranic injunction and many other instructions in the hadith, the four major schools of Islamic law, Hanafi, Hanbali, Maliki, and Shafi, all command that anyone who leaves Islam shall be put to death. This is very important. In this way, Islam only always grows because everyone converts into Islam but never out of it. Its graph, even when slow, never goes down. This has various other implications. This law of 'always in, never out' means that while the opponents of Islam need to keep winning repeatedly and endlessly until Islam is gone, Islam only needs to win once. Because after winning once, they convert opponents to Islam. And the outsider becomes the insider. This law of Islam had a profound implication on the history of the world.

It ensured that while non-Muslims needed to win eternally, Islam needed to win only once, so the Muslims just had to keep trying, and once they won, they would convert the defeated to Islam, forever.

Islam needs to win only once; non-Muslims need to keep winning forever.

Once the defeated society was converted, they became a part of Islam and started attacking others with the same or more zeal. Once defeated and converted, they would become the ambassadors and soldiers of Islam. This is how Islam has progressed in history. Arabs converted Persians; Persians converted Turks, and Turks converted many Indians, Chinese, and many others across the world.

When Islamic armies invaded and defeated the Sassanid rulers of Persia, this is the process that unfolded there. Conversions of Persians started happening at a lightning pace, at the point of the sword and through various other means. Very soon, a majority of the population became Muslim. Once a country is Muslim majority, the minority non-Muslims are eliminated through conversions, genocide, and ethnic cleansing without any special care or attention. Nobody even notices since the process is so common, so continuous, and so relentless. In any country where non-Muslims become a minority, it is just a matter of when, not if, they will disappear altogether from the face of the earth through a continuous genocide and ethnic cleansing.

This happened in Pakistan after the partition of India. There were 10 per cent Muslims in Pakistan in 1947, and now only a little more than 1 per cent remain. There were around 28–30 per cent Muslims in Bangladesh in 1947, and now less than 8 per cent remain. One of the greatest genocides of the century took place in 'peaceful Bangladesh', with almost one fourth of the Hindu population vanishing without a trace, and it is not even a news item in international news. An ongoing genocide of Hindus is going on in Bangladesh as we speak. Nigeria is another case that is undergoing a complete demographic change to the detriment of the non-Muslim population of the country.[7]

It is clear that when Islamic armies defeated and ruled non-Muslim populations in history, it was the non-Muslim populations who converted to Islam. But what happened when non-Muslim kings ruled Islamic populations? Did the non-Muslim pagans and Hindus also convert Muslims back to paganism? The answer is a clear no.

The Mongol defeat of the Abbasid Caliphate is a case of the latter variety. In this case, a pagan-Buddhist force had defeated an Islamic empire and came to rule it for centuries. But it failed in converting the Muslim population of Persia and Mesopotamia (Iran and Iraq) back to paganism or Buddhism. Not only this, but something far worse happened from the point of view of pagans and Buddhists. It is actually the pagan-Buddhist Mongol emperors of Persia who converted to Islam and not the other way around.

The so-called 'golden age of Islam' under the Abbasid Caliphate of Baghdad came to an abrupt and violent end when they were defeated by the much more chivalrous Mongols in the Siege of Baghdad by Hulagu Khan[8] in 1258 CE. The Mongols utterly destroyed the Abbasid Caliphate once and forever, causing a great massacre of the population of Baghdad.[9] The greatest leader of Islam, the Abbasid Caliph, was killed by being wrapped in carpets and then trampled upon by elephants. This was because Muslims at the court had intimated that it was a rule in their Islamic capital that the blood of the Caliph could not touch the ground. So, the Mongols respected their rule and made the carpets absorb all the blood, without letting a single drop touch the ground. It was the first dusk of Islamic power. Arabs and Persians were spent forces, and a pagan-Buddhist Turco-Mongol power had completely destroyed the political and military power of Muslims.

But did that affect Islam badly in the long run? It did not at all. It actually benefitted Islam. Hulagu Khan was a pagan-Buddhist, but like most pagans, he respected others' 'religions', failing to recognize that Islam was not just another religion. It was a religion that wanted to end all religions and dharmic sects like Tengrism, which was the indigenous dharma of Mongolia. Hulagu Khan never tried to convert Muslims. Instead, he gave them full freedom to practice their religion.

Thus, even while Islamic armies lost, and Muslims were killed en masse, Islam did not lose, as the religious configuration of the empire remained completely Islamic, as the pagan Mongol rulers never tried to convert them. Eventually Islam ended up gaining from Mongol occupation. Hulagu's son and successor, Abaqa Khan, was a Buddhist. He practiced his own dharma in peace and let his Muslim subjects practice Islam. His son Arghun Khan, the next ruler, was also a very devout Buddhist. He was more conscious of religious and dharmic boundaries and the great distinction between Buddhism and Islam. He was aware of the missionary and proselytizing nature of Buddhism, but even he did not try to convert his Muslim population.

Three generations of pagan rulers of Baghdad did not try to convert their Muslim subjects. And we would do well to remember that no Muslim ruler would ever let go of a single opportunity, let alone a generation, to convert his subjects to Islam. Islam was biding its time until the tide turned in its favour. Meanwhile, the Muslim Ummah was constantly converting the Mongol courtiers one by one to Islam. The argument that they presented to the Mongol courtiers was that it would help the Mongol rulers in ruling Muslims if both the rulers and the ruled followed Islam. They knew that once the emperor turned Islamic, they would send court armies to convert whatever few pagan Mongols were left in the country.

In typical pagan indifference and ignorance, none of these Islamist machinations and changes in demography of the Mongol court affected Arghun Khan. Arghun was a devout Buddhist, but he never thought that Muslims should convert to Buddhism. Islam was biding its time. Islam's time came when Arghun's son, Ghazan, became the fourth major emperor of the llkhanate. Ghazan was pushed by Ibn Taymiyyah, one of the most intolerant, iconoclastic, and greatest Islamic scholars of the time, to become a Muslim. And he did. In the prospect of expanding his empire and preventing his Muslim subjects from rebelling against him, he became a Muslim. And Islam finally won.

In this case, the Muslim subjects managed to convert a non-Muslim emperor after four generations of non-Muslim rulers.

The point to note here is that Islam wins when a Muslim army defeats a non-Muslim country, as Muslim kings convert non-Muslims. But Islam also wins when a non-Muslim army defeats a Muslim country, as the Muslim population converts the non-Muslim king. Islam wins in both the cases.

This is the context in which Muslims say that Islam never loses. Despite a military loss, Islam always grows in numbers through converts and through a better reproduction rate. Non-Muslims and Hindus should learn their lesson from this. A Shatrubodha point here to remember is that any practice of tolerance, chivalry, and kindness to an opponent that does not reciprocate those ethical values proves lethal to the side that practices these values. The other side uses the benefits provided to it from these values and then destroys the very same values when it wins or whenever it gets the chance. Thus, in civilizational wars, the greatest moral and ethical principle is reciprocity. Practice any value with a side that can reciprocate it. Iran, the successor of llkhanate, is still an overwhelmingly Muslim country. They never allowed any other religion or dharma to grow on their land.

So yes, the Islamic armies lose. Yes, their kingdoms and countries sometimes collaborate tactically with non-Muslim empires but always with the eye that Islam cannot lose, and they guarantee this by making sure that the converted Muslims never convert or reconvert back to their previous traditional dharma. Muslims cannot leave Islam. And non-Muslims should always be forced, appeased into Islam. They make temporary alliances with the pagans, heathens, and non-Muslims. They have a judicial allowance for that, and they call it *taqiyya* (devout deception). They collaborate only so that in the future they can convert the heathens, whenever the time is ripe.

In short, Islam only needs to win once. While non-Muslims need to keep winning forever if they want to stop Islam.

This situation can change only when non-Muslims also seek to convert Muslims whenever the situation is favourable. True balance, true harmony, and peace will be achieved only then.

A similar case of winning in loss is the case study of the demographic invasion of all of Europe by Muslims in the post-colonial era. While the great age of colonialism saw the European Christian colonial powers ruling the entire world, including the Islamic world, the impact of colonialism was very disproportionate in several of these places. While places like the Americas lost most of their population to genocide by European Christians and lost all of their pagan polytheistic character, African countries lost their religion but not their race. Their genetic stock remained more or less the same; however, theocide was as complete here as in the Americas, and the natural religions and traditions of Africa did not survive. In both of these places, the conquest of Christianity was complete by genocide in the former place and by conversion in the latter. In India, Hindus were mentally colonized and lost control of all their political, educational, and financial institutions to the British. But in the Islamic world, the impact of colonization was the least, and Islamdom almost completely retained its demography and was least impacted by colonization. As expressed above, Islam was biding its time.

After the Second World War and the fall of the great age of colonialism, Europe wanted cheap labour due to many reasons, and its population went into sharp decline in most of its countries. Muslims, however, were migrating in large numbers, with a much higher reproduction rate than Christian locals, and were converting many locals to Islam. This trend continues even now, and we see huge Muslim 'minorities' in most of the European countries, with Brussels, the capital of the European Union, having almost 25 per cent Muslim population.

Once again, Islam bided its time in defeat during colonialism, and as soon as it got the first chance to promote Islam and Islamize non-Islamic lands, it pounced upon it and is in the process of changing the demographics of Europe in favour of Islam as I write these words. The story of the conversion of Mongol emperors of

Ilkhanate of Baghdad to Islam shows how Islam sees history in long arcs and wins even when its armies lose. It teaches us how Islam bides its time during periods of defeat but keeps patient and prepares to pounce upon the first chance that it gets. This ensures that while victory on the battlefield brings gains to Islam, losing a battle is also not a loss. The only way to reverse this trend is to reconvert Muslims when non-Islamic powers come to rule Muslim subjects. There is no maintaining the status quo with Islam. Balance exists only in dynamism. Islam grows through faster reproduction rate of Muslims and by conversions. So, until non-Muslims start reconverting Muslims, it is a losing battle for them.

The Long Fall of Constantinople: How Islam Persists in Its Goals

The story of the long fall of Constantinople tells us about the other aspect of the long arc of Islam: how Islam can unflinchingly focus for centuries and millennia on just a single goal. In this case, the goal of Islam was to attack, defeat, and convert the capital of the greatest Christian empire of those times, Constantinople, to Islam. It took them 900 long years after their first attack, but they never abandoned their goal of converting the Christian capital to Islam, and they finally achieved it in 1453 CE after the great siege of Constantinople by Sultan Mehmet II of the Ottoman Empire. But we are running ahead of the story.

The city of Constantinople, also known as the New Rome, was established as the capital of the Eastern Roman Empire in 330 CE. It was the centre of Orthodox Christianity for more than 1,200 years. Within 300 years of Constantinople's establishment, Islam took advent in Arabia. When the Islamic armies broke out of the Arabian Peninsula during the reign of the Rashidun, or the four 'rightly guided Caliphs', in the East they headed towards pagan Persia and won it over in less than twenty years, while in the West they headed towards the Christian Byzantine Empire, the other great empire of the seventh century. The Byzantine Empire did not collapse entirely at the first onslaught of Islamic armies, even though it lost most of its Asian provinces like Syria. But its power was greatly reduced, and by 674 CE, the Islamic armies found the audacity to attack the Byzantine capital of Constantinople by sea route.

The Arab armies laid the first siege of Constantinople from 674–678 CE. After snatching Syria from the Byzantines after the Battle of Yarmouk, they immediately started preparing the siege of the Byzantine capital and secured bases around the great city to prepare for the war. The siege lasted for four years, since Constantinople was the most heavily fortified city of its time. Its geography made it a formidable fortress in itself, needing land defence on only one side. The Arab Muslim armies took the challenge of breaking the seemingly impenetrable defences of Constantinople. They would attack the city every spring and recede and regroup to their bases around the Anatolian seaboard during winters. This lasted for four years until the Byzantines found a new incendiary weapon called Greek fire, which repelled the Muslim armies finally, and the siege broke in 678 CE when the Arab navy receded.[10] After the defeat of the Arab navy, the Byzantine army also defeated their land armies and destroyed their bases in western Anatolia. The Muslim threat for now receded, but not for long.

This defeat did not dampen the resolve of Islam and Muslims. They regrouped for a few decades and then started attacking the border posts and towns of the Asian provinces of the Byzantine Empire. And very soon they were back at the gates of Constantinople. The second great Arab siege of Constantinople was laid in 717–718 CE under the rule of the Umayyad Caliphate of Damascus. Please note that the country of Syria and the city of Damascus were great Christian provinces just years ago. Just after falling to Islamic armies, Syria was rapidly Islamized, and its capital, Damascus, became the greatest Islamic city of those times.

This is a great Shatrubodha point: that once a land is conquered and converted to Islam, it becomes a great stronghold of Islam.

During the second siege of Constantinople by Arabs, the Christians were better prepared, and the Arab Muslim navy was destroyed just after its arrival, and the land armies that had surrounded the city from the north were sandwiched between the Bulgar attacks from the north and the Byzantine imperial army in the south. The siege ended the next year in 718 CE, once again in the defeat of the invading Islamic armies. After this siege, the Arab armies were a spent force and never attacked Constantinople again. But this was far from the end. The waning of the Arab power did not mean the waning of the Islamic power, for by the time Arabs were a spent force, Islam had managed to convert the Persians and the Turks, and they had become the flaming new sword of Islam. A point to remember is that Islam is not limited to ethnicity or even nationality. The defeat of one Muslim nation does not mean the Islamic threat has receded.

The Byzantine Empire regrouped after the second siege of Constantinople and gained some power and territories temporarily, but it could not gain its former glory because by then the provinces that were snatched from it by Arab armies had now become Islamic, and the process had become irreversible. Had things remained like this, it would not be so bad, but within two and a half centuries of the second siege, a new Islamic power emerged at the gates of Byzantium—the Seljuk Turks.

The rise of Arabs had resulted in Byzantium losing Syria as well as the eastern half of Anatolia. The Seljuk Turks were a Turkic-Persian power with their origin near the Aral Sea in Central Asia. They first spilled out in Persia and established themselves there, conquering Baghdad and many other important cities of the region. Then they started approaching the borders of the Byzantine Empire. The Seljuk Turkish Muslims picked up the war of Islam with Christendom from exactly the point where the Arab Muslims had left it. They started knocking at the gates of Byzantium in many skirmishes over the eastern border of the empire and dealt the Christian Byzantine armies a decisive blow in the famous Battle of Manzikert in 1071 CE. This battle was a turning point in the history of Christian Byzantium and Islam. It opened up entire Anatolia to Islamic conquest and conversion, and within twenty years after the Battle of Manzikert, the Byzantine Empire had lost almost all of its Asian territories and was left with just the runt of its former empire.[11]

However, its capital, Constantinople, had still not been conquered by Islam. The Seljuk Turks ruled for around two centuries until the middle of the thirteenth century and kept fighting and pushing against the Christian empire of Byzantium. For the first time, Christendom felt that its core was under threat from Islam, and this crystallized in the call for crusades by Pope Urban II. In the subsequent two centuries, Christian armies from Western Europe, mainly France, sent four crusades (religious military expeditions) to regain Jerusalem and other important ancient Christian cities that Seljuk Turks had conquered. But most of them ended in failure despite some intermediary success.

The Seljuk Turkish rule ended in 1243 CE, and Constantinople had still not been won by Islam. Two great Islamic powers had now become unsuccessful in conquering and converting the Christian imperial capital of Constantinople. But even this is not the end of the story. Like the undead, wave after wave of converted Islamic empires, thirsty for blood and conquest of non-Islamic lands, were let loose at the very heart of imperial Christianity—Constantinople.

The baton of Islam and its advance against Constantinople was next held by the Ottoman Empire. Barely fifty years after the fall of the Seljuk Turkish Empire, another empire arose in 1299 CE—the Ottoman Islamic Turkish Empire. The empire soon expanded in Europe, primarily in the Balkans, and surrounded Constantinople from almost all sides. In the next 100 years, most of the territories of the Byzantine empires were lost, and by

1400 CE, the empire was reduced to its capital—the besieged city of Constantinople. Constantinople was called the Red Apple by the Ottoman Empire because it was considered the greatest prize to be won by any Islamic army for the past many centuries. Roger Crowley says: 'The object of their offensive was known quite simply as the Red Apple, a symbol of world power. Its capture represented an ardent Islamic desire that stretched back 800 years, almost to the Prophet himself, and it was hedged about with legend, predictions and apocryphal sayings.'[12]

In 1453, Sultan Mehmet II, one of the greatest Islamic sultans ever to grace the annals of history, laid one more and final siege of Constantinople. The siege ended on 29th May 1453 CE with the breach of the great walled city. Immediately upon victory, the great churches and cathedrals of the city were destroyed and desecrated, Christian priests were massacred, and the population was converted to Islam at the point of the sword. The library of Constantinople was burnt by Ottoman Muslims, and around one lakh ancient texts were destroyed. This library had housed many texts that had survived the burning of the library of Alexandria in the fourth century by fanatic Christians. What was spared in the destruction by the first monotheism—Christianity—was consumed in the destruction by the second monotheism—Islam.

The Red Apple had fallen to Islam. The city was won over, converted, and delivered to Islam once and for all. It took them 900 long years to achieve the goal, but the Islamic armies were persistent and achieved it at last. It took them three different ethnicities and empires, but the Islamic zeal was common in all of them. This tells us that Islamic conversion of any place is a relay race, and just because one Islamic kingdom, power, or army has lost or disappeared does not mean that Islam is a spent force. Islam comes back with full or more force in the next wave of converted zealots.

Though it took them 900 years to win Constantinople, it did not even take them ten years to make the city a Muslim-majority city, with forced conversions to Islam. This proves the dictum: Islam needs to win only once; non-Muslims need to keep winning forever.

Islam's Capacity to Reverse Losses

When the Seljuk Turks won and converted large parts of Byzantine Christian lands after the Battle of Manzikert in 1071 CE, it sent a shockwave through the Western Europe. Christian leaders started thinking that things were in bad shape and the time had come to give a consolidated Christian reply to Islam and regain its lost lands by force. Pope Urban II organized a military response to Islam and mobilized many Christian nations of the time to send a military expedition to Jerusalem and other states that were lost in the war with Islam.[13] The crusades managed to regain some of the ancient Christian cities from Islamic occupation for a few hundred years, but eventually they lost, and the Islamic rule was re-established in all the crusader kingdoms.

If we study the crusades from the Islamic point of view, then we learn that without converting the local Muslim population to one's own religion and without outnumbering Muslims in demography, no non-Muslim power can hold its own if it is surrounded by Islamic nations and neighbours all around. When Pope Urban II called for the crusade, thousands of Christians answered the call to 'save the holy Christian lands from Muslims', and in 1096 CE the first crusading army arrived in the embattled Byzantine lands and Palestine. After a series of battles, they regained four important ancient Christian cities: Antioch, Tripoli, Edessa, and Jerusalem, the most important of all. Four small kingdoms were created around these cities, and for the first time in centuries, Christian armies had regained a foothold in Western Asia, where Christianity was born. The First Crusade was successful.

Islamic armies, however, started regrouping almost instantly in historical terms and started making plans to regain all the lands that were snatched temporarily by Christianity from them. In 1144

CE, the County of Edessa, the first crusading Christian kingdom that was founded fifty years ago, fell to the Islamic Seljuk forces. This precipitated a response in western Christian Europe, and Pope Eugene III called for another crusade. This time the crusade was led not by some generals or small feudal lords, but by the kings of Germany and France. But it was unsuccessful. The armies of the German and the French emperors travelled separately and were separately defeated by the Seljuk Turks. What remained of the two armies reached the remaining three crusader states but made an unsuccessful attempt to attack Damascus. In the end, Christian rule in the County of Edessa could not be recreated, and the Second Crusade failed spectacularly.

By this time, Islamic response to the crusades was getting more and more organized. A great Islamic commander had risen on the horizon—Saladin. He grew in power and in 1187 CE laid siege to Jerusalem and conquered it.[14] The second crusader state had fallen back to the Muslims. There was a complete ethnic cleansing in the city of Jerusalem, and all Christians and Jews were sent out of the city or converted.

The capture of Jerusalem triggered the third and the most famous of all crusades. It was called the kings' crusade since it was led by the kings of France and England as well as the Holy Roman emperor. It was a clash of titans, as on one hand was Richard the Lionheart, the king of England, and on the other was Saladin, the Ayyubid Islamic king. The crusaders failed to take Jerusalem but gained a lot of territory around it and restored most of the coast to Christian control. But the primary goal of retaking the holy city of Jerusalem was not completed.

This triggered the Fourth Crusade (1202–04), but due to many reasons, the crusaders attacked the Christian city of Constantinople instead of the Islamic armies and led to further decline of the Christian power in the East. After this there were many crusades, and while some parts of Jerusalem were captured in the Sixth Crusade, the Christian imprint on Western

Asia was weakening instead of strengthening as centuries passed by. Finally, the last of the Christian strongholds, the County of Tripoli, fell in 1289 CE, and with the siege and fall of Acre, the last of the crusading Christian cities, the crusades were over, and the Christian attempt to retake the heartlands of Christianity from Islam was also over. Though the crusades lasted for almost two centuries and gained control of a few important areas in the meantime and ruled a few fortified cities for some time, they failed in their goal: to re-establish a permanent Christian presence in the birthplace of Christianity.

While there are various reasons for the failure of the crusades, and one can read many books written on the subject, the Shatrubodha point to learn here about Islam is that unless permanent changes are made in the demography of a certain place that is regained from Islamic forces, the area will sooner or later revert back to Islam irrespective of the strong non-Muslim forces that were ruling there. While the crusaders fought valiantly and with great armies, they were either unable to or unwilling to convert back the local Muslims to Christianity and thus perpetually faced a sea of Muslims from all sides outside the boundaries of their small states and were just waiting for strong Islamic leaders to emerge and regain Islamic control. No matter how strong a non-Muslim power is politically, until the society becomes non-Muslim through reconversions, Islam will regain its hold over the region. The lesson being that the only way to regain control from Islam is to reconvert Muslims to the respective religion or dharma of the opponent and also to reconvert the landscape by reclaiming the sacred spaces back to the religion or dharma to which they belonged originally. Without reclaiming the people and the landscape, any reclamation from Islam is temporary.

In India, this has happened too. After the Mughal power waned after Aurangzeb's death, Hindu forces in India started regaining political power and managed to take most of the power from the hands of Muslims. The greatest power was, of course, the Marathas, but there were other regional powers all over Bharatavarsha who once again established Hindu supremacy in the country. But was this phase detrimental to Islam?

Not much. Except Chhatrapati Shivaji Maharaja, who tried to reverse many gains of Islam, almost no one else thought in these terms, and though they defended Hindu dharma with valour and courage and were noblemen, they failed to understand the true nature of Islam. While Maharaja Ranjit Singh ruled all of Punjab and many other territories, his power remained unchecked, and he failed to reconvert his Muslim subjects back to either Sikh dharma or Hindu dharma. He is famed to have banned *namaj* and some other visible markers of Muslim identity in his kingdom, but that was far from a loss to Islam and Muslims. If anything, it strengthened their resolve even more. Even the great Ranjit Singh did not try to convert Muslims back to where they belonged before conversions. As a result, when the Sikh power waned, Punjab emerged as a vicious Muslim-majority province that had no place for its Hindu and Sikh minorities. All the political power of the great Hindu kingdoms like the Marathas and the Sikhs was not enough to reverse the tide of Islam since they did not reconvert Muslims back to Hindu and Sikh dharma in sufficient numbers.

There are many small representative cases of this point in India after independence. The district of Gurdaspur in Punjab was slightly Muslim-majority in 1947 before Partition, but India demanded and got it because it provided the only plains access to their territories of Jammu and Kashmir. Partition resulted in the exchange of populations in Punjab, and Gurdaspur became a heavily Sikh–Hindu majority district. But today, the Muslim population is growing there again to reclaim their erstwhile status. In the east, the districts of Hailakandi and Karimganj in Assam were also Muslim-majority before Partition but were given to India to provide it easy plains access to the hilly states of Tripura and Mizoram. As a consequence, they became Hindu majority, but Islam, having the long arc in mind, kept repopulating it with illegal Bangladeshi immigrants after independence, and today these districts are once again Muslim majority.

The Shatrubodha point to learn is that while dealing with prophetic monotheistic sects, no change is permanent until the religious demography of a place is changed and care is taken that this is not disturbed from any cross-border Islamic long arc manoeuvers.

Unfinished Agendas of Islam

To properly understand the long arc of Islam, we also need to analyse the behaviour of the Muslim community at various percentages of demography they are at in a certain country. Islamic countries never have peaceful relations with non-Islamic neighbours. 'Islam has bloody borders,'[15] as Samuel Huntington famously said. The process of radical Islamization of every piece of land the Muslims inhabit goes on in a two-pronged strategy depending on whether they are in the majority or minority.

If the Muslims are in the majority like in Egypt, Pakistan, or Bangladesh, they keep harassing, converting, and ethnically cleansing their non-Muslim populations, citing conspiracy theories and suggesting disloyalty. In Egypt, the Coptic Christians are a peaceful minority of around 10 to 12 per cent. Even then, the Islamic majority feels threatened by it, and there are regular Islamic terror attacks on the Christian minority of the country.[16]The ongoing genocide of Hindus in Pakistan is an open case and need not be discussed here in detail. It will suffice to say that the Hindus are such second-class citizens in Pakistan that many of them are not even allowed to cremate their dead and are instead forced to bury them like Muslims.[17] Hindu girls are regularly kidnapped, molested, and forcibly converted to Islam.[18]

In Bangladesh, a silent genocide of Hindus is going on. Bangladesh had a huge Hindu minority just 100 years ago. In

1901, there were around 33.93 per cent Hindus in Bangladesh, who have now been reduced to less than 8 per cent in 2011. A quarter of the population of the country has been wiped out through forcible conversions and outright genocide, and the world watches silently. There are numerous such cases all over the world where a Muslim majority is leading genocide of its non-Muslim populations.

If the Muslims are in the minority, like they are in India or Myanmar, they cite harassment by the majority and demand a separate state. In 1947, in India, they got a separate state and are on the verge of demanding another in the twenty-first century. In Kashmir, where the Muslims were in the majority, they engaged in the genocide and ethnic cleansing of Kashmiri Hindus in the 1990s. Can any 'persecuted minority' attempt that? However, as soon as the valley was cleansed of Hindus by the majority Muslims, the narrative was changed overnight, and Muslims started posing as the 'persecuted minority', hounded by the Indian State. In the rest of India, they keep playing this card, and the states in which they are now fast becoming a majority, like in Kerala and West Bengal, their tactics are very aggressive. And India is not alone.

Muslims are 4.3 per cent in Myanmar of which the Rohingyas constitute even less. Yet, they managed to destabilize an entire country. In August 2017, a Rohingya terrorist group launched twenty-four coordinated attacks on Myanmar Army camps, leading to more than eighty dead.[19] One wonders what kind of 'most persecuted minority' is capable of pulling twenty-four coordinated attacks against one of the most dreaded armies in the world. And when the Myanmar army retaliated, the Rohingya Muslims fled to India, bypassing the Islamic heaven of Bangladesh, in order to occupy more land and resources in a 'heathen country'. But as if this was not enough, they also engaged in genocide of Hindus living in the region, killing more than 100 Hindus and dumping them in mass graves.[20] While the world demonizes Aung San Suu Kyi and racially profiles the whole country, these atrocities by Rohingya terrorist groups do not find even murmurs in the intellectual circles.

This is not an exception but a norm. In every single case, the Islamic side tries to localize the problem, often giving territorial, ethnic, or legal hue to the problem overtly and distracting attention from the fact that the Muslims have a trouble living with their non-Muslim neighbours globally, no matter where they live. However, they betray their intentions when they accuse the majority community of mistreating them on religious lines and claiming that Muslims are persecuted everywhere. It shows that the Islamic angle is never far from their mind.

The problem of radical Islam can only be understood in a global context. Viewing Muslims as local minorities is not only dangerous for the future of these countries but downright suicidal. Muslims number around two billion all over the world and have a powerful lobby at the United Nations, with more than fifty Islamic countries, enabling them to sway public opinion to the benefit of radical Islam. Radical Islam must be seen as an aggressive global majority that has no internal mechanism of peaceful coexistence with non-Muslims. Only then will solutions to this problem begin to appear.

Common Muslims are often used as cannon fodder for the colonialist and expansionist plans of radical Islam. Some Indian historians say that the frequent rioting of Indian Muslims is leading India towards another partition, calling it an unfinished agenda of the Muslim League, which lives on as IUML (Indian Union Muslim League) in Kerala but also in the attitude of radical Islamists all over India. India is not the only unfinished agenda of radical Islam in the world. We will see that in every partition in the world in which radical Islam was involved, the problem was never solved, and the non-Muslim country that came out of the partition was once again on the verge of another partition.

Let us take a case first where Muslims were a near minority of almost 44 per cent. What happens when Muslims are as strong as around 44 per cent? We do not have to imagine. We have a historical case study: Lebanon. It is a sample case of how Muslims become a majority from a minority overnight. Lebanon is a West Asian country and the only country except Israel in the region where, at least until the 1970s, a functioning democracy was in place. It is the only country where an ancient branch of Eastern Orthodox Christianity, called the Maronites, still lives. Along with some other branches of minority Christian sects, it was also home to the last Greek Orthodox and Greek Catholic communities of the Middle East. All of these Christian sects are minorities within Christendom itself and thus did not have global friends and lobby groups. It also had some minority pagan and nominally Shia sects.

In 1956, Lebanon was 54 per cent Christian and 44 per cent Muslim, with the rest of 2 per cent comprising other religions and atheists. Thus, Christians were in the majority, and Muslims were in the minority. Lebanon is a small strip of land running north to south, comprising cool mountain valleys and the narrow strip of land hemmed in between the mountains and the Mediterranean Sea. Due to its geography, it had been a refuge to the communities persecuted under the long rule of Islam. That is why the crusaders too included Lebanon in their safe haven for Christians during the Middle Ages. Even in the Ottoman times, it somehow managed to survive as a country with sizeable populations of non-Muslims. Beirut, called the Paris of the East, was a great centre for trade, and it helped Lebanon survive as a non-Muslim-majority region.

In 1920, with Turkey's defeat in the First World War, Lebanon came under the French Mandate, which included present-day Syria and Lebanon. In 1943, the Mandate was partitioned between Syria and Lebanon. Syria was Muslim majority and quickly acquired characteristics of an Islamic dictatorship. The minorities were not safe there, even though it was not officially an Islamic state. Lebanon, on the other hand, was a functioning democracy, with one of the finest educational, social, and political institutions in the Middle East. Beirut was a world-class city with a multicultural milieu and an environment that induced free trade and open culture.

But all of this was to change soon. The Lebanese, like many other non-Muslim states all over the world, made the same mistake. The democratic rights were extended to the Muslim minorities, despite the fact that the Muslims were growing at a far greater pace than the Christian communities. Little did they realize that radical Islam uses democracy as an opportunity to capture important institutions and then grab power and destroy the very same democracy. In essence, they use democracy to destroy it. The rights that are extended to the Muslims when the non-Muslims are in the majority are never extended to the non-Muslims when the Muslims become the majority. As we know, Islamic theology does not give rights to non-Muslim subjects.

A multicultural Lebanon met its end through the demographic explosion of the Muslim population. The creation of Israel gave a pretext to the Palestinian Muslims to infiltrate Lebanon. As a strategic move, Jordan, an Islamic State, evicted its Palestinian Muslim refugees in 1970 and 1971. Despite being a Sunni Muslim country and despite being the designated country for Palestinian Muslims, Jordan refused to take their fellow Muslims in and instead sent them to Lebanon. This is interesting, as Islamic countries never fail to raise their voice for any other Islamic community in the world, but when it comes to taking Muslim refugees, they are always sent packing towards non-Muslim countries. Many birds are killed with one stone here. They do not have to deal with any refugees. And the Islamic agenda of taking over non-Muslim lands is also furthered as the Muslim 'refugees' in non-Islamic countries occupy new non-Islamic lands. Jordan did the same with the Palestinian 'refugees', who were nothing more than front soldiers of Islamic terrorist groups that invaded and changed the demography of Lebanon.

Coming back to Lebanon, encouraged by the Palestine Liberation Organization and other Islamic terrorist groups, the Muslim bodies started infiltrating the democratic institutions of Lebanon. The Muslims of various sects grouped under the banner of the 'left', though more than half of these groups were directly associated with Islamic terrorists and had nothing communist, leftist, or secular about them. They were rabidly Islamist but used the label of the 'left', which came in handy in projecting the Muslims as the victims and the hapless non-Muslims as 'rightists'. After the Second World War, the word 'rightist' had become the greatest political slur, and any group that was labelled as such was considered the ultimate personification of evil by the global media dominated by the left.[21]

One by one these Islamic terrorist organizations within Lebanon, hiding under leftist labels, started taking over Lebanese cities one by one. First they took western Beirut, then Sidon, and then Tyre. They were now in a position to launch a civil war. Along with a higher growth rate, the influx of Palestinian Muslims into Lebanon also contributed to a sharp rise in Muslim numbers in Lebanon. In 1975, when the Muslims had become 44 per cent, a civil war started. Scholars have different takes on who is exactly to blame for starting the civil war, but the Muslims were growing increasingly violent and intolerant of the Christians, and thus the Maronite Christians started to defend their territory and their people with arms. Muslims quickly upped the ante, and a full-scale civil war was upon Lebanon very soon.

The civil war went on for fifteen years, and when it ended in 1990, the Muslims had become the majority, and Christians had become the minority, almost overnight. More than a lakh of people were killed, and more than a million had fled to other countries. Right now, there are 54 per cent Muslims in Lebanon (exactly the same percentage as Christians were in 1975), and Christians are now in the minority with only 40 per cent of population—even less than the Muslims' share in 1975.

Many scholars have covered the ugly story of the Lebanese Civil War, but Bridgette Gabriel has been most objective. She tells the tale of the destruction of democracy and the Christian population of Lebanon, which happened almost overnight.[22] Keeping their vision local cost a great deal to the Christian community of Lebanon. When the civil war started, Christians found themselves isolated, fighting a lone war against a global coalition of radical Islamists and Islamic terrorist groups fighting alongside the Lebanese Muslims against the Christians.

While the Christendom of the West rarely cared about or identified with the ancient leftovers of Eastern Christianity in Lebanon, the Islamic countries and organizations had long been invested in the domestic situation of Lebanon, as Islam brooks no national boundaries and has a global vision. Lebanese Christians kept thinking that the rapidly changing demography of Lebanon with an exploding Muslim population was just a local phenomenon, but the Muslims were very well aware of their Islamic goals and agendas. They were indoctrinated and radicalized to use demographic explosion as a tactic of war against the kaffir Christians of Lebanon. And so the outcome of the Lebanese Civil War was decided even before it officially started. A loose infighting coalition of local Christian militias, beleaguered by the West, was no match against the well-coordinated Muslims, backed by the Islamic countries all over the world, and with a global and millennial vision as their goal.

When the civil war officially ended in 1991, the Muslims were in such a comfortable majority that the Christians could never raise arms against them. All the Christian militias were forced to disband, but the Islamic terrorist groups like Hezbollah kept functioning, thus keeping the Christian population perpetually terrorized. Along with the Hezbollah, which fights for the Shias of Lebanon, Hamas and the PLO (Palestine Liberation Organization) have continued fighting for the Sunni Muslims, while the Christians were left to fend for themselves with little or no international protection or support. The Islamic terrorist organizations also used Lebanon as a training camp for Islamic terrorists and to launch attacks on Israel from there. Within fifteen years, an ancient multicultural democracy of the Middle East died a horrible death. It became a hellhole of Islamic terrorists. Non-Muslims were ruthlessly massacred there. Genocide of Maronite Christians was perpetrated by the Muslims. The rest began an exodus towards the Western countries, particularly France and the United States. And those Christians who dared to remain are rapidly dwindling as the growth rate of Muslims is still far higher than the Christians.

India has many frightening parallels with Lebanon. The Muslims of India are also aligned with the global and national left. In reality, under the façade of the left, they carry on their openly Islamist and racist agendas. They portray the majority Hindus as fascists, neo-Nazis, racists, and above all, rightists. In reality, India's Hindus have nothing to do with the global right either. They just want to survive against the Islamic onslaught. Islam and the left try to localize the problem of radical Islam and portray India as the aggressor and Muslims as the victims. However, looking at the situation globally, we will realize that India is just another victim of radical Islam and Islamic terrorism. While Muslims have the support of all the Islamic countries and various Islamic organizations and individuals all over the globe, the Hindus are fighting a lone fight with absolutely no friends overseas.

In Lebanon too, the neighbouring country of Syria continuously provided arms and help to Islamic terrorists of Lebanon, particularly the Hezbollah, while the Christians had almost no overseas help. Jordan, on the other hand, provided immigrants. In India, too, while Pakistan provides terrorists, Bangladesh perpetrates silent terrorism on India by sending all excess populations of Muslims to India, thereby radically altering India's demography in favour of radical Islam. In Lebanon, the Christians saw the conflict locally and thus were always infighting. The Hindus in India too are shortsighted and keep infighting, looking at the problem at a local level and thus do not see the eminent threat that radical Islam and the rapidly expanding Muslim population pose. Just like Lebanon's demography was radically altered in favour of Muslims by rapid growth rates and quick influxes from neighbouring Islamic countries, India is also experiencing the same with the growth rate of Indian Muslims much higher than Hindus and the influx of crores of Bangladeshi Muslims in India. With this deadly combination, India's demography is rapidly changing in favour of Islam, and some of its states, like Kerala, West Bengal, and Assam, are rapidly reaching the tipping point. It is granted that Lebanon was a small country and tipping the demographic balance was easier there, but India is not an impossible target for Islam. If the Hindus hope to survive as Hindus and preserve Hindu culture, civilization, and the way of living, the case of Lebanon is a grim reminder and a potent warning about what lies ahead in the path.

Turkey and Armenia are another case of an unfinished partition. But Turkey is also a case of how even a secular Muslim state is no better in treating its non-Muslim minorities than an Islamic state is. Turkey is guilty of committing the first great genocide of the twentieth century, namely the Armenian Genocide in which 1.5 million Armenian Christians were killed by Turkish Muslims and the Turkish State.[23]Armenia is an ancient country situated just to the north of the Fertile Crescent, abutting the beautiful Caucasus Mountains. Due to its geographical location, it has been at the crossroads of many empires. It lies at the boundary between Asia and Europe and has historically been caught in the crossfires of numerous empires. Yerevan, the current capital of Armenia, has been inhabited for more than 2,000 years. The sacred centre for all Armenians has always been Mount Ararat, which lies just near Yerevan. Like every other nation in the world, the Armenians were pagan once, with their spiritual life centred around Mount Ararat, which was celebrated as the place of their origin. Their ancestral religion was not very different from Zoroastrianism, though they also worshipped many other gods along with the fire god. Even after converting to Christianity, Armenia preserved many of its pagan traditions, like worshipping Mount Ararat as their sacred origin, which was essentially a pagan practice.

After the advent of Islam, it became increasingly difficult for Armenia to defend its territory, its religions, and its traditions, but it kept its Christian character alive by paying jizyah tax under the Umayyad Caliphate. It once again kept alternating between independence and serving under some great powers, most of which were now Islamic. Thus, it suffered under the Seljuk Turks, under the Mongols, and the Ottoman Turks. In the sixteenth century, Armenian lands were divided into two parts. Eastern Armenia was controlled by the Shia Persia, and western Armenia, the larger part, was controlled by Sunni Ottoman Turkey. More significantly, Mount Ararat, the sacred centre of all Armenians, came under the occupation of Sunni Ottoman Turkey. Under these occupations, Armenia suffered heavy persecution, with its people massacred, expelled, and converted to Islam regularly.

In the early nineteenth century, Eastern Armenia was annexed by Russia from Persia. There was much oppression under Russia too, but as the Russians were also Orthodox Christians, Armenian religion became safe in Eastern Armenia. This would prove to be crucial and a safe haven for all Armenians in the future. For western Armenia, unfortunately the misery continued under the Sunni Ottoman Empire. Anti-Christian pogroms, rape of Armenian women, and many other communal crimes continued under the Sunni Muslim rule of Ottoman Turkey. Coming close to modern times, in 1896, Ottoman Sultan Hamid II ordered mass massacres of Armenian Christians, killing around three lakhs of them. This was a precursor of the Armenian Genocide to come.[24]

What was even more significant was that the mass massacre of Armenians continued even after the government of Sultan Hamid II fell and a new Turkey rose to power in a revolution called the 'Young Turk Revolution' in 1908. This 'new Turkey' was supposed to be more modern, less mediaeval in approach, and more tolerant of its Christian minorities. However, in the very next year of 1909, the Adana Massacre happened in which more than 30,000 Armenian Christians were brutally massacred by Turkish Muslims. If this was the flavour of 'new Turkey', things were not hopeful in the future.[25]

When the First World War started, Turkey was fighting alongside the Germans. As soon as the war started, Turkey started killing off its Christian minorities, the largest of which were the Armenians. The excuse was the most common one that the Islamic countries give while massacring their non-Muslim minorities: that they were siding with the enemies of the Islamic State. There were a significant number of Greek Orthodox and other smaller non-Muslim minorities in the country, all of which came under fire from the Islamists and the marauding Islamic mobs. During the war, regular pogroms against non-Muslims were carried out. Christian women were raped, children were killed, and mass massacres of Christians by common Muslims were the norm of the day. In the fog of the First World War, nobody paid any attention to what the Turkish Muslims were doing to their Christian minorities. Many of them, mostly males, were directly massacred, and women and children were told to march on foot to the Syrian desert. While on the march, these Christian Armenian women were raped by soldiers and by common Turks; children were massacred; the marchers were denied any water or food, and thus almost all of them perished while walking on foot. As the war ended and Turkey lost, some hoped that the massacres would end, but it was a false hope. The massacres continued.

The Russian armies, mainly led by Armenians from Eastern Armenia, managed to capture most of western Armenia, which was suffering under the Turkish Muslim yoke. But fate had a lot more pain in store for Armenia. Out of the blue, the Russian Empire itself fell, and the Bolsheviks under Lenin came to power in the October coup. Lenin was bogged down in the civil war, and in order to show solidarity with the Islamic world, he never even tried to lay a claim to western Armenia. In 1920, the Western powers woke up to the Armenian Genocide and pledged to attach western Armenian territories too to the new Republic of Armenia. However, the 'new Turkey', which was overtly singing the secular tune, was in no mood for that, and it promptly annexed all of western Armenian lands in 1920, and the genocide of Armenian Christians continued until 1923. In total, around 1.5 million Armenian Christians were massacred in this first great genocide of the twentieth century.[26] Half of this genocide happened under 'new Turkey', which had already started to profess secularism, both in politics and society.

Turkish leaders had realized that the time of the Islamic Caliphate had finally come to an end, and it would have to abandon its non-Muslim colonies. Turkey's game in all this defeat was to carve for itself a Turkish heartland of pure Islam, containing nothing but Muslims.The Caliphate was formally abolished in 1924, but it had already become a puppet in the hands of the military generals who had excelled in the First World War. The greatest of these leaders was Mustafa Kemal Pasha, who was later to become the supreme leader of 'secular Turkey'. Since 1920, it was certain that the Caliphate would be abolished, and a 'secular state' would be created. During this overt pursuit of 'secularism', the would-be secular state of Turkey massacred and ethnically cleansed all of its non-Muslim minorities. Today, Turkey is one of the most complete Muslim countries in the world, with a Muslim majority of 99.45 per cent, greater than that of Pakistan.

For Muslims, even in Turkey, secularism was possible only when the last Christian was dead, when the last non-Muslim was massacred. The later secularism was just a political ploy to keep the more troublesome Islamic leaders in control. The West remained silent as it was itself in great trouble. The interwar years were fraught with poverty and political tensions as two new threats, that of Nazi Germany and communist Russia, were on its threshold. After the Second World War, Turkey became a member of NATO (North Atlantic Treaty Organization), acting as a bulwark against the Soviet Union, and so with the help of the United States, its crimes against humanity and its genocide of Armenian Christians were whitewashed from history.

What is most tragic is that Turkey kept Mount Ararat in its own territory, even though it is just at the border. The sacred centre of all Armenia, the spiritual pivot of Armenia, is no longer in Armenia. Yerevan, the Armenian capital, is just at the border, for precisely this reason, so that every Armenian can look wistfully at Mount Ararat, just across the border, in Muslim Turkey, which had killed half of the Armenians in the genocide. Can the situation be any more tragic for Armenians?

It was entirely possible that the almost uninhabited mountain region of Mount Ararat, which is just a few kilometres from the border, could be gifted to Armenia. Turkey had no use for it, and radical Islam considers worshipping nature as heresy. In Turkey, Mount Ararat can best be neglected with apathy and at worst can be destroyed with impunity. But Islam is not known for the generosity of heart. And thus, the sad situation is that all Armenians can only wistfully look at Mount Ararat, never knowing if the mountain itself will be desecrated by Turkey in the future.

Armenia's woes do not end here. After the absolute genocide of western Armenia, all that was left of ancient Armenia were the two small provinces of Yerevan and Artsakh (Nagorno-Karabakh) in the Russian-occupied Eastern Armenia. When Eastern Armenia became free again in 1990, its eastern province, Nagorno-Karabakh was left as an exclave inside the Shia Muslim country of Azerbaijan. This Christian exclave of Nagorno-Karabakh was completely surrounded by Muslim Azerbaijan from all sides. Azerbaijan also has an exclave of Nakhchivan, but it is surrounded by Armenia on one side and Turkey on the other. While the Muslim exclave of Nakhchivan was given to Muslim Azerbaijan and is legally a part of it, Nagorno-Karabakh was never given to Armenia and was left legally a part of Azerbaijan. Since its independence in 1990, Armenia kept its link to its eastern province alive by maintaining a small Lachin corridor to Nagorno-Karabakh, which was an enclave inside Muslim Azerbaijan. However, this Armenian exclave was constantly harassed by Islamic Turkey on one side and Azerbaijan on the other.

When Armenia tried to support this ancient region of its civilization, Muslim Azeris would thwart its designs. Whenever it tried to use the Muslim exclave of Nakhichevan as leverage, Turkey threatened military reprisals, and Armenia would once again be left out in the cold. Still, for thirty years, Armenia maintained its corridor through Azerbaijani territory to keep the supply link open to its exclave Nagorno-Karabakh. But things were changing in the meantime. While Armenia is mostly an arid land in the mountains, Azerbaijan struck oil in its Caspian oilfields and kept getting richer and stronger every passing year, while the Armenian economy was in doldrums.

In 2020, amid internal political turmoil in Armenia, Azerbaijani Muslim armies attacked the Armenian corridor to its exclave, reducing it to a very thin line. Lakhs of Armenians were displaced and sent to Armenia proper. It was the first great defeat of Armenia against Azerbaijan since its independence in the 1990s from the Soviet Union. Azerbaijan got bolder through this acceptance of defeat by Armenia and in 2023 did a complete genocide and ethnic cleansing of Nagorno-Karabakh and completely emptied it of its Armenian population. Nearly 99 per cent of the inhabitants of Nagorno-Karabkah fled to Armenia.

Thus, the ancient Armenian province, once home to Armenian Christians, was no more, and it was finally occupied by Islamic forces. Now, Armenia is reduced to just the province of Yerevan, and things look bad for the future. It is clear that Armenia is dying a long and slow death at the hands of its Islamic neighbours.

The Islamic quest, which was started by Arabs, continued first by Seljuk Turks, then by Ottoman Turks, is now taken over by Azerbaijan and Turkey. No Islamic power rests until it completely destroys its non-Muslim opponent. This is a lesson to anyone who battles Islamic states at their borders, like India does.

Many Western scholars now maintain that secularism is just an outgrowth of Christian culture and carries on many Christian attitudes, couched in neutral modern terminology. Similarly, the 'secularism of Turkey' was just a method to keep its more troublesome mullahs in check after all non-Muslims in the country were dead, converted, or exiled. 'Secular Turkey' always took great care to keep the religious composition of the new 'secular state' close to 100 per cent Muslim. Turkey has a lot more blood on its hands other than that of Armenian Christians. Many Greek Orthodox Christians, Greek Catholics, and other smaller sects of Eastern Orthodoxy suffered genocide along with the Armenians. In 1923, after a lot of massacres, Turkey expelled more than twelve lakh Greek Christians to Greece in exchange for a few Muslims left there. Another ethnic cleansing was complete.

The French Mandate after the First World War included present-day Syria, Lebanon, and also the province of Antakya. The city of Antakya is ancient Antioch and housed many Christian communities. It was also annexed by 'secular Turkey' in 1939. Then in 1974, Turkey just simply invaded the island of Cyprus and created a pure Muslim state of Turkish Cyprus on its northern shores. All Greek Christian Cypriots were ethnically cleansed from these Turkish states. All of this, to repeat, was done by 'secular Turkey'.

It proves that there is no such thing as a 'secular Muslim state' until a majority of its inhabitants publicly declare atheism. Turkish secularism is a smokescreen. The Islamic State always keeps bubbling beneath the surface, beneath the thin veneer of 'secularism'. What the case of Turkey and Armenia teaches us is that even a single non-Muslim left in an Islamic state is perceived as an existential threat to the Islamic theocratic state, and hence even that last non-Muslim has to be driven out, killed, or converted to Islam. Secularism, like all other rights in an Islamic State, can only be extended to fellow Muslims. The non-Muslim, the hated kaffir, has never had and never will have any true rights under a Muslim state, whether secular or Islamic.

What Hindus can learn from the case of Armenia and Turkey is that when non-Muslims are in a minority in any Muslim country, an outright genocide is carried out against them, and the world does not even bat an eyelid. Hindus should learn a lot from this case since this is what has happened to Hindus of Pakistan and is happening to the Hindus of Bangladesh as we speak and will happen to Hindus in India if they ever become a minority or even a near minority.

The next important case for Hindus to study is that of Greece and its partition from Turkey. Hindu nationalists often cite the case of Greece and Turkey while arguing that India should have finished partition as they did by complete population transfer. While this should have been done and was a necessary step that India never took, it is necessary but not a sufficient step, as the case of Greece and Turkey will illustrate. The partition of Greece and Turkey, it seems now, was only temporary. Greece is a case of how any partition with a radical Muslim society will always remain unfinished until Islam is fought at a global level. Greece teaches us that radical Islam is a global problem, and there are no local solutions to it.

Greece is a Balkan country. In the mediaeval ages, the Ottoman Empire, with its capital in Istanbul, had ruled almost all of the Balkan Peninsula along with many other countries of Eastern Europe. During this brutal Islamic occupation of Europe, many Christians were forcibly converted, and Turkish Muslims were also resettled in all of these lands. The demographics of many of these countries were fundamentally changed in favour of Muslims. What is Turkey now was itself Greece once. The Turkish Muslim tribes invaded from Central Asia, converted the local Greeks, and drove others away, all the while settling there in large numbers. In the modern era, Greece was a very nationalistic country, priding itself on its Christian and pagan heritage, and having fought the Balkan Wars of the nineteenth century, they knew the real nature of Islam. They had also seen the genocide of Armenian Christians and many other smaller Greek and other Orthodox Christian communities of Turkey. The then prime minister of Greece, Venizelos, proposed to the West that the Christian and Muslim populations be exchanged between Christian Greece and Muslim Turkey. This proposal was accepted, and the population transfer was completed, and it is the only case of a 'finished partition', where in a partition between an Islamic and a non-Islamic country, complete population transfer was done.[27]

Even then, Greece lost more than half of its historical land and became much smaller as a consequence. The Asian part of Greece was forever lost to Islam and became 100 per cent Muslim. Even in Europe, Turkey gained a toehold. Istanbul (former Constantinople) was claimed by Turkey. Along with that, a large part of Bulgaria, called Eastern Thrace (also in Europe), was also awarded to Turkey. Turkey had massacred all the Armenian Christians left inside its borders and expelled the Greek Orthodox Christians to Greece. What is now Muslim Turkey was once Christian Greece. But the story does not end here. One would say that at least some of Greece was salvaged and the population was transferred completely. But immediately after the partition, Muslims started trickling in and settling in

Greece. They are now officially more than 2 per cent in Greece, though the latest estimations say they are not less than 4 per cent. But the story does not end here either. A quick look at all the neighbours of Greece will quickly make the story more frightening. Greece has borders with four countries: Turkey, Bulgaria, Macedonia, and Albania.

Turkey, as we have discussed, is more than 99 per cent Muslim and is a population time bomb with numbers teeming around eight crores. Turks are just swarming all over Eastern Europe once again, exactly like in the Middle Ages when they came along with the Ottoman armies. Bulgaria is a former communist country, one of the most brutal under its communist dictatorship and one of the poorest. A huge part of its population has already migrated to Western countries, and the growth rate of the Bulgarians left in Bulgaria is dismal. The resulting population gap is being filled by Turkey, and though reports vary widely, one estimate suggests that Bulgaria, since 1990, has taken in a significant number of Muslim Turks, making up between 12 to 18 per cent of the population, with a lot of them concentrated around the border with Greece.

Macedonia is even worse. It has the highest percentage of Muslims in any Christian-majority country in Europe. And the Muslim population is literally exploding there. Muslims are now more than 34 per cent in Macedonia! Until just 2014, they were around 20 per cent. Macedonia is on its way to becoming the first country in Europe to turn Muslim majority from Christian majority in the modern era. It is bad news for Macedonia, of course, but not so good for Greece either. The fourth country bordering Greece is Albania, and it is more than 93 per cent Muslim, and just like Bangladesh, it is sending all its excess population to Kosovo, Bosnia, Serbia, and Greece. Though a lot of Albanians, carrying their communist legacy, declare themselves atheist, whenever it comes to a skirmish with other ethnicities and followers of other religions, their inner Islam quickly surfaces as the only concrete defining identity. Using this Muslim brotherhood, they are destroying the demographics of many neighbouring countries, including Macedonia, Montenegro, Serbia, and Greece. Greece, meanwhile, is one of the poorest countries in Europe, with one of the lowest growth rates. Greeks are going down in numbers, not just percentage, every year. Poor, bankrupt, with one of the highest median ages in Europe and one of the largest dependent populations, and a collapsing welfare state, Greece is in bad shape. Surrounded by either completely Islamic countries with burgeoning populations or by other countries rapidly turning Islamic, any demographic invasion in the future will be well-nigh impossible for Greece to prevent or resist.

What does this grim tale teach us? That even if a partition with a radical Muslim country is completed, it will not be enough. Sooner or later, the society in the non-Muslim country will take a turn for the worse; the sympathetic government will fall, and the situation in the neighbouring countries will change, and Islam will reinvade and reclaim the non-Muslim lands. Just like Sita Ram Goel said, it is not enough to defeat radical Islam in one country. It is necessary to defeat it globally. It is necessary to defeat it at the level of ideology. Local solutions will only be temporary against the global problem of Islam.

This morale becomes evident from another tale of another great European country: Spain. The story of Spain teaches us how the threat of radical Islam is never dead until it is dealt with globally. Spain was one of the first European countries to be overrun by Islam in eighth century. Almost as soon as the Arab conquest of Spain started in 711 CE, Christian armies started giving resistance and got their first success in 718 CE. This is categorized by the later historians as the start of the Reconquista of Spain, which lasted for around 800 years, ending with the expulsion of the Moors from Spain by Ferdinand and Isabella in 1491. Spain is the only case where a non-Muslim nation became successful in rolling back the conquest of Islam completely. Spain was able to liberate all of its land and its people from the Islamic occupation after a prolonged occupation. It is a unique tale of reclamation from Islam. But even this story has its loopholes. Just because the Reconquista of Spain by the Christians was completed once, it was no guarantee that it will not be reversed in the future.

In 2016, Muslims were once again 4 per cent in Spain. And the situation is much worse than their numbers actually reveal. When the US invaded Iraq, Spain was one of the countries supporting the US. Al-Qaeda retaliated in 2004 with the deadliest Islamic terrorist attack in Europe for decades, the Madrid train bombings, which killed 191 Christians.[28] What is more sinister is the timing of the attacks. They were done three days before the general elections. The ruling People's Party had chosen to go with the US against Muslim Iraq. The bombings frightened the Spaniards so much so that they voted in favour of the opposition party, which was socialist and appeasing towards Muslims. Since then, Spain is not in good shape. Many of its provinces want to secede from Spain, and the Islamists and Muslims support these micro-states, as it is very easy to overtake smaller chunks of bigger countries, one by one.

After 800 years of the Reconquista, just a few decades of multiculturalism destroyed the common sense of Spain, allowing Muslims to settle again and grow to a point where they could orchestrate terrorist attacks and influence governments in their favour. Spain is one of the 'unfinished agendas' of Islam, and going by the dictum 'once an Islamic land, always an Islamic land', the country remains a prime target for Muslim immigration and Islamic conquest.

Spain teaches us that Islam has a long memory.

Even if hundreds of years have passed after its defeat locally, it can invade back by using other neighbouring countries as springboards, other countries that were not successful in resisting the Islamic invasion.

Islam has a millennial approach, a global vision, and global action.

It has long-term goals and ready-made mechanisms to act in coordination worldwide. This is why it is not enough to defeat the designs of Islamic forces within our boundaries; it is also necessary to consider the global scenario. You cannot fight global powers with local thinking. Keeping it local helps perpetuate the victim narrative of the Muslims, where non-Muslims are always portrayed as evil. Seen globally, it becomes instantly clear that radical Islam is the aggressor, the perpetrator of violence and genocide, and not its victim. That is why both action and thinking about Islam must be global.

Chapter 11

Weaponization of Life

'With the grace of Prophet Mohammad and Allah, almost all Hindus at Calicut are converted to Islam. Only at the borders of Cochin State a few Hindus are still not converted. I'm greatly determined to convert this as Jihad to achieve that objective.'

—Tipu Sultan

Illustrations on the Tale of the Indian Regions Devastated by some Spaniards, Theodor De Bry, 1598. Spanish conquistadors burning alive non-Christian heathen pagans in the Americas. One of them is going to smash a baby against the wall, to death[1]

Hindus fail to recognize that they are under siege from monotheistic religions like Islam and Christianity because the latter fight what is called an 'unconventional war'. While Hindus fight at the borders, against soldiers, against men, and only in the battlefield, Islam makes every aspect of life a dimension of its war against 'accursed idolaters'. Christianity also does the same. This conversion of every aspect of life into a tool of religious warfare is called 'weaponization'. Islam and Christianity weaponize every aspect of life for religious war.

This has serious consequences on both sides of the war. While Islam and Christianity gain an unfair advantage in warfare due to the weaponization of every aspect of life, the other side, usually a Hindu or pagan side, does not even recognize that it is in a state of war because it can never imagine that something as personal as marriage or death can be an act of war. Failing to see that they are under siege from Islam and Christianity, they lose the war without even knowing they were fighting one.

That is why it is extremely important for Hindus to learn how prophetic monotheism weaponizes every aspect of life, in order to be able to see the act of war when they are in it. In a sacred tradition like Sanatana Dharma, the State is seen as an instrument of disbursing justice and not a means of furthering petty politics as is the norm in Islamic and Christian-captured States. However, Christianity sees the State as the greatest tool to further its goal, and so does Islam.

Weaponization of State

We saw in the previous chapters how Christianity converted Emperor Constantine and, through him, captured the State power of one of the strongest empires of those times—the mighty Roman Empire. It then promptly used the State power to destroy pagan sects, destroyed pagan temples, and killed any pagan priest or philosopher who dared to resist Christian conversion and destruction of classical Greco-Roman heritage. The Christian priest and the soldier went hand in hand on the battlefield. Wherever Roman armies went, the flag of Christianity started flying proudly. The same story was repeated in every single State of Europe, including the countries that we now know as France, Germany, and Britain. The State employed armies to enforce Christianity upon its populations once the king was converted. Destruction of pagan temples was ordered by the State; fanatic Christians who were destroyers of pagans were protected by law, and crimes against pagan culture and people went unpunished.[2]

The story of the Americas is the most heart-rending of all Christian conquests, as the State power was used not just to Christianize but to commit genocide of all the indigenous non-Christians. The State took control of all natural resources, or what we now call as 'commons', and made them a Christian monopoly while the surviving indigenous non-Christian tribes were left to starve to death in deserts or unforgiving forests. But Americas were far from the only continents to suffer this way. The Christianization of central, western, and southern Africa is one of the saddest stories in contemporary times. In the nineteenth century, almost the entire continent was cut up into artificial countries by the European Christian colonizers which prevented the usual movement of tribes across the continent, destroyed tribal and traditional structures, and impoverished the populations living there. Along with this, these colonial countries were used by the barbaric Christian colonizers to forcibly convert the natives to Christianity. The Christian armies of European countries did not just loot the resources of Africa but also looted their native, indigenous religions, as most Africans were converted at the point of the sword to Christianity. In the process, unlimited atrocities were committed against the African natives, as historian Thomas Pakenham writes:

> Atrocities were commonplace during the first phase of occupation by the Powers. When German brutality in South

> West Africa provoked a revolt by the Hereros, the German general, Lothar von Trotha, issued a *Vernichtungbefehl* ('extermination order') against the whole tribe, women and children included. About 20,000 of them were driven away from the wells to die in the Omaheke desert.[3]

We also saw how Christianity weaponized the State in the case of Indian states of Andhra Pradesh, Punjab, and Arunachal Pradesh among many others. The UPA (United Progressive Alliance) decade of 2004–14 was the worst decade that Hindus had ever seen in their post-independence history. With Manmohan Singh as the puppet prime minister, the country was virtually being run by Christian missionaries. The Indian State, despite having a Hindu-majority population, was weaponized for Christianity, which managed to convert sizeable populations of not one but three states to Christianity—Andhra Pradesh, Punjab, and Arunachal Pradesh.

Jagan Reddy, the Catholic chief minister of the divided Andhra Pradesh weaponized state resources for Christian conversions. He also allowed all the churches in the world to fund conversion activities by funnelling billions of dollars through indirect means in Andhra Pradesh. The Centre, ruled by another Christian-led party, collaborated heartily. The weaponization of the State did not just result in conversions of Hindus but also encouraged churches and Christian fanatics to desecrate and destroy Hindu temples. There are many instances of Hindu vigrahas destroyed surreptitiously to terrorize the Hindu population of Andhra Pradesh.[4] One should remember that even before Christianity became the state religion in the Roman Empire in the fourth century, fanatical Christians were destroying temples and vigrahas of pagan deities. The same is happening in Andhra Pradesh. These are not accusations by vested groups. Even sitting MLAs of Jagan's own party were terrorized and forced to shut up and not speak up the truth. One MLA whose conscience woke up and who spoke up had to go into hiding fearing violent Christian and church reprisals.[5]

Most new converts in Andhra Pradesh do not classify themselves as Christian in public or on paper because they do not want to lose the reservation benefits that are only allowed to Hindu populations, and under this garb rapid Christianization of the rest of the state is going on. Having sparsely populated states at the borders of India (like the northeastern states) converted to Christianity was a tragedy nevertheless, but to have a mainstream, deeply Vedic, deeply Hindu state like Andhra Pradesh fall to Christian conversions is a tragedy of monumental proportions. Christianity has a new-found zeal and a great Christian base in the core of Bharatiya Sanatana civilization and in the centre of south India.

Punjab, another state, fell to the designs of Christian missionaries during the UPA regime. Amarinder Singh, the chief minister of Punjab from 2017 to 2021, had a special affinity for Christianity and took a public vow to let Christians join the Punjab assembly.[6] During his reign, Christianity increased by leaps and bounds in Punjab through rampant conversions, particularly converting Dalit Sikhs and Hindus. This is another great tragedy since, for the first time, Christianity has found a great foothold in a major state in north India. This can lead to a tsunami of conversion activities in the north Indian hinterlands threatening the religious demography of the region.

One of the most insidious ways in which Christian plans have been succeeding in India is in the northeast. The northeast now has three, and possibly four, Christian-majority states, and the demographic balance there, along with Bangladeshi Muslim infiltration, has tilted far out of favour of the native and indigenous Hindus. In these states, the State has been weaponized to the hilt by Christianity and used as a tool to convert non-Christians. Nagaland, Mizoram, and Meghalaya have long been

Christian-majority states, and many resources and privileges are now reserved only for Christians. The Church strictly controls the State, and through this control, it virtually controls every other aspect of life in Mizoram, Nagaland, and most parts of Meghalaya.

One example of Christianity's weaponization of state power is in Mizoram's capacity to enforce Christian-only policies in the State. Mizoram is the largest Christian-majority state in India, with scarcely any other community in the state except Christians. Only the Chakmas survive as a major non-Christian community in the state, being Buddhist. But Mizoram had one Hindu-minority community called Reang (Bru). This Hindu community was ethnically cleansed and driven out of Mizoram, only to be resettled in Tripura because they were Hindus.[7] The Church made sure that the Hindu-minority community was not allowed to even live inside Mizoram. To add more to the tragedy, the Reangs, who had to run away from Mizoram because they were not Christians, finally had to convert to Christianity in Tripura due to ongoing clashes with other groups and due to lack of space and resources to subsist.

In Mizoram and Nagaland, they converted Hindus and the followers of natural religions by creating parallel systems of power and authority in the British-appointed tribal leaders (converted Christians), who got all the power and money from the British State while the dharmic leaders of the traditional sects languished in poverty and suffered from many other kinds of discrimination. Gradually, the skewed power equation made sure the British-appointed leaders converted the rest of society to Christianity. In all these cases, it was a weaponized Christian State that furthered the cause of Christianity.

In much of northeastern India, as well as many other states of India like Kerala and Tamil Nadu, State power has been weaponized by Christianity, and in the case of Kerala, by Islam too. The British Empire is wrongly seen as against the Christianization of India. In the rest of India, they adopted indirect methods of conversion, while in northeast India they actively collaborated with the Church to convert natives to Christianity. This is how Christianity weaponizes the state and makes use of it, even if for ten years there is a tandem of Christianity-promoting governments, both at the centre and in any state. An ancient Vedic state like Andhra Pradesh becomes vulnerable and has around one-fifth of its population converted to Christianity. A pristine state like Arunachal Pradesh, which had kept Christianity in check, is converted to Christianity, and the native traditions and Hindu dharma fall there like a pack of cards. And even in a state like Punjab, which was almost exclusively made up of a Hindu–Sikh population, can develop a bursting Christian nucleus.

Islam similarly weaponizes the state. Hindus were taken aback by how the Islamic invaders violated all rules of war and life and how they used the State to enforce 'religious beliefs' on the subjects. In Hindu psyche and experience, war was limited to armies and to battlefields. No Hindu king disturbed the subjects and never disrespected the dharmic tradition of the place. However, the first job of the Islamic invaders after victory on the battlefield was to destroy the temples, kill common Hindus, violate women, and enslave the children: all of this barbaric behaviour was unimaginable to the Hindus. As Sita Ram Goel writes in *The Story of Islamic Imperialism of India*:

> The Hindus advance the following seven accusations against the Muslims (invaders): 1. They kill the Brahmins and the cows; 2. They violate the chastity of Hindu women; 3. They demolish temples, and desecrate the idols; 4. They cut the tuft of hair on the head (*shikha*) and break the sacred thread (sutra); 5. They circumcise people and make them eat beef, that is, convert people by force; 6. They capture people, particularly women and children, and sell them into concubinage and slavery; 7. They plunder people's properties, and set fire to whatever they cannot carry away.[8]

While Indian media and popular culture portrayed Tipu Sultan as a brave nationalist warrior, many authors, most prominently historian Sandeep Balakrishna, exposed him as a bloodthirsty Islamic tyrant who committed genocide against Hindus and employed every form of Islamist barbarity to convert them and destroy their culture and society. In a letter that Tipu Sultan wrote to his military chief, he boasts about his conversion activity in the Calicut area of what is now Kerala: 'With the grace of Prophet Mohammad and Allah, almost all Hindus at Calicut are converted to Islam. Only at the borders of Cochin state a few Hindus are still not converted. I'm greatly determined to convert this as *Jihad* to achieve that objective.'[9]

To contrast this religious Islamic behaviour with the dharmic Hindu code of conduct, we need to know the story of the three temples in the south. In 740 CE, the Badami Chalukya king Vikramaditya II defeated the Pallava capital of Kanchipuram, leading to significant architectural inspiration. The Kailashnathar Temple in Kanchipuram, built by Pallava king Narasimhavarman II in 700 CE, showcased exquisite Dravidian architecture and sculpture. Vikramaditya II, impressed by this temple, took Pallava architects back to his capital, where his wife, Queen Lokamahadevi, commissioned the Virupaksha Temple in Pattadakal, mirroring the Kanchipuram temple's grandeur. Decades later, the Rashtrakuta king Krishna I got inspired by the Virupaksha Temple in Pattadakal and created the rockcut Kailashanatha Temple at Ellora. These events reflect a tradition of cultural and artistic exchange, where conquering kings admired and replicated the architectural marvels of their rivals, fostering a legacy of enduring artistic achievements in India.

Compare this story to the tale of death and destruction that was spread in the wake of any Islamic invasion. In fact, all three temples under discussion in this story were destroyed by one or the other Islamic invader at some point in history. It was the sacred duty of the Islamic kings to destroy the culture and dharma of the defeated Hindu kingdom. Iconoclasm, or temple destruction, was their favourite activity. Qutbud-Din Aibak destroyed at least twenty-seven Hindu and Jain temples[10] to create Qutub Minar and the mosque Quwattul Islam, which means 'the might of Islam'. It is a name that intends to humiliate Hindus for posterity and show them the strength of Islam. This story was repeated in every single small block of this land. Adhai Din ka Jhopra in Ajmer was converted from a great Sanskrit university and a temple dedicated to Saraswati in just two and a half days, because the emperor had to offer namaz in the 'newly built mosque' on the 'ruins of the temples of the kaffir'.[11]Bhojshala in Dhar is another such example among millions of cases where Hindu temples were destroyed to create a mosque.[12]

Prophet Muhammad was not just the greatest religious figure in Islam; he was also a great military leader. Thus, in Islam, the State was weaponized as a religious tool from the very beginning. It was weaponized to fight and win religious wars and spread the authority of Islam. The civil, military, and religious authority in Islam is one—the Caliph, telling us how the State is weaponized to further the cause of Islam. Pakistan sees itself as a flag bearer of Islam, and the messages on the Pakistani military at the border with India proudly declare the goal of furthering the cause of Islam. The Pakistan Army, thus, sees itself directly as a tool of furthering the cause of Islam. It is a clear case of weaponization of the State for the purpose of Islam. This is not something new but has been a persistent theme throughout Islamic history.[13] Muslim Arabs, Persians, and Turks too saw themselves as the soldiers of Islam. Conversion to Islam was seen as a necessary activity by all Islamic invaders in India. This is not an allegation made by Hindus against Muslims or Islam; it is an attitude recorded by Muslim historians themselves, as Sita Ram Goel writes:

> The Muslim historians treat every war waged against the Hindus as a *jihad* as enjoined by the Prophet and the Pious

> Caliphs. In these Muslim accounts we never notice any note of pity, or regret, or reflection over deeds of wanton cruelty and rapacity. On the contrary, the Muslim historians express extreme satisfaction and gleeful gratitude to Allah that the mission of the Prophet has been fulfilled, the light of Islam brought to an area of darkness, and idolatry wiped out. These historians go into raptures over the richness of the booty acquired for the service of the Islamic state, for distribution among the mujahids and the ulama and the sufis, for the promotion of Islamic learning, and for securing the seats of Islamic power.[14]

It is very clear from these words that the Muslim historians consider jihad and forced conversions of non-Muslims as the 'mission of Allah', and they are in the process of praising Islamic generals and soldiers in fulfilling this mission, making it clear how Islam weaponizes the State to further its conversion agenda. *The Story of Islamic Imperialism* tells the story of how the Islamic State in India destroyed Hindu society by weaponizing the State directly for the cause of Islam. This weaponization continued during the British times when Islam exacted many bargains from the British to benefit Muslim society. Hindus were now at the receiving end from both Christianity and Islam. J. Sai Deepak has charted out the history of the weaponization of the British Indian State by Islam and Muslims in his book *India, Bharat and Pakistan*. Whether it was the issue of partitioning Bengal on Islamic lines or extracting the promise and practice of separate electorates from the British, Muslims had managed to weaponize the State of India even while they were not directly ruling it. Commenting on their manoeuvers around separate electorates, J. Sai Deepak writes:

> On 1 October 1906, a deputation of thirty-five Muslim representatives headed by the Aga Khan was received by Minto in Simla, which would thenceforth be known as the Simla Deputation, which would alter the course of Bharatiya history.... The memorial submitted by the Simla Deputation

> must be read for its categorical assertion of the distinct nature of 'the Muslim Nation' ('qaum' as Syed Ahmed Khan called it), which formed the basis of the demand for separate and special treatment of Muslims.... Upon receipt of the memorial, Minto replied to it by assuring the members of the Deputation of British appreciation of Muslim loyalty and promised them the protection of Muslim interests. He also agreed with the principle of communal representation proposed by the Deputation in its memorial.... From a reading of the memorial of the Simla Deputation and Minto's reply, it becomes evident that Muslim separatism/the Two-Nation Theory had been spelt out in the clearest of terms possible and that its validity had been accepted by the British government in India at the highest levels. Not only was it here to stay, it had also entered legal and constitutional thought in a manner that could no longer be ignored.[15]

Today in independent India, the weaponization of the State happens indirectly. When Hindu temples are controlled by the State it is in a way weaponization of the Indian State for Islam and Christianity. This is because while Hindu institutions are taxed, Islamic and Christian religious institutions are subsidized. Thus, Hindus pay tax to subsidize mosques and churches and are thus funding their own conversion. This is nothing but a modern form of jizyah. Harsh Narain, the great chronicler of jizyah in India, concurs:

> We cannot resist the temptation of concluding this chapter with an unusual assessment of the Indian situation today by maintaining that the so-called majority community is still paying something as good or as bad in effect as *jizyah*, viz. that part of the taxes paid by the majority which is used exclusively in the interests of the so-called minorities.[16]

There are many more ways in which the Indian State is weaponized against Sanatana Dharma. The State is prevented by the Constitution from teaching Hindus about their dharma while Islamic and Christian institutions continue teaching the most orthodox and intolerant religious ideology under the pretext of 'minority rights', and they keep arming common Muslims and Christians with radical and fundamentalist Islamist and Christian missionary propaganda.

The 'secular' State of India is being weaponized to de-Hinduize Hindus, make Muslims better Muslims, and Christians more Christians, thus skewing the fight heavily against Hindus. Electoral democracy gives an undue advantage to any political party that is anti-Hindu, as it secures the votes of Muslims and Christians, while any Hindu party must start from zero and swim against the tide. India's official institutions, like the judiciary and the executive, are also trained in anti-Hindu propaganda. Hindus need to learn from these examples, prevent the weaponization of the State against Sanatana Dharma, and seek to declare India a Hindu rashtra.

Weaponization of Charity, Healthcare, and Education

For a Hindu, *daana* (charity) is something to be done in secret. It is considered important that one should forget what one has given in charity because the entire point of Hindu charity is to diminish the ego of the giver. It is also important to keep charity secret so as not to belittle or hurt the sentiments of the person in need. One has to help without making the helped person feel small. This was how beautifully the Hindu institution of daana (charity) helped in the material upliftment of those in need and the spiritual upliftment of the one who had in excess. Hindu charity was personal, decentralized, and one of the most important focuses of Hindu life. But everything that is sacred to a Hindu is a token of politics for Christianity and other prophetic monotheisms. While a Hindu cannot even imagine stooping as low as weaponizing charity, Christianity, the Church, and the wily missionaries are experts at doing just that.

Christianity has always weaponized charity. Christianity believes in total war, just like Islam, and total war means to weaponize every aspect of your life into a holy war. Any such force engaging in total war does not believe in fighting and winning only through war but converts daily life and all actions in life into acts of war. Thus eating, sleeping, loving, and even dying are converted into weapons of conversion. All aspects will be illuminated later, but suffice it to say that in total war, every act has dual results, one for the individual and another for the religious party for which the entire life is weaponized.

In the case of charity, when the Church weaponized charity as a tool of conversion, it used the impulse to give away money and possessions to the less needy (an individual act of compassion) to create a centralized and organized racket of conversions. This process took a leap when the great era of colonialism ended, and the State was no longer always available for direct weaponization for Christianity. Christianity found other indirect means to convert, and weaponizing charity was one of these methods. As the British Raj was settling into power positions in India, various Christian missions were opened across India with the express goal of 'doing charity in the name of Christ'. These activities were sometimes simply giving away food and other essential articles to the poor or the victims of floods and famines. The Church opened hospitals to 'treat the children of God' and to open schools to 'spread the light of education and Good News' to the uneducated and the poor. Needless to say, the 'good news' mentioned above was nothing more than thrusting Christianity down the throats of the gullible and unsuspecting victims of Christian charity.

Weaponization of charity also leads to weaponizing education and healthcare. Christianity has managed to weaponize both of these aspects and institutions in India by routing global charity money through Christian channels. Kind-hearted individuals in Western countries are exploited by showing them the 'poverty', 'disease', 'ignorance', and 'hunger' of non-Christian populations in the third-world countries, and billions of dollars are collected in donation. But this donation then becomes the tool of the church, as it all gets centralized through one or the other arm of the church. A centralized empire of conversion is built on this, controlled by the Vatican in the case of the Catholic Church and by other Christian churches in case of other denominations.

Whenever natural calamities like floods or famines happen, the Church opens soup kitchens and medical camps for the victims. While this seems like a great activity, the victims are converted in turn to Christianity. The world only gets to know of the 'charity' and the 'philanthropic activity' of the Church due to the global Christian stranglehold of communication channels, academia, and media, while the conversion racket goes on secretly, and if any victim makes a noise, then he and his supporters are hushed by branding them as those who are 'communalizing' the matter and 'vitiating the atmosphere'. As the victims are mostly like Hindus, they do not have global networks to make their voices heard, and often their own country is so much biased against them and their native dharmic traditions due to the Christian colonial influence that they have no voice in their own country either. So, their voices remain unheard, and they are branded as villains.

Christianity is the 'harvester of sorrow'. It exploits individuals, families, and social groups going through physical and emotional crises and converts them by providing them some material or psychological relief, thus 'harvesting their sorrow'. A poor mother who wants to treat her son, a father who is not able to make ends meet, a divorcee or single individual in a city who is going through depression, an entire community or area that is suffering due to a natural calamity like famine or flood: all these are 'opportunities' for Christianity to 'harvest their sorrow' and to convert them to Christianity.

This has been the case in many tribal states and areas in India where poor Hindus are converted during a natural calamity.

In peacetimes, conversions happen through offering healthcare and English education. The Christian missions, like the postal service of India, have reached every nook and corner, every district and small village in India. They open schools and hospitals and provide free healthcare and education to anyone who is open to conversion to Christianity. At first, they appear to be impartial but keep enticing the beneficiaries to convert, and once they have a sizeable number of converts in a local place, Christians are favoured over their non-Christian neighbours in everything, including education, thus creating an aspirational social ladder that entices others to Christianity. Hindus are directly discriminated against in this most undemocratic and inhuman Christian manoeuver.

In Jhabua district of Madhya Pradesh, the Church pays for the study of the Christian children but not for the Hindu children, making 'being Hindu' a really disadvantageous position financially. It puts up a hand pump and then brands in bold letters that it is the 'grace of God' and the 'love of Christ' that has put up the hand pump in the region. Yes, the Church has really no shame in touting even a single hand pump that it has ever erected and using that as a tool of conversion. This happens all over India and is happening very aggressively in states like Andhra Pradesh. The difference in the financial aid results in a skewed metric, and conversions follow due to it. *Harvesting Our Souls* by Arun Shourie explains all these aspects in great detail. The Church does not seek to solve crises like hunger, homelessness, and disease. It thrives on these calamities as they lead to conversions.

The greatest example of this is the life and works of the Albanian missionary who dedicated her life to converting poor Hindus to Christianity. She is none other than Mother Teresa. In her institution, Missionaries of Charity, many weaponizations come together: weaponization of charity, healthcare, and even education. She was hailed as a saint by world media and as a very paragon of virtue for 'helping the destitute'; however, all she did was harvest the sorrow of India's poor so that she could run a conversion racket and do 'God's work' in India. Aroup Chatterjee, in his book *Mother Teresa: The Untold Story*, exposes how Mother Teresa promoted what is now known as 'poverty porn' and how she willingly let people suffer so they could 'meet Christ'. Christopher Hitchens, one of the great atheists of the UK, criticized her hypocritical attitudes towards the Indian poor:

> Bear in mind that Mother Teresa's global income is more than enough to outfit several first-class clinics in Bengal. The decision not to do so, and indeed to run instead a haphazard and cranky institution which would expose itself to litigation and protest were it run by any branch of the medical profession, is a deliberate one. The point is not the honest relief of suffering but the promulgation of a cult based on death and suffering and subjection. Mother Teresa (who herself, it should be noted, has checked into some of the finest and costliest clinics and hospitals in the West during her bouts with heart trouble and old age) once gave this game away in a filmed interview. She described a person who was in the last agonies of cancer and suffering unbearable pain. With a smile, Mother Teresa told the camera what she told this terminal patient: 'You are suffering like Christ on the cross. So Jesus must be kissing you.' Unconscious of the account to which this irony might be charged, she then told of the sufferer's reply: 'Then please tell him to stop kissing me.' There are many people in the direst need and pain who have had cause to wish, in their own extremity, that Mother Teresa was less free with her own metaphysical caresses and a little more attentive to actual suffering.[17]

The above lines by Hitchens make it clear that the purpose of Teresa was not to absolve the suffering individuals from their pain, which is and should be the goal of any normal philanthropist. Teresa was just worried about her own Catholic registry and how many 'heathens' and 'accursed idolaters' she had converted in her lifetime. Missionaries count their own life's success by how many non-Christians they managed to convert, and this is what Teresa was also doing. Instead of wanting to end India's poverty, she sought to continue it and use it for Christian conversions. Her 'healthcare facility' was a subterfuge to convert poor Hindus. She successfully weaponized both charity and healthcare by using healthcare as a ruse to route charity by gullible good folks all over the world and divert it towards the Christian conversion racket in India.

Along with charity and healthcare, Christianity weaponizes education too. We already saw how Hindus have always done charity in history; they just preferred not to talk about it. In education too, the great Gandhian thinker Dharampal tells us in his wonderful work, *The Beautiful Tree*, how India was far more educated than the West. The British destroyed the beautiful system of Indian education by supplanting it with English Macaulayite education. By destroying our indigenous system, they impoverished Hindus in education, and when the impoverishment was complete, they presented us with the English education system: a perfect case of creating a problem and then offering a solution, gaining in both processes.

As the Indian state was weaponized against Hindu society and Sanatana Dharma, many anti-Hindus, like Islamists, missionaries, and Marxists, came together to weaponize all other aspects of Indian institutions, including education, charity, and healthcare. In education, the communists struck a bargain with the rulers of post-independence India. Jawaharlal Nehru was an inveterate communist and was head over heels in love with communism and all communist states like the Soviet Union and communist China. Sita Ram Goel reveals how deeply communist Nehru was in his magnificent work *Genesis and Growth of Nehruism*. Nehru facilitated socialist policies in India, gravitated away from the

USA, and towards the USSR and then China. His policies led to the establishment of the communist party deeper in India, and even the Chinese debacle did not open his eyes. He let many institutions of India be taken over by anti-Hindu Marxist ideologues.

Even worse happened under the prime ministership of Indira Gandhi, when many free institutions were nationalized and given a communist and anti-Hindu bent. The communists supported Indira Gandhi in politics and in exchange demanded control of India's educational institutions as well as institutions of mass communication. Dr Nurul Hasan, cherry-picked by Indira Gandhi and inducted from the Rajya Sabha, became the Union Education Minister in the fateful year of 1971. He was an avowed leftist who wore his political orientation on his sleeve. Under him, the country changed hands and was completely handed over to leftists and their paymasters. The leftists went on to capture every institution in media and academia, throwing out great scholars, genuine historians, and natural artists. Within a decade, the rout was complete. The country was painted red. The nation had turned left. We are still to recover from that.

India's textbooks are still deeply anti-Hindu. While the Vajpayee government tried to change the textbooks but failed as it lost the subsequent election, the subsequent BJP (Bharatiya Janata Party) government did not even try to remove the anti-Hindu bias from India's textbooks due to international opposition, activated by all leftist channels. We are still creating de-Hinduized Hindu youths every single day in all our schools, colleges, and universities. The British understood when they came here that the route to the conversion of Hindus is through its education. They saw a flourishing indigenous dharmic education system and set out to destroy and replace that with the English education system to prepare Hindus better for 'receiving the love of Christ'. And this is exactly what India's English education is doing.

Weaponizing Relationships and Death

The weaponization of the State, economy, charity, education, and healthcare is not, however, the extent of the weaponization by monotheistic forces in India. Christian and Islamic ideologies have also weaponized relationships as well as the most sacred phenomenon of death. Islam accepts converts but does not let them go away. Leaving Islam is punishable by death. And enticing non-Muslims to Islam is considered Allah's work, and thus certain sections of their communities are employed in enticing non-Muslims to Islam and thus ensuring that the lineage of that person, most often a girl, is bequeathed to Islam.

In Islamic ideology, women are treated as wombs to produce children. While Hindu dharma also glorified the great ability to give birth, and rightfully so, women are and cannot be limited to their reproductive ability only or reduced to their sexual and reproductive organs. The Arabic word for woman, *aurat* comes from the word *awrah*, which denotes female genitalia, so the very word reduces women to their reproductive organs. This mentality is then extended, and they are often seen as wombs to produce more children who are also followers of Islam. Shri Ram Swarup, in his brief and precise survey of the position of women in Islam, says:

> When a Muslim man and woman marry, they have their rights and duties. She cannot refuse cohabitation except on such grounds as menstruation and sickness. If she refuses to go to the husband's bed when called, 'the one in Heaven is displeased with her until the husband is pleased with her', says the Prophet according to an oft-quoted hadith.[18]

In most Islamic countries, women are often treated as nothing but means to produce male heirs, and their status suffers if they do not produce male heirs. The Quran ordains: 'Your women are a tilth for you (to cultivate) so go to your tilth as ye will, and send (good deeds) before you for your souls, and fear Allah, and know that ye will (one day) meet Him. Give glad tidings to believers, (O Muhammad).'[19]

Women of other religions are also considered legitimate targets of enticement. They are after all the 'rightful reward of *Jihad*', or as the Quran says, 'as the right hand possesses'.[20] It is considered worthy to convince anyone to accept Islam, and while others might be wary of converting to Islam, individuals who are in love are most likely to do so, and thus love has been weaponized by Islam as a tool of conversion. This is known in India as Love Jihad. The term was coined by the Syrian Christian community of Kerala, which saw that many of its girls were enticed by young Muslim boys, and when they would get ready to be married, they would be convinced to convert to Islam since that is the only condition to accept someone from other communities in their community. And thus, through marriage, love, and relationships, the lineage of an entire Hindu or Christian family would be bequeathed to Islam, and their numbers would grow.

Marriage is a most sacred contract in any traditional society, including Hindu dharma, and it is all about the two individuals, their families, and society around them, but it is never about using it as a political tool. Islamic ideology, which is more politics than religion, weaponizes something as sacred as marriage into a tool of Islamic imperialism or Islamic conquest of the world. Hindus and other non-Muslims should be aware and work towards preventing this from happening. Islamic law encourages Muslim men to take four wives so that more and more non-Muslim women can see the 'light of Islam' by marrying Muslim men. In mixed societies where Hindus and pagans cohabit with a monotheistic sect like Islam, they are sitting ducks to such enticements in marriage. But they do not even realize it because Hindus cannot imagine that something as intimate as marriage can be weaponized for the sake of politics, ideology, or religious extremism.

Most shockingly, prophetic monotheistic sects like Christianity and Islam have even weaponized death. When a Hindu dies, he is burnt to ashes in the last rites in a cremation ground. Hindu darshana says that our petty selves are nothing but just temporary patterns that are created in a flowing stream that are sure to disappear soon. An atman wears a body made of *pancha mahabhuta tattvas* or the five elements. When a person dies, his body is then burnt to death, and rituals are performed so that his soul moves on for transmigration to another body. That is why a Hindu is cremated upon death, so that his body disappears and his soul moves on in transmigration.

The philosophy behind burying a dead body after a funeral in Islamic and Christian communities is different. For them, there is no reincarnation and thus no transmigration of souls. Every individual takes birth only once, and after death, his body lies in wait for the Last Judgement (in Christianity) or *Qayamat* (in Islam). All the dead Muslims and Christians are waiting in their graves to be woken up by either Prophet Muhammad or Prophet Jesus so that they can go to heaven. Thus, the bodies are important even after death and are taken special care of. That is why Muslims and Christians bury their dead, and Christians especially bury their dead in special coffins that prevent quicker decaying of the body, and everybody has to be buried in a separate place with a separate commemorative stone and plaque.

This belief of Christianity results in land jihad even after death because, while millions of Hindus can go up in flames in the same area over many centuries, the same space will be filled up by a Christian graveyard in a matter of years or months. Even after death, Christian ideology is occupying land in India and claiming this country for Christ. At this rate, in a thousand years, all of India will be a vast Christian graveyard. That is how they have marked various other nations on earth and are employing the same strategy in Bharatavarsha.

This is the weaponization of death in peace, as Islamic ideology weaponizes death in war.

Islam has the concept of jihad, of course, and there is no need to go deeper into it right now, but jihad is an obligatory duty upon every Muslim. Jihad is a holy war against the infidels or non-Muslims. Engaging in jihad is one of the most important tasks a Muslim can undertake, and to entice more Muslims into the war machine, perks are associated with jihad. Any Muslim who dies while engaging in jihad is said to skip the wait till judgement day and go dirrectly to jannat, where they enjoy the company of the *houris*. This is a great perk for anyone who believes in Islamic ideology and does not want to wait till eternity to go to heaven.

While Hindus should not and cannot change their rituals, to fight the land jihad by such monotheistic ideologies in which they weaponize even death, they can have policies where certain areas of forest land are reserved for every Hindu who dies, and after a certain great area is reserved, a Hindu temple can be built at the centre, while the forest area is maintained all around. This can be used for the reforestation of the arid land. This will put a counter to the land jihad by ideologies like Christianity and Islam, and at the same time will not tamper with sacred Hindu rituals, and in turn improve the ecosystem by rejuvenating forest lands.

Hindus have to understand that prophetic monotheistic ideologies weaponize every single aspect of life. They do not just fight on the battlefield, or only in the day, or only against men. They fight in our streets, in our homes; they fight against men, women, and children; they fight incessantly without stopping during day and night. While Hindus give daana for destroying their ego, improving their individual karma, and selflessly helping those who are in need, Christians weaponize charity to make a harvest of pain and sorrow so that they can convert the sufferers to Christianity, notwithstanding whether their pain and suffering are alleviated or not. Muslims do charity (*zakat*) in order to further the holy war (jihad) against non-believers. While Hindus engage in medicine and healthcare purely for the alleviation of suffering, Christian missionaries like Mother Teresa use this opportunity to weaponize healthcare when individuals are vulnerable and to convert them to Christianity. While Hindus educate their children so that they can navigate through the samsara well and, on the other hand, keep moving towards the ultimate target of moksha, Christianity and Islam weaponize education to de-Hinduize Hindus and to make the State keep giving benefits to Islam and Christianity.

Hindus need to understand this deeply biased game against them and understand that it is not simply ideologies but also the institutions of contemporary India that are working against Hindu interests. Hindus need to identify, recognize, become aware of, and then dismantle all anti-Hindu institutions and create not just neutral but pro-Hindu institutions on their way to revival and reclamation.

Chapter 12

Hindu View of Secular Modernity

'Secularism in India today means denunciation of Hindu society, denunciation of Hindu culture, denunciation of Hindu history. It means denunciation of everything which is Hindu. The word "Hindu" itself has become a dirty word. This is the religion of secularism which is replacing Sanatana dharma.'

—Sita Ram Goel

Two Dominican Monks Burned at the Stake by Order of the Inquisition for Allegedly Signing Pacts with the Devil, Histoire veritable de quatre lacopins, 1549[1]

The Fault with India's Secularism

Sita Ram Goel famously said that the adoption of secularism by the Indian state was the greatest tragedy that happened to India after independence. It did not solve any problem but created many instead. It de-Hinduized the Indian state and Hindu society, promoted the delusion of sarva-dharma-samabhava, equated dharma and religion, and gave the status of dharma to Islam and Christianity. At the same time, it facilitated the successive radicalization of Muslims and Christians. Thus, while it made Hindus less Hindus, it made Muslims and Christians more Muslim and Christian, thus creating an unfair and skewed playing ground where Hindus were at a perpetual disadvantage.

Indian secularism functions as the magnet that attracts all breaking India forces. It is the rallying cry for all anti-Hindus of every hue. Sita Ram Goel maintained that secularism was unfit for Hindu society, which was open and free by its very nature, and secularism's imposition in India has become disastrous because it is a great mistake to import a concept born in an alien cultural milieu into our society without critical examination.

> When we adopt those concepts by translating them literally or even substantially in our own language and make them current in our country which has had a different ethos and history, then we not only render those concepts invalid but also corrupt and obscure the heritage of our culture. The concept of Secularism which we have made current in our politics by calling it *dharmanirpekshata* or *sarva-dharma-samabhava*, is one such concept.[2]

Sita Ram Goel rejects any need for secularism in the Indian context because the ideas, beliefs, institutions, and the religion that caused the birth of secularism in Europe were non-existent in India. The dharmic ethos that prevailed in Bharatavarsha under the aegis of Sanatana Dharma was something completely alien to the Judeo-Christian world. The two cultural milieus—the one in which secularism was born and the one on which it was forcefully superimposed without thought, i.e., India—had nothing in common. Any superimposition would not only be utterly meaningless but also extremely dangerous. Jakob de Roover, commenting upon the predicament of Hindu secularists, says that in an attempt to import an alien ideology into their native society, they destroyed a lot in the process:

> They tried to make an alien world their own, while their own world became alien to them. This is the situation of India's secularists. They also reproduce the Western discourse about India and the West, but these sets of ideas fail to make intuitive sense to them because they cannot access the experiential world within which the ideas are embedded. Worse, the same discourse also prevents them from gaining insight into their own experiences and the world they live in, including Indian experiences of conflict and co-existence.[3]

That is what Indian secularism became: dangerous to the very core of Hindu society and Sanatana Dharma, as its imposition suggested that our society also had the same deficiencies and fault lines that existed in Christian Europe. In independent India, Hindus grew up believing that dharma is religion and 'all religions are same' and that religion is the stuff of primitive society and should disappear upon the first touch of reason and logic, forgetting that Hindu dharma had entire systems of logic and rationality, including *nyaya*, and it was Christianity that rested upon blind belief and not Hindu dharma. We grew up believing that *archakas/pujaris* in Hindu temples were also like Catholic priests in Christian Europe: corrupt and degenerate. We grew up believing that in order for science to grow, we need to decrease the influence of dharma in life, because we were fooled into believing that dharma and religion are the same categories and that all religions are same—sarva-dharma-samabhava. Had secularism not been adopted in independent India and had India's constitutional foundations been closer to dharma, these fallacies would not have crept into our worldview. Sita Ram Goel says that given the non-existence of the conditions that gave rise to secularism in an Abrahamic society, the only relevance for secularism in India would be to use it to end all institutional power of Abrahamic/monotheistic sects in India.

> In such acountry (India), Secularism could have relevance only in one sense: to establish complete cultural freedom in the Hindu homeland by eliminating the fanaticism which had survived in the form of Islam and Christianity.... The right use of Secularism would have been to unmask these closed creeds and liberate the communities which had become their victims.[4]

What happened in India was the opposite since power did not pass on to the Hindu side in 1947. It passed on to a party and a leader that were Hindu in name only (HINO). As discussed above, in India monotheistic populations were mixed with dharmic populations, and the worst-case scenario played out for the dharmic sects. Islamic and Christian groups ganged up to force the Congress government to declare them as minorities in the constitution and extracted legal permission to convert Hindus to Christianity and Islam under 'minority rights'.

Islamic groups combined various tactics to once again start carving Islamic majority districts and areas inside India, essentially the same tactics that had led to the religious partition of India, with one-third of the country forever lost to Hindus. The Islamic groups forced governments to give them special rights, and on the street, they kept showing their 'power' using the street veto and threatened the Hindu majority into silence. Christianity, on the other hand, proceeded to make pathways to channel the unlimited billions of global Christian funding to convert Hindus to Christianity with the help of money and other fraudulent methods. Some brave folks tried to speak against this perversion of the meaning of secularism and other words, but they were all silenced by the Congress party in an era when democracy depended on the discretion of the Gandhi family, which was hand in glove with Islamic and Christian lobbies and meted out a stepmotherly treatment to the Hindu majority. All those who tried to speak the truth to power were denounced as 'Hindu communalists'.

> The Christian missionaries had never had any shortage of money. The mullahs also began to receive unlimited funds from Arab countries due to exorbitant increase in the price of petrol in the eighth decade of this century. And because of the campaigns mounted by Islam and Christianity, the situation has now become quite frightful.[5]

This situation kept becoming more and more frightful as Congress shut its eyes as district after district and state after state in India was Christianized and Islamized. Secularism functioned as the smokescreen under which the Islamization and Christianization of India proceeded apace. Assam was a heavily Hindu-majority state in 1951, and now it is almost a Hindu minority state. Hindus will soon be reduced to a minority in Kerala and West Bengal, and Christianity threatens to become the majority in Andhra Pradesh and Tamil Nadu in the next few decades. Hindus were subjected to unimaginable genocide in Kashmir, and every single Hindu had to flee the valley. Even states like Madhya Pradesh, Gujarat, and Chhattisgarh, which are heavily Hindu majority, saw the increase in Muslim and Christian populations everywhere. All this happened while the ruling party, the media, and academia in India kept talking about the 'aggressive and violent Hindu majority' that is 'oppressing peaceful Muslim and Christian minorities'.

It was a case of victim shaming on a civilizational scale. Hindus, the long victims of Islam and Christianity, were declared as the 'disturbers of peace'. In fact, the only thing they were trying to disturb was the monotheistic nexus of Islam, Christianity, communism, and the Congress party against the Hindu majority of India. The Gandhian slogan of sarva-dharma-samabhava was utilized to legitimize monotheistic religions as 'dharma'. It can perhaps be counted as the greatest mistake in Hindu history—to provide the status of dharma or tradition to Islam and Christianity. And this was done by the mainstreaming of the Gandhian slogan of sarva-dharma-samabhava. Gandhi could not be more wrong, and yet this legacy has damaged India heavily:

> The principle of *sarva-dharma-samabhava* has always been accepted and practised among the schools of Sanatana Dharma. But to entertain *samabhava* (equal regard) towards Islam and Christianity, by giving them the status of dharma, is to extend invitation to doom. A study of the scriptures, traditions and history of Islam and Christianity, makes it more than evident that these ideologies are not worthy of being called dharma in any sense of the term. Contrary to this, these ideologies are brimful of imperialistic ambitions. By accepting them as dharma, it becomes impossible to resist their imperialistic expansion. There should be no place for doubt in this matter. Wherever the impact of Islam and Christianity has grown, it has given fillip to treason. Afghanistan, Pakistan and Bangladesh were inseparable parts of India for ages past. Islam severed these parts from the motherland. In the North-East region of India, the increasing spell of Christianity is also inciting moves of separatism in the same way.[6]

Islam and Christianity are predatory colonial ideologies masquerading as dharma in Bharatavarsha in order to fool Hindus so that, one by one, district by district, year by year, they can all be converted to one or the other monotheistic sect. And this is becoming possible because we have adopted an ideology like secularism, which is designed to rig the game against Hindus, aiming for the actual death and destruction of Hindu society and dharma.

Then why was secularism adopted in India?

Even though it was included in the Preamble of the Constitution in 1976, it had always been the State ideology. India was most clearly not a Hindu dharmic State. It was a 'neutral' secular State. One obvious reason why secularism was adopted as the model is that the British Christians handed over the power to a party and a family that would be conducive to the continued dominance of Christianity and Christian institutions in India. But there are other reasons too. A.K. Saran says that secularism was seen as a solution to the 'Hindu–Muslim problem' and adopted as the State policy to accommodate both the populations together. This had happened before independence too.

The Hindu Renaissance was started in contemporary times by Swami Vivekananda. It was enriched by the greats like Swami Dayananda, Shri Aurobindo, Lokmanya Balgangadhar Tilak, etc. Hindu revival could be seen in public events, the display of Hindu symbols, arts, literature, and language, and in the revival of Hindu festivals. There was a general upswing in dharma across the country. This Hindu movement was a great threat to the British Raj in India. And they were looking to cull it. Even after much suppression, Hindu revival was on an upward swing. It was only derailed when the Congress party called for Hindu–Muslim unity for a united front against the British invaders, completely forgetting that Muslims were also the living representatives of the Islamic invaders and continued with the same ideology.

A neutral platform for both Hindus and Muslims was called for. In a bid to make everything neutral, the Congress party, much before India's independence, de-Hinduized the Hindu movement and stopped Hindu revival. The renaissance that the great Swami Vivekananda had started was killed by the call for Hindu–Muslim unity by the Congress party. A 'neutral' platform was created by de-Hinduizing the independent movement and all the institutions related to it, but the tragedy was that the Muslims never accepted even this 'neutral' platform, because for them no compromise on Islam is acceptable.

Hindus were left in a very pitiable and ridiculous situation. They were left with a de-Hinduized platform and identity, which they created to accommodate Muslims, but which was never accepted by Muslims. Muslims went ahead with their demand for a separate Islamic country while Hindus moved forward with a 'secular' and 'neutral' platform that was essentially anti-Hindu. Hoping against hope, Hindus kept trying to woo Muslims with their 'neutral' and 'secular' platform, never realizing that coming together was never the goal of Islam. Its goal was to carve out a separate Islamic country for Muslims and then send the remaining Hindus and Hindu areas on a wild goose chase of a 'composite society' with the ideal of 'Hindu–Muslim unity'. Hindus never realized or dared to profess that the ideal of 'Hindu–Muslim unity' failed with the Muslim rejection of it, and hence Hindus were no longer obliged to keep hoisting it on their shoulders. But it was still carried through, and Congress politicians under the disastrous leadership of Gandhi, who had no Shatrubodha, kept trying to appease Islam and kept strengthening the Church and Christian institutions. As was inevitable, Muslim demand for a separate country could not be ignored, and Jinnah got it by Direct Action Day in which lakhs of Hindus in Noakhali and other areas were brutally massacred by Islamic gangs.

The Islamic State of Pakistan was thus born. Secularism had failed. History, at the cost of millions of Hindu-Sikh lives, proved that Hindus and Muslims could not live together. Secularism as a policy should have been scrapped and banned, for it was responsible for millions of Hindu-Sikh lives. But the opposite was done. Lacking good Shatrubodha and lacking control of the

Congress party and India's new institutions, Hindus could not see the elephant in the room that Hindus and Muslims cannot live together. India did not go through with the population transfer. While Pakistan largely massacred, converted, or drove away the Hindus that were living in its domains, India gave Muslims and Christians equal rights, ignoring the fact that the problem that led to the partition of India persisted as a glaring wound inside 'secular India's' domains if they did not go through with the population transfer.

What was the result? Divided and truncated, India was once again left with the 'Islam problem', the problem that led to the division of India in the very first place. Once again, the same question of 'Hindu–Muslim unity' and 'neutral platforms' and 'secular fabric to bind Hindus and Muslims' came up, and once again the solution was to practice secularism and to de-Hinduize Hindus with the 'neutral State' and further Islamize Muslims and Christianize Christians under the name of minority rights. Islam had extracted a great Islamic country from Bharatavarsha and started on the path of another partition and another civil war. And this game continues under the garb of 'secularism'. If this is so, then why was secularism adopted by independent India?

A.K. Saran answers this by saying that secularism goes hand in hand with secular nationalism that the country had adopted since independence; that 'secular nationalism' is just a political expression of secularism. There is some truth in this assertion. This kind of secular nationalism would also believe in an 'Indian nationality' that is above and higher than Hindu, Muslim, Christian, and other religious or dharmic identities. This was something very new to the Hindu psyche. For millennia that preceded the entry of Islam on the Indian political scene, there was no identity or category greater than Sanatana Dharma. For Hindus, the priority pyramid was clear. Dharma was bigger than *desha*, and desha too had a different identity and configuration than what we denote as a country today. Hindu texts never spoke on laws of Muslims, and no available treatise on administration and governance has provisions for incorporating Muslims and Islam in any national idea.

Before Hindu thinkers could come up with provisions for Muslims inside the boundaries of a Hindu rashtra, another kind of monotheists came barging in—the British Christian colonialists. India, before the British, had not seen a collective identity comprising both Hindus and Muslims. The Muslim invaders had seen a unity only in the conversion of Hindus to Islam, but they never imagined a state where Hindus were allowed to thrive as Hindus. Even Akbar's *Din-e-elahi* required Hindus to take up a new *deen*, or 'religion', which was invented by Akbar, but which was very similar to Islam. The British came on the heels of the Islamic colonialists, and it was they who saw a collectivity in their 'Indian subjects' (that is, Hindus and Muslims together) for the first time. For the ease of administration, they created a single identity for their subjects based on their geography and their status in polity (subjects of the British Empire). This identity was called 'Indian', and for the first time, we had a national identity based on the name of our country, which included followers of monotheistic religions like Islam too. This invention of hybrid monotheistic–dharmic identity hinged around the 'Indian' nationality and had far-reaching consequences that are still reverberating in this land of Sanatana Dharma.

This does not mean that there was no collective Bharatiya or Hindu identity before the British came to India. The spirit of the Vedas, the soul of Sanatana Dharma, had sewn the diverse cultures and peoples of Bharatavarsha into one undivided unit. We had a common identity even though we did not subscribe to the narrow linguistic nationalisms that were the norm in Europe. But this common Hindu identity had no provision for incorporating monotheistic religions and populations like Islam and Muslims in it. All the Hindu states that rose before the British in India, like the Sikhs and the Marathas, vowed to fight and defeat the forces of Islam and thus had no provision for permanently incorporating Islam, a monotheistic religion, in their national polity. The creation of an overarching Indian identity comprising Hindus, Muslims, and Christians was entirely a British creation.

When India became free, this secular nationalist 'Indian' identity was used as a political counterpart of the secularist ideology. It was seen as the 'good' counter to the evil twins of 'Hindu nationalism' and 'Muslim nationalism'. In reality, secular nationalism, which was championed by the Congress party and copied by many other political parties and institutions, was used just as a ploy to prevent the rise of genuine Hindu revival movements in society and Hindu nationalism on the national scene. In theory it declared both 'Hindu nationalism' and 'Muslim nationalism' as evil, but in practice, it was a tool to suppress Hindus and encouraged Muslim nationalism in the name of 'minority rights'. Just like the 'neutral platform' was populated only by Hindus before independence, 'secular nationalism' was manned only by Hindus after India's independence. It was the worst-case scenario for Hindus, where they did not get any right to govern their own motherland according to their own dharmic fundamentals and were forced to serve the 'Indian identity', which was just a ploy to prevent the rise of a Hindu identity. This sociopolitical mix is also known to us today as Nehruvian secularism, or India's secularism, as Sita Ram Goel called it. While Muslims continued their secessionist activities in independent India, Hindus were prevented from thinking on Hindu nationalist lines by promoting secular nationalism as the good ideal.

The 'Indian' identity, which was invented, thus had no real basis on the ground because Muslims never participated in secular nationalism, just as they did not participate in the 'neutral platform' created by Congress in the run-up to the independence. The Muslims kept touting their religious Muslim identity as the supreme and only identity, while Hindus were shamed when they called for Hindu nationalism, and instead they were encouraged to see 'rashtra' as greater than 'dharma'. Even so-called fundamentalist Hindu organizations like Rashtriya Swavayamsevak Sangh (RSS) kept 'nation' higher than 'dharma', for they too were struggling with the problem of accommodating Muslims in their idea of a Hindu rashtra. They talk of 'cultural nationalism', which roots itself firmly in ancient Hindu identity, but the hierarchy of nation first and religion/ dharma later that was created by the British was not violated by even independent Hindu organizations like RSS. They came up with the trope of 'nationalist Muslim' in order to circumvent the public proclamation of ghar wapasi as their policy of creating a Hindu rashtra. This is because even the great Svatantra Veer Savarkar toyed with the idea of a 'nationalist Muslim'.

The situation has improved in the twenty-first century, and Nehruvian secularism is now an object of fervent critique. Various Hindutva thinkers have mainstreamed the critique of Nehruvian secularism and exposed its fallacies, like Anand Ranganathan, Harsh Madhusudan, and Aravindan Neelakandan, but none of them have questioned the supremacy of nation over religion/ dharma. While Madhusudan and Ranganathan have brilliantly pulled apart the evil that is Nehruvian secularism and exposed its anti-Hindu bias, they have also not disturbed the 'nation supreme' hierarchy. Aravindan Neelakandan has gone to another extreme and called for incorporating Islam and Muslims in the idea of a Hindu Rashtra through the cultural agency of what he calls as '*samanvya*' (union of Hindu and Muslim societies) in his book *Hindutva*. In another Gandhian fallacy, he thinks that Islam and Muslims can be incorporated through the sheer goodwill of Hindu society. If this idea is ever practiced, it will once again lead Hindu society and the Hindu revival movement on the path of delusion and destruction just as it did when the call for Hindu–Muslim unity first went out in the run-up to independence and second when secularism was adopted as the model of governance after independence. Here one would do well to remember the idea of the 'poison pill' of Rajiv Malhotra, where some ideas make it impossible for a system to be completely digested and incorporated in another system. Islam itself is a poison pill for a dharmic society and can never be completely incorporated in a traditional/dharmic setup. Hindus need to introduce their own poison pills to prevent their digestion by Christian ideas and institutions.

A.K. Saran says that the failure of the secular nationalist idea and its repetition again in independent India means that Indian Muslims will always have divided loyalty since it is their choice of Islam over nationalism that created Islamic Pakistan. Their divided loyalty in India as a nation results in their support of separatist politics and support for all those political parties that encourage Islamic fundamentalism and suppress the Hindu majority. Electoral democracy with a huge Muslim vote bank results in a politics that always tries to divide Hindu society into various caste/class groups and combines one or two of these castes with a huge Muslim minority that votes as a bloc. This has been the winning formula of all 'secular parties' of India. It leads to the perpetual disintegration of Hindu society and the successive strengthening of Islamic and Christian fundamentalism in India. But secularism fails on more than one count. Let us analyse its central claims and how they fare against Hindu society.

The Internal Contradictions of Secularism

The model of secularism that is being practiced in liberal democracies the world over faces many problems today and seems to have largely failed in its goals beyond European boundaries. This is not to say that it has been entirely successful in Europe either, but outside of Europe, and especially outside the realm of Western Christendom, it has miserably failed to deliver on its promises. To understand more about it, we first need to understand the two central claims and requirements of secularism.

First, secularism aims to keep the public and the private realms separate, purportedly to ensure that the private preferences of individuals do not influence the public life of the country. Secondly, secularism aims to keep the religious and the secular spheres separate, ensuring that no religion affects the secular life.

This is the claim in theory, but in practice it has been found almost without exception that it is almost impossible to completely separate the religious from the secular and also the public from the private. The case of the Shri Ram Janmabhoomi temple would be very illustrative. The dispute was purely a religious one where Islamic invaders had destroyed the Shri Rama temple that stood at the place of his birth. As was the Islamic practice, a mosque was created on the ruins of the temple in order to appropriate the sacred site of the Hindus and to make sure that the act of reclamation never happens. The case went to the court, and Shri Ram Lalla Virajaman, the deity of the temple, was made the complainant. In 1992, the disputed structure was brought down. In 2020, the court gave the site to the Hindu side, and in 2024, a grand temple was inaugurated at the same place. In all of this, many arms of the secular State, like the legislature and the judiciary, were involved in matters that were purely religious/dharmic (Islamic/Hindu).

The State has been involving itself in the religious matters, even though it claims to be secular all the time. There are many other cases to illustrate this fact. In the Shah Bano case of 1985, a Muslim woman got the right to alimony from the court, which is against the Islamic law Shariat. The Islamic lobby pressured the Muslim-appeasing government of Rajiv Gandhi-led Congress to give in to the Islamic pressure and enact a law preventing the court of law from ordering the husband to pay alimony to the divorced wife. The Islamic religious cause was furthered through the agency of the State most clearly here. Most recently, in the Sabarimala case, the courts ordered menstruating women to enter the temple, something which is against the rules of the temple or the sampradaya. There were many protests after which the judgement was reversed. This is a case in which the 'secular State' and its arm, the judiciary, inspired by judicial activism, actively tried to interfere in the private affairs of the Hindu temple. In this case, the State interfered with dharmic matters.[7]

We see that it is impossible to completely separate the religious/dharmic from the secular in a 'secular State', the most primary condition of secularism. This problem is not limited to India but exists as it is in the European society also, where the laws of the country intervene and dictate in many areas of the Church and where the Church also influences and manipulates the business of the State and, through international relations, intervenes in the internal affairs of other countries like India.

The other central claim of secularism, the claim of separating the private from the public affairs, is also not always possible. Judicial activism is basically an argument of intruding into the private affairs of the citizens on the basis of social justice theory. Many bills have been proposed that offer to intervene in the private lives of the individuals, like marriage, parenting, and other social relationships. Many laws are already in place, which prevent communities from following some of their customary laws, like dowry. To be clear, laws against dowry are absolutely necessary, but that is besides the point here. The point here is to stress that in this case too the State interferes in the personal lives of its citizens, citing ethics and morality.

We see that the two central claims of secularism are impossible to achieve in reality. But does it have an adverse effect on Hindu society? It does, because as Sita Ram Goel said, if we forcibly transpose an alien ideology in a new social setting, it creates new problems. The new problem that secularism created in India was to open Hindu society and Sanatana Dharma up for conversions to Christianity through the agency of the State.

As the religious and the secular realms do not always separate like two neat boxes, in any case where they overlapped, the State assumed the overarching authority over religion, and in India's case, over Sanatana Dharma. However, this authority of the State could not be extended to Christianity because the very idea of a secular State had developed in the Christian religious milieu, and Christianity had long safeguarded its interests against the encroachments of the State. It used its long experience with a secular State to extract benefits, perks, and special concessions from the Indian State too, while Sanatana Dharma and its followers, having no experience of a secular State, could not extract any benefits and were left completely subservient to the secular State. Hindus were fooled into believing that the secular State would do justice to all religions and dharmas and all societies, including Hindu dharma and Hindu society. We have already seen that they could not be more wrong. In 'neutral India' it is the secular State that controls and taxes the Hindu temples and redistributes the resources to the minorities and aids the Hajj pilgrimage, as well as gives a free rein and autonomy to Christian institutions in the name of 'minority rights'.

To provide an analogy from the natural world, prophetic monotheistic religions in India are like an invasive species that rapaciously destroy native dharmic sects like Sanatana Dharma. In the natural world, an invasive species is any species that is transplanted from a faraway alien continent. In its old habitat, it has a history of co-evolving and living together with different species in a state of dynamic equilibrium. But in its new habitat, the indigenous species have no defence against it as there is no previous exposure. Such an invasive species grows with leaps and bounds without any checks and balances and comes to dominate the new continent very soon. After initial destruction, however, the native species evolve defence mechanisms, and a new equilibrium is created.[8]

Sanatana Dharma in India was evolving defence mechanisms, as is evident from the Hindu Renaissance that Swami Vivekananda started. But it was prevented from doing this by the idea of secularism and the agency of the modern secular State. Secularism and the modern State are the agencies through which invasive species of Christianity and Islam grow rapidly and without checks and balances at the expense of the native traditions like Sanatana Dharma. But Sanatana Dharma is capable of great adaptations, and it can develop defence against the agency of secularism and the modern State too. That defence mechanism is none other than Shatrubodha, which identifies the invasive species of prophetic monotheism and strikes a balance in Hindu society.

But before this goal is achieved, we have to dismantle the agency of secularism itself. Secularism maybe a bad word in the intellectual circles in the budding Hindu intellectual ecosystem, but it is by and large the idea on which the entire Indian State functions. For dismantling secularism fundamentally, we need to go to its roots and investigate the religious milieu in which secularism was born.

Christian Origins of Secularism

On one hand, secularism hides the Islamist game of digesting India piecemeal by demographic invasion and higher Muslim birth rates, but on the other hand, it facilitates another game to destroy Hindu society and Sanatana Dharma, a game that is much more sinister than the Islamist agenda—the game of Christian conversion of India. This is because secularism is a Christian heresy, and wherever it is implemented, it encourages the Christianization of that society. This seems like a contradictory statement, but to know why it is true, we need to go a little deep into the origins of secularism in Europe.

One of the central tenets of secularism, the separation between the religious and the secular spheres (Church and State), is also an important doctrine of Christianity. Jesus has said: 'My kingdom is not of this world'[9] making it clear that Christianity is not about this world but the world after death, the world after the

Last Judgement. Not only this, but he has also made it clear that the physical world of reality and the metaphysical world of the Bible are two very different worlds and shall be kept separate. In the famous injunction that has been used as the foundation of secularism, Jesus told his followers to 'render to Caesar the things that are Caesar's, and to God the things that are God's'.[10]

The very thought of separating the secular and religious spheres is a fundamentally Christian thought. From the beginning, embedded in the New Testament is the thought of two separate realms that have been called the *regnum* (royal power) and the *sacerdotium* (priestly power). But this is not because Christianity had a liberal future in mind when it was evolving. The reason for this separation is very different. It is historical, opportunistic, and shows the chameleon-like ability of Christianity to change colours depending on the power situation in a certain country or civilization.

We know that Christianity was not in power in the first 300 years of its existence. Christianity first took shape as a religion around 100 years after the death of Jesus when Paul made it into a proper religion. And even after that the Christians had to wait more than 200 years to grab political power. The separation between the State and the Church became an important dogma for Christianity because for the first 300 years of its existence, Christianity was not in power. It is the theological evolution of these 300 years that explains this separation.

Christianity claimed that Jesus will come again on earth in a Second Coming and will judge individuals on the basis of their belief. All non-Christians will go to eternal hell, and those who showed unflinching belief and faith in Christ will go to eternal heaven. But Jesus never came, and the apocalypse that was predicted never came. Christians could not see any Kingdom of Heaven coming anytime soon. Instead, the 'devil-worshipping', 'idolatrous', and 'sinning pagans' of the Roman Empire were powerfully ruling the society while Christians were still a minority who were being 'persecuted'. Christian claims had not come true. The Kingdom of Heaven was nowhere in sight, and it seemed in those times that the pagan Roman Empire might never fall. It was directly in contradiction to the early Christian claims of apocalypse and the Second Coming. This had to be explained away.

In order to cope, the Church fathers claimed that worldly power is something not Christian at all and thus Christian monks and common Christians should stay away from it. They claimed that the world of religion and the world of politics could never meet. As the pagan Roman Empire did not look like going away anywhere anytime soon, it was declared by the prominent Christian monks that Christianity can be practiced only in private, while the public world of politics and power will remain pagan. Christians were instructed to tolerate this dual nature of their existence where they saw utter 'idolatrous abomination' in public while practicing Christianity and the 'one true religion' in private. Christians should thus quietly suffer the misfortunes, persecution, and torture in this world and wait till death to get to the Kingdom of Heaven.

It is in this context that the separation of the realms of Caesar and God should be seen. This dogma was created at a time when Christianity never thought it would come to power. And so, an entire theology was created to explain this lack of power: that in the clause of separation of the realms of Caesar and God, Christianity and power were never to meet. This was the first stage of the evolution of secularism. The art and literature of early Christianity are a testimony to this phase where Christ is depicted as a sacrificial lamb, who has sacrificed himself for the sake of his followers. The accidental death of Jesus Christ in the war against the Romans was converted into a dogma of atonement and sacrifice for his followers. Along with the separation of the world between the realm of Caesar and God, human beings too were divided into two realms: the temporal and the spiritual. Jakob de Roover comments:

> The temporal and the spiritual were viewed as two distinct worlds. One was the secular material world of earth, also referred to as 'this temporal world', which would last until the second coming of Christ. The other was the eternal spiritual world, also named 'the other world' or 'the heavenly kingdom'. This corresponded to a fundamental split in human existence: as bodies, we live earthly lives; as spirits, spiritual lives. The monks were expected to turn to God by moving away from the temporal carnal world to the eternal spiritual world.[11]

As a consequence, the Christian religious life became the inner, private life of the Christians, while the pagan-dominated secular life became the public life. This is how the clause of the separation of the public and the private spheres was invented. We can see how the central tenets of secularism came from a fundamentally Christian theological conundrum. The theological clause of separation of the two realms also had one practical application. By learning how to survive without power in an alien country, Christianity created the toolkit for planting Christianity in a new non-Christian land. In the coming centuries and millennia, it would practice this template almost everywhere else on earth.

The second stage in this long march to secularism came when Christianity got power. As luck would have it, Christianity did become the state religion of the Roman Empire quite unexpectedly in 330 CE with the adoption of Christianity as the State religion by Constantine. Christians promptly set out to destroy pagan traditions, temples, and customs as soon as they got power. But Christian theology found itself in a conundrum. They never quite expected to be in power and had evolved their theology to account for the lack of it. Now they had to explain Christians being in power. The trouble was that Christian theology had already claimed that Caesar's and God's realms (or the temporal and spiritual powers) were separate, but now the two realms had become one. The problem was to explain how the two realms, which were never supposed to meet, had actually met. In other words, if the spiritual (Christian) world was only to come in heaven, how come Christianity came to rule the temporal world too?

Church theologians struggled to explain the paradox but eventually found a way. They built upon the hierarchy between the two realms and claimed that the spiritual realm of God would always be superior to the temporal realm of Caesar. And since Christianity was now in power, the temporal power had to bow in front of the spiritual power; Caesar had to bow in front of God, and the State had to bow in front of the God. Thus, Christianity learnt to protect its number and strength when in the minority and out of power, but on the other hand it also learnt to increase its numbers and eliminate all non-Christian ideas and individuals when in the majority and in power. It was becoming the formidable civilizational sniper that we have already discussed.

To come back to the Middle Ages when Christianity was clamping back the authority of the Church over the State, the hierarchy of Christianity over the State was not just a matter of ideas. It was very real and very much physical, as Roover explains:

> In 1077, Pope Gregory VII forced the emperor of the Holy Roman Empire, Henry IV, to kneel in the snow near the Italian castle of Canossa and had him beg for papal absolution. This dramatic moment in the history of Western Christendom symbolized the power that would be possessed by the papacy during the next centuries. It was the culmination of a long, sometimes violent, struggle concerning the relation between secular authority and the religious authority of the Church.[12]

But how did things come to such a pass if the Church and the State had initially practiced a nice division of powers and realms? It was because, looking from the Hindu point of view, overlooking all the verbose pseudo-spiritual terminology, both the Church and the State were extremely worldly and materialistic institutions, and both the pope and the emperor were very worldly men competing for very worldly goals. This is explained by the extremely materialistic pursuits of the pope and his institution—the papacy. Sita Ram Goel throws light on one of the most ignored parts of Christian history, the materialistic degeneracy of the papacy, in his least widely known but absolutely wonderful work *Papacy, Its Doctrine and History*:

> Some of the Popes stand out as hardened criminals instigating secret assassinations and hair-raising cruelties. Some others are imbeciles, pressed into service by powerful political factions or wealthy families. There are some abominable fanatics who institute inquisitions, order the burning of numerous heretics and witches, and incite mobs for committing massacres and pogroms. There are plenty of profligates who lead a life of luxury and lust after taking vows of poverty and chastity. They sire any number of illegitimate children with a clean conscience. They specialize in milking rich maidens, sponsoring wills which leave vast amounts of wealth to them, and poisoning cardinals in order to inherit the latter's estates. They can be credited with every conceivable crime, even if we do not take into account such deeds as have been declared cardinal sins by the Catholic Church.[13]

If the papacy was so given to the pursuit of materialistic goals, we can understand that it would run into the crosshairs of the State, which was very much an instrument of power. After the adoption of Christianity by Constantine, for the next 500 to 600 years, both the State and the Church (the emperor and the pope) worked very well together, except for a few skirmishes and mishaps, because the external enemy—the hated, idolatrous pagan—remained a common target of both to conquer. But once most of Europe was converted to Christianity, this arrangement between the State and the Church started breaking down, and bloody religious wars between emperors and kings on one hand and the pope and his minions on the other started. After all, for all the verbose terminology, both the powers were functioning very much within the realm of the physical world, seen from a Hindu point of view. Sita Ram Goel writes with utmost clarity on the arrangement between the Church and the State:

> So long as the continent of Europe retained communities which were yet to be converted to Christianity, cooperation between the Church and the State continued smoothly. The Church had given absolute liberty to the kings to expand their domains in the name of spreading Christianity. The kings also used the sword, as far as practicable, for converting the non-Christians to Christianity or for slaughtering them or for trampling them under foot in other ways. The Church applauded the kings wholeheartedly for their services. In turn, the kings also claimed that they were striving heart and soul in order to save the pagans from hellfire. In this sinister alliance, both the kings and the Church extended their dominions and domination. Dissensions also cropped up between the two from time to time, but cooperation was so beneficial that conflicts continued to be resolved. Thereafter, a time came at the end of the fifteenth century when the Whole of Europe became Christianized. The kings were no more in need of blessings from the Church in order to augment their power. The State began to feel restless against the stranglehold which the Church had imposed on it.[14]

As this arrangement started falling apart, more and more clashes between the Church and the State started cropping up everywhere in Europe. Despite the growing discomfort of the kings about the overarching authority of the Church, the Church kept staking its claim and its supremacy over the 'realm of the Caesar' and the authority of the spiritual over the temporal.

Their claim to supremacy was derived from monastic Christianity. In the early years of Christianity, when it was not the State religion, Christian monks created monasteries, and by confining themselves in their walls, practiced extreme austerities. They lived very frugally, prayed constantly, ate tolerably, and constantly punished themselves physically to become 'worthy of the love of God'. This monastic process was also called conversion. In general, conversion meant converting a non-Christian to Christianity, but those who took vows as monks carried the process of conversion further and became more and more Christian by monastic austerities. The monks attained great respect in Christian society by their austerities. However, at the same time they would be extremely cruel to any non-Christian and openly favoured massacre of pagans and other non-Christians. And when the Church came to power after the conversion of Constantine, it was these monks who came out of their monasteries, became bishops, and started governing the affairs of the Church, and through it, the affairs of the State.

When Christianity was not in power, the Christian monks favoured withdrawal from the world and seclusion inside monasteries. However, when Christianity came to power, they advocated for the 'reform' of common Christian society through the spiritual power and authority that monks had attained due to their austerities. This decision to come out of their monasteries and involve themselves in worldly affairs was called the Papal Revolution. The idea was to 'monastize the Church' and to make it more powerful from within. But the basic urge was to maintain control over politics by making it subservient to religion. It was this 'spiritual' (Christian) authority of the monks that the Church used to claim supremacy over the State.

Hence, while the two realms were separate, they were united in the hierarchy of the Church over the State. This is how the theologians reconciled the problem of Christianity grabbing State power while keeping the clause of the separation of the two realms. This readjustment of Christian theology to accommodate Christianity being in power was the second step in the development of secular ideas.

The supremacy of the Church over the State proceeded through many stages in which the pope kept arrogating power after power to himself and his institution. This process reached extremes during the turn of the millennium when Pope Gregory VII forced the Holy Roman emperor to kneel, symbolizing the utter subjection of the State in front of the Church. But it had a long history. Initially the Church was too happy to support Emperor Constantine, as the Roman Empire under him was very powerful, and the Church was just tasting blood (of power), but as the Roman Empire in the West started crumbling, the pope and the church leaders started shifting powers to the Church through a series of blatantly forged documents, the greatest of which was the 'Donation of Constantine', which was 'discovered' in the ninth century to prove that Emperor Constantine had ceded supreme powers to the Church. Sita Ram Goel writes:

> It was the most formidable forgery ever fabricated by the Popes. The Popes had every reason to be audacious, once they discovered that their pretensions were being accepted promptly by the princes and people of West Europe, without suspicion or protest. The Donation of Constantine depicted the first Christian Emperor of the Roman Empire prostrating himself before Pope Sylvester I (314–335) and holding the bridle of the papal horse for a few steps. Next, the Emperor was made to take off his imperial robes and surrender them to the People along with other imperial insignia and symbols, including the crown, the scepter, the globe and the lance.... Finally, the Emperor was made to express a wish for removing his own seat to Constantinople because he thought himself to be too small to reside in the same city as the Successor of St Peter![15]

Based on this forged document, the pope forced the State to cede more and more powers to the Church, and Christianity became supremely powerful at the height of the Dark Ages. It is not a coincidence that the height of the Dark Ages coincides with the height of Christianity's unbridled power. Church leaders became extremely arrogant and corrupt and started selling 'salvation' and 'indulgence', which meant an exemption from punishment in hell by paying a certain fee. Christianity never had a spiritual practice like meditation. And dogmas inevitably degrade to this ridiculous level of corruption. Catholic Christianity had reached that point. Such unbridled power was sure to bring some backlash, and it would come in a storm that would wipe out many existing structures. This new storm was the Protestant Revolution, and it marks the third stage in the evolution of secular ideas.

At the beginning of the sixteenth century, the dam broke. Christian thinkers like Martin Luther made European society aware of the corruption of Christian priests and the Church and showing that they were far from the ideal 'spiritual' authority that people had come to believe in. He called upon common Christians to revoke the authority of the Church and priests. He argued that the process of internal conversion through which monks attained their authority should be open to all Christians.

> The Protestant Reformation extended the medieval process of conversion to all believers. Before, the monks and priests had been the true Christians because of their vocation and conversion. Now God called all believers to conversion. All were priests. Through this monasticizing of everyday life, Christianity began to pervade society at a much deeper level than it ever had before. At times, the Reformers explicitly stated this goal. A Lutheran pastor suggested that every household had to be transformed into a monastery. Calvin remarked that every family of the pious ought to be a church.[16]

This does not mean that European Christian society became open and liberal. Only the authority of the Catholic Church and priests was overthrown. The dissenters were also fanatical and orthodox Christians, who placed dogma or belief over action or practice. In fact, Luther went to extremes to prove that faith alone was enough: 'Yes, since faith alone suffices for salvation, I need nothing except faith exercising the power and dominion of its own liberty. Lo, this is the inestimable power and liberty of Christians.'[17] While monks favoured high austerities to prove their spiritual authority, Luther declared that no good action or deed was required for spiritual authority; only faith, blind and naked faith, was enough. It was inevitable that such dogmatic belief would bring more strife, religious fanaticism, oppression, and persecution in Christian society. And this is what happened:

> In the sixteenth century, widespread revolts broke out against the Church and Christianity got splintered into several sects. But the reformist sects of Christianity proved to be far more intolerant, and a terrible carnage took place all over Europe in the name of religion. The State in one country, by aligning with one sect, began to suppress the other sects, while the State in another country, by aligning with another sect, began to suppress all others. And wars began to be fought among different countries in the name of religion.[18]

Questioning the authority of the Church and priests opened up the Christian dogma to a wide variety of individuals and institutions. Once the stranglehold of the Catholic Church was over, various individuals and groups started defining what 'Christian truth' was. Many Christian sects developed their own interpretations of the Bible and the 'truth' that it contained. Every sect believed that it, and it alone, held the sole path to God and every other path was wrong. Thus, only in principle did Calvin and Luther say that every person is a priest. It was just a way to dissent and break the established authority, but as soon as these dissenters came to power, they created their own orthodoxy, and the Christian tyranny continued.

It was not, however, simply the transfer of tyranny from one authority to another. The Protestant Revolution resulted in thousands of Christian sects establishing rival churches like Lutheran, Anglican, Baptist, Anabaptist, Calvinist, and many others, each one of which claimed the sole authority on truth. The Europe of the fifteenth and sixteenth centuries got divided into numerous small kingdoms, each one of which adopted one of these Christian sects as the State religion and started religious persecution of all other sects. It gave birth to religious conflict of a scale the world had never seen. A copious amount of blood was spilt, and numberless Christians were burnt alive or killed in many different ways just because they followed a branch of Christianity that was not the State-approved branch in any particular kingdom. Not only Catholics persecuted Protestants and vice versa. One sect of Protestants persecuted other Protestant sects too. It was the greatest religious orgy of bloodshed the world had ever seen, and this was happening within Christendom.

Among this barbaric bloodshed, foundations for modern secularism were also being laid. Luther interpreted the theory of two kingdoms in a different way. He said that the separation of the two kingdoms was within every human being. 'All men lived in the spiritual and the temporal sphere at the same time.'[19] Calvin believed the same. They said that while our souls were completely free, our flesh was governed by the temporal laws because flesh is eternally corrupt. Since the soul functions in the spiritual kingdom and the spiritual kingdom is invisible, the freedom of the soul must be exercised in private, while in public the temporal authority has to hold sway. As the soul was considered pure, while the flesh was considered corrupt, it was thought that the flesh should suffer under the yoke of temporal authority.

This is the foundation of the clause of the separation between public and private life, the second clause of modern secularism.

The first clause of secularism was based on the separation of the religious and secular realms in early Christianity; the second clause of secularism was based on the separation of public and private life, a product of Protestant Christianity.

The third major clause of secularism is that of 'toleration' of other sects. However, this too is a very Christian concept. The argument for 'toleration' rose in mediaeval Europe when heresies were appearing and being persecuted everywhere. When the bloodshed and persecution reached their peak during the Protestant wars of religion, the clause of 'toleration' of other sects was brought in to prevent all Christians from killing each other to extinction, but this toleration was limited only to recognizable Christian sects that sported the dogmas of one true god, the last prophet, divided humanity, time, and space, etc. This 'toleration' was certainly not extended to pagans or non-Christians.

How does it affect Hindus?

Because to 'tolerate' a sect, it had to be defined as a religion, and as we know, that dharma is not religion, when the British came to India and started 'tolerating' Hindu dharma, they started the process of turning Hindu dharma into a religion by looking for the 'law book', for 'scripture', and for 'dogma' and central authority. Just by this 'looking' or 'studying', they distorted Hindu dharma and created an artificial 'Hindu religion' in the image of Christianity, which follows a text, a law book, and has recognizable religious features. This is what sent British lawmakers on a wild goose chase of the 'Hindu law book' and resulted in the elevation of certain texts and textual practices at a level above their place in a dharmic ecosystem where practices dictated the texts and not the other way around.

The impact of British colonialism on Hindu society was not unlike the impact that a meteorite makes on earth's surface. The high temperature and pressure instantaneously create a stone called impactite. The British Christian impact created a new class in itself: a group of Hindus who started seeing Hindu tradition from a Christian lens and saw Biblical revelation in shabda pramana, law books in Smritis, clergy in archakas, and recommended going back to the 'pristine age', whatever it meant. This is how secularism hurts the dharmic fabric of Bharatavarsha in many ways. Not only does it disadvantage Hindu dharma in a game created for monotheistic sects, but it also seeks to rebuild what is left of Hindu dharma in the image of prophetic monotheistic religions. If Sanatana Dharma has to survive in Bharatavarsha, then secularism has to go. Dharma and secularism are mutually incompatible ideas.

The Problem of Secular Modernity

Secularism is not a standalone concept or a legal clause. It has far-reaching cultural consequences. Since it establishes religion (and mistaking dharma as religion) as a private affair and relegates it completely to the discretion of the individual and remakes public life in a completely new image, it inevitably clashes with the tradition of a certain culture and place. The process of secularization is nothing but the universalization of Christian beliefs and attitudes by shedding some of their particularistic features but retaining the fundamental Christian spirit.

The process of secularization results in the decay of culture and tradition and a whole-scale adoption of Western culture and lifestyle. This process has been collectively called modernization, which seems to be an inevitable companion of secularization. Modernity, the quality of being modern, is understood as being 'contemporary' or given to a 'new' understanding of the world that is contemporary and perpetually pitted against the 'ancient', 'old', or 'regressive' understanding of the traditional culture. 'Historically modernization has been a search for a new world-view to replace the decaying traditional world-view.'[20]

This was true in many ways in Europe, where Christianity sought to ossify customs and practices in a bygone era, but in a society like Bharatavarsha, it meant nothing because Sanatana Dharma does not ossify anything in the past. It is the eternal tradition. It is neither old nor new. It always keeps changing and adapting according to the changing needs of the times, but also at the same time, keeps alive the fundamental and universal values that create its core. To impose a perpetual change-making process like modernization on a society that had eternal change as its internal design is disastrous. Just like the imposition of secularism created problems in Indian society that did not exist before, the implementation of modernization on a traditional society was bound to decay and distort Hindu tradition simultaneously. While the process of decay of Hindu tradition directly benefitted monotheistic religions like Islam and Christianity, the process of its distortion that modernity causes lets enemies of Hindu society to blame all social evil on tradition, leading to further erosion of trust and further decay of Sanatana Dharma.

Sanatana Dharma is ever-changing while keeping the universals alive. The Hindu tradition incorporates in itself the mechanisms of change and reform. This is more than evident if one just cursorily glances at Indian history. Reform is a constant theme, and it goes along with conservation. Dharma is eternal balance, as we know, and as it is dharma that ruled Hindu society, it meant that we would always balance reform and conservation, creation and preservation, and innovation and maintenance. Conservation is the very soul of civilization because if we do not continue what has been previously created, then we have nothing to stand upon. This fact was never lost on a deeply dharmic society like India. But we also understood that changing times and context means new customs and practices, and we never shied away from this constant churn. We even developed institutions that incorporated reform in their very structure. Kumbh Mela is one such institution.

Gandhian scholar Shri Banvari says that Kumbh Melas were not just for spiritual pursuit. It was, of course, their primary goal, but a gathering of crores of Hindus accomplished much more. It had many other social roles. In Kumbh Melas, our society corrected the flaws that had crept into it over the past few years. Social customs and practices that were prevalent were talked about, and decisions were taken whether they could continue as they were, or they needed some change, or a complete scrapping. Every single community of Bharatavarsha camped on the banks of a sacred Hindu river for about a month, forgetting all differences for a while, and came together in the greatest gathering on earth. For a month, the sense of Sanatana, the sense of being Hindu, was so palpable in the air that it dominated all. Here, Shri Banvari says the sages advised the kings, and the kings advised the sages, but it was not limited to that. Every varna, jati, and community interacted, advised, and corrected each other. It was one place where the entire world of Sanatana came together for a month to adapt and move forward, as well as conserve and continue the tradition.

The greatest of all Kumbhs is held at Prayag, the confluence of the two most sacred rivers of Hindus, the Ganga and the Yamuna. The land is provided by the rivers every twelve years when the waters recede, and after the Mela is done, the land is reclaimed by the eternal flow of water, and *Sanatana Ganga Pravaha*, both literally and metaphysically, continues, and the great and eternal tradition, Sanatana Dharma, continues.

And just like the land that is provided by the great rivers is reclaimed by the flow of the rivers once the job of Kumbh Mela is done, similarly, the institution of Kumbh Mela also disappears for twelve years, to reappear once again on the newly vacated land by the Ganga and the Yamuna. It signifies the very nature of Santana Dharma and its institutions that the institution and authority appear only when it is necessary and disappear when the need for it subsides.

It is the institution that never is.

Once again, it was no dogma that guided this mechanism of continuous reform in Sanatana Dharma. No 'book', no normative ethics dictated what custom stayed and what was scrapped. Incredulous as it seems, it was people themselves, in crores, in the greatest act of democracy ever seen in the history of humankind, who kept updating, adapting, and reforming their customs and values without any need for normative ethics or an overarching dogma. This society needed no 'book' and not even a written constitution because dharma was that great operating principle that sufficed for all. Like Dr Kapil Kapoor says, India had one-word unwritten constitution—dharma.

Kumbh Mela was one of the greatest mechanisms of change and reform, but it was far from the only one. Our saints, outside the realm of all social structures, led the reform as well as conservation. These jnanis and jivanmuktas were outside the boundaries of the society, varnashrama dharma, or any other structure that Hindus ever practiced. But it is the testimony of the greatness of Sanatana Dharma that it was them that all communities and individuals looked up to as the ultimate resort. We discussed in the Svayambodha section that it is the word of the jivanmuktas or jnanis that is considered as the final authority on anything. As a consequence, we see a long line of saints who led the reform from within Sanatana Dharma: Shri Ramanujacharya, Shri Madhvacharya, Goswami Tulsidas, Shri Chaitanya Mahaprabhu, Shri Namdev, Shri Tukaram, and many more. The list is endless. While one set of the jnanis as rishis ensured that the values are conserved and tradition continues, the jnanis outside the tradition, the roaming mendicants, took care that no ossification was ever possible, and no stagnation was ever allowed in society.

This is why Sanatana Dharma is ever fresh, ever new, while being eternal.

The British, through the agency of colonialism, made Hindus forget about these dynamic, contemporaneous aspects of the Hindu tradition and handed them the toy of modernity. By arrogating all rights of change to itself, modernity patented reform while confining tradition to its conservative role. Taking modernity to be synonymous with contemporaneity and change, followers of Hindu and other dharmic traditions thought that change and reform can only be possible in a modern paradigm, forgetting that conservation is only half of the role of a tradition, with the other half pertaining to creation, innovation, reform, and change. Imposing modernity as it is on the Hindu society gave Hindus the impression that their tradition was also ossified, archaic, and regressive like Christianity. It made them believe that their dharma was also oppressive of women, minorities, allergic to science, and regressive in outlook.

The Hindus were also convinced by their colonial masters that it is Hindu tradition that is fixed in time and modernity led by secular Christian values, which is contemporaneous. Hindus forgot that in Bharatavarsha, it is the opposite: that it is tradition, the glorious Eternal Tradition, or Sanatana Dharma, which is ever new and modernity, which is fixed in time. Modernity is the product of Enlightenment Europe, inspired by Judeo-Christian ideas, and represents a 'forward-looking' 'future-forming' outlook as it was born in Europe, where a superstition and barbarity-ridden Christian society was navigating ways to move forward while adjusting Christian theology, which was proved wrong in both its physics and metaphysics.

Just because modernization was the need of the hour in the Judeo-Christian Enlightenment in Europe does not imply that the same would be true in every culture because its tradition was ever dynamic. Bharatavarsha, as explained above, never needed it. The implementation of modernization in India actually interrupted the continuous cycle of ever-changing tradition and instead imposed a time, place, and culture-dependent outlook. This is why modernization in India is culturally very destructive.

In other words, people think that 'being modern' means living in the present or being updated and adapted to the time and place, while being traditional means being outdated, regressive, and archaic, and living in the past. They do not know that it is actually the opposite.

It is by following Tradition that one can live in the eternal present. By following modernity, one is only following a specific ideology fixed in a certain time and place.

Secularism, Modernity, and Liberal Atheism through the Lens of Pancha Rnas

Having known the origins of secularism and the attendant ideas, let us put them through the lens of the pancha rnas. To start with the first, secularism obviously fails in deva rna. Continuing in the Judeo-Christian tradition, it rejects the dharmic and pagan idea of the divine. It does recognize the Judeo-Christian idea of God but relegates it to the private sphere. Considering Hindu dharma to be just another religion, it also thinks that it has the similar idea of God and similarly relegates it to the private sphere. In any case, it fails to imbue society with the idea of the divine. The desacrality of secularism is rooted in its reliance on liberal atheism. While liberal atheism was a boon to Europe, which was coming out of the Christian Dark Ages, it is irrelevant at the least and dangerous at most in the Indian context. India had its Charvakas, who had a materialistic view of the samsara, and it found very little use of its philosophy. Shri Ram Swarup sums up the Indian attitude towards Charvakas:

> India has known its *Charvakas* and *Jabalis*, but has found their definition of man, and consequently their ethical thinking too, as inadequate and unacceptable. Sanatana dharma teaches that materialism and hedonism in their exclusive demands are very

> unsatisfactory, that cultures based on a purely psycho-physical definition of man are neurotic, that they cannot provide the basis of a truly stable society. These cultures lack vision and sympathy; they are violent. Think of all their meat industries and their slaughter-houses and even their laboratories and experiments.... And behind and supporting all this wastefulness and cruelty, one can also see the mindlessness of the whole prevailing system, its forgetfulness (*vismriti*) of any higher dimension.[21]

Secularism and its attendant ideologies fare a little better in rishi rna. Although they have no concept of the divine or any indigenous methodology of meditation, liberalism is open to suggestions from science. In the absence of any *adhyatmika* epistemology, the West developed science, which does not seek or give ways of discovering the absolute truth, but it has developed excellent mechanisms to explore the material world. Liberalism honours great scientists, who are like the rishis of the West. They are, of course, nowhere near a jivanmukta or a jnani, but they have a great commitment to truth and a methodology of exploration that roots itself in experience and not dogma. As liberalism and secular cultures honour science and have created great institutions to support scientists and scientific pursuit, we can say that secularism does respect rishi rna.

Modernity presents itself as the eternal victor in its battle with religious/dharmic tradition, and in this bid it rejects most ideas from the past and focuses only on the future. In this way, we can say that modern secular cultures largely disrespect pitra rna. They have no concept of pitra as Hindus do, obviously, but as the past has come to be synonymous with the Christian Dark Ages for most secular countries today, there is always a negative association with ancestors and ancestral tradition. It is pertinent to say here that Christianity also vehemently rejected the past and ancestors, and secular cultures carry some of that attitude too. They just add orthodox Christianity to the long array of things and ideas to be rejected as 'ancestral' and thus 'useless' in modern life.

Encouraging individualism and considering the individual to be the most basic unit of society, secular societies have always advocated and led to the decay of traditional social structures of family, clan, community, etc. Focusing on human rights predicated upon the belief of individuals having basic rights, with very little focus on duties, is a fundamental reorientation of the kartavyabodha of the Hindu universe, where human relationships as well as institutions are built upon the idea of duties and not rights. From this point of view, secularism and its attendant ideas do not respect nru or manushya rna, even though it makes great pomp and show about 'caring for the individual'. This 'care' is only for his material and not the spiritual well-being and results in a lopsided worldview, which eventually brings more pain in every sphere of life.

The greatest violation by secularism is that of the bhuta rna, where it has failed spectacularly to respect ecology and ecosystems. While discovering scientifically the truth about the destruction of ecosystems, the secular Western society is unable to act upon its knowledge and bring eco-consciousness into the behaviour of its individuals because it has no mechanism to transfer knowledge into behaviour. Thus, it violates bhuta rna too. In this way, secularism has a very limited utility for Hindu society. As Sita Ram Goel said, one use of it should be to expose and banish the influence of prophetic monotheism from a dharmic society like India.[22] While scientific epistemology that has evolved in secular cultures is of great use and value to Hindu society and should be cherished, on all other counts, secularism and its attendant ideologies of modernity, atheism, liberalism, and all their mutations are of no use to Hindu society.

Fig. 2 The Svayambodha–Shatrubodha Circle

Chapter 13

The Svayambodha–Shatrubodha Scale

'Fundamentalism is not accidental but essential to Islam. It is inherent in those religious ideologies which are built on a narrow spiritual vision, have a limited psychic base, and which emphasise dogma and personalities, other than experience and impersonal truth.'

—Shri Ram Swarup

Rama and Hanuman Fighting Ravana, Tanjore or Trichinopoly, Tamil Nadu, India, c. 1820, The British Museum. A scene from the Ramayana, with Shri Rama killing Asura Ravana[1]

Having gained both Svayambodha and Shatrubodha, now we proceed to look at the world. We need to look at our history, our civilization, our leaders and thinkers, our friends, and our enemies from this lens. We need to look at geopolitics, international relations, and India's place in this world from the deeply Hindu vision of Svayambodha and Shatrubodha. To be world leaders, Hindus need to have an opinion on everything under the sun. The Svayambodha–Shatrubodha scale will give us that worldview, that Vishwabodha.

The Shatrubodha Scale

The Hindu society, as the great Sita Ram Goel said, is under siege from not just one, but many enemies. He listed them as mullahs, missionaries, Marxists, Macaulayites, and indirectly he also included modernists in his list. We have now done a purva paksha of all these enemies of Sanatana Dharma. We know what forces want to destroy Hindu society, Sanatana Dharma, and Bharatiya civilization.

The ultimate goal of having Shatrubodha is to have a clear view of the 'in-group' and 'out-group'. No Hindu shall ever be confused about which religious ideology is a friend of Hindu civilization and which is the enemy. Hindus need to have a crystal clear mental map of who they are, who their friends are, and who their enemies are. Once again, we are talking about ideologies and not individuals.

Figure 2 shows the Svayambodha–Shatrubodha circle which clearly indicates what constitutes 'us' and which ideologies are our 'friends' and which are 'enemies'.

All the institutions and ideologies that are inside the Svayambodha circle are the in-group, and all those who are outside the Svayambodha circle are the out-group. Not all 'out-groups' are hostile. Outside the Svayambodha circle, there is a *Mitrabodha* circle. 'Friends of Hindus' lie in this circle. In case of any active hostility, when a binary worldview is necessary, the Mitrabodha circle will fold into the Svayambodha circle, and the inhabitants of both of them will be fighting against the ideologies in the Shatrubodha circle.

All prophetic monotheistic religions that want to convert Hindus to either Christianity or Islam are clear out-groups since they want to grow at the expense of Sanatana Dharma. Religious ideologies of Islam and Christianity, and more specifically Islamists and Christian missionaries, are thus clear out-groups and lie in the outermost circle of Shatrubodha.

Judaism is also an out-group as a religion, since it is the fountainhead of all anti-polytheistic, anti-dharmic, and anti-traditional ideologies that the world suffers from now. Jews are great friends of India so far, due to their hostility to the Islamic world, but they are also a monotheistic society, and even in symbolism Judaism remains hostile to the very idea of natural indigenous dharmic sects like Sanatana Dharma.

Jewish society and Israel as a nation are a different case. They are friends of Hindus since the Jews no longer follow the literal meaning of the Bible and do not want to convert Hindus to Judaism.

Any other monotheistic ideology or religion like Bahais, Ahmaddiyas, and Mormons are also out-groups. Some tactical alliances can be made with some of them for a brief time in the more immediate and larger fight of Sanatana Dharma against Islamic ideology and Christianity but otherwise as ideology they remain in the Shatrubodha circle.

Buddhism is not an 'in-group' but far from an 'out-group'. It is a dear friend, almost like a brother, coming from the same font of Indian dharmas. In the Shatrubodha–Svayambodha circle, it lies between the Svayambodha circle and the Shatrubodha circle, in the Mitrabodha circle.

All pagan, polytheistic, native, and indigenous religions of the world (outside Akhanda Bharata territory), like Shinto,

Sendo, Chinese ancestral religions, African religions, native religions of Southeast Asia, East Asia, etc., and revivalist pagan religions of the Americas, Australia, and New Zealand, are friends, and Hindus have to create a common cause with them to fight the onslaught of prophetic monotheistic religions.

The pagan, polytheistic, desiya religious sects of the tribal communities in India's northeast and many other states like Jharkhand, Chhattisgarh, and Madhya Pradesh are the closest friends of Hindu dharma and Hindu society. While many of them do not call themselves Hindus, they are deeply dharmic in their philosophy and ways of life. Donyi Polo, Heraka, Hnam Sakhua, Sarna, etc., are some of these dharmic sects. They come under the Sanatana umbrella, while maintaining their distinct dharmic identity.

But are political entities ruling pagan societies outside India also friends of Hindus? When it comes to the States that rule pagan, polytheistic, or Buddhist societies, it is a different case. Some of them are friends, and some of them are enemies at any given time. For example, today, Japan is a friend, and China is an enemy. This might not remain the case forever since China might lose its communist government, and a non-communist government might be India-friendly. China is an enemy today at the level of State, but if it solves its border disputes with India it might well become a friend, as it should be, since that would be the greatest, pagan, polytheistic, dharmic alliance against monotheistic forces of the West and Islam. Similarly, Japan once committed atrocities against Indians in Andaman, Nagaland, and Manipur because India was a British colony then, but now it is a great friend.

Myanmar is and should be a friend, as are Bhutan, Thailand, and other Southeast Asian countries that do not play Chinese politics. Laos, which is now virtually a Chinese stooge, shall be seen as an enemy at the level of the State. But civilizationally and religiously speaking, Hindu society has to be friends with all non-monotheistic societies, for we have much in common, and most of all, the ideological enemy of all the pagan, polytheistic, indigenous religions and societies is one, as they have the common enemy in the religious ideologies of Islam and Christianity.

All political, social, economic, and educational ideologies that want to damage Hindu society by destroying its social and religious institutions are enemies.

An education system that refuses to let Hindus teach their youth about dharma in schools and colleges and that lies about the history of Islamic invasions and Christian missions in India is an enemy.

Any ideology like secularism, communism, socialism, leftism, liberalism, and wokeism that wants to dismantle Hindu social institutions and reduce Hindus to hapless individuals at the mercy of the State and global forces, are perpetual enemies of Hindu society and dharma and can never be friends.

Any ideological trend, like radical feminism or intersectional activism, that just aims to dismantle existing Hindu institutions is also an enemy.

An economic system that disregards dharma and says that only 'artha' matters is not dharmic and has to be adapted to conform to the purushartha hierarchy to achieve a proper Hindu rashtra. Sanatana Dharma has artha as one of the four purusharthas and believes in increasing the individual as well as collective prosperity of society, but economic prosperity has to be in keeping with dharmic values for it to be sustainable. Such an economic system is also hostile to the Hindu dharmic order now but can be adapted and edited to suit dharmic needs.

A political system that does not have the fundamentals of Svayambodha or Sanatana Dharma at its core will also be inimical to Hindu society in the long run, and in the future, it has to be adapted to suit Hindu needs. In other words, any political system has to be particularized and adapted to the needs of a Hindu polity in a Hindu rashtra. It is also an enemy since it harms

Hindu society right now but can be adapted in a particularistic democracy to suit dharmic needs.

Any legal system just based on the narrative of rights is sure to fracture and divide Hindu society into small sub-groups, which can then be used as vote banks or lobby groups, for it is in the nature of rights to infringe upon each other. Thus, a Hindu rashtra shall have a legal system that incentivizes social behaviour centred on the narrative of duties and should empower and partner with intermediary Hindu social institutions for social welfare. It is not a friend of Hindus today since it harms Hindu society right now but can be adapted in a particularistic democracy to suit dharmic needs.

Any social ideology or rights activism aiming at the welfare of one or the other Hindu group based on the narrative of rights and not duties will ultimately pull apart Hindu society until it is no more. Any such ideology might sound nice but is not a friend of Hindu dharma. Any social welfare or justice has to be done in a dharma-centric way, using the Hindu social institutions of the temple, the community, and the family, supported by a respectful State. The State by all means, shall help, but by incentivizing and empowering the intermediate Hindu social institutions.

Once again, this map is about ideas, ideologies, and institutions and not individuals. Christianity is an inveterate enemy of Hindu society, but common Christians can only be viewed with empathy. The same is the case with Islam and Muslims. It is the ideology that exhorts an individual for good or bad acts. As Dr Koenraad Elst says, for Hindus, Muslims have to be treated as captives of hostile ideologies, to be rescued by ghar wapasi.[2] All those whose ancestors were Hindus thus have to be welcomed back eventually with ghar wapasi. And even those Christians and Muslims who do not come from Indic cultural backgrounds can be offered the undeniably better option of Sanatana Dharma.

Those Hindus who serve enemy ideological institutions and follow those ideologies have to be treated with sympathy, as most of them are innocent and deracinated Hindus who genuinely think they are doing good to Hindu society. Most of them are useful idiots who serve the enemy without knowing that they are. A few of them are genuinely in service of the enemy and are just paid mercenaries. We need to identify them but be considerate in our approach.

The SS Scale about Historical Leaders

While the Shatrubodha circle was used to create a mental map of Hindus and their place in the world, the SS scale is to assess whether a historical personality has enough Svayambodha and Shatrubodha. Without this scale we tend to either accept or reject historical leaders and personalities in total. But we can choose what is good and reject what is bad in the case of every individual. The Svayambodha–Shatrubodha scale helps us do exactly that.

Before we discuss historical personalities, let me assure the readers that it is beyond my capability to judge any great historical personality from Bharatavarsha who was also involved in spiritual sadhana. I am not at all making any judgements on historical personalities or their spiritual or intellectual calibre, as that is simply out of my reach. I am simply using the Svayambodha–Shatrubodha scale to help Hindus navigate in finding out, in case of any such historical personality, what is helpful to the Hindutva project today and what is not.

For example, let us take the example of Mahatma Gandhi. He is the one responsible for misleading Hindu society on the path of secularism from which it is still recovering and which damaged Hindu dharma and society a lot. He gave the slogan of *sarva dharma samabhava*, giving Islam and Christianity the same pedestal as Sanatana Dharma. Any common Hindu, like Kalicharan, doubts the dharmic credentials of Islam and Christianity, feeling that they are fundamentally different from what a Hindu knows as dharma. But all these doubts were quashed and overpowered by his slogan of *sarva dharma samabhava* in which he gave equal status to prophetic monotheism on one hand and dharmic sects on the other. In this he did not just commit a great factual blunder but also made Hindus complacent and thus sitting ducks for the missionary and conversion goals of Islam and Christianity. He distorted the classical respect that a Hindu has for different sects and extended it to Islam and Christianity, thus confusing them into thinking that these two are also just two other dharmic sects, which are in millions in Hindu dharma. He even distorted classical Shri Rama bhajans like '*Raghupati Raghava Raja Rama*' and made them into secular melodies like '*Ishwar Allah tero naam*'.

He whitewashed the crimes of Islamic invaders and jihadis of his own time. Only in the rarest of moments did he accept that 'Hindus are cowards and Muslims bullies'. But even then, he recommended no action to develop any Shatrubodha. In fact, he did not even think that missionary prophetic monotheistic religions were enemies of Sanatana Dharma. Far from developing Shatrubodha, he obfuscated it, harming Hindus in the process.

He was more critical of Christianity. Shri Sita Ram Goel describes in *History of Hindu–Christian Encounters* how he was very critical of Christianity and ripped apart the arguments of Christian missionaries who wanted him to convert. But even there he recommended no course of action and did not evolve his criticism of Christian missionaries into a purva paksha of Christianity itself. Mahatma Gandhi symbolizes the destruction of the tradition of purva paksha in Hindus, leading to the destruction of Shatrubodha and eventually to a disintegration of Hindu society in front of its most dangerous enemies. Shri Sita Ram Goel summarizes Gandhi's contribution to the perception of Christianity and Islam among Hindus:

> It has to be admitted that Mahatma Gandhi's prolonged dialogue with Christian theologians, missionaries, moneybags, and the rest, left the Hindus at home more defenseless vis-a-vis the Christian onslaught than they had been ever before. Whatever laurels the Mahatma may have won abroad, he has proved to be a disaster for the Hindus in India. The sorry turnout can be traced to three basic infirmities from which his position vis-a-vis Christianity and its missions had suffered. Firstly, he coined and made fashionable the utterly thoughtless slogan of *sarva-dharma-samabhava* vis-a-vis Christianity (and Islam). Secondly, he upheld an unedifying character like Jesus as a great teacher of mankind, and glorified no end the sentimental nonsense that is the Sermon on the Mount. Thirdly, he failed to see the true character of Christian missionaries, and nourished the illusion that he could tame them by his reasonableness and good manners.[3]

Even after figuring out how dangerous the Christian missionaries were and even after knowing their conversion designs, he did not recommend any course of action to combat their advances and to reverse them. We can safely say that Gandhi's Shatrubodha was extremely poor. If we were to plot it on a scale of zero to ten, one would say that Gandhi's Shatrubodha was at best one, as he knew some tricks of Christian missionaries.

But was Gandhi also this bad in Svayambodha? It turns out that this is not the case. When it came to knowing and asserting who he was, as a Hindu, Gandhi was confident in putting forward Hindu values. For example, he always thought that the indigenous method of education in India was far better than the one that the British wanted to transplant it with. It is his remark to the British that inspired a generation of Hindus to work on indigenous Indian methods of education. Dharmapal, the great Gandhian educationist and thinker, quotes Gandhi in his book on indigenous education *The Beautiful Tree*:

> I say without fear of my figures being challenged successfully, that today India is more illiterate than it was fifty or a hundred years ago, and so is Burma, because the British administrators, when they came to India, instead of taking hold of things as they were, began to root them out. They scratched the soil and began to look at the root, and left the root like that, and the beautiful tree perished.[4]

Today many Gandhian educationists are working on similar lines. They are one of the few alternatives to the English education system that has become the norm now. By advocating the indigenous education system of Bharatavarsha, Gandhi was advocating an ancient Indian knowledge system. In the economy, too, he mistrusted the overwhelmingly materialistic system that is the norm today and advocated a system in which people mattered as much as profit, and which had a balance of economic, social, and spiritual growth of individuals and communities.

E.F. Schumacher, one of the greatest thinkers in alternative economy, who wrote the wonderful work on economy keeping human beings at the centre, *Small Is Beautiful*, was inspired by Gandhi. The subtitle of the book expressed the core Gandhian message in economy: 'A Study of Economics as if People Mattered.' Even today many economists who dare digress with the reigning economic wisdom refer to Gandhi as a contemporary pioneer in the field. Gandhi managed to mainstream many core principles of Hindu economic thought with his advocacy. Ivan Illich, one of the greatest thinkers of the West, who has done a brilliant critique of some of the core institutions of the West, was also inspired by Gandhi. Illich critiqued the day job, Western medicine, modern education, and modern housing. To look for alternatives in economy and education, he looked towards Gandhi and through Gandhi towards the Indian knowledge system. Wendell Berry, another great thinker on native alternatives to Western lifestyle, was also inspired by Gandhian views on economy and education.

In terms of viewing one's own system, Gandhi never employed a foreign prism to Hindu institutions. Even though he was primarily an activist-thinker, he never pushed to destroy Hindu institutions like many left-liberal thinkers and radical liberal right thinkers tend to do. In the case of social justice, he recognized that certain communities in India were marginalized and discriminated against. He identified the problem and the communities that had suffered and worked to better their condition, both intellectually and also on the ground. On the other hand, he never blamed core Hindu institutions for the condition of these communities. Thirdly, he adopted a very core Hindu method of upliftment of the downtrodden. He called these discriminated communities 'harijans', people of the god, thus raising their status by claiming them to be closer to deities. This was the standard way of all the great bhakti saints in their efforts to raise the fallen communities. This is what Shri Ramanujacharya, Shri Madhvacharya, Shri Namadeva, and others did. Their method was to raise a community or an individual by clocking them closer to God and not by taking them away from the divine, the sacred centre of Sanatana Dharma. This is what Gandhi followed. Maybe he had not elevated himself spiritually as much as the other bhakti saints had, but his method of social justice was deeply Hindu. The four great systems of Sanatana Dharma, four varnas, four ashrams, and four purusharthas, Gandhi did not discard totally. Thus, we can say that his Svayambodha was not bad, if not very good. Plotting on the scale of zero to ten, we can say that his Svayambodha was six. So Svayambodha–Shatrubodha score of Gandhi would be around 6/1.

Let us analyse another important twentieth-century leader Dr B.R. Ambedkar on the Svayambodha–Shatrubodha scale. He is a dear leader for many and yet a controversial figure for others. However, for any future building process, we should respectfully discuss all our cultural icons without letting our emotions sway our minds either way. This is not the place to go deep into the analysis of his work, but even a cursory reading of his work will tell us that Dr Ambedkar had a problem with some of the most central ideas and core institutions of Sanatana Dharma, including varnashrama dharma. He has written scathing criticism of Hindu institutions and even deities. It is not doubted that his experiences with many other sections of Hindu society were definitely bitter, but other leaders from other downtrodden communities and his own community did not exhibit the level of resentment that his writings show. His views about 'higher castes' were not charitable. His disgust at the social exploitation grew so much that during the last years of his life he converted to Buddhism and chose to go out of the fold of Sanatana Dharma. All of this tells us that he is not a figure to learn Svayambodha from.

Like Gandhi, he also correctly identified that some communities in India had lost self-respect and dignity as well as economic status too. But unlike Gandhi, he blamed their condition squarely on the very nature of Sanatana Dharma. And thirdly, he chose to find a solution by going out of the fold of Sanatana Dharma and not by remaining within it. The word that he chose to denote the marginalized communities, 'dalit', locks its followers into a permanent victim mentality. If the very name of a community is 'dalit', how many chances are there that its followers will ever start feeling that they are not being discriminated against, even when the situations have improved?

On the other hand, his Shatrubodha was good enough, and even when he left the fold of Sanatana Dharma, he did not choose Islam or Christianity but Buddhism, which is a friend in the bodha circle. His views on Islam and Muslims were also very clear, and he made some prescient and clear observations about Islam and the behaviour of Muslims. He did not make the mistakes that Gandhi did regarding the relations of Hindus and Muslims and accepted the facts about Islam without trying to distort them. So we can say that his Shatrubodha was good, but his Svayambodha was not good. His score on Svayambodha–Shatrubodha scale would be 1/6.

It is one of the greatest tragedies of independent India that we learnt wrong bodhas from both Gandhi and Ambedkar. We copied the Shatrubodha of Gandhi and the Svayambodha of Ambedkar and thus met disasters in both. What needs to be done is the exact opposite: to copy and follow the Svayambodha of Gandhi and the Shatrubodha of Ambedkar.

This blunder was also facilitated by the kind of electoral democracy that prevails in India. It incentivizes dividing the majority community of Hindus into many sub-groups and sub-identities and prioritizes the unification of minority communities of Muslims and Christians into deeply united, close groups that can be promptly used as vote banks. Generally, the formula in Indian politics, before the BJP, was to splinter Hindu society into various sub-groups, combine one or two dominant castes with Muslim and Christian vote banks, and keep winning elections based on this formula. Congress and other secular parties perfected this method. BJP, coming from the RSS background, fought and won over Hindu unity politics by swimming against the tide, but if the demographic trend of decreasing Hindu population and increasing Muslim population continues, then the day is not far when the politics that divides Hindu society into myriad small sub-groups will come to rule again since the current form of electoral democracy incentivizes that. This does not mean that electoral democracy is bad in itself. But we have to adapt and particularize it in ways in which some fundamentals of Sanatana Dharma are declared as fundamental values that every party has to follow.

To move on to other great Hindu leaders, let us analyse Swami Dayananda. To clarify once again, this book is not the place to properly analyse these great figures on the Svayambodha–Shatrubodha scale. It is a work for the future. Here we are just giving a tentative idea of where the great leaders stand in both the bodhas, so that we can take the best from every leader for a future course for Hindus. Swami Dayananda was one of the greatest leaders to come out during the British colonial era.

He was the first to do a proper purva paksha of both Islam and Christianity. He put the rational-logical lens on Christianity and Islam and ripped apart their theological claims, proving them to be utterly wrong and obviously unfit for Hindus to follow. Swami Dayananda's critique of prophetic monotheism is still one of the best that the Hindu society has produced.

He was not just an ivory tower thinker but a great activist too. He knew the dangers that the Hindu society faced from the proselytizing religions of Islam and Christianity. He knew that until Hindu society finds ways to accept converted Muslims and Christians back to the Hindu fold, we will not be able to survive in the future, as without Hindus taking converted Muslims and Christians back into their own fold, the social balance that is needed will not be achieved.

He gave Hindu society the revolutionary idea of 'shuddhi'—the ritual by which the Hindu society takes the converts to Islam and Christianity back into the Hindu fold. It is the single greatest idea and action plan that the Hindu society has offered against the onslaught of prophetic monotheism. No other pagan, polytheistic society in the world has even thought of institutionalizing the reconversion of those folks who have converted to one or the other monotheistic religion. It is only Hindu dharma that has popularized this idea and has also practiced it, albeit in a very low number. And this idea was given and popularized in contemporary times by Swami Dayananda. When the Sangh Parivar and the BJP talk about ghar wapasi, it is the same concept as that of shuddhi that Swami Dayananda and Arya Samaj gave.

Therefore, the Shatrubodha of Swami Dayananda was very high. We can say that on a scale of zero to ten, his Shatrubodha was nine. The only thing that was lacking in his critique of Islam and Christianity was the spiritual lens. He analysed, critiqued, and rejected prophetic monotheism completely from the rationalist lens, which is a great intellectual achievement in itself and quite enough to discard and disprove the claims of Islam and

Christianity, but to a Hindu that is not enough. Since Islam and Christianity claim to be religions, it is necessary to explain in a spiritual way what exactly is wrong with them and what is right, from the point of view of yogic chitta bhumis. This spiritual analysis of Islam and Christianity had to wait for another 100 years. It was the great Shri Ram Swarup Ji who placed prophetic monotheistic gods on the scale of yogic chitta bhumis and told us that the monotheistic gods arise from kshipta and vikshipta yogic chitta bhumis, which explains why they are involved with so much violence and strife. Thus, the only fault with the Shatrubodha of Swami Dayananda was the lack of a spiritual lens.

On the other hand, his Svayambodha had many problems. He and the Arya Samaj took the Vedas to be the only authentic Hindu texts and considered anything that came outside and after the Vedas to be a corruption of the great Vedic dharma. While accepting the *nigama* tradition of Bharatavarsha, they completely rejected the *agama* tradition. Considering Puranas and Itihasas to be spurious stories concocted by wily Brahmins to fool common poor folks, they rejected the entire Puranic tradition. They considered temples to be nothing but degeneration of the great Vedic dharma and thought that priests were nothing more than corrupt swindlers. Having such a view of the Puranas, the Agamas, and the temples, they recommended 'going back to the Vedas', to the 'pure Hindu age'.

This 'back to the Vedas' call of the Arya Samaj and Swami Dayananda was very similar to the Protestant call of 'back to the roots' in which they claimed that the Christian society had to go back to the literal interpretation of the Bible since it had been corrupted by the middlemen—the Catholic Christian priests. While there is great truth in saying that the Catholic priests were very corrupt and had made a business out of religion, in their corruption they had come to adapt to local, indigenous, and sometimes even pagan belief systems, practices, and customs. When the Protestants said that the Catholicism and the Catholic priests were 'corrupt', their meaning of 'corruption' was not just financial and moral corruption. The 'corruption' that they were most horrified by and which they most vehemently and violently opposed was the 'corruption' of 'adopting pagan practices' like institutionalizing pilgrimage, worshipping icons of the Virgin Mary and other apostles, and adopting various pagan rites under Christian garb. To be clear, Catholicism is also deeply Christian and as rapacious against other religions as Protestantism is, but it also adapts and adopts many indigenous practices. The Protestant Church, on the other hand, is very Islamic in its approach, with an extremely literal approach to the Bible. In the Christian context, the Protestant appeal makes sense, as the basic idea of Christianity was to ossify scriptures, beliefs, customs, and practices in a certain historical time and place. The evolution of social mores and customs was never in the plan. It was an anathema. It was tolerated by the Catholic Church as there was no other way to grow, and it had to make compromises.

Sanatana Dharma is ever evolving and also absolute. There is no 'pure original state' that has to be achieved again. Dharma proceeds in different ways through different ages, and the cycle of time brings back the same time again, but by the same logic, nothing can stay in that stage forever. There is no ossification of attitudes and customs, as well as there is no hangover of a golden age. This is why the Puranas are not degraded versions of the Vedas. They fulfill a dharmic need, just as the Vedas do. Similarly, the 'Puranic age', if we can call it that, was not a degeneration of the great and pure Vedic age. It was what the times needed. The temples provided a way to take the message and phala (result) of the Vedas to all when it was no longer possible to do so just with the yajnas. Temples are not the fallen versions of yajnas. They continue the same rituals in a different way. The priests are not middlemen. They are the Puranic/Agamic counterpart of someone performing yajna in the Krita Yuga.

This fact was lost on the Arya Samaj and Swami Dayananda. Putting the same rationalist lens on our own tradition, as they put on the historical religions of Islam and Christianity, they came up with the conclusion that temples, the Puranas, and the Agamas are corruptions of the pure Vedic dharma, and hence it is the duty of the Hindus to go back to the Vedas. This is essentially a Protestant urge to 'reform' religion in a way that restores the supposed 'original'. Anyone who understands the ever-evolving nature of Sanatana Dharma will not entertain these thoughts. So, in the case of Svayambodha, Swami Dayananda would not fare as well as he did in the case of Shatrubodha. In Svayambodha, his score would be three out of ten.

About Swami Vivekananda, it would be folly to analyse him on any scale, but as discussed, this is to help Hindus navigate the future path by taking the best from each great Hindu leader. Swami Vivekananda was the great yogi who kick started the Hindu Renaissance. In many ways, Hindutva starts from him when he gives the call to Bharatavarsha to rise again by raising Sanatana Dharma. He arrived at the scene during one of the darkest periods of Indian history, when Hindu society was broken and poor, when Sanatana Dharma was receding under the dual threat of Islam and Christianity, and when the colonial State was destroying the very spirit of being Hindu. Swami Vivekananda, the great yogi disciple of a jnani guru, Shri Ramakrishna Paramhamsa, gives the clarion call of the Hindu Renaissance from the holy ghats of the Ganga on the other side of the great Dakshineshwar Temple, in Belur Math, and our society, at the beck and call of a yogi, starts to rise.

Like all great Hindu leaders, he never disrespected the eternal tradition of Sanatana Dharma. At the same time, he recognized that Hindu society had become too impoverished, divided, and broken, and so he set out to give them confidence and necessary fundamentals to exist through reigniting the great concept of Hindu charity. He wrote and spoke extensively on yoga, dhyana, and sadhana and illumined some of the most central concepts of Advaita Vedanta like a great guru. On the other hand, his Shatrubodha was also excellent. His understanding of the faults of the enemies of Sanatana dharma was great. He recognized the missionary mischief of Christianity and the jihadi danger of Islamic ideology. He fought the missionary arguments tooth and nail, sought to explain to the Hindus the evil dangers of missionaries and jihadis, and exhorted the common Hindu to rise and fight against the monotheistic danger faced by Hindu society:

> Now, if you had the same positive feeling for your religion, your true mother, you could never see any Hindu brother converted to Christianity. Yet you see this occurring every day, and you are quite indifferent. Where is your faith? Where is your patriotism? Every day Christian missionaries abuse Hinduism to your face, and yet how many are there amongst you whose blood boils with righteous indignation and who will stand up in its defense?[5]

He defended all core practices of Hindu dharma and attacked all central ideas of monotheism. He was as much an expert in Hindu darshana, as he was practiced in creating social institutions to help raise the living standards of the poor Hindus. Both his Svayambodha and Shatrubodha are 9/9. No one can take away from his Svayambodha, but I have reserved one last point to differentiate jnani gurus like his own guru Shri Ramakrishna Paramhansa and others like Shri Ramana Maharishi and Shri Nisargadatta Maharaja.

The only thing that is missing in his body of work regarding Shatrubodha is that, being a big public figure, he had to sit with Christian missionaries and Islamic scholars a lot and thus had to adapt to certain crowds in some of his speeches, which are now quoted out of context to prove that he was secular. He was not, but due to being a great activist, his potential to do a ruthless purva paksha was limited, and that was something that was left for other spiritual and intellectual leaders to come, like Shri Aurobindo and Shri Ram Swarup.

Shri Aurobindo, in many ways, represents the pinnacle of scholar saints like Swami Vivekananda and Swami Dayananda, who illuminated the path forward for Hindus by their deep spiritual power and who were yet intellectually brilliant. He is one of the greatest thinkers to come out of Bharatavarsha in the past 150 years. He was a deep sadhaka, a great philosopher, thinker, intellectual, activist, poet, dramatist, and spiritual and political leader. He was a firebrand revolutionary, as well as a great thinker who cogitated on every important aspect of Hindu civilization and all the challenges and problems it faced.

His Shatrubodha was deep and sharp. He did not suffer from the Shatrubodha blindness that Mahatma Gandhi suffered from. He was also not reticent in his criticism and seldom had a good view of prophetic monotheistic religions. In sadhana, he was profound, and along with abiding by the fundamental principles and practices of Sanatana Dharma, he also experimented anew. His Svayambodha–Shatrubodha score would also be similar to Swami Vivekananda.

Before we talk about perfect scores, let us also talk about some 'thinkers' who got zero in both the bodhas and yet whose impact on India's future was immense. Jawaharlal Nehru, unfortunately the first Prime Minister of India, was in that category, who had no clue about what it meant to be a Hindu and no clue about the enemy of any kind, religion like Christianity, ideologies like communism, or states like China. He was perfectly zero in his Svayambodha, and he was also perfectly zero in his Shatrubodha, as is evident from his cluelessness before the Chinese invasion of India. Nehru's score on the Svayambodha–Shatrubodha scale is 0/0.

To look at the other end of the spectrum, is it possible for some of our leaders to have perfect Svayambodha? Absolutely! Great saints like Shri Ramana Maharishi and Shri Nisargadatta Maharaja have perfect Svayambodha because they have reached the highest goal ascribed to a Hindu—*moksha*. Having perfect atmabodha (self-knowledge of the highest kind), they are incapable of having flaws in any bodha. Thus, they have perfect Svayambodha and perfect Shatrubodha.

Outside the category of jivanmuktas and jnanis like Shri Ramana Maharishi, Shri Nisargadatta Maharaja, Papaji, and Mata Amritanandamayi Maa from contemporary times and Shri Ramakrishna Paramhamsa, the great gurus of the countless great guru-shishya traditions of Bharatavarsha, is it possible to have perfect Svayambodha? I believe that without having reached the ultimate state of self-knowledge, absolute Svayambodha is impossible, but most like Shri Aurobindo and Swami Vivekananda get quite close.

But is it possible to have perfect Shatrubodha? It turns out it is, as our enemies are not of that high a spiritual calibre, and knowledge about them can be gained without achieving the highest states of consciousness. However, a great Svayambodha always helps any other bodha, including Shatrubodha. Shri Ram Swarup comes in that category. His sadhana was also very profound, like Shri Aurobindo, and it was his high spiritual state that let him have a perfect ten score in Shatrubodha. How?

Because it is Shri Ram Swarup, who, for the first time in history, plots the gods of various dharmas like Sanatana Dharma and pagan sects, and the gods of prophetic monotheisms like Islam and Christianity on the chitta bhumi scale. He says that the gods of Islam and Christianity rise in kshipta and vikshipta chitta bhumis.

With one stroke he solves many problems. First of all, he reverses the gaze and gives a Hindu/dharmic view of prophetic monotheism. Second, he does not limit himself to the rationalist/logical lens to analyse prophetic monotheism. But he goes many steps ahead of his predecessors in purva paksha of monotheism. He incorporates the very existence of monotheistic gods in a Hindu worldview and explains the very phenomenon of prophetic monotheism from the point of view of yoga and sadhana. This is an amazing feat, as no other Hindu before him had used one of the great darshanas of India to analyse monotheism critically. He killed many birds with one shot. He used one of the six darshanas, Yoga, to explain monotheism and thus applies a very Indic, very Hindu technique on a very novel and alien subject. Thus, he uses a very traditional Hindu philosophical system to analyse monotheism. At the same time, he does not 'accept' monotheism as a valid dharmic sect and manages to reject it by calling their gods having originated in vikshipta chitta bhumis. He simultaneously rejects monotheism while Hinduizing its criticism. Before him the opposite had happened. Those who chose to comment on monotheism did not analyse it from a Hindu lens and yet accepted them as valid practices, thus simultaneously blinding Hindus from the threat that monotheism proposes and, at the same time, approving them as valid sects by giving them the status of religion.

Rejecting monotheism, while Hinduizing its criticism, shall remain one of the greatest intellectual achievements of the Hindu thinkers for many decades and centuries to come. And that was the achievement of Shri Ram Swarup. That is why his Shatrubodha has a perfect score of ten.

His colleague and great friend Shri Sita Ram Goel was another great visionary whose Shatrubodha was also extremely good. He completely believed in the analysis of Shri Ram Swarup and analysed the very nature and modus operandi of the enemy in great detail. At the same time, he also gave us a way out, having chalked out a plan of the 'defense of Hindu society'. Thus, his Shatrubodha score can also be said to be ten.

It is an attempt of this work and the Svayambodha–Shatrubodha scale to be able to reinterpret and analyse our past leaders as well as important leaders and thinkers of contemporary times in a way that maximally benefits Hindu revival. I hope that by understanding our enemy (having perfect

Shatrubodha) and understanding our own civilization (having great Svayambodha), we will simplify the process for Hindus of understanding their great leaders and using their work to forge a crystal clear and extremely unambiguous action plan for the future. The 'score' here is just relative and is not more than a prop to understand relatively how our great leaders and thinkers fare on both the bodhas.

The Spectrum of the Hindu Movement and the SS Scale

The Svayambodha–Shatrubodha scale is useful in analysing the spectrum of the Hindu movement itself. A detailed analysis of the Hindu movement would need another book. Here we will discuss the characters of various Hindu sub-groups on the Svayambodha–Shatrubodha scale. While secularists, communists, left liberals, and woke activists are clear enemies, we also need to analyse our own Hindu side to have an idea of how developed various ideologies are in Svayambodha and Shatrubodha, ideologies that are inside the spectrum of the Hindu movement.

While some may want to restrict the meaning of the word 'Hindutva', it is more reasonable to address the entire movement for Hindu revival as the Hindutva movement. Hindutva has been defined recently by many of its proponents as 'Hindutva is Hinduism that resists'. While there are many objections to that, we do not need to go into this. Hindutva can be the broad umbrella under which all Hindu revival attempts are made. Referring to the quality that the word 'Hindutva' denotes, it simply means 'Hinduness', to bank more on the etymological meaning of the word.

Having said that, there is a certain group inside the Hindutva movement that is inspired by the vision and words of the great freedom fighter Veer Savarkar and Guru Golwalker of the RSS; this group is most commonly known as the Hindutvaites. To be more accurate, we will call them Hindu nationalists, coming under the broad umbrella of Hindutva. These Hindu nationalists gathered around Veer Savarkar, the RSS leaders Dr Hedgewar and Guru Golwalker, but after independence it was mostly the leaders and members of the RSS and its political affiliates, the Jan Sangh and the BJP, who were known by this tag, until the Ram Janmabhoomi movement picked up speed in the 1980s, when independent saints, scholars, activists, leaders, thinkers, authors, and journalists started identifying with the word 'Hindutva' and everything that it denoted. The great groundswell for the Ram Janmabhoomi movement mainstreamed the Hindutva movement in Hindu society and Indian politics.

Today it encompasses a broad swath of intellectuals, activists, and thinkers, but the core of Hindu nationalists is still inspired by the ideas of Veer Savarkar and other nationalists. The Hindu nationalists consider 'rashtra' or 'nation' to be sacrosanct and believe that every other feeling and identity should be secondary to the idea of the rashtra. This was the foundation of Veer Savarkar's thought of 'nationalist Muslims' who pledge their allegiance to Hindu rashtra. The idea of Hindu rashtra as the overarching Hindu identity was created to accommodate the 'Muslim problem'—namely the problem of accommodating and incorporating Muslims in Indian society. While Congress had de-Hinduized itself and all the platforms it controlled in the call for Hindu–Muslim unity, the Sangh and the Hindu nationalists imagined a Hindu rashtra that would be inclusive enough to inspire Muslims to become nationalists.

According to the Svayambodha–Shatrubodha scale, there are a few problems with this concept of a Hindu nation. Shatrubodha tells us that Muslims and Christians do not and cannot aspire to any idea of Indian nationalism, let alone Hindu nationalism, until the idea of Islam and Christianity, respectively, is deeply alive in their imagination. For them, nation means nothing; only religion is important, and Islam trumps every other priority. That is the reason that they feel closer to their co-religionists in Pakistan and Bangladesh than they do to the Hindus of India. So, there is no such thing as a 'nationalist Muslim' or a 'nationalist Christian' because their religions simply do not allow this. This is not to say that no Muslim or Christian is a nationalist, but their nationalism is despite their religion and not because of it. A 'good Muslim' or a 'good Christian' will not love or like the idea of a Hindu-majority India at all. Only someone who does not practice Islam or Christianity properly will be able to love the idea of India. So there are many individuals in India who were born Muslim or Christian and who are great nationalists and love India, but it is because they are not sufficiently inspired by their respective religions. In short, they are good Indians but 'bad Muslims' or 'bad Christians'. The only situation in which Muslims and Christians can be properly nationalist in India, while remaining true to their religious affiliation, is when India becomes a Muslim-majority or a Christian-majority nation.

Hence the idea of a 'nationalist Muslim' and a 'nationalist Christian' is a pipedream. A proper Shatrubodha, which is a proper knowledge of Islam and Christianity, will tell us that a Christian can have one but not both: nationalism in India or Christianity. The Hindu nationalists, for all the bad press that they get, fall short in their Shatrubodha. They are deeply nationalist, very devoted, and very inclusive, to the point that it becomes dangerous to their own side. The entire point of having a perfect Shatrubodha is not to include an idea that will destroy the very religion or institution which is tolerating and including it.

In Svayambodha, the Hindu nationalists pay more attention to Hindu unity and, for that sake, ignore many distinctions and diversity within the Hindu fold. It is correct that these are the times of emergency, and Hindus have to get their act together, especially when they are reduced to less than 78 per cent population in India (if we count the crypto-Christians). If Hindus do not unite now, the day is not far off when they are reduced to a minority in the only country they have. But the only way they can perfectly unite is to have a perfect Shatrubodha.

Only having unity without knowing the shatru very well will not achieve the goal. Unity is necessary but not sufficient. It is Shatrubodha that makes Hindu unity sufficient.

Neglecting diversity and some of the fundamental social institutions of Sanatana Dharma for the sake of unity leads to the conclusion that Svayambodha, of core group of Hindu nationalists, is not perfect. This is not to say that they do not have Svayambodha. This group is so diverse that one will find all kinds of folks in it, from strict ritualists to near-atheists, but suffice it to say here that on the Svayambodha–Shatrubodha scale the Hindu nationalists' score would be 7/8. Their Svayambodha lacks some core ideas but is not bad. Their Shatrubodha is good but not complete.

There is another group on the so-called 'right' of India that goes by the tag of nationalism. They are the centre-right, econ-conservatives. Their line starts with Dadabhai Naoroji and continues to the group of centre-right folks who focus on the economy and oppose Nehruvian secularism. Their main ploy is economic conservatism, and they wholeheartedly support Western capitalism over any socialist idea or any alternative idea of the economy. They do not subscribe to Nehruvian secularism and have no use for appeasement politics. They believe in all-round development and progress and believe that economic prosperity coupled with liberal social values will wean away the troublesome behaviour of some minority groups.

Their Svayambodha is quite low since they trace their lineage and origins in the font of European conservatism and the Burkean tradition. Sanatana Dharma and its core institutions have very little to do with this kind of nationalism. Their Shatrubodha is average since they avoid leftist, socialist, and communist ideologies like plague and make a scathing critique of Nehruvian secularism but fail to do a proper purva paksha of Islam and Christianity and at best offer Enlightenment solutions to the problem of Islamism in India and the world. In their pursuit of limitless 'artha', they invert the purushartha paradigm completely, making dharma subservient to artha. We can call them '*artha sarvopari* Hindus', considering that they consider artha to have veto over dharma whenever the aims and interests of the two purusharthas clash. We can say that their Svayambodha–Shatrubodha score is 4/6.

A small group of the Hindu nationalists adopt all liberal values of the West and reject most of the values of Sanatana Dharma and Hindu society. They do not see much value in ancient Hindu tradition, particularly the Puranic/Agamic tradition of the Middle Ages, and their inspiration does not go much beyond the great Hindu leaders of the nineteenth century. They see tradition as something ossified in the past and thus worthy of leaving behind. They favour liberal revolution in Hindu dharma, arguing for assigning some of the most fundamental aspects and institutions of Hindu dharma to the dustbin of history. They jettison some of the most central Hindu ideas, like moksha, favouring 'enlightenment here', or 'nirvana through material possession'. Perpetual reform, for its own sake, is their argument, and they consider tradition to be 'obscurantist', 'ossified', 'dead', 'casteist', and 'regressive'. Unlimited economic progress is their mantra in the economy. They build their ideology on the foundation of Hindutva but go against some of its central principles and practices. Electoral politics makes them more important than they are, but their ideas do not hold water, lack cogitation of mind or dedication of bhakti, and, of course, have very little background in sadhana. However, their Shatrubodha is reasonably good but does not go beyond the rationalist lens of Swami Dayananda. On the Svayambodha–Shatrubodha scale, they would score 2/6.

There is another group that is deeply nationalist and positively views the rise of Hindutva politics in India but does not trace its origin to the Hindutva movement. These are the real traditionalists of Bharatavarsha, the individuals and communities who are still following Sanatana Dharma and their own community and individual dharma in all its aspects, including all the rituals attendant on them. We can call them 'cultural traditionalists'. These are mostly the priestly communities of India (both Brahmin and non-Brahmin) and some great scholar-saints who follow a very deep ritualistic Hindu lifestyle. Their sense of *saundaryabodha* is very high, and their lives are rich and full of culture.

One important feature of this group is that they do not see a complete break in tradition in India, all the while recognizing that Sanatana Dharma has been reduced to too few spheres of influence, as compared to its days of glory. They also recognize that many dharmic institutions now no longer exist on the scale that they used to, and some have ceased to exist altogether. But they are themselves self-conscious witnesses of the fact that eternal tradition, or Sanatana Dharma, is far from dead, as they are still practicing it as it is. They are not averse to reforms and parallel systems of organization either, given that the reform is not mindlessly for its own sake and that these reforms do not disturb the fundamentals of Sanatana Dharma. They see themselves as the eternal firekeepers of Hindu civilization and Sanatana Dharma, whose job is to continue the ancient traditions of Bharatavarsha as they are. They are the Sengol bearers of dharma, who hold their positions without fail, becoming a pole star to anyone who wants to know what tradition and dharma mean in practice.

Thus, their Svayambodha is quite high. Their Shatrubodha is also not bad, but in this they rely mostly on the Hindutva leaders. They would score 9/7 on the Svayambodha–Shatrubodha scale.

There is another group, mainly visible on the internet, which goes by the tag of 'trad'. This group also swears in the name of tradition, but unlike the cultural traditionalists, they maintain that the tradition is no more, continuity is broken, and Sanatana Dharma is dead for all practical purposes. They maintain that varnashrama dharma and Sanatana Dharma are synonymous, and since varnashrama dharma is no longer followed by the larger Hindu society, they conclude that Sanatana Dharma too is no more. And we are no longer Hindus for all practical purposes. They recommend that varnashrama dharma has to be reinstated completely and followed by everyone, and only then can Hindu dharma be said to have revived or restored to its former glory. They are completely averse to reform and say that tradition has to be defended as it is, as they consider reform or any great change in lifestyle as degeneration. Many of them see even bhakti as a degeneration of *charya* and clock the beginning of the degeneration in the mediaeval ages when bhakti saints and tantra started creating new pathways to sadhana and charya. Due to their opposition to any reform, they are highly critical of Hindutva and its incorporation of reform in its agenda.

It is better to define them as 'neo-trads', since theirs is not a continuance of tradition but a coming back to it. They themselves are mostly non-practicing Hindus and maintain that the social structure makes it impossible for them to realize their Hinduness and live a Hindu life. They see a complete break in tradition and want to restore it. They do not like a society in which everyone, including them, is forced to seek independent jobs and individual glory and thus want to restore Hindu society to its status before the bhakti saints arrived on the scene in the mediaeval ages. Like any neo-movement, they identify the varnashrama dharma society before the bhakti era as the golden era of Hindu society and want to go back to it without any change.

In their pursuit of following the Shastras literally, they also refuse to consider any loka tradition and thus miss the entire half of the Bharatiya tradition. In pursuit of *marga* that has been lost, they discount all of *desa*, forgetting the famous assertion of Dr Ananda Coomaraswamy that during the mediaeval ages when Bharatiya and Hindu marga were under attack, it ran away and took refuge in desa, and thus today a lot of desiya traditions reflect Sanatana marga more faithfully than what we can understand by reading the texts just literally. They see many causes behind the breakdown of tradition, one of which is the onset of the bhakti era, but another major reason is the coming of the British and the introduction of the modern economy, which fundamentally changed Indian society by breaking down varnashrama dharma. The onset of the Industrial Revolution in India and the resultant re-arrangement of Hindu society is seen by them as the greatest tragedy to have ever struck Hindu society.

Their Shatrubodha is quite weak as they include both Islam and Christianity in tradition, and far from seeing fundamental problems with their theology, they consider these monotheistic religions to be valid paths to divinity or God. They see modernity, however, as the number one enemy of Hindu society. Modern West, Industrial Revolution, and liberal modernity are seen by them as the primary enemies of Hindu dharma.

While they indeed are reactionary, they identify some real problems with modernity and the ways in which it has been adopted hook, line, and sinker by the Indian State and its econ-right leaders after India's independence. Some of the scholars, from whom they get inspired, like Dr A.K. Saran, have made excellent critiques of modernity, liberalism, and secularism and have made contributions to critiquing European institutions that are sold as universal to Hindus and all other traditional societies. Their inclusion of Islam and Christianity as tradition and the exclusion of most of the desiya sects, practices, and customs is the major problem in their Shatrubodha and also Svayambodha. On one hand, they refuse to see Islam and Christianity as outsiders, thus missing on Shatrubodha, and on the other hand, they exclude pagan traditions of the world as well as the dharmic sects in India from Svayambodha. This group particularly falters in finding friends of Hindus and inverts the SS paradigm by considering enemies to be friends and friends to be enemies by rejecting pagan polytheistic traditions and accepting monotheistic traditions as friends. Their Svayambodha–Shatrubodha score would be 4/0.

There is another group within the larger umbrella of Hindutva, which professes atheism as its ideology but considers itself within the sphere of 'cultural Hinduism' as some of them trace the inspiration of their atheism in the ancient sect of Charvaka or Lokayata. They think of Hindu unity as the greatest goal of Hindutva and maintain that the nationalist Hindu identity should be the one-stop identity for all Hindus, even if it means the destruction of the manifest diversity of Sanatana Dharma and Hindu society; they also do not believe in any good aspect of caste and prefer its absolute destruction or 'annihilation' over time.

Their Shatrubodha is good, and they do a proper purva paksha of Islam and Christianity, but as their tool to dismantle the enemy is only rational, some of them find a common cause with the Western atheists. However, being only rational, their Shatrubodha fails to reach the level of Shri Ram Swarup. The Svayambodha–Shatrubodha score of the Hindu atheists would be 1/5. They get some points in Svayambodha because they correctly identify the dogmatic nature of prophetic monotheism and its absence in Hindu dharma. On the other hand, their Shatrubodha is good but is only rational and does not include modernity, liberalism, and atheism even partly as the causes of decay in Hindu society, and this takes some points off their Shatrubodha.

This analysis is far from watertight and far from complete. The readers are invited to start the process of mentally analysing individuals, ideas, and ideologies on the basis of this scale to have a far greater clarity in their worldview while working for the great Hindu revival.

Re-establishing Pax Sanatanica

Shatrubodha helps us rediscover the discrimination between dharma and adharma. The Svayambodha–Shatrubodha scale helps us reinterpret the ideas of individuals and institutions in a way that helps us create a Sanatana world order and a Hindu Bharatavarsha. For global peace and well-being, India needs to be Hindu, and the world needs the Sanatana umbrella. Monotheistic religions like Christianity destroyed the *pax deorum*, the peace or order of the gods, almost two thousand years ago. That peace, which was broken in hundreds of countries all over the world, needs to be re-established in the global world today under the Sanatana umbrella, or Pax Sanatanica. Pax Sanatanica is a more comprehensive and spiritually elevating form of *pax deorum*. In the pre-Christian era, the world was full of various local *pax deorums*. In the post-monotheistic era, the world needs a global Pax Sanatanica, where Sanatana Dharma gives abhaya to every local dharmic sect to be what they want to be without any condition. No one should be forced to give up their way of life or gods.

Only a Sanatana world order will ensure maximum freedom and diversity. Only Hindu universalism is true universalism, as it is rooted in the idea of non-dualism. Every other 'universalism' is 'counterfeit universalism' in the words of Sita Ram Goel, for they are nothing but tribal cults claiming universality. True universalism nourishes diversity and freedom and does not destroy it. True universalism is sourced in the unity of knowledge, like the Hindu idea of involution and evolution. True universalism is sourced in non-dualism, the only universalism that generates diversity and does not kill it. That is why the world needs a Sanatana world order.

Pax Sanatanica will ensure that no monotheism or monotheistic idea ever becomes strong and capable of destroying dharmas, traditions, and ways of life of others. Like the horse of the *Ashwamedha Yajna* of the *Chakravarti Samrata*, Pax Sanatanica will spring into action only if a counterfeit universalism of the monotheistic variety tries to raise its head and destroy the dharmic freedom of the world.

Hindu cosmology has stories that show that Sanatana Dharma is capable of pre-empting such a monotheistic counterfeit universalism and crushing it in the beginning. We all know Shri Narasimha, the avatar of Shri Vishnu. We know that Shri Vishnu appeared in the Narasimha avatar at the behest of his great devotee Prahlada, who had an asuric father, Hiranyakashipu. If we analyse the characteristics of Hiranyakashipu, we will find that it has striking similarities to a monotheistic cult.

Hiranyakashipu sounded uncannily similar to early Christian monks and saints who asked the pagans of the Roman Empire: Where is your Vishnu? If he is real, why does not he appear in front of me? Why should I believe in something I cannot see? If your god is everywhere, then is he in this stambha (pillar) in front of me too? Why does he not come to your help if he is so powerful?

These are some of the questions that Hiranyakashipu asked his Prahlada. We will remember that early Christian fathers, priests, and missionaries asked the same questions of pagans: 'How can god be in an "idol"? How does he not appear when we desecrate his images? He must be powerless then. It is superstition to offer sacrifices to invisible god.'

The Christians instead asked the pagan to honour the 'living God', that is, Jesus Christ, who 'rose in body and flesh to heaven' after having sacrificed himself to 'atone for the sins of humankind'. Hiranyakashipu, anticipating the fanatic and barbarian Christian monks, would ask Prahlada, 'Your Vishnu is powerless. One cannot even see him. Honor me! Worship me! For I am all powerful! I hold strength, power and money! I am the one who holds real power in the real world! I am the one who is visible! So worship me!'

One finds the demands of Yahweh (and also of Jesus) not very dissimilar to the demands of Hiranyakashipu. Yahweh is a jealous god, and he wants his followers to exclusively worship him. Hiranyakashipu also wants the same. Jesus is a 'living god', as Hiranyakashipu claims his own power to be real and living. One can see that the Sanatana tradition wanted to present an example of monotheism, what its qualities are, and how it can be defeated. Shri Vishnu, being everywhere and everything, springs from the stambha and kills Hiranyakashipu, who embodies the monotheistic idea, thus crushing a monotheistic cult in its very birth.

There are many more similarities in this story. Hiranyakashipu seems extremely powerful and undefeatable, as all the paths of the gods to kill him are blocked by the boons that he received.

But dharma finds a way to kill Hiranyakashipu, for the asura demanded only what he could imagine from his mind, but reality is far beyond the capacities and tendencies of a human mind. What it tells us Hindus today is that no matter how powerful adharma is, dharma will always find a way to kill it.

The Pyramid of Shatrubodha

Hindu Itihasas, Puranas, and the storytelling tradition of Bharatavarsha are full of stories that warn us about shatrus and teach us Shatrubodha. It is all there in our great and eternal tradition. We just need to rediscover it, and there is not a force on this earth that will be able to defeat or dominate dharma. The Hindus suffer from the 'Hanuman syndrome', as Prof. Kapil Kapoor puts it. We have all the strengths in ourselves; we just need to remember them. Once Hindus remember their strengths, there is no power on earth that can defeat them. Like Swami Vivekananda said: 'Arise! Awaken! And stop not until the goal is achieved!'

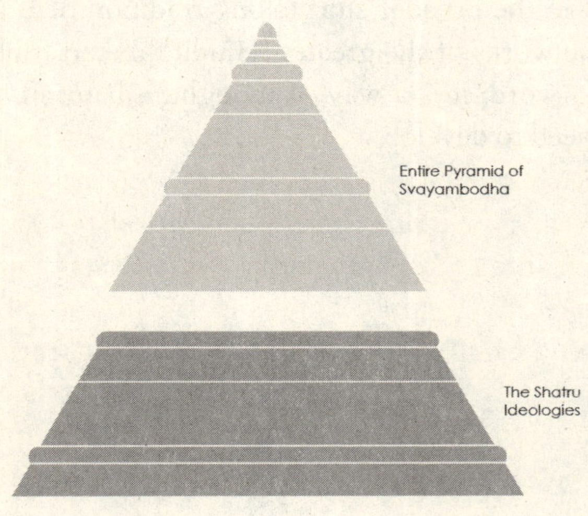

Fig. 3 The Pyramid of Shatrubodha

Hindus just need to remember the pyramid of Shatrubodha. Never shall we prioritize the enemy ideologies and institutions over our own society and dharma. Figure 3 illustrates that. Never shall the Hindus prioritize the out-group over the in-group. And in this there are no exceptions. Hindu society is under siege from prophetic monotheism. It is in a war. And in a war the only morality is victory. Ethics, morality, and humanity will get abhaya the world over once the Sanatana world order is established in Bharatavarsha and then the world. For that, the Hindus need to defeat all the prophetic monotheistic forces that are trying to destroy Sanatana Dharma. And for that we need to have a clear order of priorities. Never prioritize the enemy over our own society and our dharma.

This book is an attempt to rekindle the forgotten Shatrubodha in Hindus. Neither did the effort start with it, nor will it end. As far as my own efforts are concerned, this book is just the first one in the series of books on Shatrubodha. While the first book introduces the framework and the template of looking at the world through the lens of Svayambodha and Shatrubodha, the next few books will present Shatrubodha in Hindu Itihasas, Puranas, in the broader storytelling tradition of Bharatavarsha, and in the works of the greatest Hindu thinkers. Shatrubodha is not just a word; it is a way of thought, a habit of mind, which Hindus need to develop.

Prologue to the Hindu Renaissance

'Nothing that has any truth in it can be destroyed.'

—Shri Ram Swarup

The first *bhava* that arises in a Hindu's heart when he becomes aware of his great heritage is that of immense gratitude towards Sanatana Dharma. When we realize what our ancestors had to sacrifice so that we could be Hindu today, we start feeling the weight of our tradition on our shoulders. A natural kartavyabodha arises in our heart, and we feel obliged to make our contribution to the dharma yajna that goes on eternally. Countless Hindus before us have felt this kartavyabodha, and that is the reason that we are still here. Sanatana Dharma is still alive, and Bharatavarsha lives on. We act for dharma because we feel obliged by it. But in the course of our action, our bhavas go through many ups and downs. To be aware of the landscape of the battle for dharma also means to soak up all the tragedy and trauma that comes with it. And Hindus cannot look at this battle for dharma from the point of view of a historian or an observer distant in time and place. For Hindus, the battle for dharma is as real as war is for a soldier on a battlefield. It comes with all its colours, including macabre.

Such a conscious Hindu starts observing a thousand attacks on dharma every day. Two Hindu children butchered by their neighbouring Muslim barber in their own house in Budayun, just for being Hindu.[1] Hindu temples being destroyed in Bangladesh;[2] Hindu women molested;[3] Hindu teenagers lynched for exercising freedom of expression;[4] Hindu girls kidnapped and forcibly married to old Muslim men in Pakistan.[5] A conscious Hindu observes with concern how Kerala is being held hostage by Islamists and how the Muslim League is once again active and supporting a national party like Congress. He watches with terror as the whole of Lower Assam becomes an extension of Bangladesh and how the chicken neck becomes populated by illegal Bangladeshis.

This Hindu observes the Christianization of many parts of India; the mushrooming of churches in every single village of Andhra Pradesh;[6] the breaking up of Hindu families, with young women being lured away by the Church to Christianity; sons of temple priests being converted with money during sickness; crosses visible from inside the temple premises; buses to Tirupati sporting ads for Jerusalem;[7] and Christian officials of TTD (Tirumala Tirupati Devasthanams) mixing beef fat in Tirupati prasadam.[8] He is shocked to realize how one of the largest churches in Asia is being built in Punjab, of all places,[9] and he watches with dismay as Hindus do not even get grounds for cremation in Meghalaya,[10] an Indian state. He observes with pain that the last Hindu tribe of Mizoram, the Brus, have to flee because Mizoram, as a Christian state, does not tolerate any Hindu minorities.[11]He watches in quiet anger as government officials in Nagaland vow to convert the last Nagas to Christianity.

He watches in vain as Hindus in states with huge Islamic/Christian minorities turn towards left-liberal ideology. His heart cries out looking at how Marxism destroys Manipur valley, the minds of Kerala and Bengali Hindus, and the pristine forests of Chhattisgarh, Odisha, and Andhra Pradesh. He looks at the dominance of anti-Hindus in almost every other institution of

India, with a thousand insults daily of Hindu gods and goddesses. He watches with disbelief how the woke brigade aligns with Islamists against Hindus. He watches how Hindus still pay informal jizyah as Hindu temples have to pay taxes while Islamic and Christian institutions get subsidies from the Indian state.

When dharma is attacked constantly from all sides, it might become overwhelming sometimes. It is not something rare, and it happens to all good folks who fight for dharma or any other fight to preserve what is good and what is sustainable. I would like to tell you three anecdotes that sum up our dilemma and tell us why we do not need to despair at all.

Scientists and thinkers who fight to preserve ecosystems are usually in a boat, similar to Hindus. Waking up to the destruction that surrounds them, they become a little too aware for the sanity of their minds. Constant information of loss can become psychologically corrosive, leading to despondence. Loren Eiseley, one of the greatest thinkers of the West, in one of his best works *The Firmament of Time* laments the destruction of both nature and culture in the West. Discussing the loss and decay, he becomes despondent for a while, but then, happily remembers that while species are disappearing all around, they are but various mutations of types that are safe in the common gene pool of many other species. So, even while many species are dying off today, when the era of great destruction is over, many new forms will spring from the common gene pool still extant in the few species that survived, and the game of evolution will kick-start once again, replenishing species diversity very soon. This thought would settle Eiseley into spiritual peace.

> At such times a great peace settles on me, and with the office door closed, I can sleep as lemurs sleep tonight, huddled high in the great trees of two continents. Let the storms blow through the streets of cities; the root is safe, the many-faced animal of

> which we are one flashing and evanescent facet will not pass with us. When the last seared hand has flung the last grenade, an older version of that hand will be stroking a clinging youngster hidden in its fur, high up under some autumn moon. I will think of beginning again, I say to myself them, sleepily. I will think of beginning again, in a different way.[12]

Eiseley, in a way, remembers the Brahman of evolution, that one source from which all diversity springs forth. Through some anugraha, he realizes the unity of all existence and gets comforted in the knowledge that the seed of life is well nigh indestructible, and while the outer forms are lost in the temporary fires of destruction, the seed remains secure in the eternal *hiranyagarbha*, the cosmic egg, to spring back once again when the times and conditions are so conducive. Eiseley, even though born an American, intuitively understood that the seed of all evolution was in the process of involution.

Seven seas away, quite unconnected to Eiseley, there lived another great thinker, rishi, and sadhaka, who is one of the inspirations of this book—Shri Ram Swarup. And in a quite unconnected subject, but in an uncannily similar way, he talks about another great destruction and another great source of comfort. In *The Word as Revelation* he discusses theocide, the destruction of natural religions by Islam and Christianity all over the world. It is a dismal story of how thousands of gods and goddesses now remain forgotten; their temples destroyed; their shrines and sacred groves burnt; their chants forgotten; and their followers converted to either Islam or Christianity. But Shri Ram Swarup is far from announcing despair. He, like any dharmic thinker, is a harbinger of hope. He assures us that the pagan gods are not dead. They are not gone anywhere. It is just us humans who have lost paths of access to them. And if we were to rediscover these paths of access by mantra, japa, and ritual, then these gods will come alive to us again.

> If there is sufficient aspiration, invoking, and soliciting, there is no doubt that even gods apparently lost could come back again. They are there all the time. For nothing that has any truth in it can be destroyed. It merely goes out of manifestation; but it could reappear under propitious circumstances. So could the old Gods come to life again in response to new summons.[13]

And it is the job of the Hindus, as the greatest living dharmic tradition, to rise and provide guidance to the new followers of these lost traditions and help them arise and awaken their gods. This is the call to action that Shri Ram Swarup gives Hindus in his greatest work *The Word as Revelation*. He does not see doom when he encounters loss. Rather, he sees reclamation, not out of hope, but out of a deep sense of dharma. While every word that Shri Ram Swarup has ever written is calming, these words especially settle me in a deep sense of peace.

The third and last anecdote is deeply personal to me. When I first became aware of the wonder that is the Hindu temple, the sheer joy that all that uplifting beauty provided was overwhelming. But that joy soon turned into pain and despair as I saw in temple after temple the signs of Islamic vandalism and iconoclasm. Every temple was destroyed; every *murti* desecrated; every goddess had her breasts hacked off; every god his head.[14] Every contemporary student of Hindu architecture and sculpture has to deal with the tale of destruction simultaneously with the saga of creation, with destruction landing on him more forcefully. Many respond to it by compartmentalizing creation and destruction in two different mental boxes, with the box containing the story of destruction permanently locked up. Most books on Hindu temple architecture and sculpture pretend as if all Hindu temples and all Hindu murtis stand today un-desecrated and nothing bad ever happened in the Hindu temples. But I did not have that luxury of denial and insomnia. My guru and the great gurus like Shri Ram Swarup Ji and Shri Sita Ram Ji had woken me up to the destruction of Hindu heritage. I had to face it with all the pain that it entailed.

I flew into a rage full of despair one day and went to my guru and asked, 'Do you not see how we have irretrievably lost the great Hindu heritage of sculpture, architecture, and many other arts?'

He looked at me with that calm gaze, which was permanent on his face, and gave me a reply that I could never forget:

> It is not irretrievably lost. No Hindu art of sculpture, architecture and iconography, and no Hindu science is ever truly lost. Do you know why? Because the seed of all this creation lies inside the heart of a yogi. Hindu art has its seed in the *yogic chitta bhumis* of great *sadhakas*. And this is why it is never truly dead. When the time so comes, all this creation, in art, science and life, will spring back once again from the *ekagra chitta* of yogis.

With the eternality of an apta vakya, his reply would reverberate in my mind in the next two decades of my journey with Hindutva and would keep comforting me whenever I felt a little overwhelmed by the intensity of the battleground of dharma. And upon every such remembrance a great peace would descend on me, a peace not unlike that of Eiseley or that of Shri Ram Swarup; a peace that descends from the unity of all existence; a peace that transcends the transience of time and the ephemerality of context; a peace that is eternal, like satya. And in that moment, I would 'know' that dharma cannot lose, that dharma cannot disappear. Dharma does not need any saving. It is already saved. It is us who save ourselves by serving dharma; it is our chittas that are cleansed by serving dharma, and that is the greatest purpose of engaging in *dharmayuddha*.

These three anecdotes illuminate the most central goals of dharmayuddha: the protection of seed. That when one feels overwhelmed by the access of information that is natural of any battleground, that when a Hindu asks the question, what to save and protect from all the things that he sees under attack, the answer is always: the seed. Hindu cosmology is full of symbols and anecdotes that stress this point. I will once again tell three anecdotes, this time from our eternal shastras.

The *Ganesha Purana* tells the story of the contest between Shri Ganesha and his brother Shri Kartikeya. The goal is to circumambulate the entire cosmos 108 times. Kartikeya, more interested in prakriti or manifestation, literally goes around the cosmos 108 times, but Ganesha, given more to the study of the principle, goes around his parents, Shiva and Parvati, because he considers them to be his entire universe. This story is not about finding shortcuts or being smart. It is a contemplation of the seed, the siddhanta. It does not put down the understanding of abhivyakti or prakriti. The fight for dharma manifests in every walk of life and has to be fought in all those arenas. But at the same time there is another approach to save dharma—protecting the seed. And that is the import of the story.

There is another story from the Upanishads that takes a similar approach. In the *Mundaka Upanishad*, Shaunaka, a *grihastha* disciple, asks the great rishi Angiras: 'What is that by the knowing of which all this becomes known?' Shaunaka, here, is asking the question of all questions. He is not lazy or short of time. He is not even uninterested in the affairs of the world. But he realizes the theoretical impossibility of getting to know the one by knowing many, and so he asks the ultimate question: how to know many (everything) by knowing that one, Brahman or absolute truth. It is a question about the key to a subject, the seed of a problem.

Finally, anyone who despairs about the victory of dharma for any reason, they should remember the story of Savitri and Satyavana in the 'Vana Parva' of the Mahabharata. Savitri marries Satyavana even though he is cursed to die young. The moment arrives, and Yama, the god of death, takes the soul of Satyavana. Even then, Savitri does not lose hope. After following

Yama for a while, she gains five boons from him and ultimately accomplishes the inconceivable—Satyavana returns from death. She is not just saving a dying Satyavana; she manages to save an already dead Satyavana. This is perhaps the greatest story demonstrating the resolve of dharma—the power of dharmic sankalpa.

If Savitri could bring Satyavana back from the dead, the job in front of us dear Hindus is far easier. Sanatana Dharma is alive and kicking and on the rise. We just need to keep up the momentum. Develop Shatrubodha and strengthen Svayambodha, and the victory of dharma is a foregone conclusion.

At last, let me flip the Shaunaka question from the Svayambodha point of view: 'What is that by saving which everything else worth saving becomes saved?'

The answer is the guru-shishya parampara and the practice of meditation or sadhana.

Sanatana Dharma is not located in an institution, or a book, or a place, or a language. Of course it is in all these things, but most critically and centrally, Sanatana Dharma flows through the guru-shishya parampara, in the nadis of the meditating yogis. If that is saved, everything else worth saving becomes saved or springs back to life, like Satyavana did. This is the Svayambodha seed to save.

To give another flip to the Shaunaka question from the Shatrubodha point of view: 'What is that by fighting which everything else worth fighting becomes fought?'

The answer is prophetic monotheism.

We have seen how it is the monotheistic tendency that is at the root of all problems that the world and Bharatavarsha suffer from today. It is the grand siddhanta behind every manifest problem today, including the problem of ecology. By fighting the monotheistic spirit and ideology, we will be able to fight all that is bad with this world.

This brings us to the end of this book and to the new beginning we shall make: to make Hindus more aware of Svayambodha and Shatrubodha. Here and now, we begin our *dharma yuddha*. Because the battle for dharma is eternal, and every moment, every awakening, is a new beginning. This battle has always been going on and always will go on. And in an eternal fight that goes in circles, every point is point zero, where it all starts.

Shri Rama has come back to rule in his capital of Ayodhya, the great city. The very word Ayodhya means 'that which cannot be won in *yuddha*'. Ayodhya can only be conquered spiritually, by getting moksha, as it is a *moksha nagari*. It can never be won militarily. No matter how many times the asuric forces take it, it will come back to Sanatanis, to Hindus. And it has now. Ayodhya is a great victory for Hindus and the greatest defeat of prophetic monotheism so far. No other pagan power, no other natural religion, no other dharmic sect has ever been able to reclaim its most sacred site with sheer assertion, as the Hindus did with Ayodhya. This is the first instance of its kind. Moreover, for a total system like the Islamic mutation of prophetic monotheism, one defeat like this can be devastating.

Ayodhya is the Stalingrad of prophetic monotheism. From here, dharma rises. From here monotheism falls.

With the *sankalpa* of Savitri, the *kshaatra* of Arjuna, the *prajna* of Shaunaka, and the *dharma buddhi* of Krishna, we, the Hindus, ascend.

Acknowledgements

Everything I know is the anugraha of my guru, and it is not enough to thank him in the dedication. His influence on my life and understanding is infinitely greater than that. Though, being a physicist, he would instantly object to my use of 'infinitely' here, saying I mean 'huge' and not 'infinite', I get my quota of mistakes in imprecision, and I insist on using the word 'infinitely' and the bhava that it conveys. My guru is the fountainhead of all that is good in me. I landed at his lotus feet when I was a Kapital-thumping Marxist—angry and frustrated at the world, disappointed with life and the state of affairs in society; irreverent, rebellious, and clueless about what to do with all the books I had read, all the information I had gathered. My life was not unlike the area downstream of a broken dam: there was so much information, so much that I had known and so much still to know, but no way to organize it. Most importantly, I had no way to channelize my knowledge into behaviour. It is my guru who taught me how to do that. He taught me that knowledge must convert into behaviour; otherwise, from a Hindu point of view, it is not knowledge. What he really means to me is inexpressible in words and would take tomes, even if I tried, but in short, he is my inner compass, that voice of dharma, that dharma drishti, which keeps me and my behaviour in balance, at all times and in all places. More than a decade after he stopped being a daily presence in my life, his voice—his aptavakyas—reverberates in my mind, keeping my compass alive. It is his prajna that lets me wade through the battlefield of dharma without falling into either extreme. This book, in a way, is his voice, adulterated by faults arising from my own limited understanding. In expressing my immense gratitude to him, I fulfill my kartavya owing to rishi rna, albeit limitedly, of course.

I have no wish to violate the order of the *rnas*, but in acknowledgements, I can take some liberty. Without *deva anugraha*, no life is possible, of course, but in my life, I became aware of all this only through my guru and the great gurus who were introduced to me through his anugraha. Thus, I pay obeisance to the great rishis, gurus, and *acharyas* in my life, who taught me, directly or indirectly. My guru introduced me to the great rishis of Voice of India first—Shri Sita Ram Goel and Shri Ram Swarup. It led to my deracination and de-Hinduization. It was the start of my return to Sanatana Dharma. Next in importance to my guru's contribution to my understanding are the works of Shri Sita Ram Goel and Shri Ram Swarup. Like the fast-flowing waters of the Ganga cleanse our body and soul of impurities, the words of Shri Sita Ram Goel washed away the Christianizing force of secularism from my mind. The *aavega* of his words was so much that it did not just wash away the impurities but provided me with the passion and purpose of *dharma yuddha*. The clarity of his thought was most conducive to action. And what Shri Ram Swarup gave me was the spiritual reason for dharma yuddha. He is a *shishta*, as the texts describe Shri Hanuman: polite, humble, and empathetic. Yet, none of these qualities blur his clarity, because all of them come from a *chittabhumi* deep in *sadhana*. He has written on almost every important subject for Hindus, yet his entire written corpus hardly exceeds 2,000 pages. He taught me brevity, clarity, and simplicity of words and thought. The Voice of India publications by Shri Sita Ram Goel and Shri Ram Swarup changed my life. I was never the same again. I cannot thank these gurus enough.

Sita Ram Goel gathered a band of great scholars, thinkers, historians, and journalists who, defying all odds—like an anti-Hindu punitive State, media, academia, and Hindu elite—produced a body of literature that shattered the myths about Hindu culture, history, and civilization, and illumined upon the greatness of our civilization. They did this while the Ram Janmabhoomi movement was going on. While the groundswell of *bhakti* for our beloved Shri Rama changed this country forever, Voice of India created the intellectual backbone of the movement for Hindutva. Their contribution to the battle for dharma will be remembered as one of the great herculean attempts that succeeded against all odds. Today, most of the Hindus fighting the battle for dharma stand on the intellectual backbone of the great rishis and savants of Voice of India.

I cannot also miss mentioning the other greats of Voice of India, including Padma Bhushan Shri Vamadeva Shastri (aka David Frawley), Belgian Indologist Dr Koenraad Elst, ancient Indian historian Shrikant Talageri, N.S. Rajaram, Harsh Narain, Arun Shourie, etc. I have had the great fortune of meeting and recording the great talks of Shri Frawley, Shri Elst, Shri Talageri, and Shri Rajaram, learning from them in person. It is the wisdom of these gurus and thinkers that flows through this book.

Another great living guru I had the great fortune to learn from is Professor Kapil Kapoor, whose unmatchable humour and zest for life are so infectious that you cannot escape them once you have met him. For me, he is one of the best representatives of the great oral tradition of Bharatavarsha. Refusing to confine knowledge to books, he learnt his dharma from life as it is lived in this great land of Sanatana Dharma, and that is how he transmits knowledge to others—by speaking, in context, on dharma. And that, in my view, is the crux of dharmic living.

I learnt about the *Natyashastra* and, in general, aesthetics from Dr Bharat Gupt, who is a living embodiment of what a true *nagarika* is. I learnt what history writing truly is from Padma Shri Dr Meenakshi Jain, but it was her motherly love and care for a young man that showed me what true intellect is. I learnt the nuances of communism and its sister ideologies from

Shankar Sharan, who carries the legacy of Voice of India even today and, at great personal cost, serves Hindi along with dharma. I learnt what rigour and discipline is in this work from Padma Shri Dr. Meenakshi Jain. It is to all these rishis, gurus, and acharyas that I owe a great debt. Without them, my understanding would have been impossible.

Nothing is possible without deva anugraha, and this is as true in my life as in others'. It is the presence of Shri Hanuman that has given me strength and power in some of the weakest moments of my life. Shri Rama overshadows my life in more ways than I can recount here. He surrounds my life in many ways through many individuals and through my guru. While most of us are obviously far from realizing his instructions, he functions as the pole star—not just when things are in our control but also when they are not. The icon of Maa Tripurasundari commands the *puja* space in front of which I sit daily.

One belongs to tradition by accepting rna of the ancestors. But for me, these ancestors were a little different. In the dark alleys of my childhood, before I had met my gurus, it was literary giants from all over the world who held me, nurtured me, taught me, comforted me, and took care of me while at the same time opening up a world so breathtakingly beautiful, I could never come out from that deep sense of beauty. It was in the neighbourhoods of Premchand, the forts of Vrindavan Lal Verma, the barges of Tagore, the battlefields of Tolstoy, the minds of Dostoyevsky's heroes, the palatial colonial villas of Austen, and the streets of Dickens, the travels of Naipaul, the starry nights of Loren Eiseley, the rainforests of Wade Davis, that flung my horizons so far and wide that the petty tragedies of my own personal life seemed what they were—petty only. It was in the lanes of literature that I found pathways to the world, and it was the voice of my guru that never let me forget my centre. These literary pitras took good care of me until the rishis and gurus arrived. Without them,

I would not have a sense of beauty or a worldview. This book owes a lot to them.

The list of manushya rnas would be long, for I have been more than fortunate in having friends who are no less than angels, and strangers whom I met on this journey and who helped me deeply for no reason and became great friends. Then there are the families who virtually adopted me and gave me shelter. The first would be Dr Bharati Karnik, Shri Tushar Dighe, and dear Dhruv, who provided me a home and an anchor, making their house a banyan tree under which I could lie down. The human perspective that is at the core of this book would not have existed without them. To them, I owe a debt that can never be repaid.

Shri Raghava Krishna, dearest friend and the founder of Bṛhat, my organization, is the man who single-handedly inspired me to write this book. He made me focus, not just with words but with everything he could gather, and told me that what I had to say was important and that I should say it in a book. Without his constant encouragement and his overestimation of my ability, I would not have taken on this project. This book, in a way, started one day when I was discussing some organization problems with him, when he stopped me and said: 'You just write. I will handle else.' One wishes that every author had such a kind and able friend. Reena George, co-founder of Bṛhat, cannot be behind in this list of folks who worked really hard in the organization so that I could focus on the book. To them and everyone else in Bṛhat, I cannot be thankful enough. Two more names from Bṛhat merit special mention: Akshay Jha, who read through many shastras to give me references and proofread my drafts, was a constant mainstay; and Anshuman Panda, who gave me good insights into the works of Swami Vivekananda and Shri Aurobindo.

Ami Ganatra, another dear friend, is the one who had been encouraging me for years to publish. She is the one who introduced me to my agent, Shri Praveen Tiwari, and the print world.

During the course of writing my book, she read drafts and gave valuable insights and suggestions. Her expert knowledge of Itihasas was, of course, something without which my view of them would have remained incomplete in this book. I cannot thank her enough.

And it would be a folly not to thank Shri Praveen Tiwari from BluOne Ink. There is a proverb about heroes that fits perfectly on him: not all heroes hold swords; some hold the door. Praveen is that hero who threw the door of publishing wide open for nationalist Hindus and those who were fighting to establish truth. This man single-handedly fought the print establishment for what was right and what should have seen the light of the day. Without him, this fight for dharma in print would have been much harder. He was extremely patient with my frequent delays, kind and considerate in his advice, and at the end of the day, he wants the truth to get out. One can never thank such unsung heroes enough. I also take this opportunity to thank the other great folks at BluOne Ink who brave the unforgiving world of publishing and dare to publish the truth. Without them, my voice would reach far fewer people.

Shivakumar G.V. is that elder brother who has seen more of life than you and gives you perspective on texts that one cannot get just from reading them. But that's not it. His wonderful hold on Itihasas, particularly the Mahabharata, has given me insights I could not have arrived at on my own. Without him, some critical elements in my understanding would have been incomplete. For that, I thank him deeply.

Hari Shanker Kannan is the great friend of Bṛhat, who perceived that we are working for dharma and proceeded to help us sustain and still does. Without him, Bṛhat would not be where it is now, and I would not be writing these words. I am deeply grateful to him.

The list does not and should end here. There are various other fellow travellers who are not named here but who are battling to establish truth and give justice to Hindus. It is their struggles and conviction that have added to the growing confidence among Hindus that the truth will one day come out—that what is right will be vindicated, and one day Hindus will get justice and their due place under the sun. They are all the reason I have written this book.

My wife and kids are the reason I am able to do any of this. A peaceful home should not be a rare thing, but it is. I have one, and it is all thanks to them. They shall remain unnamed, but without them, none of this would have been possible.

At last, I cannot miss the bhuta rna. Long before I started understanding people and portraits, I had a deep relationship with prakriti and landscapes. Misty mornings, hazy nights, dusty evenings, and hopeful dawns spoke more to me than humans. Even in the dense urban landscape where I was born, nature reached through to me with its unruffled magnificence. That love for the natural world has never receded in my heart, irrespective of the human quests I have taken on in my lifetime. And it is because the glorious tradition of Sanatana Dharma seeks to protect this natural world that it is perhaps the greatest personal reason for me to protect dharma. By serving Hindu dharma, I serve the nature gods. And nothing makes me happier.

All that is good in this book is due to the eternal tradition of Sanatana Dharma and its great guru-shishya parampara. And all that is wrong is due to the individual faults and frailties of my nature. Do forgive me for any mistakes, and do write to me on any social media platform if you have any suggestions.

Notes

INTRODUCTION

1 There are some more examples of this behaviour. Anyone who was politically conscious during the Cold War knew about global communism and its power. Anyone who was impressed by socialist and communist ideas was aware of the famous slogan of Lenin, 'Workers of the world, unite!' This call given to workers of the world cut through national, religious, linguistic, cultural, and civilizational boundaries. Interestingly, this call was also centred on an abstract idea based in a book called *Das Kapital* by Marx. In limited ways, modern democracy based on liberal and humanist ideas is not very dissimilar, for it calls for a universal application anchored in the authority of one book—the Constitution. Although the constitutions of different countries are different, the idea and category remain the same. (It is not a blanket statement on democracy as such but is only limited to the modern form of democracy created and forged in the crucible of the Enlightenment. Democracy in various other forms has existed all over the globe, including ancient India and Greece, and is not included in this assessment.)

2 Aparajit. 'Gandhi—A Sainthood That Never Existed'. MyVoice, OpIndia, 24 January 2022. myvoice.opindia.com/2022/01/gandhi-a-sainthood-that-never-existed/ (accessed 26 November 2024).

3 Literature has examples. In *Lord of the Rings*, Saruman is initially on the good side and is given the charge of studying the evil side. He becomes so immersed in it that he starts liking the evil side and eventually becomes them by going over to the evil side. This happens in a context, which, though in a fairy tale, comes from a Judeo-Christian cultural context. It is possible to become the other by studying the other only when you do not know who you are. If

you are very sure of your own roots, where you come from, and where your cultural, religious, and civilizational centre is, there is no danger of turning into the other by studying the other.

CHAPTER 1 FUNDAMENTAL AXIOMS OF SANATANA DHARMA

1 https://commons.wikimedia.org/wiki/File:KailasanatharTemple-Kanchipuram-Tamilnadu-JM12.jpg (accessed 29 Mar. 2025).

2 Raghavan, M., H. Simha, and C.R. Ramaswamy. *Elements of Indic Knowledge Systems and Heritage*. HTSR Institute, 2023. pp. 39–40.

3 Bryant, Edwin. F. *The Yoga Sutras of Patanjali*. Macmillan, 2009. p. 158.

4 Raghavan, M., H. Simha, and C.R. Ramaswamy. *Elements of Indic Knowledge Systems and Heritage*. HTSR Institute, 2023. pp. 41–42.

5 Ibid., p. 42.

6 Ganesh, R., and Hari Ravikumar. *The Essential Sanatana Dharma*. Prekshaa Pratishthana, 2023. p. 41.

7 Ganesh, Shatavdhani R. *Your Dharma and Mine*. Subbu Publications, 2021. pp. 24–25.

8 Raghavan, M., H. Simha, and C.R. Ramaswamy. *Elements of Indic Knowledge Systems and Heritage*. HTSR Institute, 2023. p. 44.

9 'Circadian Rhythms'. *National Institute of General Medical Sciences*. U.S. Department of Health and Human Services. https://www.nigms.nih.gov/education/fact-sheets/Pages/circadian-rhythms.aspx (accessed 2 October 2024).

10 Ganesh, R., and Hari Ravikumar. *The Essential Sanatana Dharma*. Prekshaa Pratishthana, 2023. p. 20.

11 Raghavan, M., H. Simha, and C.R. Ramaswamy. *Elements of Indic Knowledge Systems and Heritage*. HTSR Institute, 2023. p. 47.

12 Kane, P. V. *History of Dharmashastras*. Vol IV. BORI, 1997. p. 2.

13 Ganesh, Shatavdhani R. *Your Dharma and Mine*. Subbu Publications, 2021. p. 21.

14 Goel, Sita Ram. *India's Secularism*. Voice of India, 1999. p. 9.

15 Davis, Wade. *The Wayfinders: Why Ancient Wisdom Matters in the Modern World*. House of Anansi Press, 2009. pp. 123–24.

16 Swarup, Ram. *On Hinduism: Reviews and Reflections*. Voice of India, 2000. p. 11.

17 The Bhagavada Gita, 2.22.

18 *The Isha Upanishad*, Verse 2.

19 More on moksha is explained in chapter 4 of section 1 where purusharthas are explained.
20 Swarup, Ram. *On Hinduism: Reviews and Reflections*. Voice of India, 2000. p. 1.
21 The Bhagavada Gita, 2.20.
22 *The Mandukya Upanishad*, 1.2.
23 *The Brihadaranyaka Upanishad*, 1.4.10.
24 *The Shiva Sutras*, 1:1.
25 *The Avadhuta Gita*, 1.13.
26 *The Aitareya Upanishad*, 3.3.
27 Saraswati Swami, Shri Chandrashekharendra. *Hindu Dharma: The Universal Way of Life*. Bharatiya Vidya Bhavan, 2022 (reprint), p. 39.
28 *The Vivekachudamani*, Verse 20.

CHAPTER 2: THE ASCENT AND DESCENT OF CONSCIOUSNESS

1 https://commons.wikimedia.org/wiki/File:Siete_chakras.jpg (accessed 13 Mar. 2025).
2 Raghavan, M., H. Simha, and C.R. Ramaswamy. *Elements of Indic Knowledge Systems and Heritage*. HTSR Institute, 2023. p. 22.
3 Ganesh, Shatavdhani R. *Your Dharma and Mine*. Subbu Publications, 2021. p. 36.
4 Anirvan. *Mandukya Upanishad and Prasna Upanishad*. Akshaya Prakashan, 2020. p. 15.
5 Ibid., p. 2.
6 Many texts mention a fifth state of consciousness, called *turiyateeta*. This is even beyond turiya, where nothing exists but Shiva, or just 'knowingness'. Shri Ramana Maharishi would keep mentioning this state in his talks with his disciples. In Hindu cosmology and iconography, the five states of consciousness are personified in many ways. In the *Pancharatra Agama* (one branch of Vaishnava Agamas), Shri Vishnu is imagined as having five avataras. One is the Mahavishnu himself, who is the very cause of entire creation and is the equivalent of the Brahman, or the Parashiva. He then takes four avataras called Vasudeva, Sankarshana, Pradyumna, and Aniruddha, and together they represent the five states of consciousness, with Mahavishnu being the highest causal state

of consciousness. In Hindu iconography, both the four and five states of consciousness are codified and represented all over Bharatavarsha. In the Kalachuri caves in Elephanta near Mumbai, the most famous rock-cut *vigraha* of three-faced Shiva is known. However, he does not have three but five faces. One on the back is obviously not visible or carved, and one, representing the turiyateeta state of consciousness, is supposed to be invisible at the top. *Panchamukhi Shivalingas* are famous all over India, like Gudimallam in Andhra Pradesh, Orchha in Madhya Pradesh, etc. Panchamukhi forms of various deities, including Shiva, Vishnu, Hanuman, etc., are famous and represent the same story of the five states of consciousness.

7 Raghavan, M., H. Simha, and C.R. Ramaswamy. *Elements of Indic Knowledge Systems and Heritage*. HTSR Institute, 2023. p. 82.

8 *TheShiva Sutras*, 1.6.

9 Chaudhri, Ranjit. *TheShiva Sutras.* Fingerprint Publishing, 2019. p. 26.

10 Raghavan, M., H. Simha, and C.R. Ramaswamy. *Elements of Indic Knowledge Systems and Heritage*. HTSR Institute, 2023. p. 64.

11 Some Hindus, perhaps copying the fundamentalist Christians in the West, oppose the theory of evolution in vain, thinking of it as something opposite to the Hindu idea of involution. But this is not true. While biologists working in scientific disciplines of course deny any existence of absolute truth or supreme consciousness, the field of evolutionary biology is limited to explaining the process of evolution once there is single-celled life on earth. It is mostly occupied with explaining how this unicellular organism differentiated into the entire gamut of flora and fauna that we see in nature. In as much, evolution is of course true without any shadow of doubt. So, the story of evolution is not a wrong story. It is just an incomplete story, as it does not tell the story of involution. It tells us how one becomes many at the level of organisms, but it does not tell us how many can also become one. This is also obvious since the process of involution is subtle, cannot be seen with the naked eye, or cannot be sensed with the five senses, and is not even grabbed easily with the mind. It has to be felt during the yogic process where our *indriyas* turn inwards and we realize our true

nature. Thus, instead of rejecting the theory of evolution, which is obviously true, we should complete the story with involution.

12 *The Taittiriya Upanishad*, 2.8.

13 Raghavan, M., H. Simha, and C.R. Ramaswamy. *Elements of Indic Knowledge Systems and Heritage*. HTSR Institute, 2023. p. 70.

14 *The Yoga Sutras*, 1.2.

15 Sastry, Trilochan. *The Essentials of Hinduism*. Viking, 2022. p. 89.

16 Ibid., p. 90.

17 Raghavan, M., H. Simha, and C.R. Ramaswamy. *Elements of Indic Knowledge Systems and Heritage*. HTSR Institute, 2023. p. 103.

18 Ganesh, R. and Ravikumar, Hari. *The Essential Sanatana Dharma*. Prekshaa Pratishthana, 2023. p.61.

19 Goel, Sita Ram. *Defense of Hindu Society*. Voice of India, 1987. p.7.

20 Swami Vivekananda. 'The Essence of Religion', *The Complete Works of Swami Vivekananda, Vol. 8*. www.ramakrishnavivekananda.info/vivekananda/volume_8/volume_8_contents.htm (accessed 20 November 2024).

21 Raghavan, M., H. Simha, and C.R. Ramaswamy. *Elements of Indic Knowledge Systems and Heritage*. HTSR Institute, 2023. p. 136.

Chapter 3: Diversity in Unity

1 https://en.wikipedia.org/wiki/File:Vishnu_Vishvarupa.jpg (accessed 29 Mar. 2025).

2 *Rig Samhita*, 10.90.16.

3 Raghavan, M., H. Simha, and C.R. Ramaswamy. *Elements of Indic Knowledge Systems and Heritage*. HTSR Institute, 2023. p. 112.

4 Raghavan, M., H. Simha, and C.R. Ramaswamy. *Elements of Indic Knowledge Systems and Heritage*. HTSR Institute, 2023. p. 100.

5 Ganesh, Shatavdhani R. *Your Dharma and Mine*. Subbu Publications, 2021. p. 100.

6 *The Taittiriya Upanishad*, 1.11.3.

7 Swarup, Ram. *The Word as Revelation*. Voice of India, 2001 (reprint). p. 15.

8 Ibid., pp. 16–17.

9 Ibid., p. 97.

10 Eight stages of Ashtanga Yoga as described in the *Yoga Sutras*: *Yama*, *Niyama*, *Asana*, *Pranayama*, *Pratyahara*, *Dharana*, *Dhyana*, and *Samadhi*.

11 Swarup, Ram. *The Word as Revelation*. Voice of India, 2001 (reprint). pp. 145–54.

12 Ganesh, R., and Hari Ravikumar. *The Essential Sanatana Dharma*. Prekshaa Pratishthana, 2023. p. 51.

CHAPTER 4: A DYNAMIC BALANCE OF OPPOSITES

1 https://en.wikipedia.org/wiki/File:Standing_Ardhanari_c.1800.jpg (accessed 29 Mar. 2025).

2 Ganatra, Ami. *Mahabharata Unravelled—II.* Bloomsbury India, 2024. p. 9.

3 Ganesh, R., and Hari Ravikumar. *The Essential Sanatana Dharma*. Prekshaa Pratishthana, 2023. p. 28.

4 Swarup, Ram. *On Hinduism: Reviews and Reflections*. Voice of India, 2009. p. 9.

5 From G.V. Shivakumar's upcoming book *Purushartha Papers: Stories from Mahabharata*.

6 Ganesh, R., and Hari Ravikumar. *The Essential Sanatana Dharma*. Prekshaa Pratishthana, 2023. p. 33.

7 Ibid., p. 93.

8 To take an aside, the Islamic invaders, always keen on destruction, knew this truth about architecture and thus would pull out the keystone in all the temples that they destroyed, making their job easier, as pulling out the keystone would make the entire structure collapse with less effort, and with the desecration of the garbhagriha and vigraha, the job of the Islamists would be done.

9 *The Yoga Sutras*, 4.34.

10 Ganesh, R., and Hari Ravikumar. *The Essential Sanatana Dharma*. Prekshaa Pratishthana, 2023. p. 46.

11 Low, Sidney. *History of Dharmashastras*, Vol. II, Part 1. BORI, 1997. p 20.

12 There is an argument that 'caste' is not 'jati' and vice versa and that caste was introduced in India by the Europeans. There is some truth in this assertion, but broadly the institution that is referred to by the word 'caste' overlaps with the fundamental Hindu institution of 'jati'. This is not a denial of the fact that the British and the Europeans introduced many distortions in our society and changed many institutions fundamentally, including the system of jati and varna.

13 Swarup, Ram. *On Hinduism: Reviews and Reflections*. Voice of India, 2009. p. 29.
14 Coomaraswamy, Ananda. *The Dance of Shiva*. Rupa Publications, 2013. pp. 12.
15 Toffler, Alvin. *Power Shift: Knowledge, Wealth and Violence at the Edge of the 21st Century*, Chapter 2, Part 1. Bantam Doubleday, 1991. pp. 12–14.
16 Haidt, Jonathan. *The Happiness Hypothesis*. Perseus Books Group, 2006. p. 233.
17 Saraswati Swami, Shri Chandrashekharendra. *Hindu Dharma: The Universal Way of Life*. Bharatiya Vidya Bhavan, 2022 (reprint). p. 83.
18 Ibid., p. 4.
19 *The Manu Smriti*, 10.31.
20 Raghavan, M., H. Simha, and C.R. Ramaswamy. *Elements of Indic Knowledge Systems and Heritage*. HTSR Institute, 2023. p. 153.
21 Saraswati Swami, Shri Chandrashekharendra. *Hindu Dharma: The Universal Way of Life*. Bharatiya Vidya Bhavan, 2022 (reprint). p. 91.
22 *The Natyashastra*, 1.12.
23 Kramrisch, Stella. *The Hindu Temple*, Vol. I. Motilal Banarsidas, 2015 (reprint). p. 11.
24 *TheShukla Yajur Veda*, 26.2
25 *The Yoga Sutras*, 2.31.
26 Bryant, Edwin. F. *The Yoga Sutras of Patanjali*. Macmillan, 2009. p. 159.
27 Ganesh, R., and Hari Ravikumar. *The Essential Sanatana Dharma*. Prekshaa Pratishthana, 2023. pp. 49–50.
28 *The Avadhuta Gita*, 1.34.
29 *The Avadhuta Gita*, 1.45.
30 *The Ashatavakra Gita*, 1.5.
31 Ganesh, Shatavdhani R. *Your Dharma and Mine*. Subbu Publications, 2021. p. 93.
32 Ibid.

CHAPTER 5: WE, THE HINDUS

1 https://commons.wikimedia.org/wiki/File:Krishna_Arjuna_Gita.jpg (accessed 29 Mar. 2025).

2 The *Mundaka Upanishad* explains in Verse 1.1.5 that *apara* vidya (lower knowledge) contains the knowledge of the Vedas themselves, and the para vidya (higher knowledge) is comprised of knowing the Brahman itself. Though the Vedas and Upanishads are also about para vidya, it is a way of saying that the texts are a means to attain knowledge and not the goal in itself, and it is ultimate knowledge that is the goal.
3 TheBhagavada Gita, 1.40–43.
4 The Bhagavada Gita, 2.4.
5 The Bhagavada Gita, 18.66.
6 The Bhagavada Gita, 2.42.
7 Swarup, Ram. *The Word as Revelation*. Voice of India, 2001. p. 94.
8 *Chanakya Niti Sara*. Verse 3.10.
9 The Mahabharata. Adi Parva. Verse 140:38. Gita Press.

SECTION B: SHATRUBODHA

1 https://youtu.be/Oj8yzvNaWyU?si=amBPM6n7Z_qBE2Ql

CHAPTER 6: ENEMIES OF SANATANA DHARMA

1 https://drive.google.com/file/d/1w5rmhOhHzaJZ27tJRj3yOmWbQ3gobZNi/view (accessed 4 April 2025).
2 Goel, Sita Ram. *Hindu Society under Siege*. Voice of India, 1992. p. 1.
3 Ibid.
4 Dixit, Sanjay. *All Religions Are Not the Same*. Garuda, 2023, p. 25.
5 Goel, Sita Ram. *The Story of Islamic Imperialism in India*. Voice of India, 2001 (reprint). p. 27.
6 Durant, Will. *Our Oriental Heritage: The Story of Civilization—Part 1*. Simon and Schuster, 1954. p. 459.
7 Goel, Sita Ram. *The Story of Islamic Imperialism in India*. Voice of India, 2001 (reprint). p. 18.
8 Misra, Ram Gopal. *Indian Resistance to Early Muslim Invaders Up to 1206 AD*. Anu Books, 1983. p. 9.
9 Lal, K.S. *Growth of Scheduled Tribes and Castes in Medieval India*. Voice of India, 1995. p. viii.
10 Lal, K.S. *Growth of Scheduled Tribes and Castes in Medieval India*. Voice of India, 1995. p. vi.
11 Swami Vivekananda. 'On the Bounds of Hinduism'. *Sri Ramakrishna and Swami Vivekananda*, www.ramakrishnavivekananda.info/

vivekananda/volume_5/interviews/on_the_bounds_of_hinduism.htm (accessed 26 November 2024).

12 Goel, Sita Ram. *Hindu Society under Siege*. Voice of India, 1992. pp. 9–10.

13 Goel, Sita Ram. *Hindu Society under Siege*. Voice of India, 1992. p. 8.

14 This is not a fringe thought but a well-established academic and literary theory, which is also a palpable daily reality in the Muslim world. Tamim Ansary, a great Muslim scholar, lecturer, and public speaker living in the United States, has written a book called *Destiny Disrupted* in 2009, which laments the fact that the West disrupted the destiny of Muslims to rule the world.

15 Goel, Sita Ram. *Hindu Society under Siege*. Voice of India, 1992. p. 14.

16 Miranda, J.C. Barreto. *Quadros Historicos de Goa*. Cadernete I, 1863. p. 145.

17 Pandey, Geeta. 'India's "last Electrified Village" Leisang Still Fighting Darkness'. BBC News, 29 March 2019, www.bbc.com/news/world-asia-india-47721497 (accessed 26 November 2024).

18 Shourie, Arun. *Missionaries in India: Continuities, Changes, Dilemmas*. HarperCollins, 2000 (reprint). p. 109.

19 Goel, Sita Ram. *Jesus Christ: An Artifice for Aggression*. Voice of India, 1994. p. 68.

20 Pipes, Richard. *Communism: A History of the Intellectual and Political Movement*. Orion Publishing Group, 2002. p. 155.

21 Applebaum, Anne. *Gulag: A History*. Anchor Books, 2004. p. 6.

22 Service, Robert. *Comrades: Communism—A World History*. Pan Macmillan, 2007. p. 138.

23 Brown, Archie. *The Rise and Fall of Communism*. HarperCollins, 2010. p. 198.

24 Quoted by Shourie, Arun. *The Only Fatherland: Communists, 'Quit India' and the Soviet Union*. ASA Publications, 1992. pp. 22, 27, 34.

25 Goel, Sita Ram. *Genesis and Growth of Nehruism: Volume 1—Commitment to Communism*. Voice of India, 1993. p. 35.

26 Andrew, Christopher and Vasili Mitrokhin. *The World Was Going Our Way: The KGB and the Battle for the Third World*. Basic Books, 2005. p. 318.

27 Ibid., p. 322.

28 Shourie, Arun. *Eminent Historians: Their Technology, Their Line, Their Fraud*. ASA Publications, 1998. p. xi.
29 Goel, Sita Ram. *Hindu Society under Siege*. Voice of India, 1992. p. 33.
30 Goel, Sita Ram. *Hindu Society under Siege*. Voice of India, 1992. p. 25.
31 The Bible: Authorized King James Version. Oxford University Press, 1997. Leviticus, 20:13.

CHAPTER 7: FUNDAMENTALS OF PROPHETIC MONOTHEISM

1 https://commons.wikimedia.org/wiki/File:The_Slave_Market_by_Otto_Pilny.jpg (accessed 6 Oct. 2024).
2 Many good books have been written on this topic by great historians and scholars like Sita Ram Goel, Ram Swarup, Rajiv Malhotra, and many others. Anyone wanting to delve into this topic deeper can refer to their works.
3 This seems to be counter-intuitive to Hindus of the twenty-first century, as we have been schooled in believing that the Christian ideas are universal ideas.
4 Goel, Sita Ram. *India's Secularism*. Voice of India, 1999. p. 11.
5 Sri Nisargadatta Maharaj. *I Am That: Talks with Sri Nisargadatta Maharaj*. Chetana Prakashan, 2006 (reprint). p. 306.
6 Swarup, Ram. *Hindu View of Christianity and Islam*. Voice of India, 1992. pp. 23–24.
7 'You shall not bow down to them or serve them, for I the Lord your God am a jealous God, visiting the iniquity of the fathers on the children to the third and fourth generation of those who hate me, but showing steadfast love to thousands of those who love.' (Exodus 20:5–6)
8 Nixey, Catherine. *The Darkening Age: The Christian Destruction of the Classical World*. PanMacmillan, 2017. p. 170.
9 Swarup, Ram. *Hindu View of Christianity and Islam*. Voice of India. 1992. p. 16.
10 Ibid., p. 40.
11 The Bible: Authorized King James Version. Oxford University Press, 1997. Matthew, 11:27
12 Elst, Koenraad. *Psychology of Prophetism: A Secular Look at the Bible*. Voice of India, 1993. p. 10.

13 Swarup, Ram. *Hindu View of Christianity and Islam*. Voice of India, 1992. pp. 21–22.
14 Goel, Sita Ram. *India's Secularism*. Voice of India, 1999. p. 12.
15 Goel, Sita Ram. *Jesus Christ: An Artifice for Aggression*. Voice of India, 1994. p. 68.
16 The bhajana that is being referred to here is titled *Ud Jayega Hans Akela* by Kumar Gandharva, a great devotional singer of the Udaseena Sampradaya from Devas, Madhya Pradesh.
17 Swarup, Ram. *On Hinduism: Reviews and Reflections*. Voice of India, 2000, pp. 6–7.
18 Elst, Koenraad. *Psychology of Prophetism: A Secular Look at the Bible*. Voice of India, 1993. p. 136.
19 Gonzalez, Justo L. *The Story of Christianity: The Early Church to the Dawn of the Reformation*. HarperOne, 2010. p. 94.
20 Goel, Sita Ram. *India's Secularism*. Voice of India, 1999. p. 17.
21 The Bible: Authorized King James Version. Oxford University Press, 1997. Genesis, 9:3.
22 The Dvaita Madhva sampradaya does have a concept of permanent hell, which is an aberration and is not replicated in any other system. There are various theories on this. One says that it was a response to the Islamic theology, and the other says that there is always the possibility of a dogmatic view rising in any society. Most often in Sanatana society, it is blocked and defeated in its infancy. Moreover, the object of Madhva samradaya's focus is Shri Krishna, thus making intolerance impossible.
23 The Bible: Authorized King James Version. Oxford University Press, 1997. Matthew, 10:28; Mark, 9: 43; Luke, 16:19–31; Revelation, 20:10.
24 Quoted by Swarup, Ram. *Understanding Islam through Hadith: Religious Faith or Fanaticism?* Voice of India, 2001 (reprint). p. 207.
25 Ibid., p. 206.
26 Whenever the term 'religion' is used for Sanatana Dharma, it is only to stress the contrast with other religions, and it is always used with the words 'natural' or 'indigenous'. Otherwise, dharma is not religion, as is explained later in the book.
27 Malhotra, Rajiv. *Being Different: An Indian Challenge to Western Universalism*. HarperCollins, 2013 (reprint). p. 6.
28 Goel, Sita Ram. *India's Secularism*. Voice of India, 1999. p. 13.

29 Swarup, Ram. *Hindu View of Christianity and Islam*. Voice of India, 2020 (reprint). p. 40.

30 The Quran, edited by Shahi International. Al-muntada Al-islami, 2004. Surah 48 Ayat 29. 'Muḥammad is the Messenger of Allāh; and those with him are forceful against the disbelievers, merciful among themselves.'

31 Joseph, Josy. 'Third Millennium Will Witness Harvest of Faith in Asia: Pope', *Rediff on the Net*, Rediff. m.rediff.com/news/1999/nov/07pope3.htm (accessed 2 October 2024).

32 Goldenberg, Suzanne. 'Pope Heralds Mission to Convert Asia', *The Guardian*, 8 November 1999. www.theguardian.com/world/1999/nov/08/millennium.uk (accessed 26 November 2024).

33 Swarup, Ram. *Hindu View of Christianity and Islam*. Voice of India, 1992. p. 110.

34 Goel, Sita Ram. *Papacy, Its Doctrine and History*. Voice of India, 1986. p. 6.

35 Macintosh, Douglas Clyde. 'The New Christianity and World-Conversion', *The American Journal of Theology*, Vol. 18, no. 3, 1914, pp. 337–54. JSTOR, http://www.jstor.org/stable/3154526 (accessed 5 September 2024).

36 The Bible: Authorized King James Version. Oxford University Press, 1997. Matthew, 28:18–20.

37 Swarup, Ram. *Hindu View of Christianity and Islam*. Voice of India, 1992. p. 77.

38 The Bible: Authorized King James Version. Oxford University Press, 1997. Exodus,23:24, 34:13; Numbers 33:52; Deuteronomy 7:5, 25–26.

39 Goel, Sita Ram. *Hindu Temples: What Happened to Them 1, A Preliminary Survey*. Voice of India, 1990. p. 37.

40 Swarup, Ram. *Hindu View of Christianity and Islam*. Voice of India. 1992. p. 80.

41 Goel, Sita Ram. *Hindu Temples: What Happened to Them 1, A Preliminary Survey*. Voice of India, 1990. p. 32.

42 Ibid.

43 Ibid., pp. 17–18.

44 Aparajit. 'Gandhi—A Sainthood That Never Existed'. MyVoice, OpIndia, 24 January 2022. myvoice.opindia.com/2022/01/gandhi-a-sainthood-that-never-existed/ (accessed 26 November 2024).

45 The Quran, edited by Shahi International. Al-muntada Al-islami, 2004.Surah 2: Ayat 221.

46 Narain, Harsh. *Jizyah and the Rise of Islam*. Voice of India, 1990. p. 2.

47 Swarup, Ram. *Understanding Islam through Hadith: Religious Faith or Fanaticism?* Voice of India, 2001 (reprint). p. 202.

48 Narain, Harsh. *Jizyah and the Rise of Islam*. Voice of India, 1990. p. 2.

49 Ye'or, Bat. *The Dhimmi: Jews and Christians under Islam*, translated by David Maisel et all. Fairleigh Dickinson University Press, 1985. pp. 396–97.

50 'Catechism of the Catholic Church'. *The Holy See*. Libreria Editrice Vaticana. www.vatican.va/archive/ENG0015/__P1C.HTM (accessed 3 Octobe 2024).

51 Nixey, Catherine. *The Darkening Age: The Christian Destruction of the Classical World*. PanMacmillan, 2017. p. 29.

52 In later chapters on secularism, the consequences of this binary will be discussed in more detail.

53 Although it is Chapter 13, 'The Monotheistic Cocktail', that deals with the origin of the dogma of the People of the Book, here we will try to understand the meaning of the dogma itself.

54 The Quran, edited by Shahi International. Al-muntada Al-islami, 2004.Surah 9: Ayat 29.

55 Narain, Harsh. *Jizyah and the Spread of Islam*. Voice of India, 1990. p. 12.

56 Swarup, Ram. *Understanding Islam through Hadith: Religious Faith or Fanaticism?* Voice of India, 2001 (reprint). p. 103.

57 Narain, Harsh. *Jizyah and the Spread of Islam*. Voice of India, 1990. p. 13.

58 Barani, Ziauddin. 'Tarikh-i Firoz Shahi', *Khalji Kaleen Bharat*. Sabda Mahima, 1998. p. 70.

59 Narain, Harsh. *Jizyah and the Spread of Islam*. Voice of India, 1990. pp. 1–2.

60 Naipaul, V.S. *Beyond Belief: Islamic Excursions Among the Converted Peoples*. Viking, 1998. p. 50.

61 Balgangadhara, S.N., and Jhingran, Divya. *Do All Roads Lead to Jerusalem? The Making of Indian Religions*. Manohar, 2023 (reprint). p. 38.

62 Origen. *Contra Celsum*, translated by Henry Chadwick. Cambridge University Press, 1965. 5.25: p. 283.
63 Eusebius. *Preparation for the Gospel*, translated by E.H. Gifford. Oxford, 1903. https://topostext.org/work/230 (accessed 26 November 2024).
64 The Bible: Authorized King James Version. Oxford University Press, 1997. Leviticus, 24:16.
65 Ellerbe, Helen. *The Dark Side of Christian History*. Morningstar and Lark, 2004. p. 78.
66 Gaddis, Michael. *There Is No Crime for Those Who Have Christ*. University of California Press, 2015. p. 151.
67 Ellerbe, Helen. *The Dark Side of Christian History*. Morningstar and Lark, 2004. p. 82.
68 'Hindu Boy Mob-Lynched in Bangladesh over Allegations of Blasphemy: Report'. *Deccan Herald*. www.deccanherald.com/world/hindu-boy-mob-lynched-in-bangladesh-over-allegations-of-blasphemy-report-3179602 (accessed 3 October 2024).
69 Ellerbe, Helen. *The Dark Side of Christian History*. Morningstar and Lark, 2004. pp. 83–84.
70 Mulligan, Hugh A. 'Columbus Saga Sinking Fast'. *Associated Press*, 8 March 1992.
71 Delumeau, Jean. *Catholicism between Luther and Voltaire*. Burns and Oats, 1977. p. 85.
72 Stannard, David E. *American Holocaust: The Conquest of the New World*. Oxford University Press, 1992. p. x.
73 Helps, Arthur. *The Spanish Conquest in America*. John Lane, 1900. pp. 264–67.
74 The Bible: Authorized King James Version. Oxford University Press, 1997. 1 Corinthians, 7:1.
75 Ibid., 1 Peter, 3:7.
76 Starr, Tama. *The 'Natural Inferiority' of Women*. Poseidon Press, 1991. p. 45.
77 Smith, Joan. *Misogynies: Reflections on Myths and Malice*. Fawcett Columbine, 1989. p. 66.
78 Ibid., p. 68.
79 Nigg, Walter. *The Heretics: Heresy through the Ages*. Dorset Press, 1962. p. 277.

80 Walker, Barbara G. *The Woman's Encyclopedia of Myths and Secrets*. Harper & Row, 1983. p. 1004.
81 Robbins, Rossell Hope. *The Encyclopedia of Witchcraft and Demonology*. Bonanza Books, 1981. p. 3.
82 Levack, Brian P. The *Witch-Hunt in Early Modern Europe*. Longman, 1987. p. 21.
83 Nixey, Catherine. *The Darkening Age: The Christian Destruction of the Classical World*. PanMacmillan, 2017. p. 78.
84 'The Aten Appears'. Episode 110, *The History of Egypt Podcast*, 3:59. egyptianhistorypodcast.com/the-aten-appears-episode-110/ (accessed 3 October 2024).
85 Swarup, Ram. *Hindu View of Christianity and Islam*. Voice of India, 1992. p. 49.
86 Chadwick, Henry. *The Early Church: The Penguin History of the Church 1*. Penguin, 1993 (reprint). pp. 18–19.
87 Chadwick, Henry. *The Early Church: The Penguin History of the Church 1*. Penguin, 1993 (reprint). p. 11.
88 Kulikowski, Michael. 'Christians Were Strangers'. *Aeon*. www.aeon.co/essays/how-an-obscure-oriental-cult-converted-a-vast-pagan-roman-empire (accessed 3 October 2024).

CHAPTER 8 HINDU VIEW OF PROPHETIC MONOTHEISM

1 https://upload.wikimedia.org/wikipedia/commons/7/7f/Geromeslavemarket.jpg (accessed 6 Oct. 2024).
2 It is not just the converts who break deva rna or any other rna upon conversion. Christianity and Islam, by their very nature, are disruptive of deva rna. But since both of them are artificial and historical religions, it helps to see the process of the destruction that happens upon conversion.
3 The Bible: Authorized King James Version. Oxford University Press, 1997. Exodus, 20:3–6.
4 Ibid., Deuteronomy, 12:3.
5 Garnsey, P. 'Religious Toleration in Classical Antiquity', *Persecution and Toleration (Studies in Church History)*, Vol. 21. Oxford University Press, 1984. p. 17.
6 Russell, N. *Theophilus of Alexandria*. Routledge, 2007. p. 69.
7 Nixey, Catherine. *The Darkening Age: The Christian Destruction of the Classical World*. PanMacmillan, 2017. p. 87.

8 Goel, Sita Ram. *Catholic Ashrams: Sannyasins or Swindlers*. Voice of India, 1994. p. 10.

9 Nixey, Catherine. *The Darkening Age: The Christian Destruction of the Classical World*. PanMacmillan, 2017. p. 95.

10 Ibid., p. xxxi.

11 Ibid., pp. xx–xxi.

12 Shaheen, Kareem. 'ISIS Destroys Tetrapylon Monument in Palmyra', *The Guardian*, 20 January 2017. www.theguardian.com/world/2017/jan/20/isis-destroys-tetrapylon-monument-palmyra-syria (accessed 26 November 2024).

13 Elliot, Henry Miers. *The History of India, as Told by Its Own Historians: The Muhammadan Period*, edited by John Dowson. Cambridge University Press, 2013. pp. 44–45.

14 Goel, Sita Ram. *Islam vis-à-vis Hindu Temples*. Voice of India, 1993. p.8.

15 Ibid.

16 Goel, Sita Ram. *Hindu Temples What Happened to Them I, A Preliminary Evidence*. Voice of India, 2009 (reprint). pp. 17–18.

17 The Basavkalyan fort in Bidar district of Karnataka and the Padawali fort in Morena, Madhya Pradesh, are just two of many such forts where one can see desecrated vigrahas of deities used as footstones and in walls randomly, but care is taken to display them to Hindus for posterity.

18 Nixey, Catherine. *The Darkening Age: The Christian Destruction of the Classical World*. PanMacmillan, 2017. p. 110.

19 Swarup, Ram. *Hindu View of Christianity and Islam*. Voice of India, 1992. p. 39.

20 Ambedkar, B.R. *Writings and Speeches—Volume 3*. Government of Maharashtra, 1987. p. 229.

21 Nixey, Catherine. *The Darkening Age: The Christian Destruction of the Classical World*. PanMacmillan, 2017. pp. xxxi–xxxii.

22 Canfora, Luciana. 'The Vanished Library: A Wonder of the Ancient World', *The Darkening Age: The Christian Destruction of the Classical World*. PanMacmillan, 2017. p. 88.

23 Nixey, Catherine. *The Darkening Age: The Christian Destruction of the Classical World*. PanMacmillan, 2017. p. 152

24 Marcellinus, Ammianus. *The Later Roman Empire (AD 354–378)*, translated by Walter Hamilton, Introduction by A. Wallace-Hadrill.Penguin, 1986. p. 29.1.35.
25 Nixey, Catherine. *The Darkening Age: The Christian Destruction of the Classical World*. PanMacmillan, 2017. p. 157.
26 Celsus quoted by Catherine Nixey. Ibid., p. 38.
27 Ibid., pp. 135–36.
28 The Bible: Authorized King James Version. Oxford University Press, 1997. Ecclesiastes, 9:5–6.
29 Sahih Muslim 203, Book 1: *The Book of Faith*.
30 The Quran, edited by Shahi International. Al-muntada Al-islami, 2004. Surah 9: Ayat 113.
31 The Bible: Authorized King James Version. Oxford University Press, 1997. Daniel, 12:2.
32 Naipaul, V.S. *Beyond Belief: Islamic Excursions Among the Converted Peoples*. Viking, 1998. p. 1.
33 The Bible: Authorized King James Version. Oxford University Press, 1997. Matthew, 10:35–38.
34 Ellerbe, Helen. *The Dark Side of Christian History*. Morningstar and Lark, 2004. p. 139.
35 Regenstein, Lewis. *Replenish the Earth*. Crossroad, 1991. p.72.
36 Smith, John Holland. *The Death of Classical Paganism*. Charles Scribner, 1976. p 246.
37 Nixey, Catherine. *The Darkening Age: The Christian Destruction of the Classical World*. PanMacmillan, 2017. p. 104.
38 Lechner, Peter. 'The Life and Times of St Benedict', *Making and Breaking the Gods: Christian Responses to Pagan Sculpture in Late Antiquity*. Aarhus University Press, 2013. pp. 86–87.
39 Gonzalez, Justo L. *The Story of Christianity: The Early Church to the Dawn of the Reformation*. HarperOne, 2010. p. 278.
40 Schaff, Phillip, editor. *Nicene and Post-Nicene Fathers: First Series Volume I—The Confessions and Letters of St Augustine*. Cosimo Classics, 2007. Augustine, Letter 47.
41 The Bible: Authorized King James Version. Oxford University Press, 1997. Deuteronomy, 12:3.
42 Ibid., Genesis, 9:3.
43 White, Lynn. 'The Historical Roots of Our Ecologic Crisis'. *JSTOR*, vol. 155, no. 3767, 10 March 1967, pp. 1203–07. https://

doi.org/10.1126/science.155.3767.1203 (accessed 26 November 2024).

44 Swarup, Ram. *Meditations: Yogas, Gods, Religions*. Voice of India, 2000. p. 1.

45 *Kathopanishad*. Verse. 2.1.1.

46 *The Yoga Sutras*, 1.2.

47 Swarup, Ram. *Hindu View of Christianity and Islam*. Voice of India, 1992. pp. 101–02.

48 Ibid., pp. 103–04.

49 Ibid., pp. 104–05.

50 Ibid., p. 105.

51 Ibid., p. 104.

52 Ibid., pp. 45–46.

53 Ibid., pp. 46–47.

CHAPTER 9 THE LONG ARC OF CHRISTIANITY

1 https://commons.wikimedia.org/wiki/File:AnnaCharboniere-Tortured.jpg (accessed 6 Oct. 2024).

2 During 1990s, after the fall of the Soviet Union, Fukuyama predicted in *The End of History (1992)* that the world will become flat, the economy and trade will boom and will equalize the world, and major wars will become a thing of history as liberal democracy will settle in as the final form of governance. On the other hand, Samuel Huntington predicted in *The Clash of Civilizations (1996)* during the same time that the world will soon be divided into eight spheres of influence mainly divided by religion: Western (Catholic-Protestant), Confucian, Japanese, Islamic, Hindu, Slavic (Orthodox), Latin American, and African. He divided the Christian world into two spheres, one led by the USA, which is Protestant-Catholic, and another led by Russia, which is Orthodox. And there is some overlap in the African category where it is both Christian and Islamic. Also, Confucian and Japanese are not very far from each other. However, these are largely the fault lines along which the world is divided today, and these fault lines are created only by religion, and particularly prophetic monotheistic religions, which are picking fights with everyone for lands, resources, and people. Fukuyama was proven wrong like no man before, and Huntington was vindicated like

no man before when the world realized with shock during 9/11 that we are under siege by Islamic terrorism. The next decade saw one after another religious war flaring like never before, reorganizing the world on largely religious lines. And yet, it is a testimony to the standing hypocrisy and humbug of global academia that Fukuyama is still taught in most universities while Huntington is considered a pariah. Fukuyama's lens is very Abrahamic and religious, where he imposes his dogmatic theory of life (peaceful trade forever) on the world without thinking whether it fits reality or not. On the other hand, Huntington (despite coming from a Christian background) observes reality and then creates a credible theory about it. While Fukuyama clings to dogma like prophetic monotheists, Huntington is humbled by reality and builds his theory based on reality.

3 The world religion is used here for the sake of its familiarity; however, the pagan traditions and sects of the Roman Empire were more like dharmic sects.

4 Clement. 'The Absurdity and Shamefulness of the Images by Which the Gods Are Worshipped', *Exhortation to the Heathen*. https://www.newadvent.org/fathers/020804.htm (accessed 27 November 2024).

5 Chadwick, Henry. *The Early Church: The Penguin History of the Church 1*. Penguin, 1993 (reprint). p. 25.

6 Symmachus, Quintus Aurelius. 'Memorandum', *The Last Pagans of Rome*. Oxford University Press, 2011. p. 37.

7 MacMullen, R. *Christianizing the Roman Empire AD100–400*. Yale University Press, 1984.

8 We now all go by a calendar that is hitched to the acclaimed and supposed birth of the cult leader of Christianity, Jesus Christ.

9 Gonzalez, Justo L. *The Story of Christianity: The Early Church to the Dawn of the Reformation*. HarperOne, 2010. p. 15.

10 Chadwick, Henry. *The Early Church: The Penguin History of the Church 1*. Penguin, 1993 (reprint). p. 24.

11 Ibid., p. 30.

12 Nixey, Catherine. *The Darkening Age: The Christian Destruction of the Classical World*. PanMacmillan, 2017. p. 31.

13 Chadwick, Henry. *The Early Church: The Penguin History of the Church 1*. Penguin, 1993 (reprint). p. 29.

14 Nixey, Catherine. *The Darkening Age: The Christian Destruction of the Classical World*. PanMacmillan, 2017. p. 95.

15 It is an irony of fate that this city would not always remain Christian either, and just like the Christians converted the ancient pagan Greek city to Christianity, one day the Ottoman Islamic armies would conquer and convert it to Islam in 1453, but we are running ahead of the story.

16 Nixey, Catherine. *The Darkening Age: The Christian Destruction of the Classical World*. PanMacmillan, 2017. p. 106.

17 Ibid.

18 Ellerbe, Helen. *The Dark Side of Christian History*. Morningstar and Lark, 2004. p. 41.

19 Pandey, Amritanshu. 'Artificial Intelligence Is Here—Part 1, from Before to Now', *Dhiti*, Brhat, 2 June 2023. www.brhat.in/dhiti/artificialintelligence (accessed 26 November 2024).

20 Tertullianus. 'On the flesh of Christ', *Tertullian's Treatise on the Incarnation*. Wipf and Stock. 2016. pp. 4–81.

21 Gonzalez, Justo L. *The Story of Christianity: The Early Church to the Dawn of the Reformation*. HarperOne, 2010. p. 369.

22 Ibid.

23 Ibid., p. 370.

24 Ibid., p. 379.

25 Goel, Sita Ram. *Catholic Ashrams: Sannyasins or Swindlers*. Voice of India, 1994. p. 6.

26 Griffiths, Bede. *Christ in India*. Christ Publications, 1986. p. 24.

27 Goel, Sita Ram. *Catholic Ashrams: Sannyasins or Swindlers*. Voice of India, 1994. pp. 16–17.

28 Swami Vivekananda. 'On the Bounds of Hinduism', *Complete Works of Swami Vivekananda*, Vol. 5. https://www.ramakrishnavivekananda.info/vivekananda/volume_5/interviews/on_the_bounds_of_hinduism.htm (accessed 26 November 2024).

29 Chol-Hwan, Kang. *The Aquariums of Pyongyang: Ten Years in the North Korean Gulag*. Atlantic Books, 2008. p. xxiv.

30 https://www.theguardian.com/uk/2009/apr/16/letters-environment-cocoa-ghana

31 Sharma, Shakshi. 'Proselytisation in Punjab: How Mazhabi Sikhs and Valmiki Hindus Are Being "lured" into Christianity', *News18*, 1 April 2023. www.news18.com/opinion/

proselytisation-in-punjab-how-mazhabi-sikhs-and-valmiki-hindus-are-being-lured-into-christianity-7440811.html (accessed 2024).

32 Shourie, Arun. *Harvesting Our Souls: Missionaries, Their Designs, Their Claims*. ASA Publications, 2000. p. 26.

33 Ibid., p. 28.

34 Ellerbe, Helen. *The Dark Side of Christian History*. Morningstar and Lark, 2004. p. 1.

35 Shourie, Arun. *Harvesting Our Souls: Missionaries, Their Designs, Their Claims*. ASA Publications, 2000. p. 26.

36 Wanglat, James. *The Rise of Christianity in Arunachal Pradesh*. Clever Fox, 2020. p. 16.

37 SamuelJohnson quoted in *The Darkening Age: The Christian Destruction of the Classical World*. PanMacmillan, 2017. p. xxxvii.

38 Singh, Rohit Kumar. 'Rachel Turns Rajeshwari to Marry Tejashwi but Uncle Sadhu Yadav Is Not Happy', *India Today*, 10 December 2021. www.indiatoday.in/india/story/rachel-turns-rajeshwari-to-marry-tejashwi-but-uncle-sadhu-yadav-not-happy-1886573-2021-12-10. (accessed 24 November 2024).

39 '"I am proud to be a Christian, Sanghis will burn after learning this," says "atheist" DMK leader Udhayanidhi Stalin at a Christmas event', OpIndia, 23 December 2022. https://www.opindia.com/2022/12/atheist-dmk-leader-udhayanidhi-stalin-says-he-is-a-proud-christian (accessed 25 November 2024).

40 'Udhayanidhi Stalin's "eradicate Sanatan Dharma" remark sparks row; BJP hits out', *The Indian Express*, 03 September 2023. https://indianexpress.com/article/cities/chennai/udhaynidhi-stalin-sanatan-dharma-row-bjp-genocide-8921845/(accessed 24 November 2024).

41 Nixey, Catherine. *The Darkening Age: The Christian Destruction of the Classical World*. PanMacmillan, 2017. p. 31.

42 Ibid., p. 68.

43 Shourie, Arun. *Harvesting Our Souls: Missionaries, Their Designs, Their Claims*. ASA Publications, 2000. p. 29.

CHAPTER 10 THE LONG ARC OF ISLAM

1 https://commons.wikimedia.org/wiki/File:Normand,_Ernest_-_The_Bitter_Draught_of_Slavery_-_1885.jpg (accessed 6 Oct. 2024).

2 Narain, Harsh. *Jizyah and the Spread of Islam*. Voice of India, 1997 (reprint). p. 9.
3 Paranjape, Makarand R. 'Bitterest Truth of History: Raliv, Tsaliv ya Galiv', *The New Indian Express*, 9 April 2022. https://www.newindianexpress.com/opinions/2022/Apr/08/bitterest-truth-of-history-raliv-tsaliv-ya-galiv-2439752.html (accessed 24 November 2024).
4 *Sahih al-Bukhari*, 6924, 6925 (Book 88, Hadith 7).
5 *Sahih al-Bukhari*, 4557 (Book 65, Hadith 79).
6 The Quran, edited by Shahi International. Al-muntada Al-islami, 2004. Surah 16: Ayat 106.
7 Center for Preventive Action. 'Violent Extremism in the Sahel', *Council on Foreign Relations*. www.cfr.org/global-conflict-tracker/conflict/violent-extremism-sahel (accessed 3 October 2024).
8 Khan, contrary to public perception, is not originally an Islamic title. It is a pagan Mongol-Turkic title of the Central Asian and Siberian tribes that spread out in Asia and Europe in the Middle Ages. They were so influential that many Islamic countries adopted their title to show pedigree and nobility.
9 Lewis, Bernard. *The Middle East: The Brief History of the Last 2000 Years*. Scribner, 2003. p. 97.
10 Theophanes. *The Chronicle of Theophanes: Anni Mundi 6095–6305 (AD 602–813)*, translated by Harry Turtledove. University of Pennsylvania Press, 1982. p. 53.
11 Runciman, Steven. *A History of the Crusades Vol. I. The First Crusade and the Foundation of the Kingdom of Jerusalem.*Cambridge University Press, 1951. p. 64.
12 Crowley, Roger. *1453: The Holy War for Constantinople and the Clash of Islam and the West*. Hyperion. 2005, p. 4.
13 Stark, Rodney. *God's Battalions: The Case for the Crusades*. HarperOne, 2009. pp. 2–4.
14 Tyerman, Christopher. *God's War: A New History of the Crusades*. Penguin, 2007. pp. 350–52.
15 https://www.foreignaffairs.com/articles/united-states/1993-06-01/clash-civilizations
16 Eltahawy, Mona. 'Egypt's Cruelty to Christians', *New York Times*, 22 December 2016. https://www.nytimes.com/2016/12/22/

opinion/egypts-cruelty-to-christians.html (accessed 24 November 2024).

17 Sehgal, Manjeet. 'Hindus, Sikhs compelled to bury dead in Pakistan as cremation grounds vanish', *India Today*, 6 January 2014. https://www.indiatoday.in/india/north/story/hindus-sikhs-bury-dead-pakistan-cremation-grounds-lahore-161274-2014-01-05 (accessed 24 November 2024).

18 PTI, 'Minor Hindu girl abducted, married off to elderly man and converted to Islam in Pak's Sindh province', *Indian Express*, 12 September 2024. https://indianexpress.com/article/pakistan/hindu-girl-abducted-married-converted-to-islam-in-sindh-pakistan-9564788/# (accessed 24 November 2024).

19 Lone, Wa, and Shoon Naing. 'At least 71 killed in Myanmar as Rohingya insurgents stage major attack', *Reuters*, 25 August 2017. https://www.reuters.com/world/middle-east/israel-strikes-heart-beirut-killing-six-2024-10-02/ (accessed 24 November 2024).

20 'Myanmar: New evidence reveals Rohingya armed group massacred scores in Rakhine State', Amnesty International, 22 May 2018. https://www.amnesty.org/en/latest/news/2018/05/myanmar-new-evidence-reveals-rohingya-armed-group-massacred-scores-in-rakhine-state/ (accessed 24 November 2024).

21 Gabriel, Brigitte. *Because They Hate: A Survivor of Islamic Terror Warns America*. Macmillan, 2016. pp. 17–18.

22 Gabriel, Brigitte. *They Must Be Stopped: Why We Must Defeat Radical Islam and How We Can Do It*. Macmillan, 2016. p. 15.

23 Jones, Sophia. '100 Years Ago, 1.5 Million Christian Armenians Were Systematically Killed. Today, It's Still Not A "Genocide"', *Noema*, 23 April 2015. https://www.noemamag.com/100-years-ago-1-5-million-christian-armenians-were-systematically-killed-today-its-still-not-a-genocide/ (accessed 20 November 2024).

24 Adalian, Rouben Paul. *Historical Dictionary of Armenia*. Lanham, Scarecrow, 2010. p. 154.

25 Kévorkian, Raymond H. 'The Cilician Massacres, April 1909' in Armenian Cilicia, *UCLA Armenian History and Culture Series: Historic Armenian Cities and Provinces, 7*. Mazda Publishers, 2008. pp. 339–69.

26 Lewis, Martin. 'The Many Armenian Diasporas, Then and Now', *GeoCurrents*, 6, 2012. https://www.geocurrents.info/blog/2012/02/06/the-many-armenian-diasporas-then-and-now/ (accessed 20 November 2024).

27 Shields, Sarah. 'The Greek-Turkish Population Exchange: Internationally Administered Ethnic Cleansing', Middle East Report, no. 267, 2013, pp. 2–6. *JSTOR*, http://www.jstor.org/stable/24426444 (accessed 3 October 2024).

28 Ray, Michael. 'Madrid Train Bombings of 2004', *Encyclopædia Britannica*, 4 September 2024. www.britannica.com/event/Madrid-train-bombings-of-2004 (accessed 24 November 2024).

CHAPTER 11 WEAPONIZATION OF LIFE

1 https://commons.wikimedia.org/wiki/File:De_Bry_1c.JPG (accessed 6 Oct. 2024).

2 Nixey, Catherine. *The Darkening Age: The Christian Destruction of the Classical World*. PanMacmillan, 2017. p. 107.

3 Pakenham, Thomas. *The Scramble for Africa*. Abacus, 1991. p. xxv.

4 Pandey, Ashish. '400-Year-Old Lord Rama Idol Vandalised at Andhra's Ramateertham Temple, Triggers Protest', *India Today*, 31 December 2020. www.indiatoday.in/india/story/lord-rama-idol-vandalised-ramateertham-temple-1754778-2020-12-31 (accessed 25 November 2024).

5 'Explosive Confession: Rampant Christian Conversions in AP, Admits YSRCP MP Raju Ramakrishna', *Telugu 360*, 27 May 2020. www.telugu360.com/rampant-christian-conversions-in-ap-admits-ysrcp-mp-raju-ramakrishna/ (accessed 24 November 2024).

6 'Will Ensure Presence of Christians in Assembly, Says Capt Amarinder Singh', *Indian Express*, 18 September 2016. www.indianexpress.com/article/india/india-news-india/will-ensure-presence-of-christians-in-assembly-says-capt-amarinder-singh-3036865/ (accessed 23 November 2024).

7 'Amit Shah Leads Historic Settlement of Bru Refugees: How the Persecuted Hindu Tribe Has a New Lease of Life', *Swarajya*, 17 January 2020. www.swarajyamag.com/news-brief/amit-shah-leads-historic-settlement-of-bru-refugees-

how-the-persecuted-hindu-tribe-has-a-new-lease-of-life (accessed 23 November 2024).

8 Goel, Sita Ram. *The Story of Islamic Imperialism in India*. Voice of India, 1994. p. 27.

9 Balakrishna, Sandeep. *Tipu Sultan: The Tyrant of Mysore*. Rare Publications, 2014. p. 112.

10 Goel, Sita Ram. *Hindu Temples What Happened to Them Volume II, The Islamic Evidence*. Voice of India, 1991. pp. 76–77.

11 Goel, Sita Ram. *The Story of Islamic Imperialism in India*. Voice of India, 1994. p. 48.

12 Goel, Sita Ram, editor. *Hindu Temples What Happened to Them Volume I, The Preliminary Evidence*. Voice of India, 1990. p. 57.

13 Fair, Christine. *Fighting to the End: Pakistan Army's Way of War*. Oxford University Press, 2014. p. 39.

14 Goel, Sita Ram. *The Story of Islamic Imperialism in India*. Voice of India, 1994. pp. 28–29.

15 Deepak, J. Sai. *India, Bharat and Pakistan*. Bloomsbury, 2022. pp. 187, 197.

16 Narain, Harsh. *Jizyah and the Spread of Islam*. Voice of India, 1990. p. 37.

17 Hitchens, Christopher. *The Missionary Position: Mother Teresa in Theory and Practice*. Verson, 1995. pp. 41–42.

18 Swarup, Ram. *Woman in Islam*. Voice of India, 2000. p. 12.

19 The Quran, edited by Shahi International. Al-muntada Al-islami, 2004. Surah 2: Ayat 223.

20 Ibid., Surah 4: Ayat 3, Surah 4: Ayat 24, Surah 23: Ayat 5–6, Surah 33: Ayat 50, Surah 70: Ayat 22–30.

Chapter 12 Hindu View of Secular Modernity

1 https://commons.wikimedia.org/wiki/File:Burned_at_Stake.jpg (accessed 6 Oct. 2024).

2 Goel, Sita Ram. *India's Secularism*. Voice of India, 1999. p. 21.

3 De Roover, Jakob. *Europe, India and the Limits of Secularism*. Oxford University Press, 2015. p. 220.

4 Goel, Sita Ram. *India's Secularism*. Voice of India, 1999. pp. 24–25.

5 Ibid., p. 26.

6 Ibid., p. 28.
7 And as the Indian State does not differentiate between religion and dharma, the same paradigm of non-involvement of the State in religious matters applies to dharmic matters too.
8 In fact, Christianity has a lot to do with disturbing the ecological balance of various species in the continents of North America, South America, and Australia. The Europeans 'discovered' these new continents and brought many plants and animal species with them, like the apple tree in flora and rabbit in fauna. These species grew rapidly in the new continents of the Americas and Australia because the native environment did not have species that could stem the tide of their growth. In 1859, ten rabbits were brought to Australia. By 1920, there were 10 billion rabbits in Australia, which destroyed crops and pretty much everything else on the continent, at the expense of the native species. Thus, European Christian colonialism did not just affect the human society of these places. They also affected the nature of these places directly. This phenomenon is called ecological imperialism and is explained beautifully by Alfred Cosby in his book *Ecological Imperialism: The Biological Expansion of Europe*. Christian colonialism was the agency through which ecological imperialism was carried through.
9 The Bible: Authorized King James Version. Oxford University Press, 1997. John, 18:36.
10 Ibid., Luke, 20:20, Mark, 12:17.
11 De Roover, Jakob. *Europe, India and the Limits of Secularism*. Oxford University Press, 2015. pp. 89–90.
12 Ibid., p. 91.
13 Goel, Sita Ram. *Papacy, Its Doctrine and History*. Voice of India, 1986. p. 17.
14 Goel, Sita Ram. *India's Secularism*. Voice of India. 1999. pp. 22–23.
15 Goel, Sita Ram. *Papacy, Its Doctrine and History*. Voice of India, 1986. pp. 21–22.
16 De Roover, Jakob. *Europe, India and the Limits of Secularism*. Oxford University Press, 2015. pp. 97–98.
17 Luther, Martin. *Martin Luther's Basic Theological Writings*. Fortress Press, 1989. p. 607.
18 Goel, Sita Ram. *India's Secularism*. Voice of India, 1999. p. 23.

19 De Roover, Jakob. *Europe, India and the Limits of Secularism*. Oxford University Press, 2015. p. 102.

20 Saran, A.K. *On Theories of Secularism and Modernization*. Central Institute of Higher Tibetan Studies, 2007. p. 159.

21 Swarup, Ram. *On Hinduism: Reviews and Reflections*. Voice of India, 2000. pp. 18–19.

22 Goel, Sita Ram. *India's Secularism: New Name for National Subversion*. Voice of India. 2003, p. 25.

CHAPTER 13 THE SVAYAMBODHA–SHATRUBODHA SCALE

1 https://commons.wikimedia.org/wiki/File:Rama_and_Hanuman_fighting_Ravana,_an_album_painting_on_paper,_c1820.jpg (accessed 29 Mar. 2025).

2 Nanda, Meera (11 July 2009). 'Hindu Triumphalism and the Clash of Civilisations'. *Economic and Political Weekly*, 44 (28): 106–114.

3 Goel, Sita Ram. *History of Hindu–Christian Encounters*. Voice of India, 1996. p. 235.

4 Mahatma Gandhi. *The Collected Works of Mahatma Gandhi (digital), Vol. XLVIII*. Publications Division Government of India, 2005. pp. 199–200.

5 Swami Nikhilananda. *Vivekananda: A Biography*. Advaita Ashram, 2010. p 114.

PROLOGUE TO THE HINDU RENAISSANCE

1 Jauhri, Rajesh. 'Badaun Killings: Murder of Trust by the Islamists', *Organiser*, 2 April 2024. organiser.org/2024/04/02/230634/bharat/badaun-killings-murder-of-trust-by-the-islamists/ (accessed 24 November 2024).

2 Bisht, Shrishti. 'Bangladesh Violence: Hindu Temples Vandalised amid Ongoing Political Unrest', *Financial Express*, 6 August 2024. www.financialexpress.com/world-news/bangladesh-violence-hindu-temples-vandalised-amid-ongoing-political-unrest/3575280/ (accessed 24 November 2024).

3 'Bangladesh: Mob Rapes Hindu Woman in Satkhira after Fall of Sheikh Hasina Govt', OpIndia, 16 August 2024. www.opindia.com/2024/08/hindu-woman-gang-raped-satkhira-bangladesh/ (accessed 24 November 2024).

4 'Hindu Youth Utsav Mondal Lynched over "Blasphemy" in Presence of Police, Army by Islamist Mob in Bangladesh: Reports', *Swarajya*, 6 September 2024. swarajyamag.com/news-brief/hindu-youth-lynched-in-presence-of-police-army-and-navy-by-islamist-mob-in-bangladesh-over-blasphemy (accessed 23 November 2024).

5 PTI. 'Minor Hindu Girl Abducted, Married off to Elderly Man and Converted to Islam in Pak's Sindh Province', *Indian Express*, 12 September 2024. indianexpress.com/article/pakistan/hindu-girl-abducted-married-converted-to-islam-in-sindh-pakistan-9564788/ (accessed 24 November 2024).

6 C., Surendranath. 'The Real Number of Andhra Pradesh Christians Is Grossly Understated: Here's Why', *Swarajya*, 16 February 2021. swarajyamag.com/politics/the-real-number-of-andhra-pradesh-christians-is-grossly-understated-heres-why (accessed 23 November 2024).

7 'Ads of Jerusalem, Haj on Tirupati Bus Tickets, BJP Demands Action for "Hurting Hindu Sentiments"', *India TV*, 23 August 2019. www.indiatvnews.com/news/india-advertisements-of-jerusalem-haj-on-tirupati-bus-tickets-544315 (accessed 23 November 2024).

8 Roushan, Rahul. 'Tirupati Laddu Controversy, Beef Tallow and the Mockery of the Hindu Idea of Pure Vegetarianism', OpIndia, 27 September 2024. www.opindia.com/2024/09/tirupati-laddu-controversy-beef-tallow-mockery-of-the-hindu-idea-of-pure-vegetarianism/ (accessed 23 November 2024).

9 Banerji, Aparna. 'Jalandhar: Rarity a Decade Ago, Churches in Villages Now Common Sight', *Tribune*, 1 February 2023. www.tribuneindia.com/news/jalandhar/rarity-a-decade-ago-churches-in-villages-now-common-sight-475420/ (accessed 23 November 2024).

10 'Hindus Denied the Right to Cremate in Meghalaya', *Haindava Keralam*, 7 June 2015. haindavakeralam.com/hindus-denied-right-2-hk21072 (accessed 23 November 2024).

11 'The Persecuted Religious, Ethnic Minority Bru Casts Votes in Christian Dominated Mizoram in 2018 Assembly Elections', *Swarajya*, 16 December 2018. swarajyamag.com/insta/the-persecuted-religious-ethnic-minority-bru-casts-votes-

in-christian-dominated-mizoram-in-2018-assembly-elections (accessed 23 November 2024).

12 Eiseley, Loren. *The Firmament of Time*. Bison Books, 1999. p. 86.

13 Swarup, Ram. *The Word as Revelation*. Voice of India, 2001. p. 142.

14 It is true there were some rare temples and murtis that survived, but my point stands.

Bibliography

Adalian, Rouben Paul. *Historical Dictionary of Armenia*. Scarecrow, 2010.

Andrew, Christopher, and Vasili Mitrokhin. *The World Was Going Our Way: The KGB and the Battle for the Third World*. Basic Books, 2005.

Anirvan. *Inner Yoga*. Voice of India, 1988.

———. *Mandukya Upanishad and Prasna Upanishad*. Akshaya Prakashan, 2020.

Applebaum, Anne. *Gulag: A History*. Anchor Books, 2004.

Aurobindo, Sri. *Karmayogin*,Complete Works of Sri Aurobindo, Vol. 8. Sri Aurobindo Ashram Publication Department, 1997.

Balakrishna, Sandeep. *Tipu Sultan—The Tyrant of Mysore*. Rare Publications, 2014.

Balgangadhara, S.N., and Divya Jhingran. *Do All Roads Lead to Jerusalem? The Making of Indian Religions*. Manohar, 2023 (reprint).

Brown, Archie. *The Rise and Fall of Communism*. HarperCollins, 2010.

Bryant, Edwin F. *The Yoga Sutras of Patanjali*. Macmillan, 2009.

Chadwick, Henry. *The Early Church: The Penguin History of the Church 1*. Penguin, 1993 (reprint).

Chatterjee, Abhas. *The Concept of Hindu Nation*. Voice of India, 1995.

Chol-Hwan, Kang. *The Aquariums of Pyongyang: Ten Years in the North Korean Gulag*. Atlantic Books, 2008.

Coomaraswamy, Ananda. *The Dance of Shiva*. Rupa Publications, India, 2013.

Crowley, Roger. *1453: The Holy War for Constantinople and the Clash of Islam and the West*. Hyperion, 2005.

Dasgupta, Swapan, et al. *The Ayodhya Reference: The Supreme Court Judgment and Commentaries*. Voice of India, 1995.

Davis, Wade. *The Wayfinders: Why Ancient Wisdom Matters in the Modern World*. House of Anansi Press, 2009.

De Roover, Jakob. *Europe, India and the Limits of Secularism*. Oxford University Press, 2015.

Deeb, M. *Syria's Terrorist War on Lebanon and the Peace Process*. Palgrave Macmillan, 2003.

Deepak, J. Sai. *India, Bharat and Pakistan*. Bloomsbury, India, 2022.

Delumeau, Jean. *Catholicism between Luther and Voltaire*. Burns and Oats, 1977.

Dixit, Sanjay. *All Religions Are Not the Same*. Garuda, 2023.

Dubashi, Jay. *The Road to Ayodhya*. South Asia Books, 1992.

Durant, Will. *Our Oriental Heritage: The Story of Civilization—Part 1*. Simon and Schuster, 1954.

Eiseley, Loren. *The Firmament of Time*. Bison Books, 1999.

Ellerbe, Helen. *The Dark Side of Christian History*. Morningstar and Lark, 2004.

Elliot, Henry Miers. *The History of India, as Told by Its Own Historians: The Muhammadan Period*, edited by John Dowson. Cambridge University Press, 2013.

Elst, Koenraad. *Ram Janmabhoomi vs Babri Masjid: Case Study in Hindu–Muslim Conflict*. Voice of India, 1990.

———. *Ayodhya and After: Issues before Hindu Society*. Voice of India, 1991.

———. *Negationism in India: Concealing the Record of Islam*. Voice of India, 1992.

———. *Psychology of Prophetism: A Secular Look at the Bible*. Voice of India, 1993.

———. *Bharatiya Janata Party vis-à-vis Hindu Resurgence*. Voice of India, 1997.

———. *The Demographic Siege*. Voice of India, 1998.

———. *Decolonizing the Hindu Mind: Ideological Development of Hindu Revivalism*. Voice of India, 2001.

———. *Ayodhya: The Case against the Temple*. Voice of India, 2002.

———. *Who Is a Hindu?* Voice of India, 2002.

———. *The Problem with Secularism*. Voice of India, 2007.

Fair, Christine. *Fighting to the End: Pakistan Army's Way of War*. Oxford University Press, 2014.

Frawley, David. *Hinduism: The Eternal Tradition*. Voice of India, 1995.

———. *Hinduism and the Clash of Civilizations*. Voice of India, 2001.

Gabriel, Brigitte. *Because They Hate: A Survivor of Islamic Terror Warns America*. Macmillan, USA, 2016.

———. *They Must Be Stopped: Why We Must Defeat Radical Islam and How We Can Do It*. Macmillan, USA, 2016.

Gaddis, Michael. *There Is No Crime for Those Who Have Christ*. University of California Press, 2015.

Gage, Matilda Joslyn. *Women, Church and State*. Voice of India, 1997.

Ganatra, Ami. *Mahabharata Unravelled—II*. Bloomsbury, India, 2024.

Ganesh, R., and Hari Ravikumar. *The Essential Sanatana Dharma*. Prekshaa Pratishthana, 2023.

Ganesh, Shatavdhani Dr R. *Your Dharma and Mine*. Subbu Publications, 2021.

Goel, Sita Ram. *Perversion of India's Political Parlance*. Voice of India, 1984.

———. *Papacy, Its Doctrine and History*. Voice of India, 1986.

———. *Defense of Hindu Society*. Voice of India, 1987.

———. *Muslim Separatism: Causes and Consequences*. Voice of India, 1987.

———. *Hindu Temples What Happened to Them: Volume I—The Preliminary Evidence*. Voice of India, 1990.

———. *Hindu Temples What Happened to Them: Volume II—The Islamic Evidence*. Voice of India, 1991.

———. *Hindu Society under Siege*. Voice of India, 1992.

———. *Genesis and Growth of Nehruism: Volume 1—Commitment to Communis*m. Voice of India, 1993.

———. *Hindus and Hinduism: Manipulation of Meanings*. Voice of India, 1993.

———. *How I Became a Hindu*. Voice of India, 1993.

———. *Islam vis-à-vis Hindu Temples*. Voice of India, 1993.

———. *Stalinist 'Historians'Spread a Big Lie*. Voice of India, 1993.

———. *Catholic Ashrams: Sannyasins or Swindlers*. Voice of India, 1994.

———. *Jesus Christ: An Artifice for Aggression*. Voice of India, 1994.

———. *The Story of Islamic Imperialism in India*. Voice of India, 1994.

———. *Time for Stock Taking Whither Sangh Parivar?* Voice of India, 1994.

———. *History of Hindu Christian Encounters (AD 304–1996)*. Voice of India, 1996.

———. *Freedom of Expression*. Voice of India, 1998.

———. *Vindicated by Time: Niyogi Committee Report*. Voice of India, 1998.

———. *India's Secularism*. Voice of India, 1999.

———. *The Calcutta Quran Petition*. Voice of India, 1999.

———. *History of Heroic Hindu Resistance to Early Muslim Invaders*. Voice of India, 2001.

———. *The Story of Islamic Imperialism in India*. Voice of India, 2001 (reprint).

———. *Pseudo-Secularism, Christian Missions and Hindu Resistance*. Voice of India, 2004.

Gonzalez, Justo L. *The Story of Christianity: The Early Church to the Dawn of the Reformation*. HarperOne, 2010.

Haidt, Jonathan. *The Happiness Hypothesis*. Perseus Books Group, 2006.

Helps, Arthur. *The Spanish Conquest in America*. John Lane, 1900.

Hiro, Dilip. *Lebanon: Fire and Embers: A History of the Lebanese Civil War*. Palgrave Macmillan, 1993.

Hitchens, Christopher. *The Missionary Position: Mother Teresa in Theory and Practice*. Verson, 1995.

Jadunath, Sarkar. *A Short History of Aurangzib*. M.C. Sarkar & Sons, 1930.

Kak, Subhash. *India at Century's End: Essays on History and Politics*. Voice of India, 1994.

Kamra, A. J. *The Prolonged Partition and Its Pogroms: Testimonies on Violence against Hindus in East Bengal 1946–1964*. Voice of India, 2000.

Kane, P. V. *History of Dharmashastras, Vol. II, Part 1*. BORI, 1997

———. *History of Dharmashastras, Vol. IV*. BORI, 1997.

Kanjamala, Fr Augustine, and Arun Shourie. *Arun Shourie and His Christian Critics*. Voice of India, 1995.

Kramrisch, Stella. *The Hindu Temple, Vol. I*. Motilal Banarsidas, 2015 (reprint).

Lal, K.S. *Indian Muslims: Who Are They?* Voice of India, 1990.

———. *The Legacy of Muslim Rule in India*. Voice of India, 1992.

———. *Muslim Slave System in Medieval India*. Voice of India, 1994.

———. *Growth of Scheduled Tribes and Castes in Medieval India*. Voice of India, 1995.

———. *Theory and Practice of Muslim State in India*. Voice of India, 1999.

Levack, Brian P. *The Witch-Hunt in Early Modern Europe*. Longman, 1987.

Lewis, Bernard. *The Middle East: The Brief History of the Last 2000 Years*. Scribner, 2003.

Luther, Martin. *Martin Luther's Basic Theological Writings*. Fortress Press, 1989.

MacMullen, R. *Christianizing the Roman Empire* AD *100–400*. Yale University Press, 1984.

Maharaj, Sri Nisargadatta. *I Am That: Talks with Sri Nisargadatta Maharaj*. Chetana Prakashan, 2006 (reprint).

Mahatma Gandhi. *The Collected Works of Mahatma Gandhi (digital)*, Vol. XLVIII. Publications Division, Government of India, 2005.

Majumdar, R.C., editor. *History and Culture of the Indian People*. Vol. I, *The Vedic Age*. Bhartiya Vidya Bhavan, 1977.

———. *History and Culture of the Indian People*. Vol. II, *The Age of Imperial Unity*. Bhartiya Vidya Bhavan, 1977.

———. *History and Culture of the Indian People*. Vol. III, *The Classical Age*. Bhartiya Vidya Bhavan, 1977.

———. *History and Culture of the Indian People*. Vol. IV, *The Age of Imperial Kanauj*. Bhartiya Vidya Bhavan, 1977.

———. *History and Culture of the Indian People*. Vol. V, *The Struggle for Empire*. Bhartiya Vidya Bhavan, 1977.

———. *History and Culture of the Indian People*. Vol. VI, *The Delhi Sultanate*. Bhartiya Vidya Bhavan, 1977.

———. *History and Culture of the Indian People*. Vol. VII, *The Mughul Empire*. Bhartiya Vidya Bhavan, 1977.

———. *History and Culture of the Indian People*. Vol. VIII, *The Maratha Supremacy*. Bhartiya Vidya Bhavan, 1977.

———. *History and Culture of the Indian People*. Vol. IX, *British Paramountcy and Indian Renaissance, Part 1*. Bhartiya Vidya Bhavan, 1977.

———. *History and Culture of the Indian People*. Vol. X, *British Paramountcy and Indian Renaissance, Part 2*. Bhartiya Vidya Bhavan, 1977.

———. *History and Culture of the Indian People*. Vol. XI, *Struggle for Freedom*. Bhartiya Vidya Bhavan, 1977.

Majumdar, Suhas. *Jihad: The Islam Doctrine of Permanent War*. South Asia Books, 1994.

Malhotra, Rajiv. *Being Different: An Indian Challenge to Western Universalism*. HarperCollins, 2013 (reprint).

Margoliouth, D.S. *Mohammed and the Rise of Islam*. Voice of India, 1985.

Miranda, C. Barreto. *Quadros Historicos de Goa*. Cadernete, 1863.

Misra, Ram Gopal. *Indian Resistance to Early Muslim Invaders Up to 1206 AD*. Anu Books, 1983.

Mookerji, Radha Kumud. *Indian Shipping: A History of the Sea-Borne Trade and Maritime Activity of the Indians from the Earliest Times*. Life Span Publishers & Distributors, 2020.

Mookerji, Radha Kumud. *Local Government in Ancient India*. Life Span Publishers & Distributors, 2020.

———. *Nationalism in Hindu Culture*. Life Span Publishers & Distributors, 2020.

———. *The Fundamental Unity of India*. Life Span Publishers & Distributors, 2020.

———. *Glimpses of Ancient India*. Gyan Publishing House, 2024.

———. *Hindu Civilization: From the Earliest Times Up to the Establishment of the Maurya Empire*. Gyan Publishing House, 2024.

Muir, William. *The Life of Mahomet*. Voice of India, 1992.

Mukherjee, Sardindu. *Subjects, Citizens and Refugees: Tragedies in the Chittagong Hilltracts (1947–1998)*. Voice of India, 2000.

Naipaul, V.S. *Beyond Belief: Islamic Excursions Among the Converted Peoples*. Viking, 1998.

Narain, Harsh. *Jizyah and the Spread of Islam*. Voice of India, 1990.

———. *Myth of the Composite Culture in India*. Voice of India, 1990.

Nigg, Walter. *The Heretics: Heresy through the Ages*. Dorset Press, 1962.

Nixey, Catherine. *The Darkening Age: The Christian Destruction of the Classical World*. PanMacmillan, 2017.

Origen. *Contra Celsum*, translated by Henry Chadwick. Cambridge University Press, 1965.

Paine, Thomas. *The Age of Reason*. Hindu Writers Forum, 2000.

Pakenham, Thomas. *The Scramble for Africa*. Abacus, 1991.

Panikkar, K.M. *Malabar and the Portuguese*. Voice of India, 1997.

Pipes, Daniel. *The Rushdie Affair: The Novel, the Ayatollah and the West*. Voice of India, 1998.

———. *In the Path of God: Islam and Political Power*. Voice of India, 2001.

Pipes, Richard. *Communism: A History of the Intellectual and Political Movement*. Orion Publishing Group, 2002.

Prime, Ranchor. *Hindus and Ecology*. Motilal Banarsidass Publications, 1994.

Priolkar, A.K. *The Goa Inquisition: The Terrible Tribunal for the East*. Voice of India, 1991.

Raghavan, M., Simha, H., and C.R. Ramaswamy. *Elements of Indic Knowledge Systems & Heritage*. HTSR Institute, 2023.

Rajaram, N.S. *A Hindu View of the World*. Voice of India, 1998.

———. *Christianity's Scramble for India*. Hindu Writers Forum, 1999.

Regenstein, Lewis. *Replenish the Earth*. Crossroad, 1991.

Robbins, Rossell Hope. *The Encyclopedia of Witchcraft and Demonology*. Bonanza Books, 1981.

Runciman, Steven. *A History of the Crusades. Vol. I, The First Crusade and the Foundation of the Kingdom of Jerusalem*. Cambridge University Press, 1951.

Saran, A.K. *On Theories of Secularism and Modernization*. Central Institute of Higher Tibetan Studies, 2007.

Saraswati Swami, Pujyasri Chandrasekharendra. *Hindu Dharma: The Universal Way of Life*. Bharatiya Vidya Bhavan, 2022 (reprint).

Sastry, Trilochan. *The Essentials of Hinduism*. Viking, 2022.

Service, Robert. *Comrades: Communism—A World History*. Pan Macmillan, 2007.

Sharan, Ishwar. *The Myth of Saint Thomas and the Mylapore Shiva Temple*. Voice of India, 1991.

Shourie, Arun. *The Only Fatherland: Communists' Quit India and the Soviet Union*. ASA Publications, 1991.

———. *A Secular Agenda: For Strengthening Our Country, for Welding It*. HarperCollins, India, 1993.

———. *Eminent Historians: Their Technology, Their Line, Their Fraud*. ASA Publications, 1998.

———. *Harvesting Our Souls: Missionaries, Their Designs, Their Claims*. ASA Publications, 2000.

———. *Missionaries in India: Continuities, Changes, Dilemmas*. HarperCollins, 2000 (reprint).

———. *Falling over Backwards: An Essay against Reservations and against Judicial Populism*. ASA Publications, 2006.

Smith, Joan. *Misogynies: Reflections on Myths and Malice*. Fawcett Columbine, 1989.

Smith, John Holland. *The Death of Classical Paganism*. Charles Scribner, 1976.

Stannard, David E. *American Holocaust: The Conquest of the New World*. Oxford University Press, 1992.

Stark, Rodney. *God's Battalions: The Case for the Crusades*. HarperOne, 2009.

Swami Nikhilananda. *Vivekananda—A Biography*. Advaita Ashram, 2010.

Swami Vivekananda. *The Essence of Religion*, Complete Works of Swami Vivekananda, Vol. 8.

Swarup, Ram. *Buddhism vis-à-vis Hindus*. Voice of India, 1984.

———. *Whither Sikhism?* Voice of India, 1991.

———. *Hindu View of Christianity and Islam*. Voice of India, 1992.

———. *Pope John Paul II on Eastern Religions and Yoga: A Hindu-Buddhist Rejoinder*. Voice of India, 1995.

———. *Meditations: Yogas, Gods and Religions*. Voice of India, 2000.

———. *On Hinduism: Reviews and Reflections*. Voice of India, 2000.

———. *Woman in Islam*. Voice of India, 2000.

———. *The Word as Revelation*. Voice of India, 2001 (reprint).

———. *Understanding Islam through Hadith: Religious Faith or Fanaticism?* Voice of India, 2001 (reprint).

Symmachus, *Memorandum*, quoted in Cameron, Alan. *The Last Pagans of Rome*. Oxford University Press, 2011.

Talageri, Shrikant. *The Aryan Invasion Theory and Indian Nationalism*. Voice of India, 1993.

Talib, S. Gurbachan Singh, and Ram Swarup. *Muslim League Attack on Sikhs and Hindus in the Punjab 1947*. Voice of India, 1991.

The Cultural Heritage of India, 8 vols. The Ramakrishna Mission Institute of Culture, 2013.

Toffler, Alvin. *Power Shift: Knowledge, Wealth and Violence at the Edge of the 21st Century*. Bantam Doubleday Dell Publishing Group, 1991.

Tyerman, Christopher. *God's War: A New History of the Crusades*. Penguin, 2007.

Walker, Barbara G. *The Woman's Encylopedia of Myths and Secrets*. Harper & Row, 1983.

Wanglat, James. *The Rise of Christianity in Arunachal Pradesh*. Clever Fox, 2020.

Ye'or, Bat. *The Dhimmi: Jews and Christians under Islam*, translated by David Maisel et al. Fairleigh Dickinson University Press, 1985.

Religious and Dharmic Books Consulted

The Aitareya Upanishad.

The Avadhuta Gita.

The Brihadaranyaka Upanishad.

The Isha Upanishad.

The Mandukya Upanishad.

The Natyashastra.

The Rig Samhita.

The Shiva Sutras.

The Shukla Yajur Veda.

The Taittiriya Upanishad.

The Vivekachudamani.

The Yoga Sutras.

The Bhagavada Gita.

The Bible: Authorized King James Version. Oxford University Press, 1997.

The Quran, edited by Shahi International. Al-muntada Al-islami, 2004.

About the Author

Pankaj Saxena is a leading Hindu thinker and author. His writing explains the beauty of Sanatana Dharma and Hindu culture, contrasting the dharmic worldview with the Judeo-Christian paradigm. He has observed and documented the Hindu renaissance movement for more than two decades. Having a deep interest in Hindu arts, aesthetics, and, particularly, Hindu temple architecture, he has visited and documented more than fourteen hundred ancient Hindu temples in Bharata. He has been writing in various magazines and journals for the past several years. He is the co-founder of Bṛhat, an organization dedicated to the revival of Indian knowledge system and linking India's policy with Hindu culture. This is his first book in a series of books on Shatrubodha.